VOLUME
9

HOW CAN YOU MAKE INSTANT RAMEN TASTE BAD?

Silver Spoon

HIROMU ARAKAWA

STORY & CHARACTERS

YUUGO HACHIKEN

A first-year student at Ooezo Agricultural High School, enrolled in the Dairy Science Program. A city kid from Sapporo who got in through the general entrance exam. He's started to see the fun side of the agriculture industry, but he's also recently become aware of the harsh realities of dairy farming...

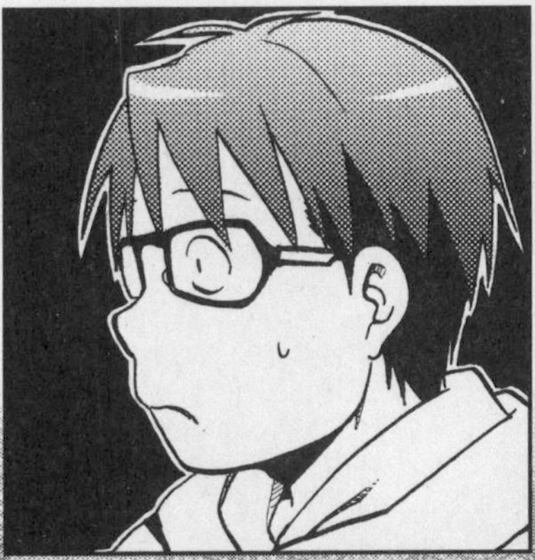

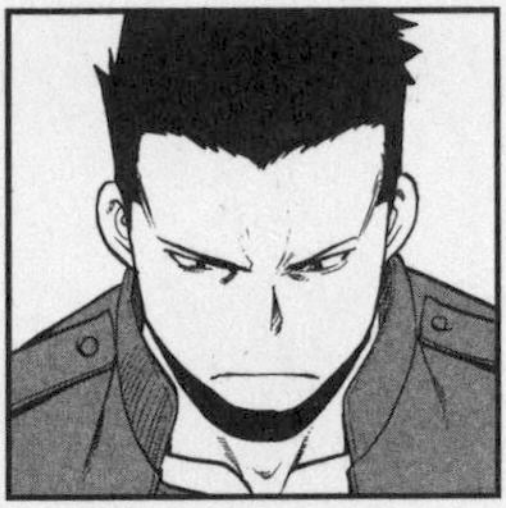

ICHIROU KOMABA

A first-year student at Ooezo Agricultural High School, enrolled in the Dairy Science Program. He had planned on taking over the family farm after graduation before it went out of business.

AKI MIKAGE

A first-year student at Ooezo Agricultural High School, enrolled in the Dairy Science Program. Her family keeps cows and horses and expects her to carry on the business, but now she's confessed her true feelings to her family...

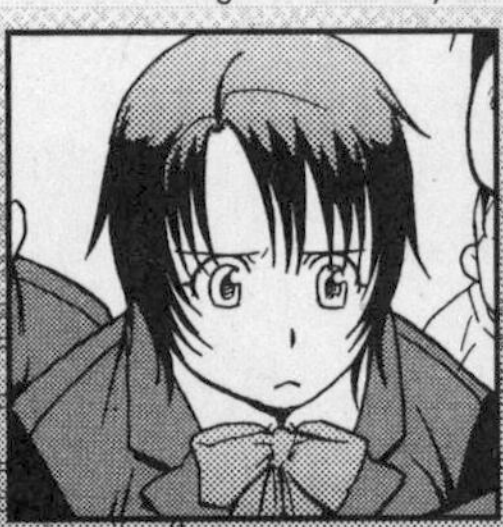

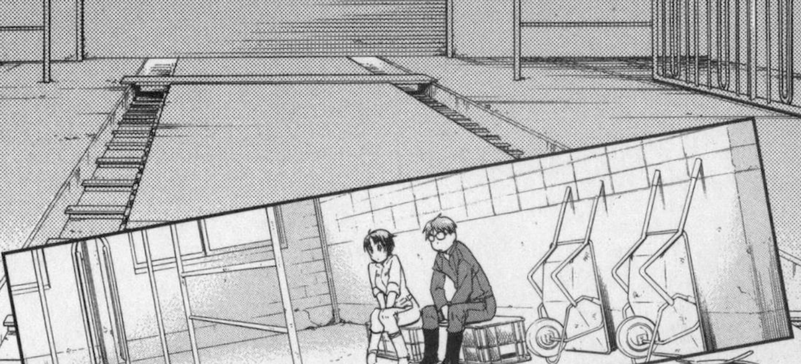

AYAME MINAMIKUJOU

Aki's childhood friend. Started an Equestrian Club at Shimizu West High School to compete with Aki. Sees Hachiken as a rival...for some reason.

TAMAKO INADA

A first-year student at Ooezo Agricultural High School, enrolled in the Dairy Science Program. Her family runs the megafarm. A complete enigma.

The Story Thus Far:

Just when agriculture was starting to get fun...it turns out reality isn't so simple. The harsher side of farming is thrust before Hachiken when the Komaba family is forced to give up farming. Komaba drops out of Ezo Ag to help pay back their debts. Their difficulties also threaten the Mikage family, who were the Komabas' guarantors. Now the Mikages will have to sell off the horses that Aki loves so much. A powerless Hachiken challenges the resignation to the status quo, and his spirit draws out Aki's true feelings...

SHINNOSUKE AIKAWA

A first-year student at Ooezo Agricultural High School, enrolled in the Dairy Science Program. His dream is to become a veterinarian, but he can't handle blood.

KEIJI TOKIWA

A first-year student at Ooezo Agricultural High School, enrolled in the Dairy Science Program. Son of chicken farmers. Awful at academics.

CONTENTS

Silver Spoon

Chapter 71:
Tale of Winter ⑧

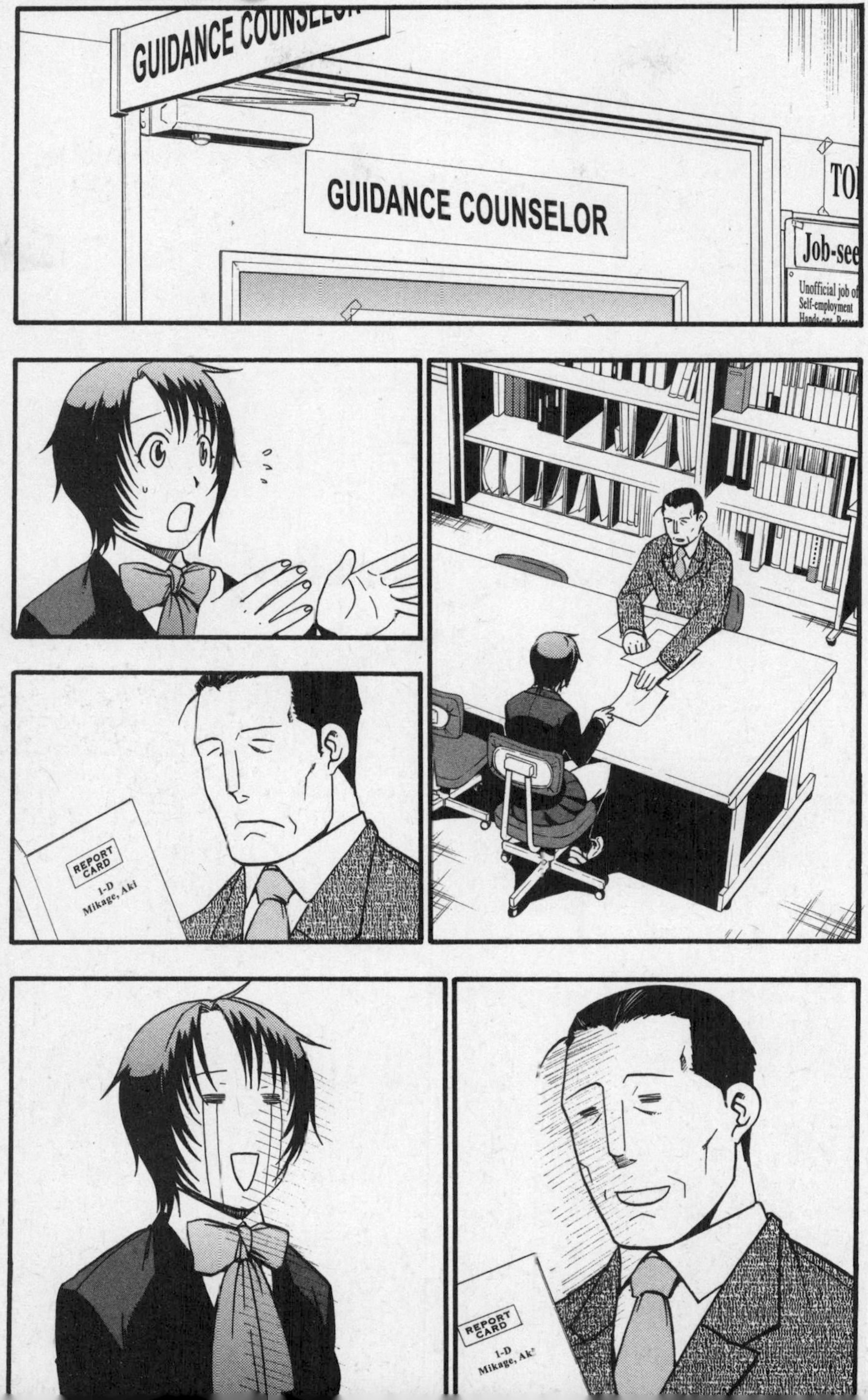
GUIDANCE COUNSELOR
GUIDANCE COUNSELOR
Job-see
Unofficial job of
Self-employment
REPORT CARD
1-D
Mikage, Aki
REPORT CARD
1-D
Mikage, Ak

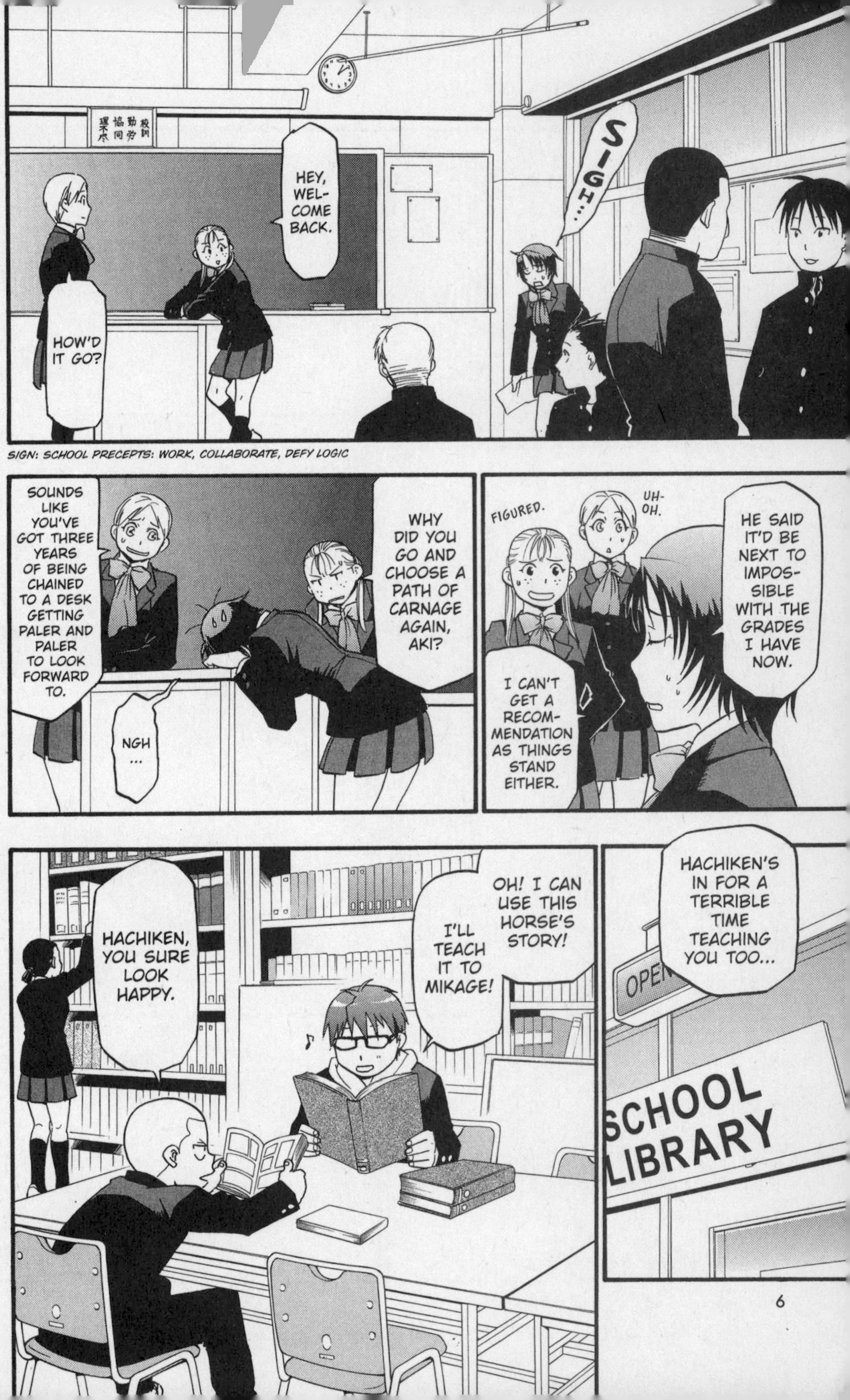
SIGH...
HEY, WELCOME BACK.
HOW'D IT GO?
SIGN: SCHOOL PRECEPTS: WORK, COLLABORATE, DEFY LOGIC
HE SAID IT'D BE NEXT TO IMPOSSIBLE WITH THE GRADES I HAVE NOW.
UH-OH.
FIGURED.
I CAN'T GET A RECOMMENDATION AS THINGS STAND EITHER.
WHY DID YOU GO AND CHOOSE A PATH OF CARNAGE AGAIN, AKI?
SOUNDS LIKE YOU'VE GOT THREE YEARS OF BEING CHAINED TO A DESK GETTING PALER AND PALER TO LOOK FORWARD TO.
NGH...
HACHIKEN'S IN FOR A TERRIBLE TIME TEACHING YOU TOO...
SCHOOL LIBRARY
OH! I CAN USE THIS HORSE'S STORY!
I'LL TEACH IT TO MIKAGE!
HACHIKEN, YOU SURE LOOK HAPPY.

Chapter 71:
Tale of Winter ⑧

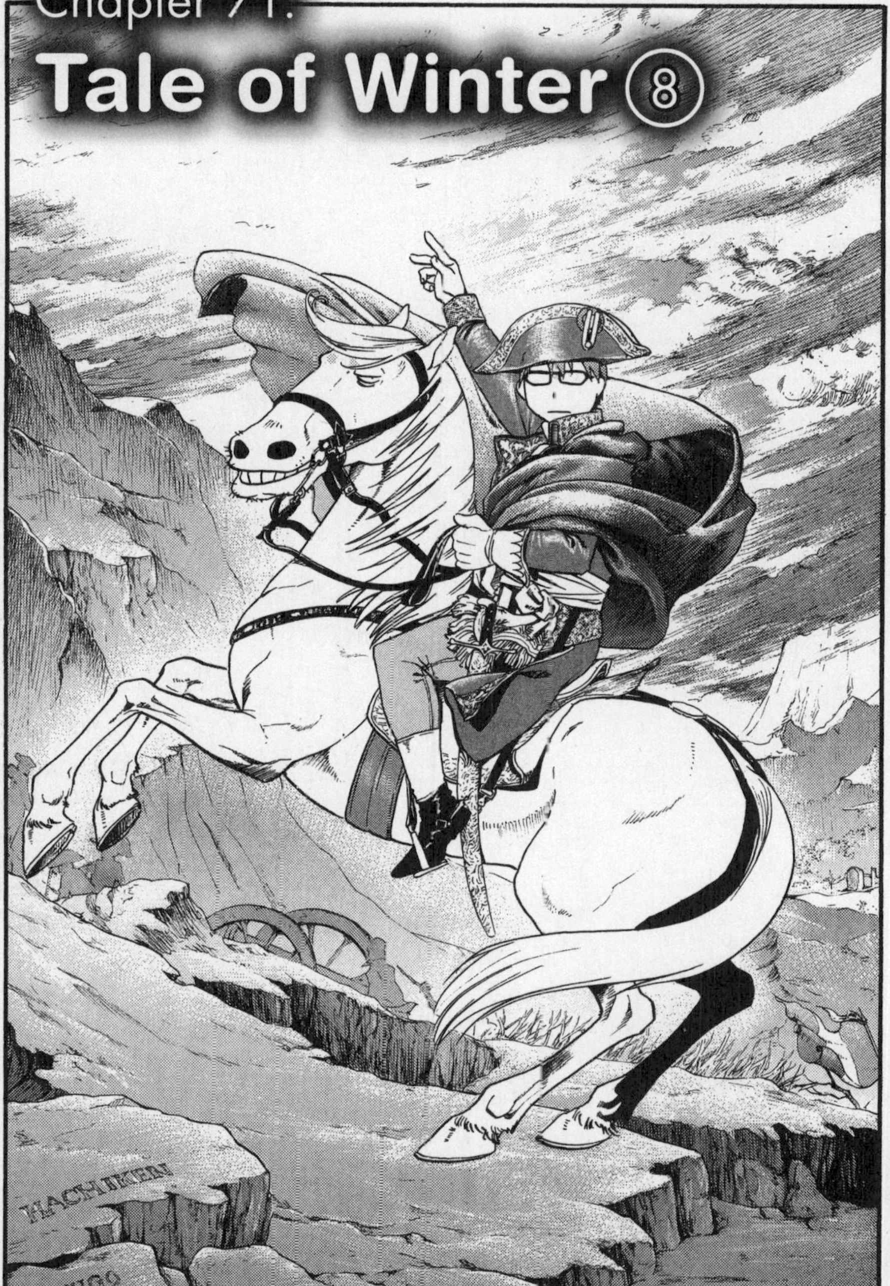
HACHIKEN
YUGO

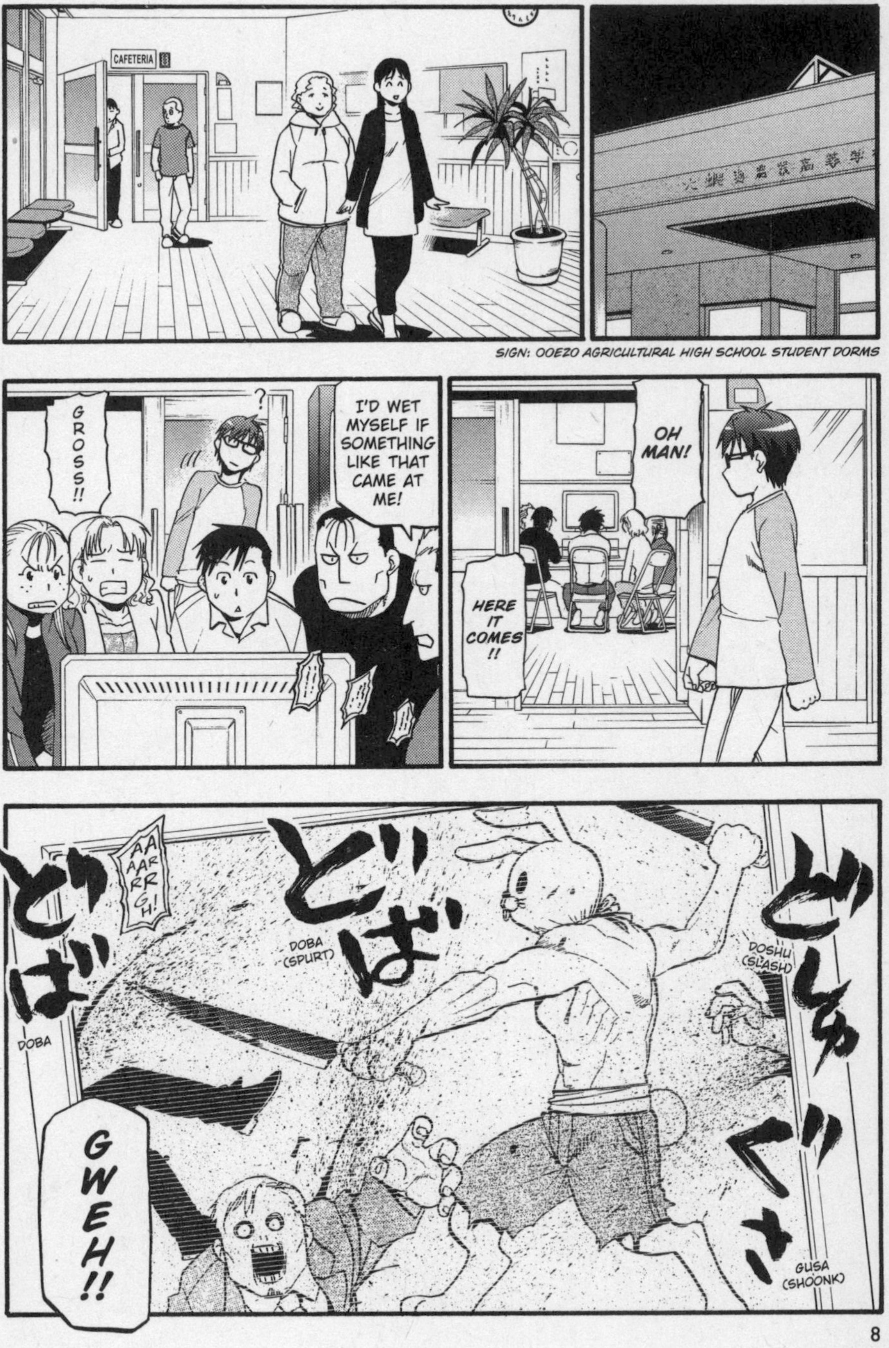

CAFETERIA
SIGN: OOEZO AGRICULTURAL HIGH SCHOOL STUDENT DORMS
OH MAN!
HERE IT COMES!!
I'D WET MYSELF IF SOMETHING LIKE THAT CAME AT ME!
?
GROSS!!
DOSHU (SLASH)
GUSA (SHOONK)
DOBA (SPURT)
AAAARRRGH!
DOBA
GWEH!!

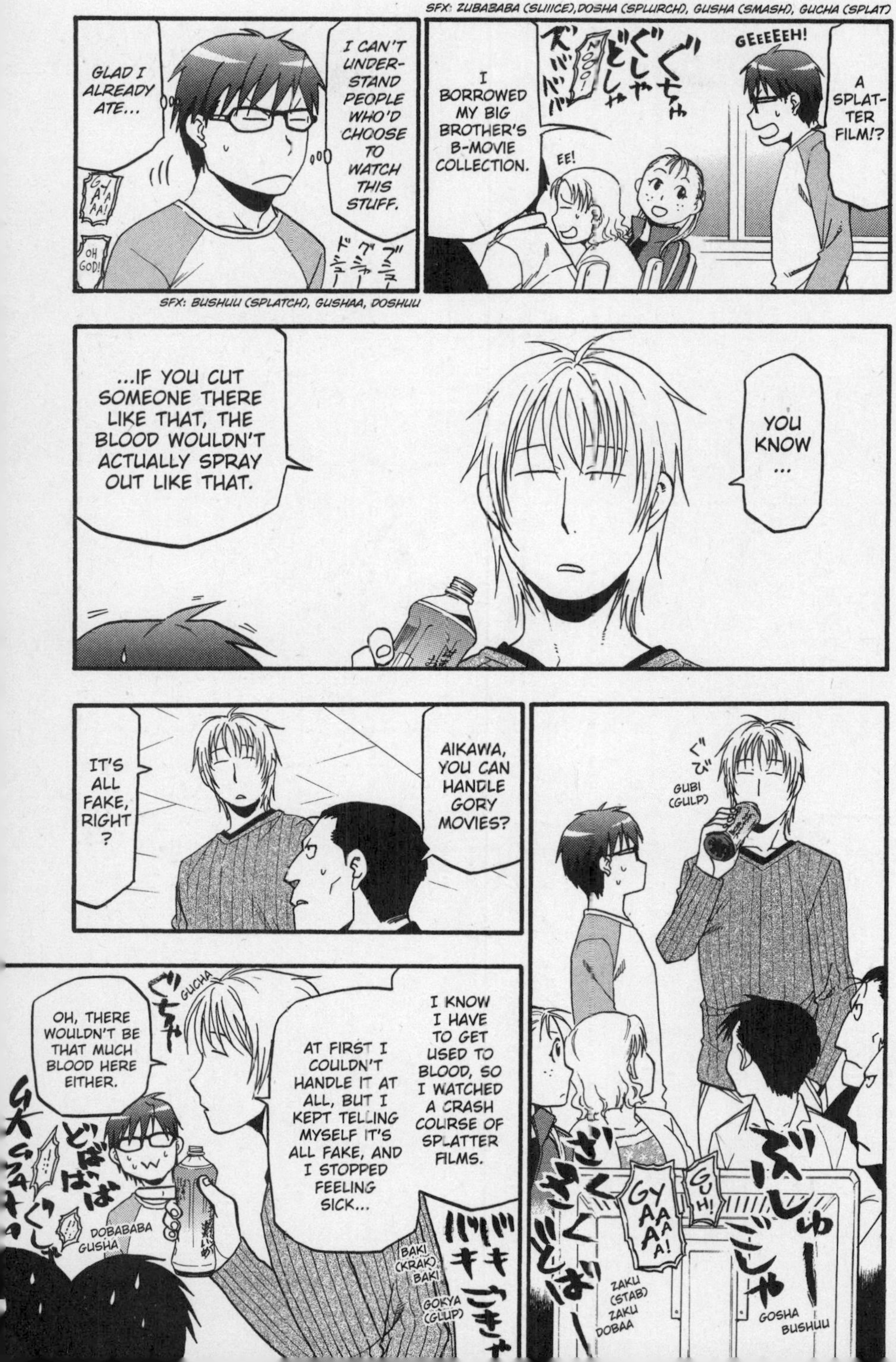

SFX: ZUBABABA (SLIIICE), DOSHA (SPLURCH), GUSHA (SMASH), GUCHA (SPLAT)
GEEEEEH!
A SPLATTER FILM!?
I BORROWED MY BIG BROTHER'S B-MOVIE COLLECTION.
NOOO!
EE!
I CAN'T UNDERSTAND PEOPLE WHO'D CHOOSE TO WATCH THIS STUFF.
GLAD I ALREADY ATE...
GYAAA!
OH GOD!
SFX: BUSHUU (SPLATCH), GUSHAA, DOSHUU
YOU KNOW...
...IF YOU CUT SOMEONE THERE LIKE THAT, THE BLOOD WOULDN'T ACTUALLY SPRAY OUT LIKE THAT.
GUBI (GULP)
GUH!
GYAAAA!
GOSHA BUSHUU
ZAKU (STAB) ZAKU DOBAA
AIKAWA, YOU CAN HANDLE GORY MOVIES?
IT'S ALL FAKE, RIGHT?
I KNOW I HAVE TO GET USED TO BLOOD, SO I WATCHED A CRASH COURSE OF SPLATTER FILMS.
AT FIRST I COULDN'T HANDLE IT AT ALL, BUT I KEPT TELLING MYSELF IT'S ALL FAKE, AND I STOPPED FEELING SICK...
GUCHA
OH, THERE WOULDN'T BE THAT MUCH BLOOD HERE EITHER.
BAKI (KRAK) BAKI
GOKYA (GLUP)
DOBABABA GUSHA

SFX: GUCHA (SQUELCH) GUCHA, BUCHI (BLRCH) BUCHI

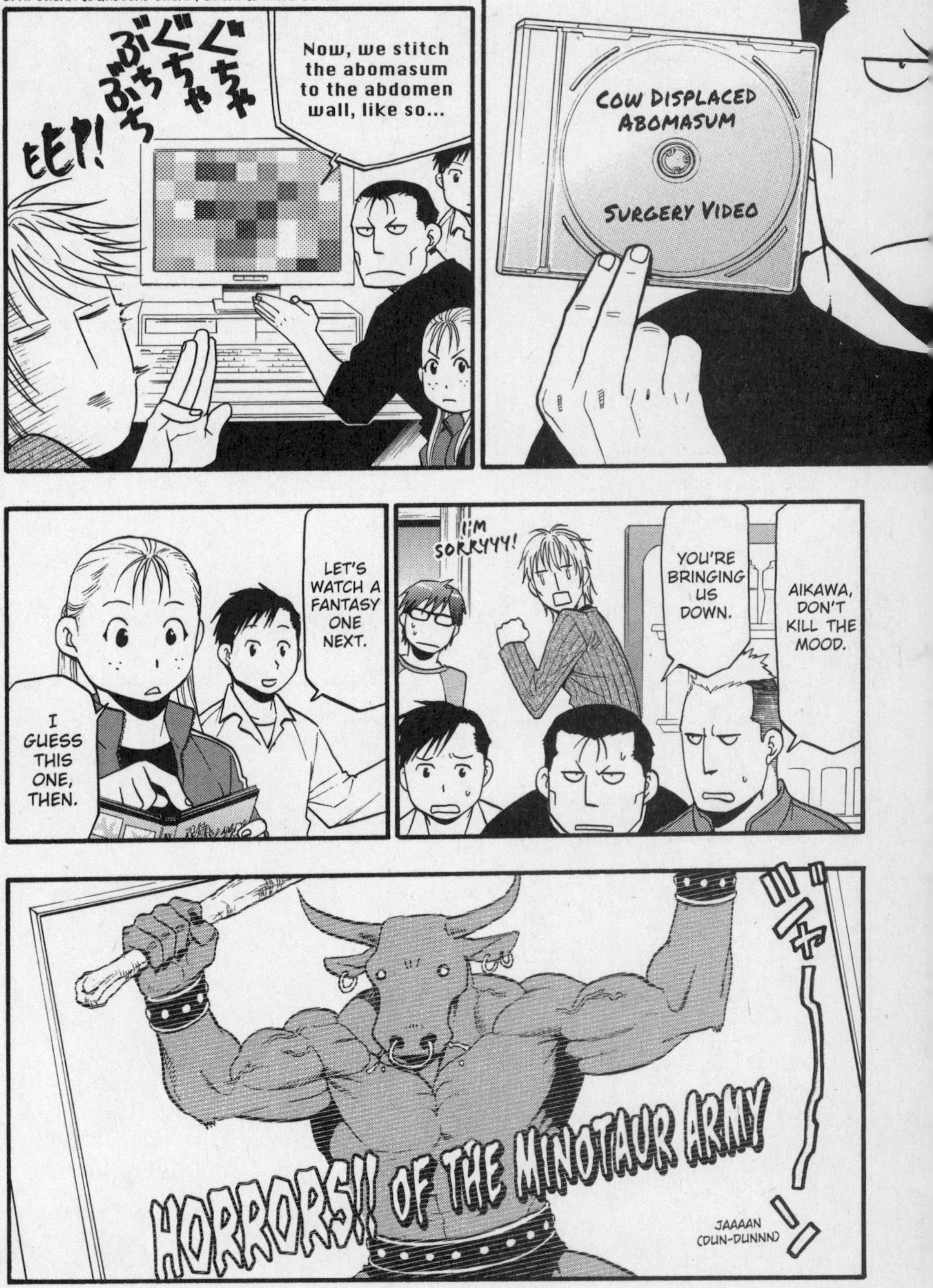
COW DISPLACED ABOMASUM
SURGERY VIDEO
Now, we stitch the abomasum to the abdomen wall, like so...
ぐちゃぐちゃ
ぶちぶち
EEP!
AIKAWA, DON'T KILL THE MOOD.
YOU'RE BRINGING US DOWN.
I'M SORRYYY!
LET'S WATCH A FANTASY ONE NEXT.
I GUESS THIS ONE, THEN.
HORRORS!! OF THE MINOTAUR ARMY
ジャーン
JAAAAN (DUN-DUNNN)

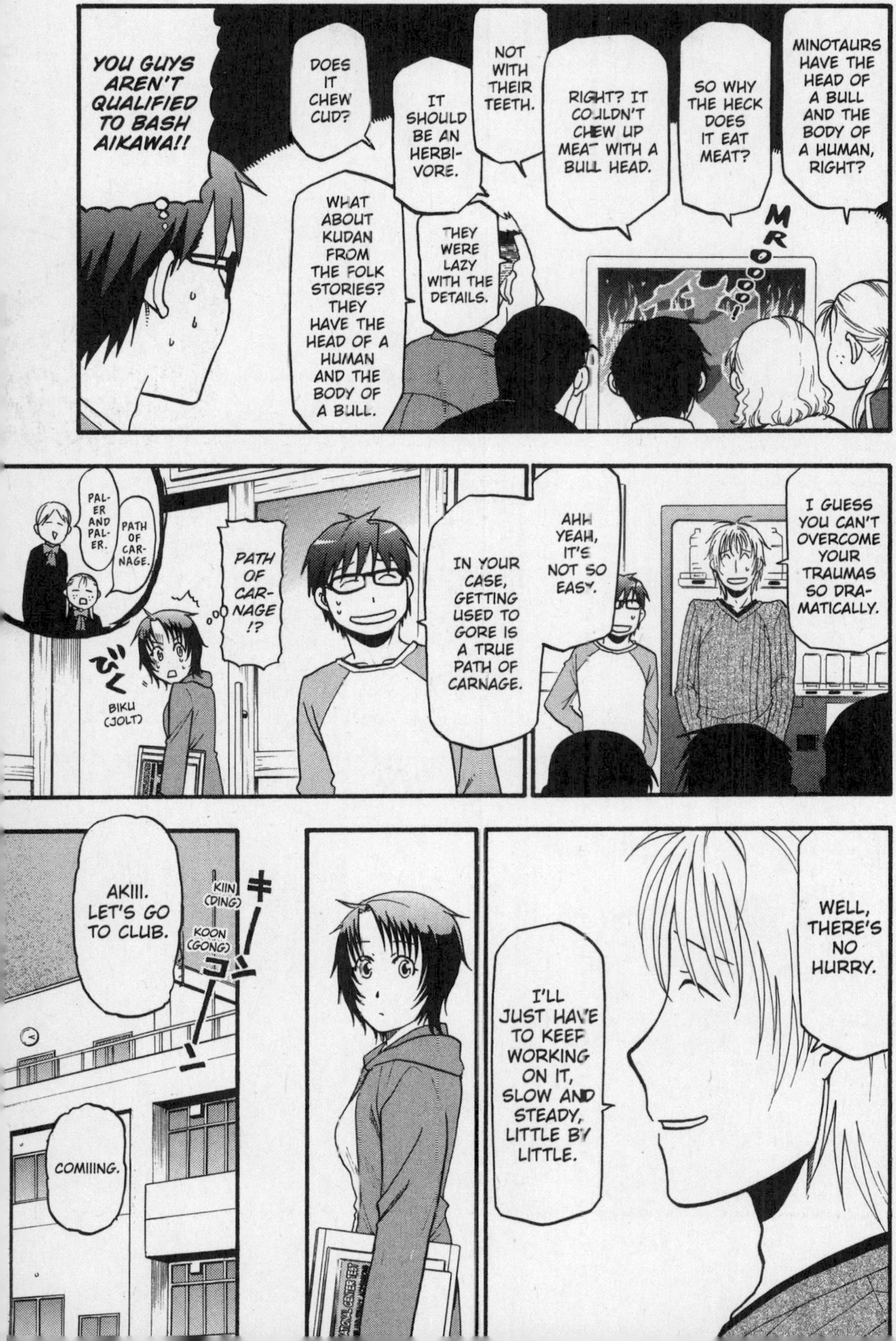
MINOTAURS HAVE THE HEAD OF A BULL AND THE BODY OF A HUMAN, RIGHT?
MROOOOO!
SO WHY THE HECK DOES IT EAT MEAT?
RIGHT? IT COULDN'T CHEW UP MEAT WITH A BULL HEAD.
NOT WITH THEIR TEETH.
IT SHOULD BE AN HERBIVORE.
DOES IT CHEW CUD?
THEY WERE LAZY WITH THE DETAILS.
WHAT ABOUT KUDAN FROM THE FOLK STORIES? THEY HAVE THE HEAD OF A HUMAN AND THE BODY OF A BULL.
YOU GUYS AREN'T QUALIFIED TO BASH AIKAWA!!
I GUESS YOU CAN'T OVERCOME YOUR TRAUMAS SO DRAMATICALLY.
AHH YEAH, IT'S NOT SO EASY.
IN YOUR CASE, GETTING USED TO GORE IS A TRUE PATH OF CARNAGE.
PATH OF CARNAGE!?
PALER AND PALER.
PATH OF CARNAGE.
BIKU (JOLT)
WELL, THERE'S NO HURRY.
I'LL JUST HAVE TO KEEP WORKING ON IT, SLOW AND STEADY, LITTLE BY LITTLE.
AKIII. LET'S GO TO CLUB.
KIIN (DING)
KOON (GONG)
COMIIING.

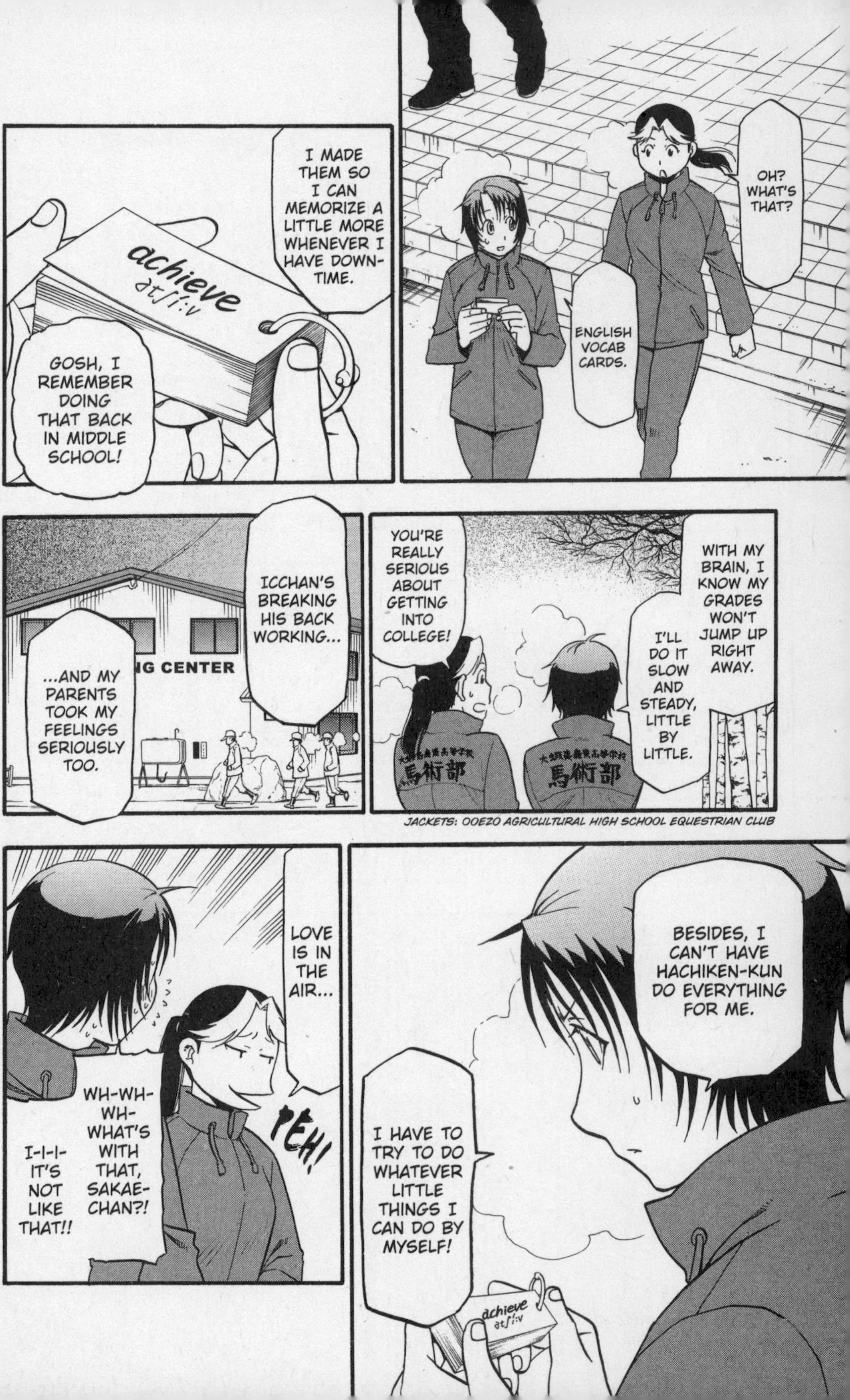
OH? WHAT'S THAT?
ENGLISH VOCAB CARDS.
achieve
I MADE THEM SO I CAN MEMORIZE A LITTLE MORE WHENEVER I HAVE DOWN-TIME.
GOSH, I REMEMBER DOING THAT BACK IN MIDDLE SCHOOL!
WITH MY BRAIN, I KNOW MY GRADES WON'T JUMP UP RIGHT AWAY.
I'LL DO IT SLOW AND STEADY, LITTLE BY LITTLE.
YOU'RE REALLY SERIOUS ABOUT GETTING INTO COLLEGE!
ICCHAN'S BREAKING HIS BACK WORKING...
...AND MY PARENTS TOOK MY FEELINGS SERIOUSLY TOO.
BESIDES, I CAN'T HAVE HACHIKEN-KUN DO EVERYTHING FOR ME.
I HAVE TO TRY TO DO WHATEVER LITTLE THINGS I CAN DO BY MYSELF!
achieve
LOVE IS IN THE AIR...
PEH!
WH-WH-WH-WHAT'S WITH THAT, SAKAE-CHAN?!
I-I-I-IT'S NOT LIKE THAT!!
JACKETS: OOEZO AGRICULTURAL HIGH SCHOOL EQUESTRIAN CLUB

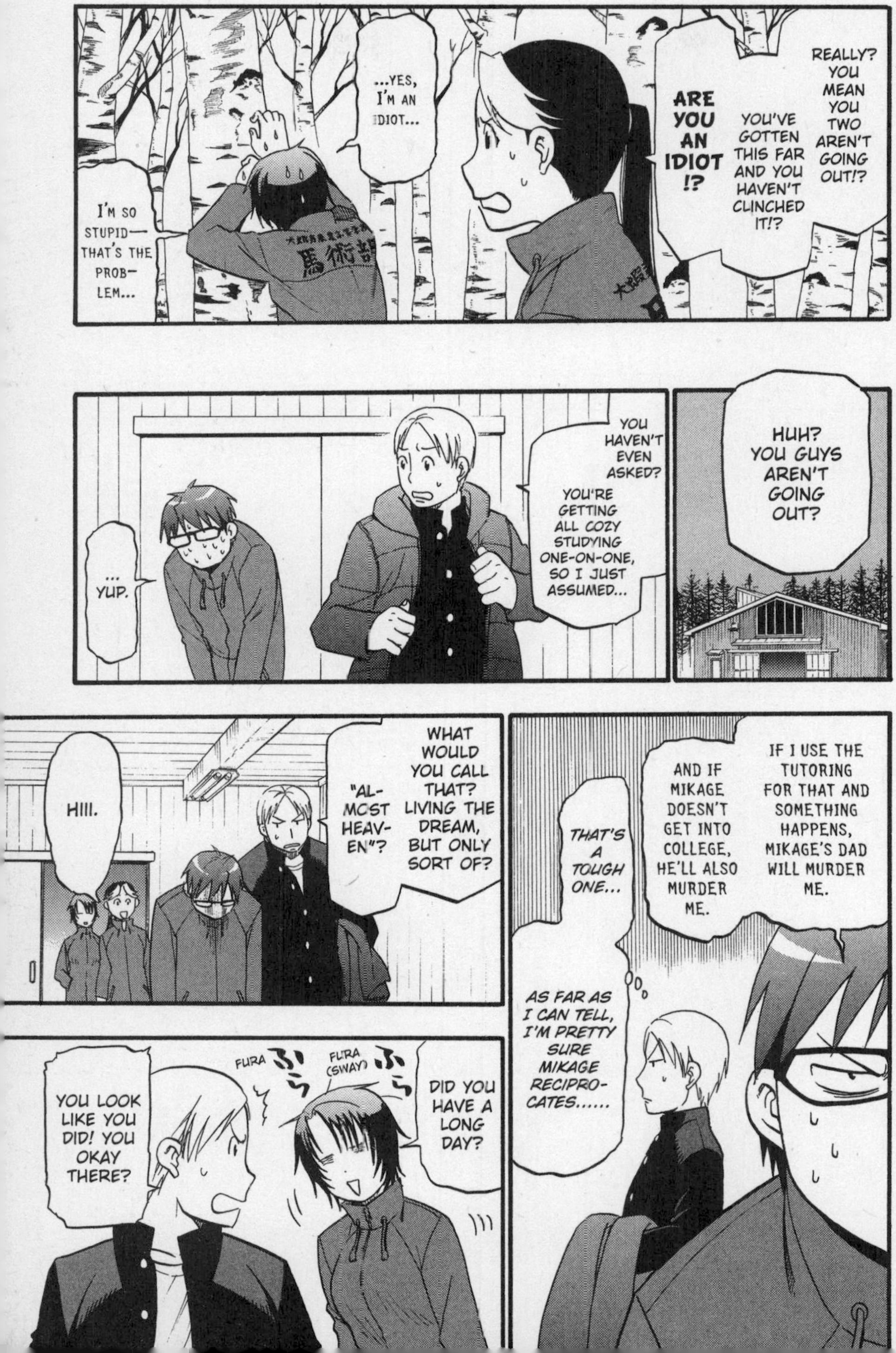
REALLY? YOU MEAN YOU TWO AREN'T GOING OUT!?
YOU'VE GOTTEN THIS FAR AND YOU HAVEN'T CLINCHED IT!?
ARE YOU AN IDIOT!?
...YES, I'M AN IDIOT...
I'M SO STUPID—THAT'S THE PROBLEM...
HUH? YOU GUYS AREN'T GOING OUT?
YOU HAVEN'T EVEN ASKED?
YOU'RE GETTING ALL COZY STUDYING ONE-ON-ONE, SO I JUST ASSUMED...
...YUP.
IF I USE THE TUTORING FOR THAT AND SOMETHING HAPPENS, MIKAGE'S DAD WILL MURDER ME.
AND IF MIKAGE DOESN'T GET INTO COLLEGE, HE'LL ALSO MURDER ME.
THAT'S A TOUGH ONE...
AS FAR AS I CAN TELL, I'M PRETTY SURE MIKAGE RECIPROCATES......
WHAT WOULD YOU CALL THAT? LIVING THE DREAM, BUT ONLY SORT OF?
"ALMOST HEAVEN"?
HIII.
ふら FURA (SWAY)
ふら FURA
DID YOU HAVE A LONG DAY?
YOU LOOK LIKE YOU DID! YOU OKAY THERE?

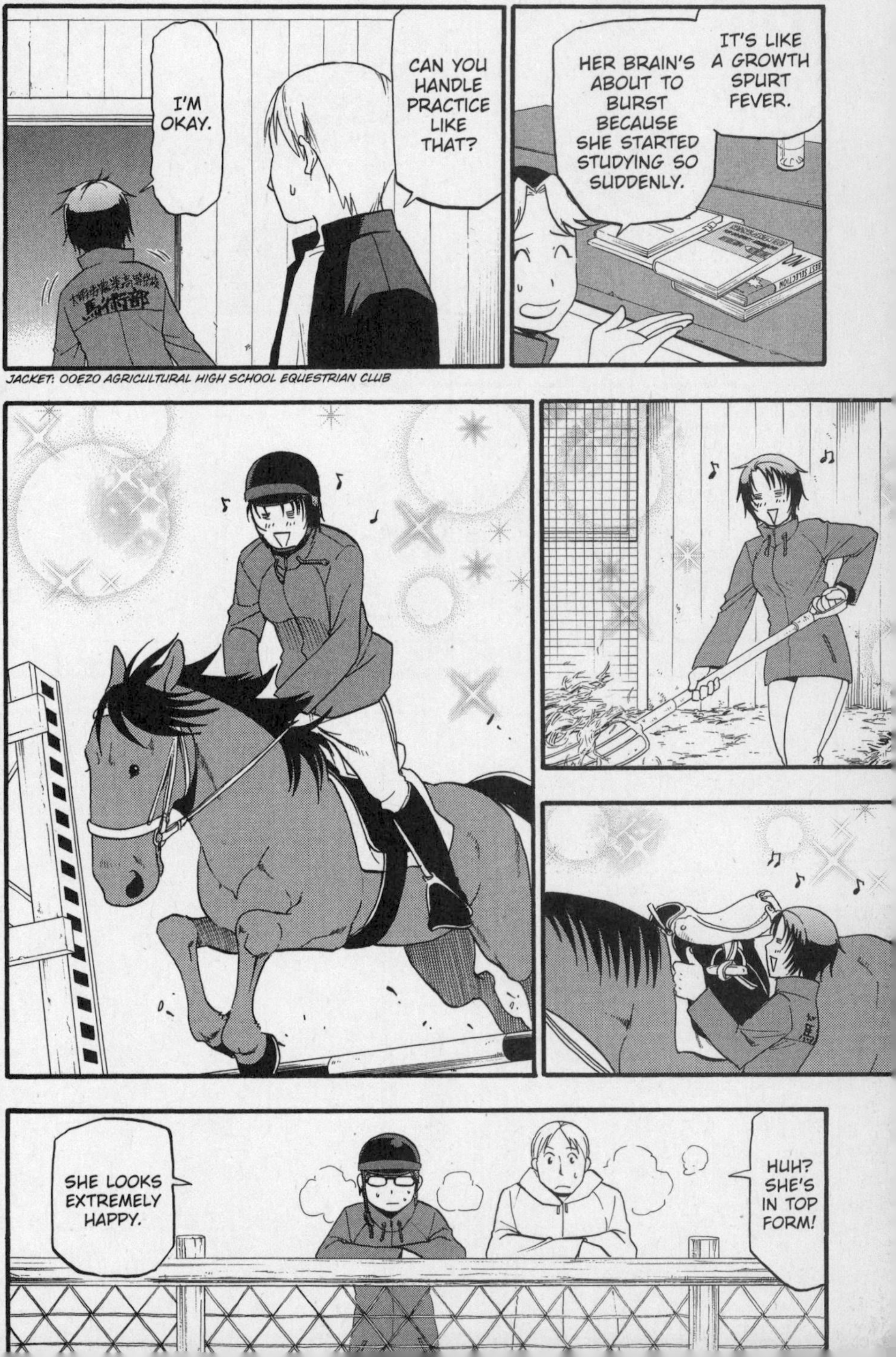
IT'S LIKE A GROWTH SPURT FEVER.
HER BRAIN'S ABOUT TO BURST BECAUSE SHE STARTED STUDYING SO SUDDENLY.
CAN YOU HANDLE PRACTICE LIKE THAT?
I'M OKAY.
JACKET: OOEZO AGRICULTURAL HIGH SCHOOL EQUESTRIAN CLUB
HUH? SHE'S IN TOP FORM!
SHE LOOKS EXTREMELY HAPPY.

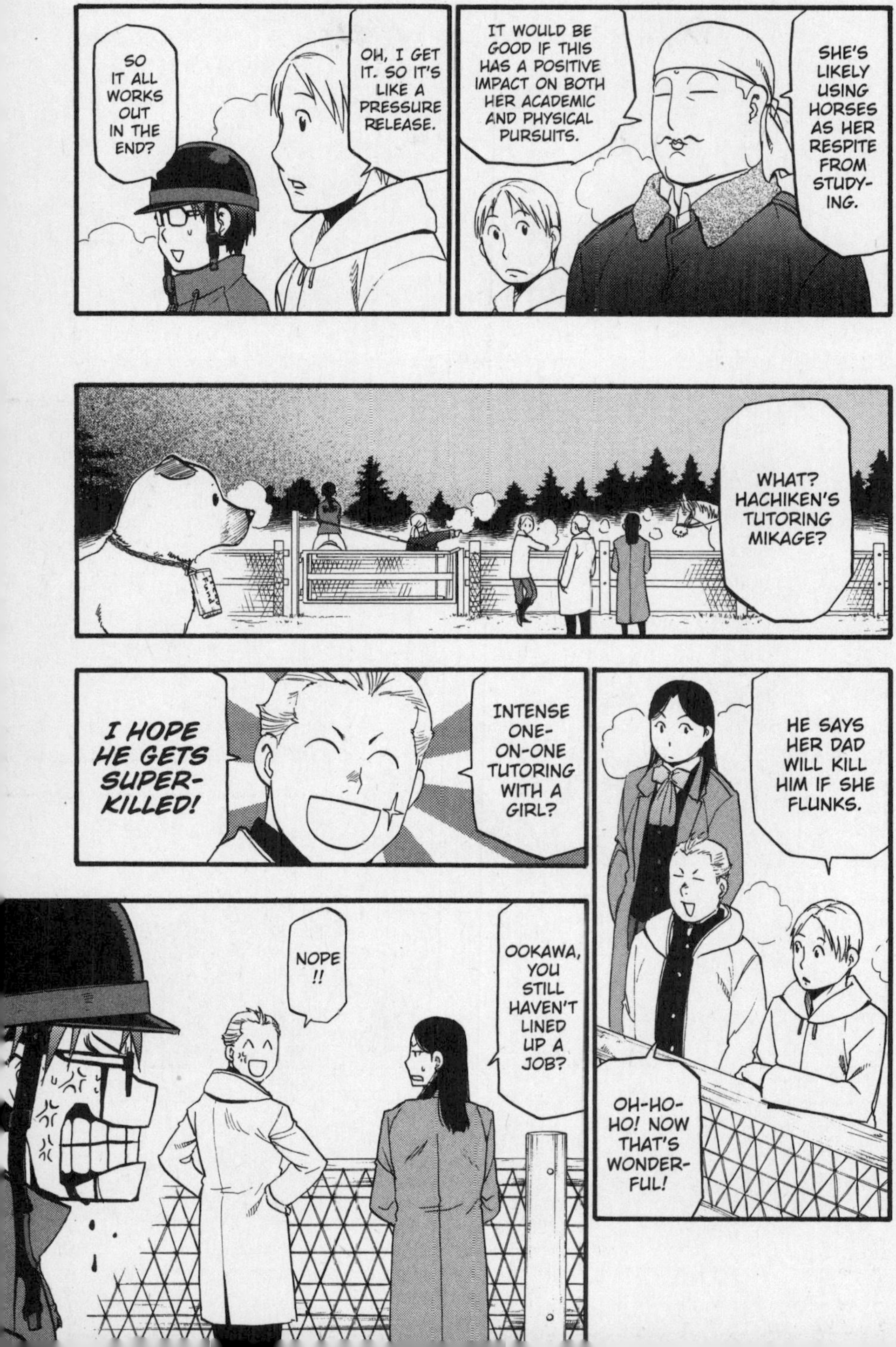
SHE'S LIKELY USING HORSES AS HER RESPITE FROM STUDYING.
IT WOULD BE GOOD IF THIS HAS A POSITIVE IMPACT ON BOTH HER ACADEMIC AND PHYSICAL PURSUITS.
OH, I GET IT. SO IT'S LIKE A PRESSURE RELEASE.
SO IT ALL WORKS OUT IN THE END?
WHAT? HACHIKEN'S TUTORING MIKAGE?
HE SAYS HER DAD WILL KILL HIM IF SHE FLUNKS.
OH-HO-HO! NOW THAT'S WONDERFUL!
INTENSE ONE-ON-ONE TUTORING WITH A GIRL?
I HOPE HE GETS SUPER-KILLED!
OOKAWA, YOU STILL HAVEN'T LINED UP A JOB?
NOPE!!

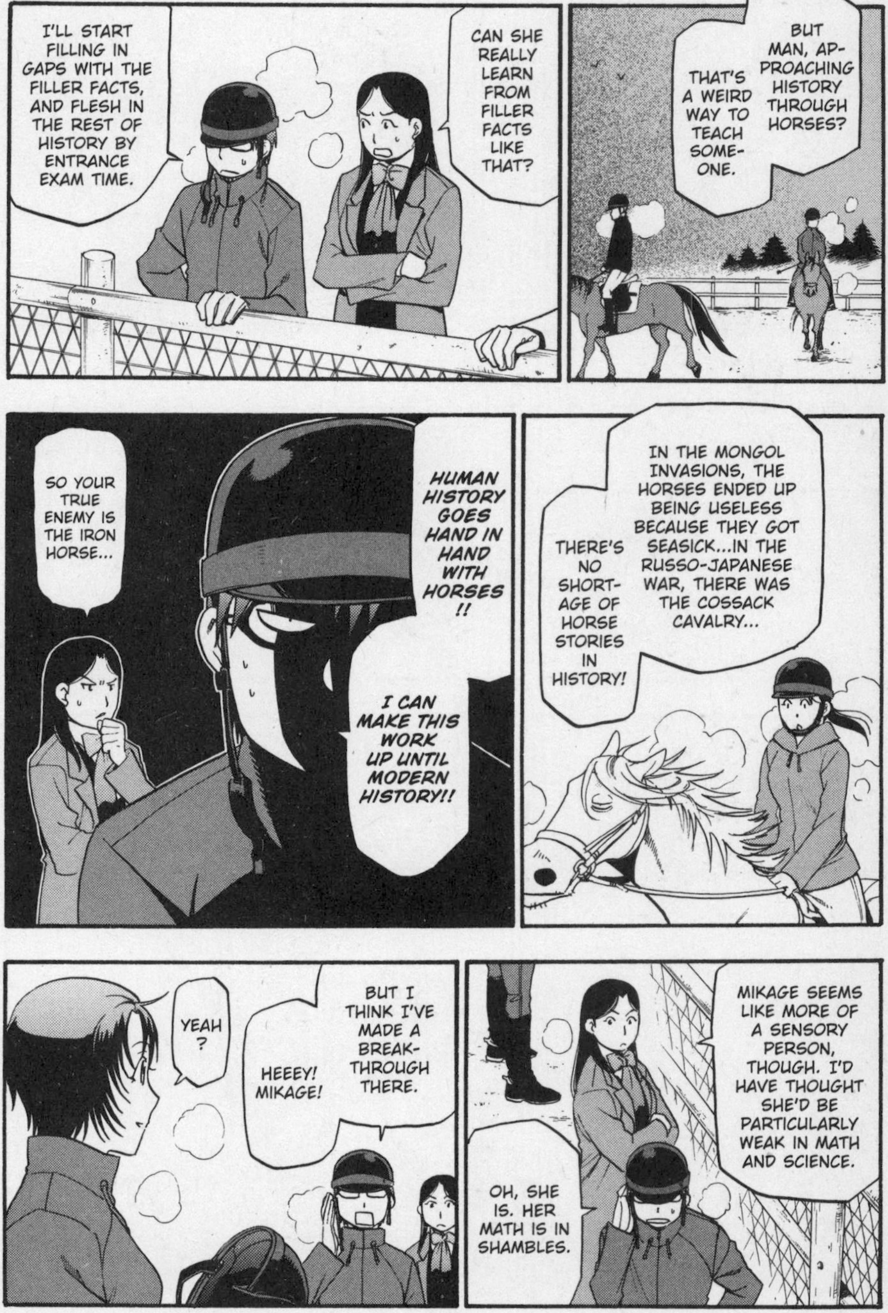
BUT MAN, APPROACHING HISTORY THROUGH HORSES?
THAT'S A WEIRD WAY TO TEACH SOMEONE.
I'LL START FILLING IN GAPS WITH THE FILLER FACTS, AND FLESH IN THE REST OF HISTORY BY ENTRANCE EXAM TIME.
CAN SHE REALLY LEARN FROM FILLER FACTS LIKE THAT?
IN THE MONGOL INVASIONS, THE HORSES ENDED UP BEING USELESS BECAUSE THEY GOT SEASICK...IN THE RUSSO-JAPANESE WAR, THERE WAS THE COSSACK CAVALRY...
THERE'S NO SHORTAGE OF HORSE STORIES IN HISTORY!
HUMAN HISTORY GOES HAND IN HAND WITH HORSES!!
I CAN MAKE THIS WORK UP UNTIL MODERN HISTORY!!
SO YOUR TRUE ENEMY IS THE IRON HORSE...
MIKAGE SEEMS LIKE MORE OF A SENSORY PERSON, THOUGH. I'D HAVE THOUGHT SHE'D BE PARTICULARLY WEAK IN MATH AND SCIENCE.
OH, SHE IS. HER MATH IS IN SHAMBLES.
BUT I THINK I'VE MADE A BREAKTHROUGH THERE.
HEEEY! MIKAGE!
YEAH?

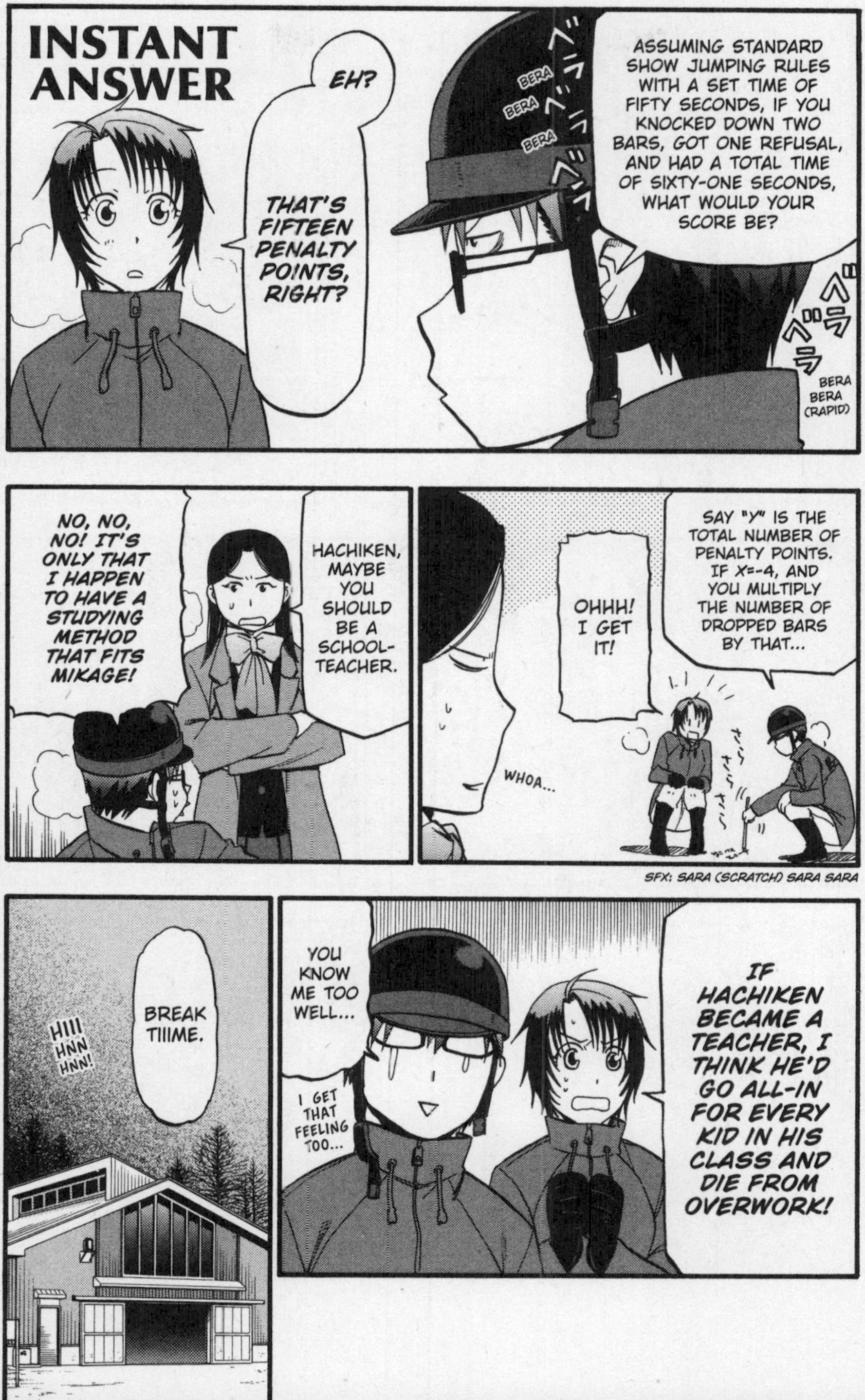
INSTANT ANSWER
ASSUMING STANDARD SHOW JUMPING RULES WITH A SET TIME OF FIFTY SECONDS, IF YOU KNOCKED DOWN TWO BARS, GOT ONE REFUSAL, AND HAD A TOTAL TIME OF SIXTY-ONE SECONDS, WHAT WOULD YOUR SCORE BE?
BERA BERA BERA
BERA BERA (RAPID)
EH?
THAT'S FIFTEEN PENALTY POINTS, RIGHT?
SAY "Y" IS THE TOTAL NUMBER OF PENALTY POINTS. IF X=-4, AND YOU MULTIPLY THE NUMBER OF DROPPED BARS BY THAT...
OHHH! I GET IT!
WHOA...
SFX: SARA (SCRATCH) SARA SARA
HACHIKEN, MAYBE YOU SHOULD BE A SCHOOL-TEACHER.
NO, NO, NO! IT'S ONLY THAT I HAPPEN TO HAVE A STUDYING METHOD THAT FITS MIKAGE!
IF HACHIKEN BECAME A TEACHER, I THINK HE'D GO ALL-IN FOR EVERY KID IN HIS CLASS AND DIE FROM OVERWORK!
YOU KNOW ME TOO WELL...
I GET THAT FEELING TOO...
BREAK TIIIME.
HIIII HNN HNN!

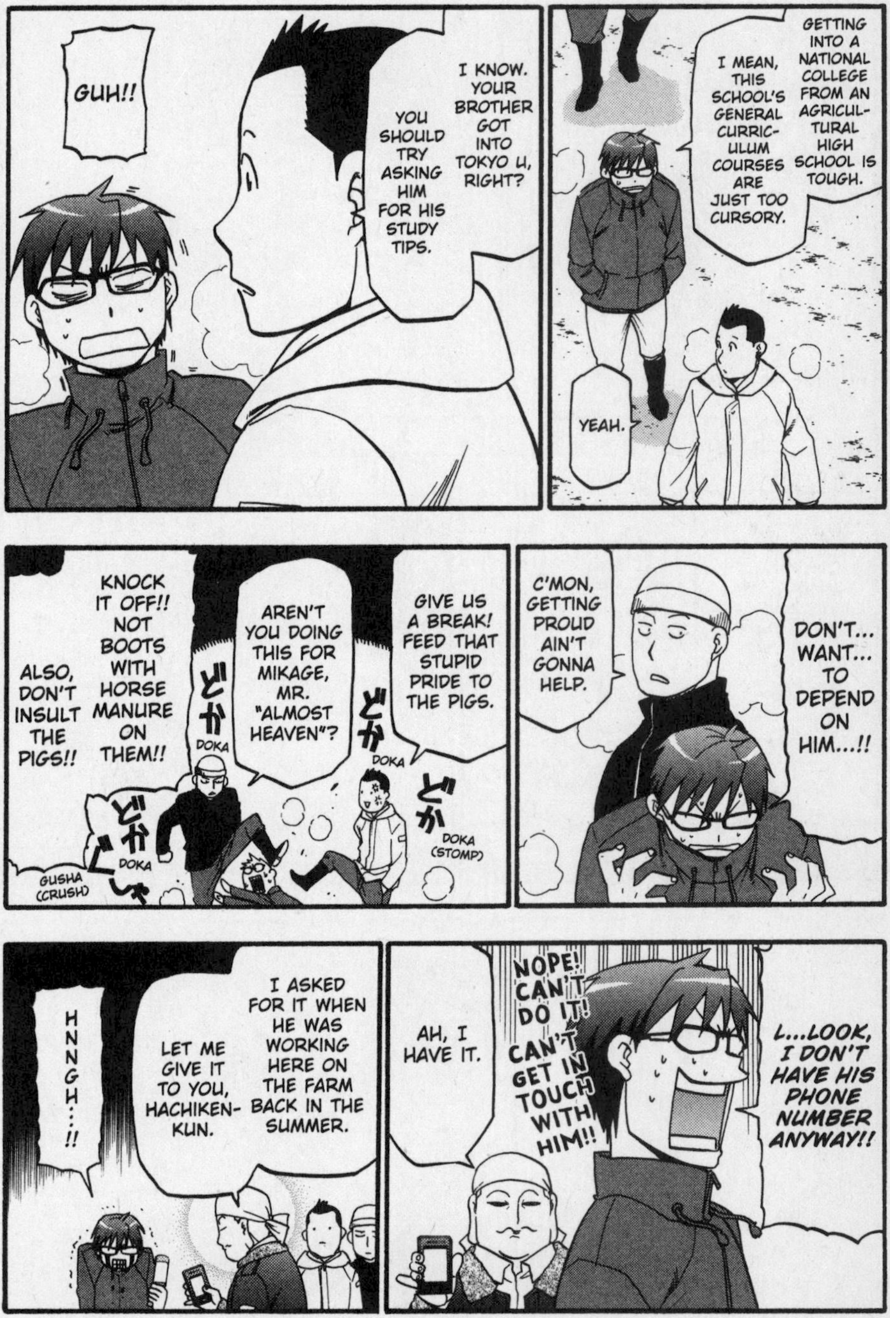
GETTING INTO A NATIONAL COLLEGE FROM AN AGRICUL-TURAL HIGH SCHOOL IS TOUGH.
I MEAN, THIS SCHOOL'S GENERAL CURRIC-ULUM COURSES ARE JUST TOO CURSORY.
YEAH.
I KNOW. YOUR BROTHER GOT INTO TOKYO U, RIGHT?
YOU SHOULD TRY ASKING HIM FOR HIS STUDY TIPS.
GUH!!
DON'T... WANT... TO DEPEND ON HIM...!!
C'MON, GETTING PROUD AIN'T GONNA HELP.
GIVE US A BREAK! FEED THAT STUPID PRIDE TO THE PIGS.
どか
DOKA (STOMP)
どか
DOKA
AREN'T YOU DOING THIS FOR MIKAGE, MR. "ALMOST HEAVEN"?
どか
DOKA
KNOCK IT OFF!! NOT BOOTS WITH HORSE MANURE ON THEM!!
ALSO, DON'T INSULT THE PIGS!!
どか
DOKA
ぐしゃ
GUSHA (CRUSH)
L...LOOK, I DON'T HAVE HIS PHONE NUMBER ANYWAY!!
NOPE! CAN'T DO IT! CAN'T GET IN TOUCH WITH HIM!!
AH, I HAVE IT.
I ASKED FOR IT WHEN HE WAS WORKING HERE ON THE FARM BACK IN THE SUMMER.
LET ME GIVE IT TO YOU, HACHIKEN-KUN.
HNNGH...!!

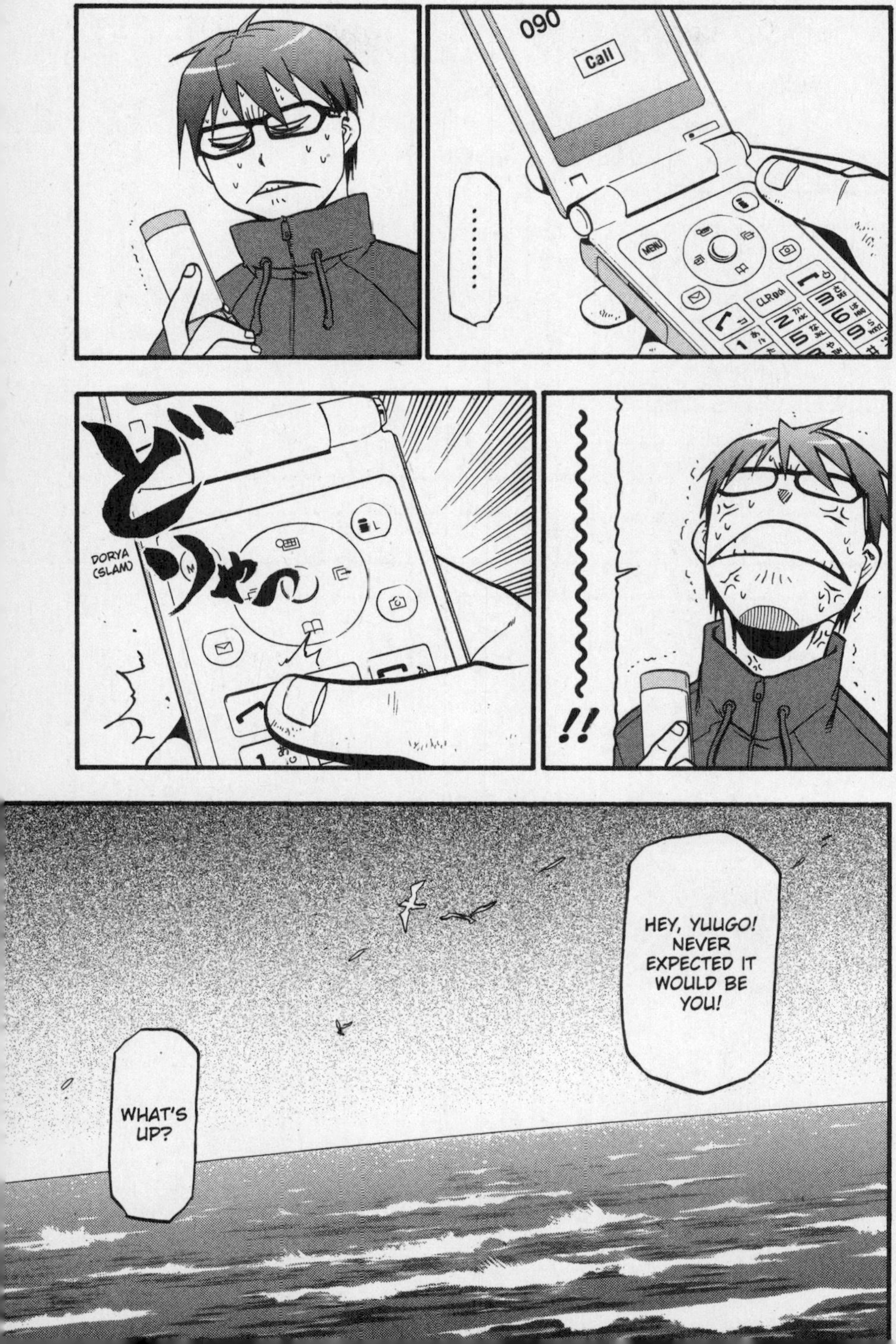
090
Call
......
!!
DORYA (SLAM)
HEY, YUUGO! NEVER EXPECTED IT WOULD BE YOU!
WHAT'S UP?

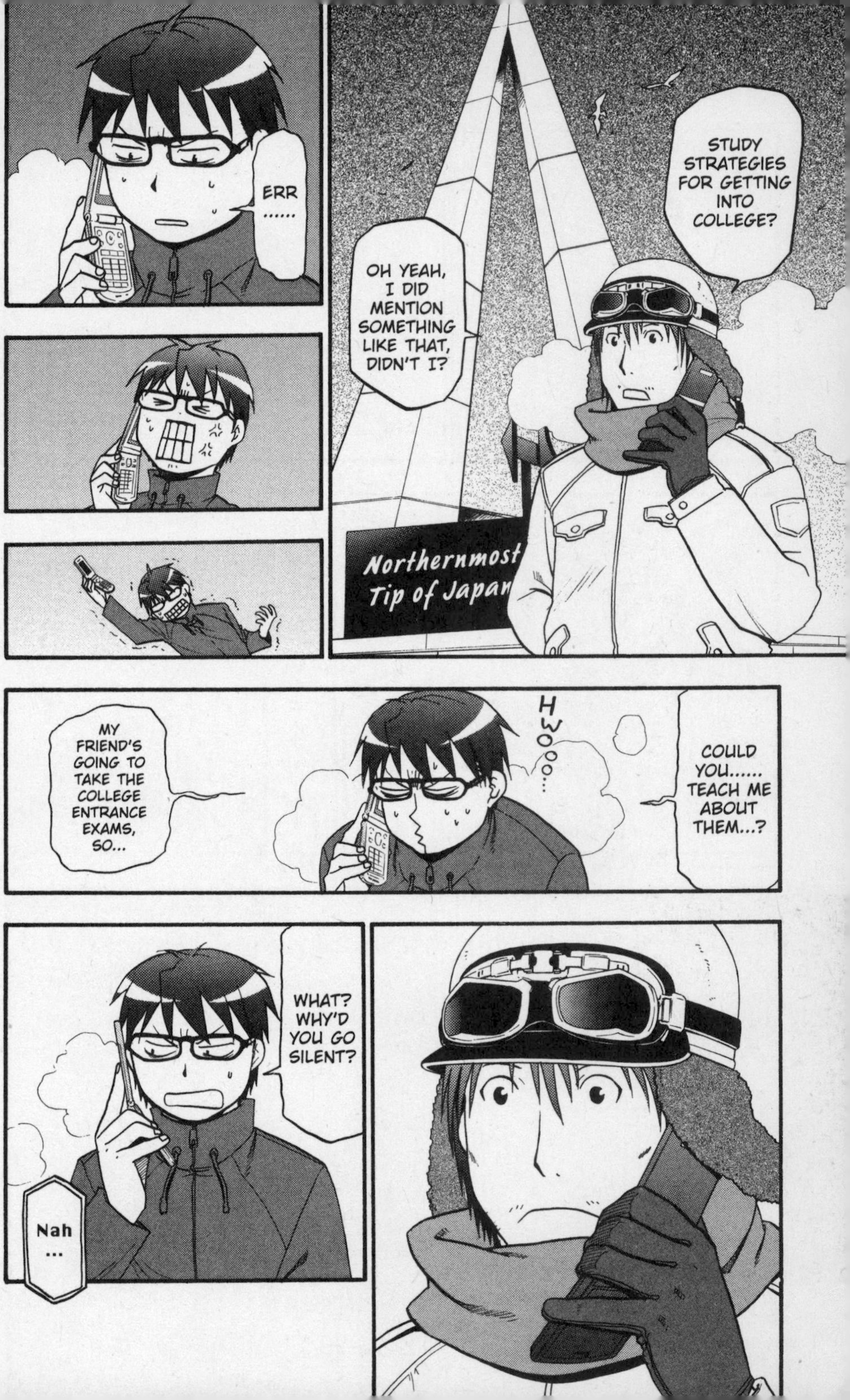
STUDY STRATEGIES FOR GETTING INTO COLLEGE?
OH YEAH, I DID MENTION SOMETHING LIKE THAT, DIDN'T I?
Northernmost Tip of Japan
ERR ......
COULD YOU...... TEACH ME ABOUT THEM...?
HWOOOO...
MY FRIEND'S GOING TO TAKE THE COLLEGE ENTRANCE EXAMS, SO...
WHAT? WHY'D YOU GO SILENT?
Nah ...

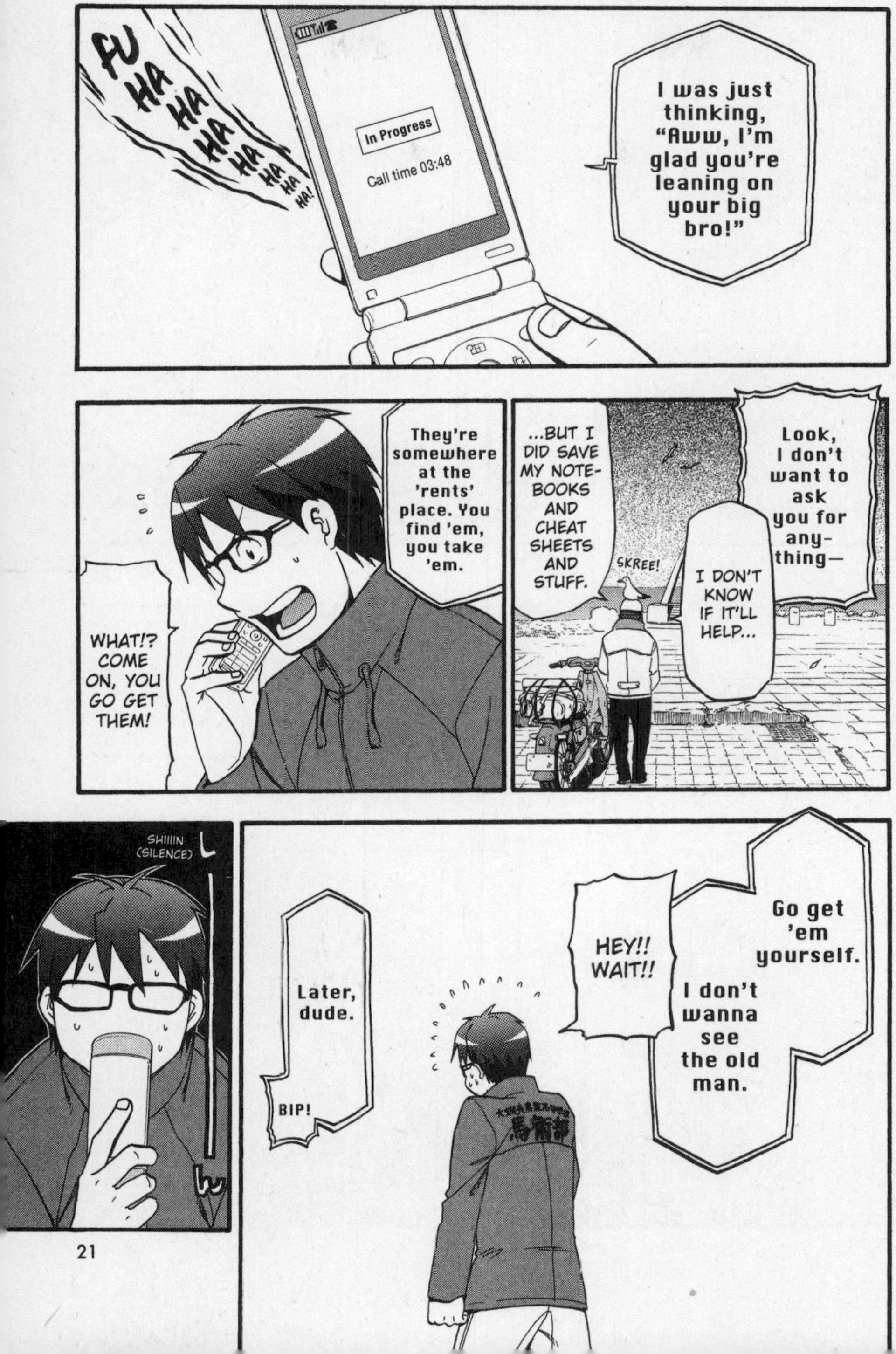

I was just thinking, "Aww, I'm glad you're leaning on your big bro!"
In Progress
Call time 03:48
FU HA HA HA HA HA HA HA!
Look, I don't want to ask you for anything—
I DON'T KNOW IF IT'LL HELP...
SKREE!
...BUT I DID SAVE MY NOTE-BOOKS AND CHEAT SHEETS AND STUFF.
They're somewhere at the 'rents' place. You find 'em, you take 'em.
WHAT!? COME ON, YOU GO GET THEM!
Go get 'em yourself.
I don't wanna see the old man.
HEY!! WAIT!!
Later, dude.
BIP!
SHIIIIN (SILENCE)

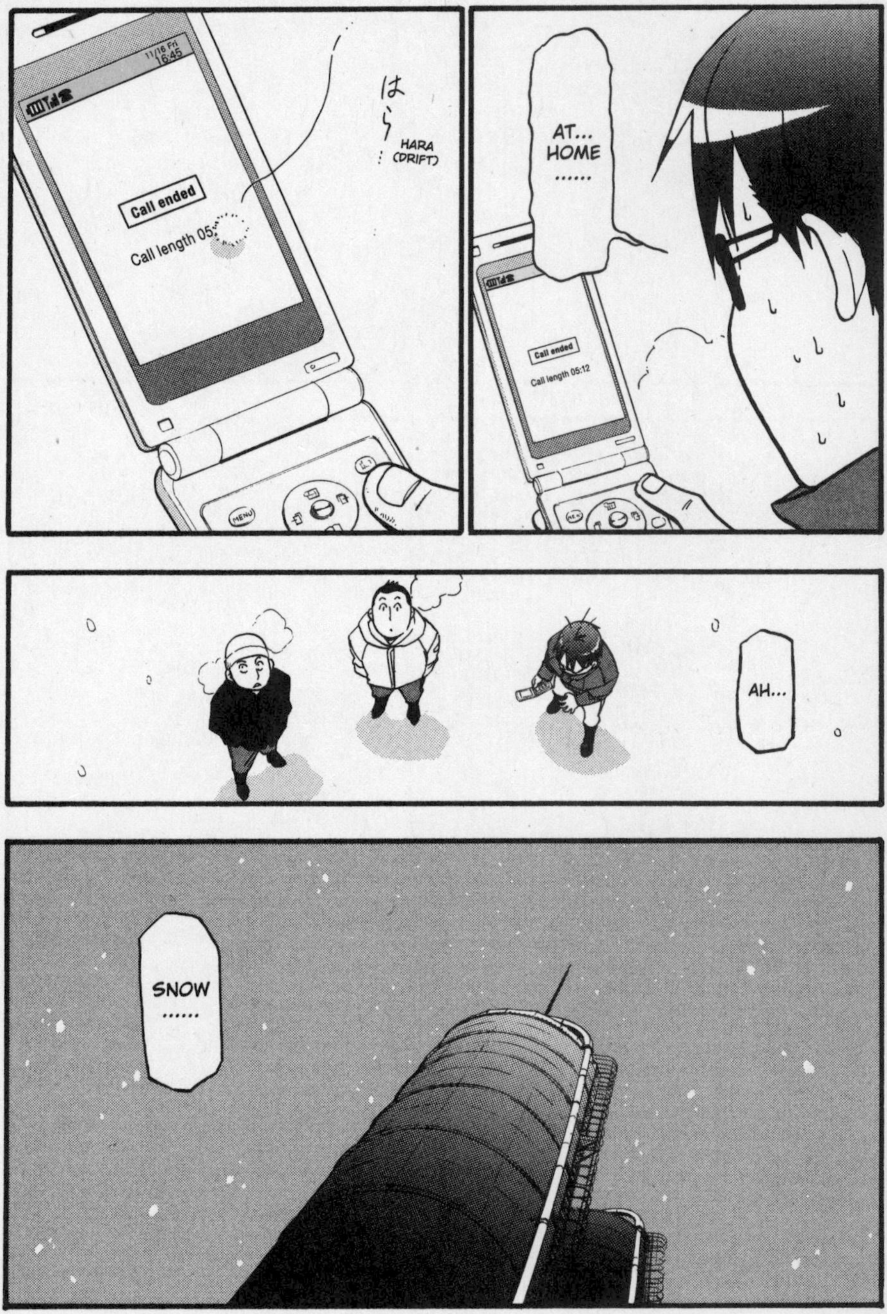
AT... HOME ......
Call ended
Call length 05:12
11/16 Fri 16:45
Call ended
Call length 05:
はら
HARA (DRIFT)
AH...
SNOW ......

Silver Spoon

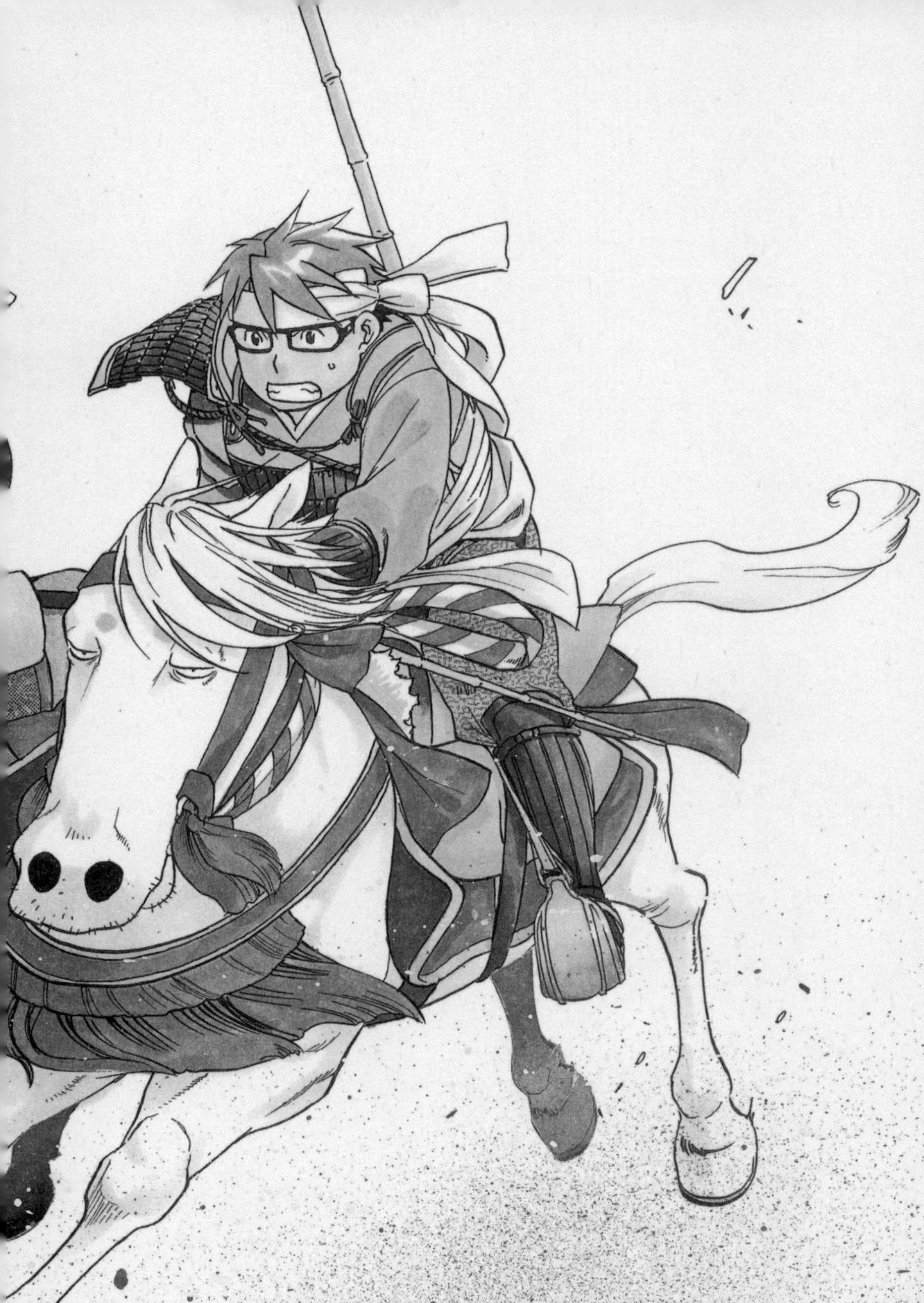

Chapter 72:
Tale of Winter ⑨

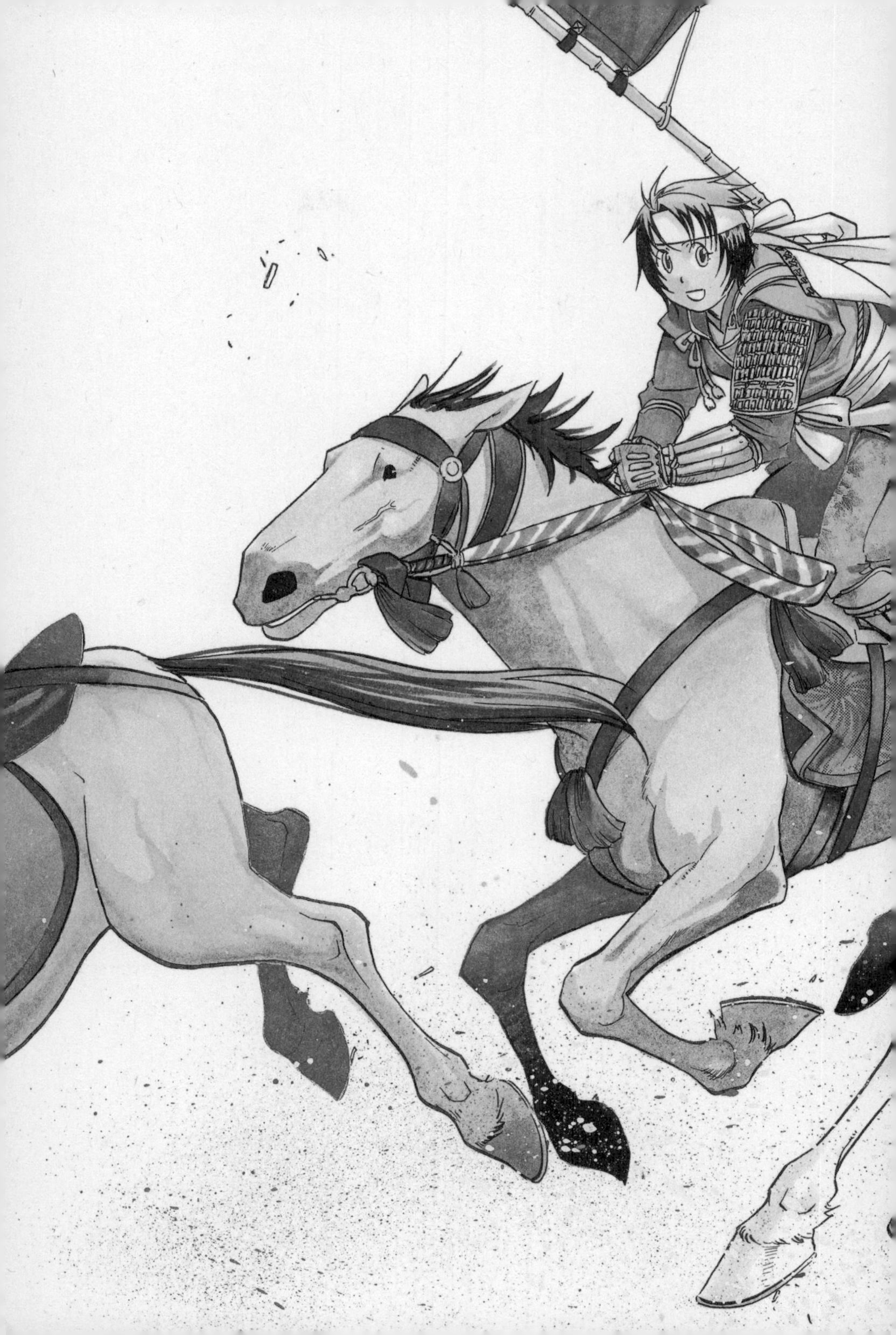

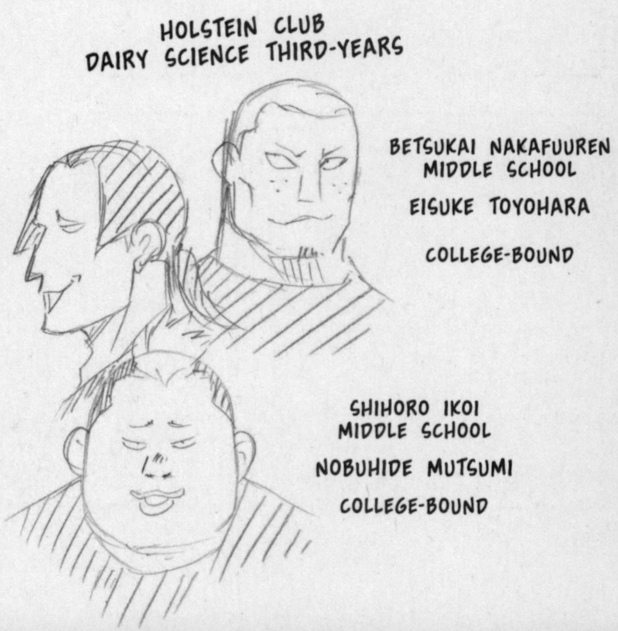

HOLSTEIN CLUB
DAIRY SCIENCE THIRD-YEARS
BETSUKAI NAKAFUUREN MIDDLE SCHOOL
EISUKE TOYOHARA
COLLEGE-BOUND
TAIKI CENTRAL MIDDLE SCHOOL
MAKOTO KAISHIN
WORK-BOUND
SHIHORO IKOI MIDDLE SCHOOL
NOBUHIDE MUTSUMI
COLLEGE-BOUND

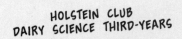

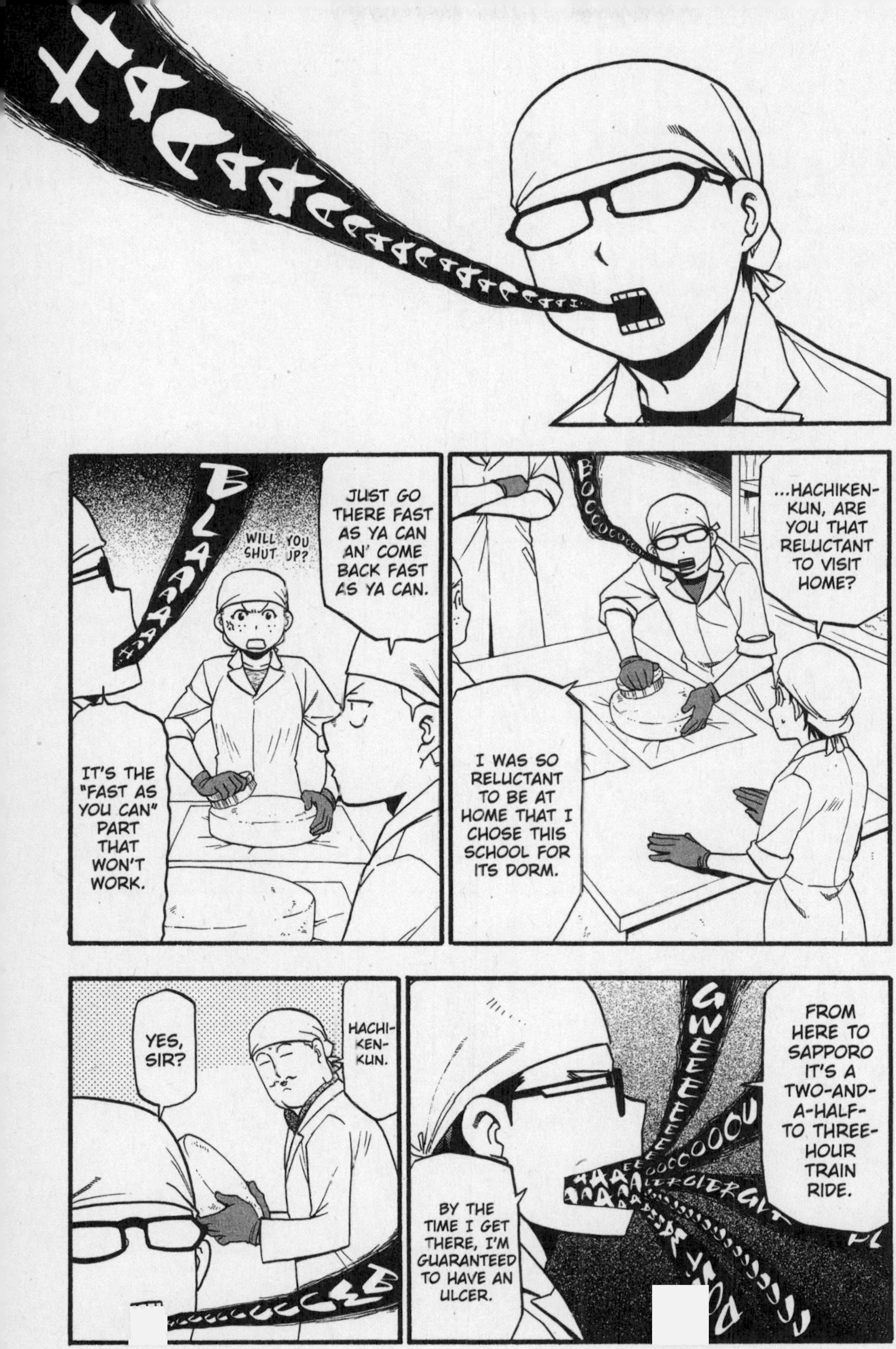
...HACHIKEN-KUN, ARE YOU THAT RELUCTANT TO VISIT HOME?
I WAS SO RELUCTANT TO BE AT HOME THAT I CHOSE THIS SCHOOL FOR ITS DORM.
JUST GO THERE FAST AS YA CAN AN' COME BACK FAST AS YA CAN.
WILL YOU SHUT UP?
IT'S THE "FAST AS YOU CAN" PART THAT WON'T WORK.
FROM HERE TO SAPPORO IT'S A TWO-AND-A-HALF-TO THREE-HOUR TRAIN RIDE.
BY THE TIME I GET THERE, I'M GUARANTEED TO HAVE AN ULCER.
HACHI-KEN-KUN.
YES, SIR?

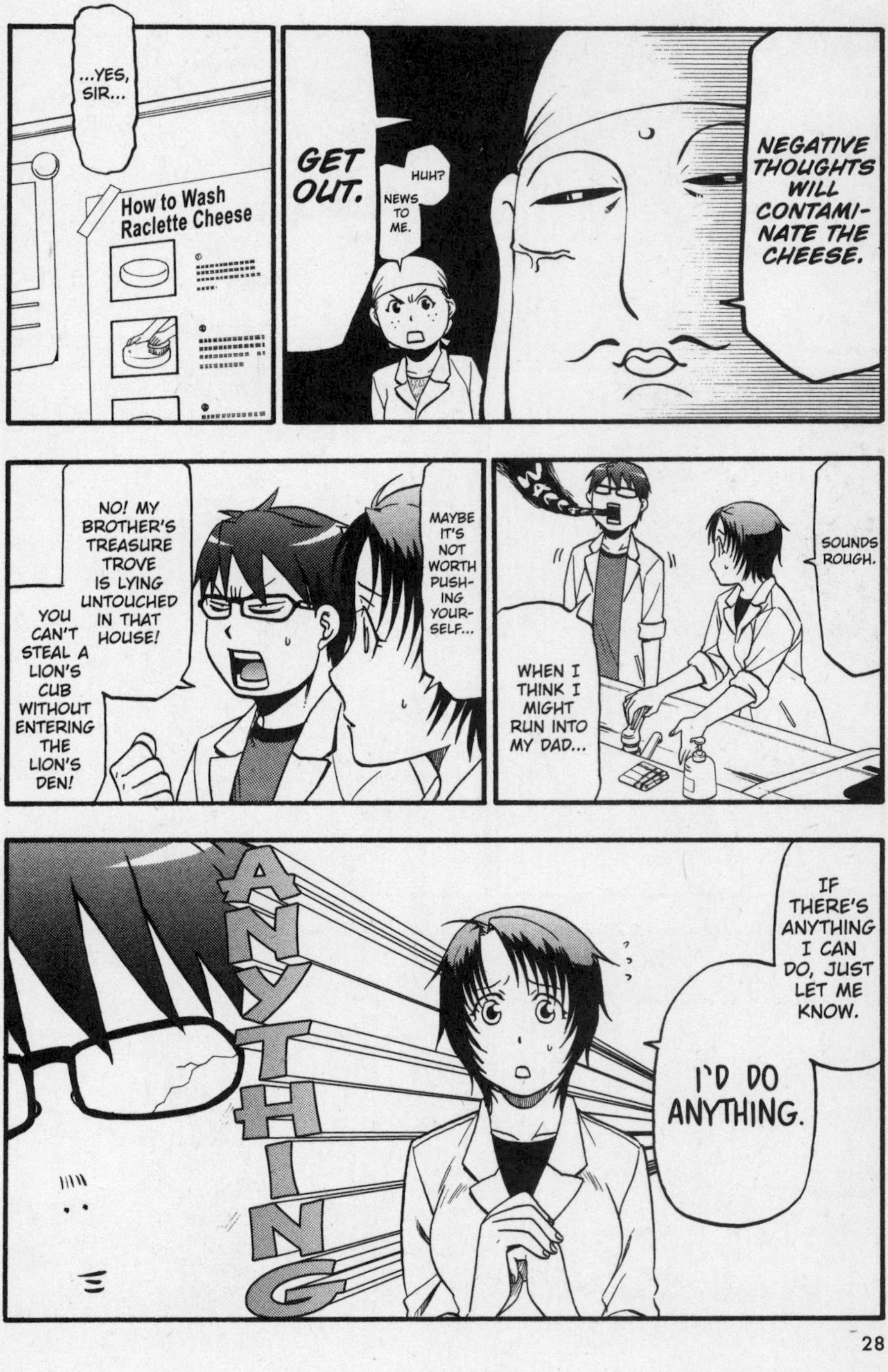
NEGATIVE THOUGHTS WILL CONTAMINATE THE CHEESE.
GET OUT.
HUH? NEWS TO ME.
...YES, SIR...
How to Wash Raclette Cheese
SOUNDS ROUGH.
WHEN I THINK I MIGHT RUN INTO MY DAD...
MAYBE IT'S NOT WORTH PUSHING YOURSELF...
NO! MY BROTHER'S TREASURE TROVE IS LYING UNTOUCHED IN THAT HOUSE!
YOU CAN'T STEAL A LION'S CUB WITHOUT ENTERING THE LION'S DEN!
IF THERE'S ANYTHING I CAN DO, JUST LET ME KNOW.
I'D DO ANYTHING.
ANYTHING

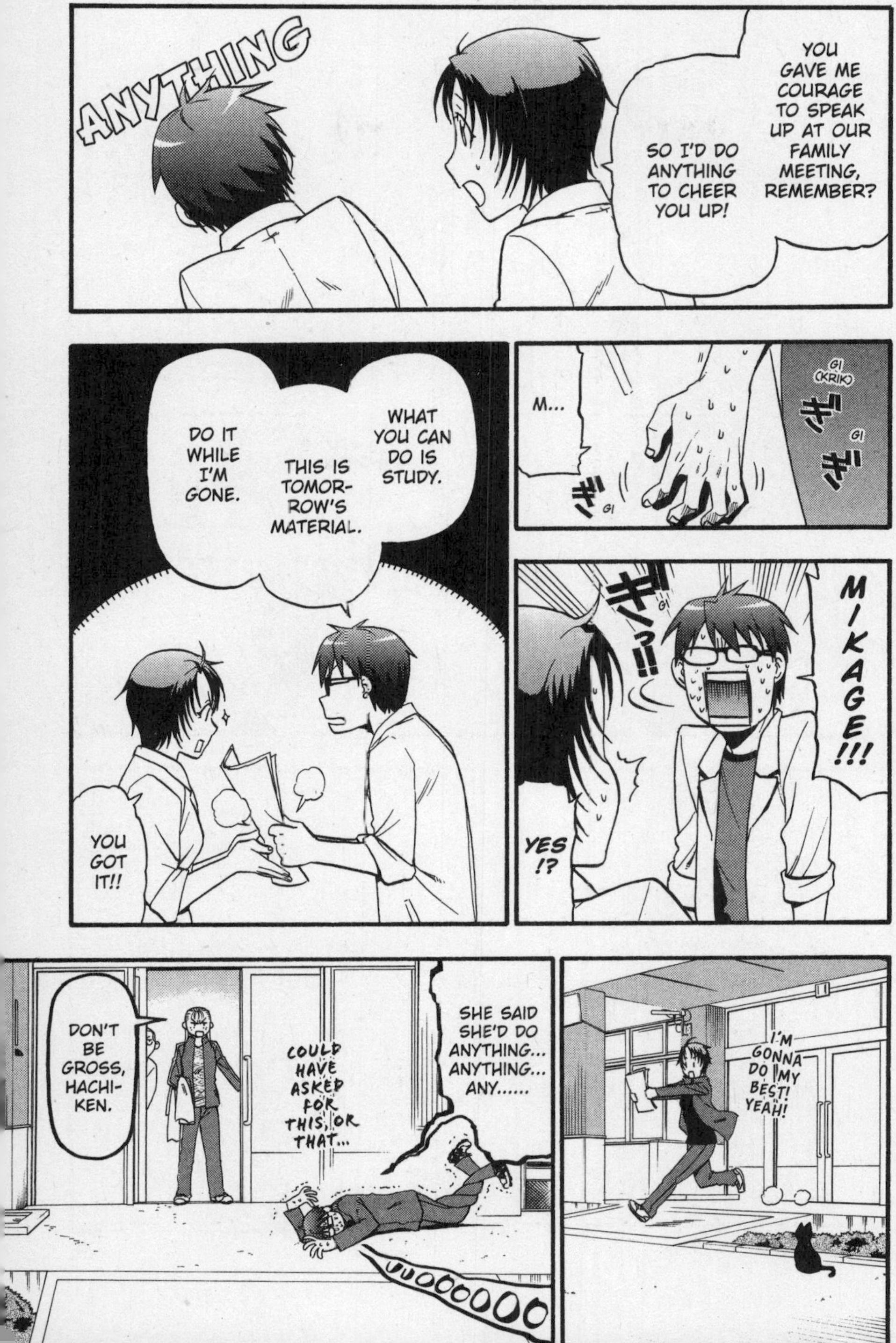
YOU GAVE ME COURAGE TO SPEAK UP AT OUR FAMILY MEETING, REMEMBER?
SO I'D DO ANYTHING TO CHEER YOU UP!
ANYTHING
GI (KRIK)
GI
M...
GI
MIKAGE!!!
GI
YES !?
WHAT YOU CAN DO IS STUDY.
THIS IS TOMORROW'S MATERIAL.
DO IT WHILE I'M GONE.
YOU GOT IT!!
I'M GONNA DO MY BEST! YEAH!
SHE SAID SHE'D DO ANYTHING... ANYTHING... ANY......
COULD HAVE ASKED FOR THIS, OR THAT...
UUOOOOOOO
DON'T BE GROSS, HACHIKEN.

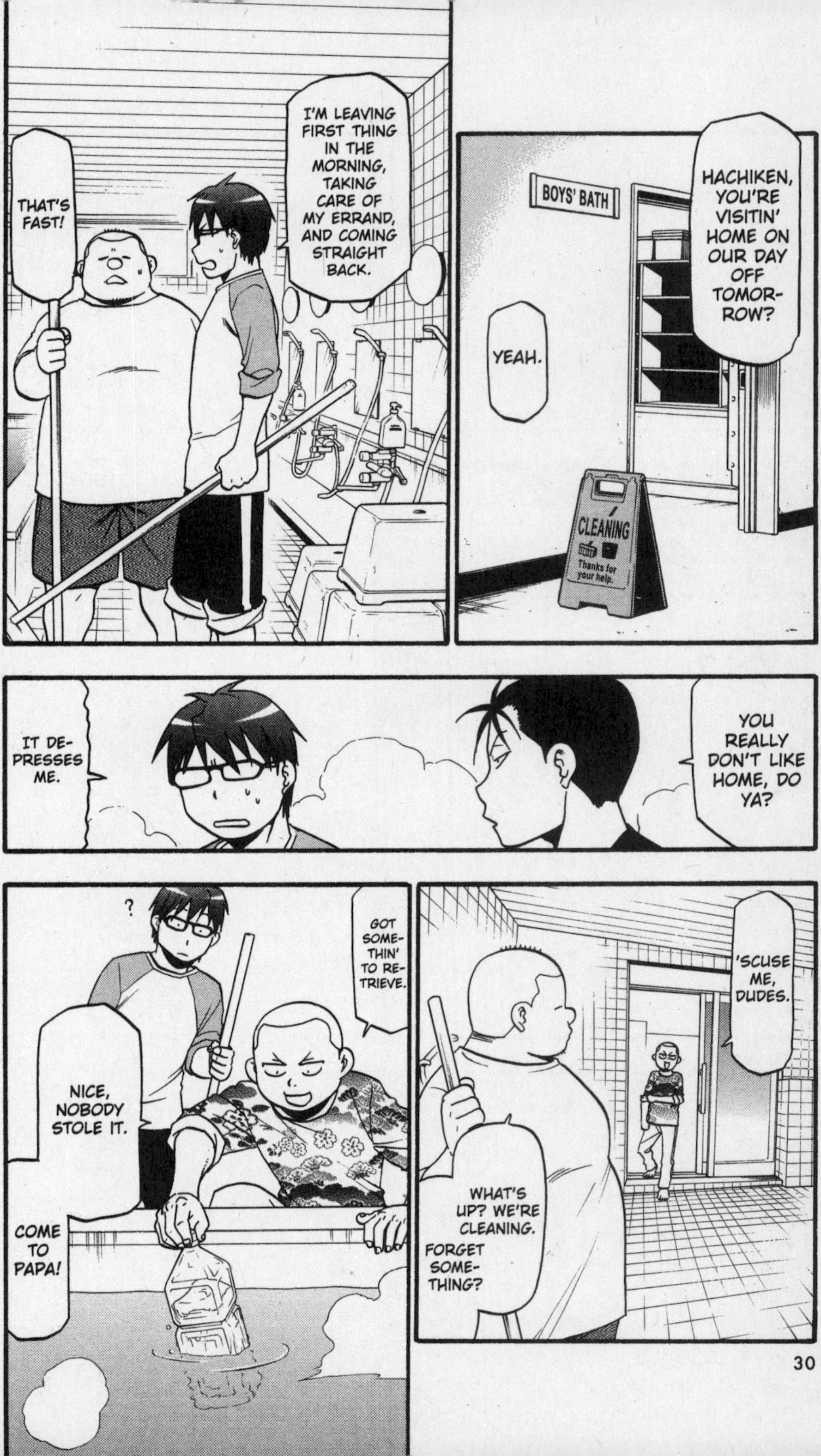
HACHIKEN, YOU'RE VISITIN' HOME ON OUR DAY OFF TOMORROW?
BOYS' BATH
CLEANING
Thanks for your help.
YEAH.
I'M LEAVING FIRST THING IN THE MORNING, TAKING CARE OF MY ERRAND, AND COMING STRAIGHT BACK.
THAT'S FAST!
YOU REALLY DON'T LIKE HOME, DO YA?
IT DEPRESSES ME.
'SCUSE ME, DUDES.
WHAT'S UP? WE'RE CLEANING.
FORGET SOMETHING?
GOT SOMETHIN' TO RETRIEVE.
?
NICE, NOBODY STOLE IT.
COME TO PAPA!

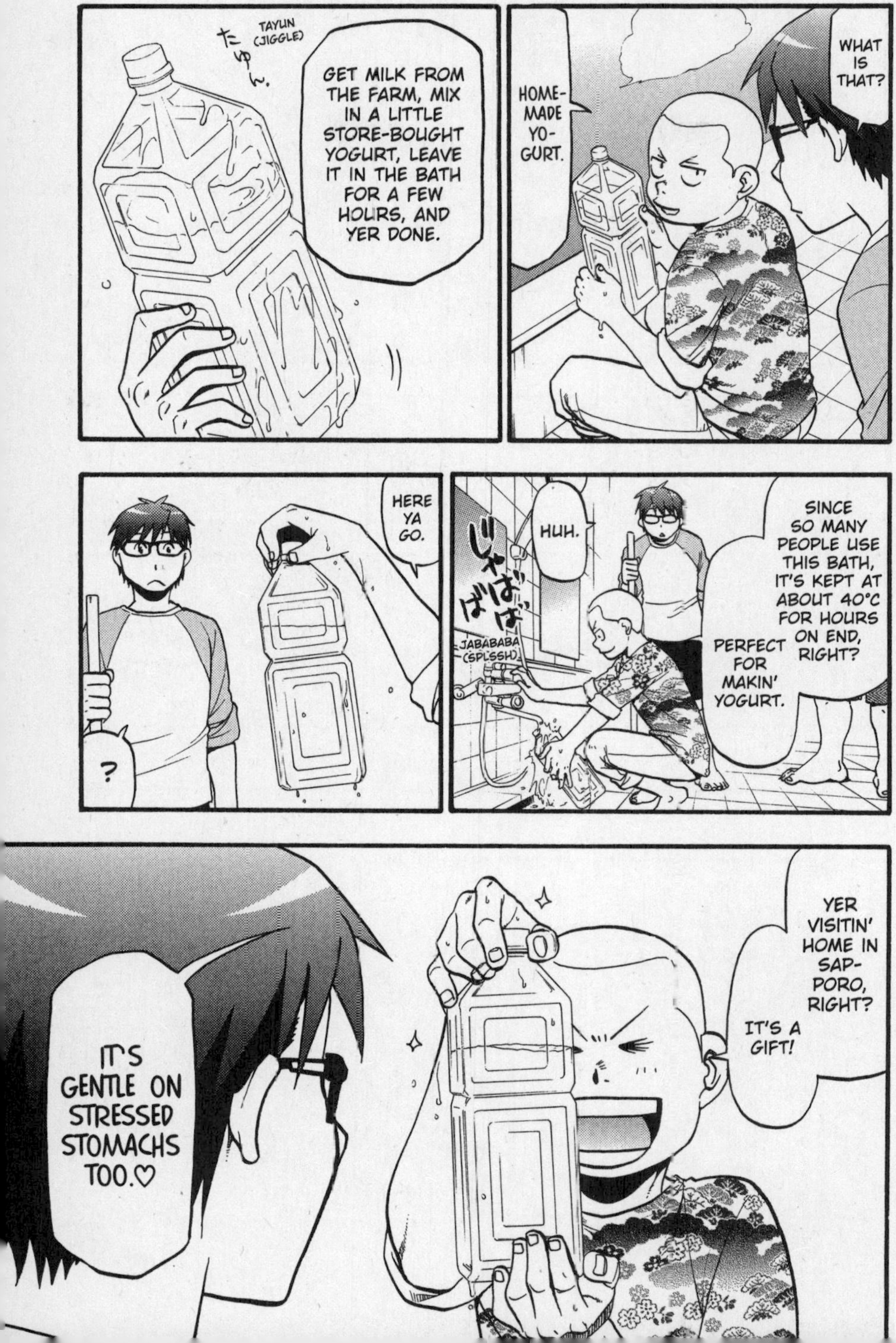
WHAT IS THAT?
HOME-MADE YO-GURT.
たゆん
TAYUN (JIGGLE)
GET MILK FROM THE FARM, MIX IN A LITTLE STORE-BOUGHT YOGURT, LEAVE IT IN THE BATH FOR A FEW HOURS, AND YER DONE.
SINCE SO MANY PEOPLE USE THIS BATH, IT'S KEPT AT ABOUT 40°C FOR HOURS ON END, RIGHT?
PERFECT FOR MAKIN' YOGURT.
HUH.
じゃばば
JABABABA (SPLSSH)
HERE YA GO.
?
YER VISITIN' HOME IN SAP-PORO, RIGHT?
IT'S A GIFT!
IT'S GENTLE ON STRESSED STOMACHS TOO.♡

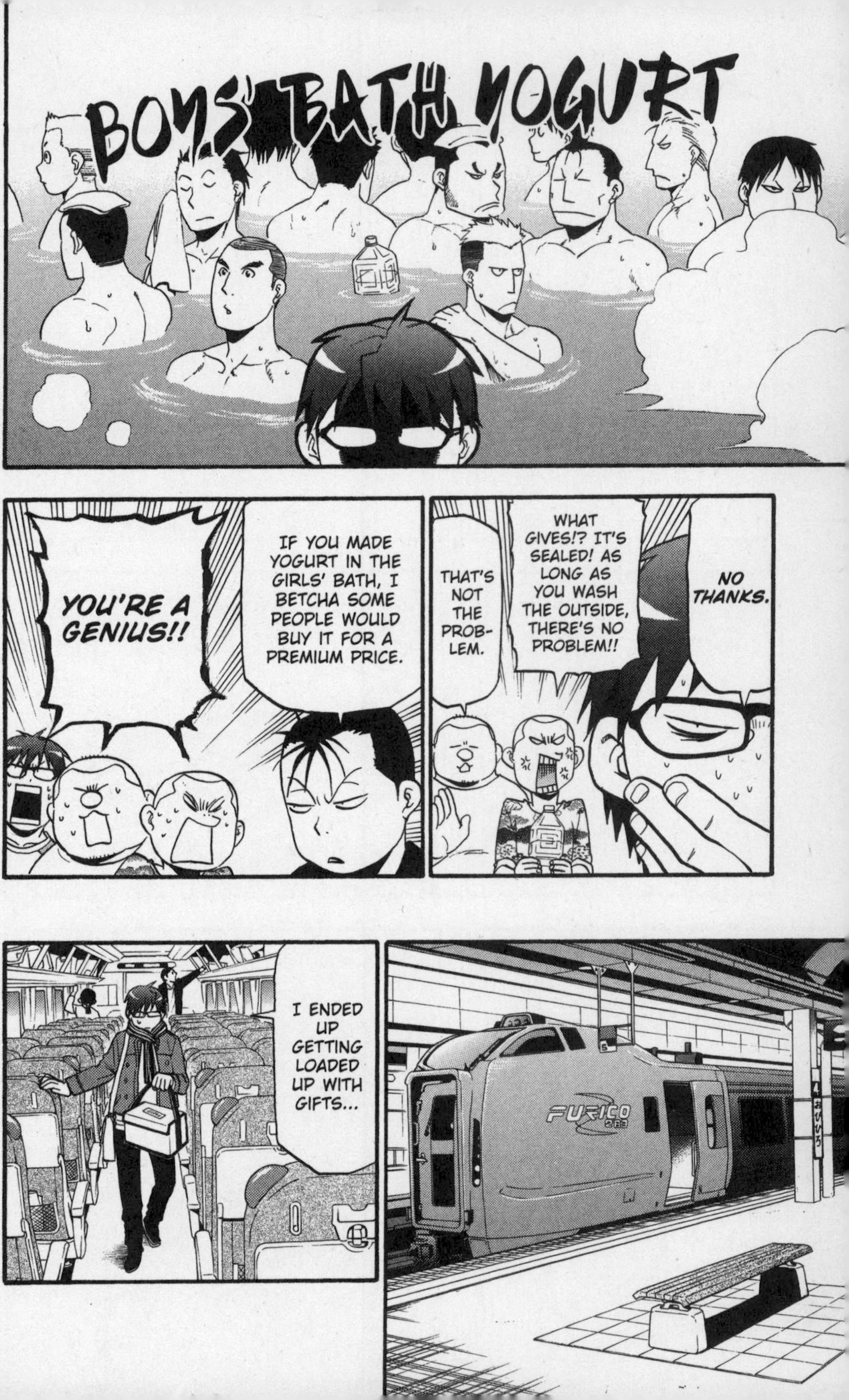
BOYS' BATH YOGURT
NO THANKS.
WHAT GIVES!? IT'S SEALED! AS LONG AS YOU WASH THE OUTSIDE, THERE'S NO PROBLEM!!
THAT'S NOT THE PROB-LEM.
IF YOU MADE YOGURT IN THE GIRLS' BATH, I BETCHA SOME PEOPLE WOULD BUY IT FOR A PREMIUM PRICE.
YOU'RE A GENIUS!!
FURICO 283
I ENDED UP GETTING LOADED UP WITH GIFTS...

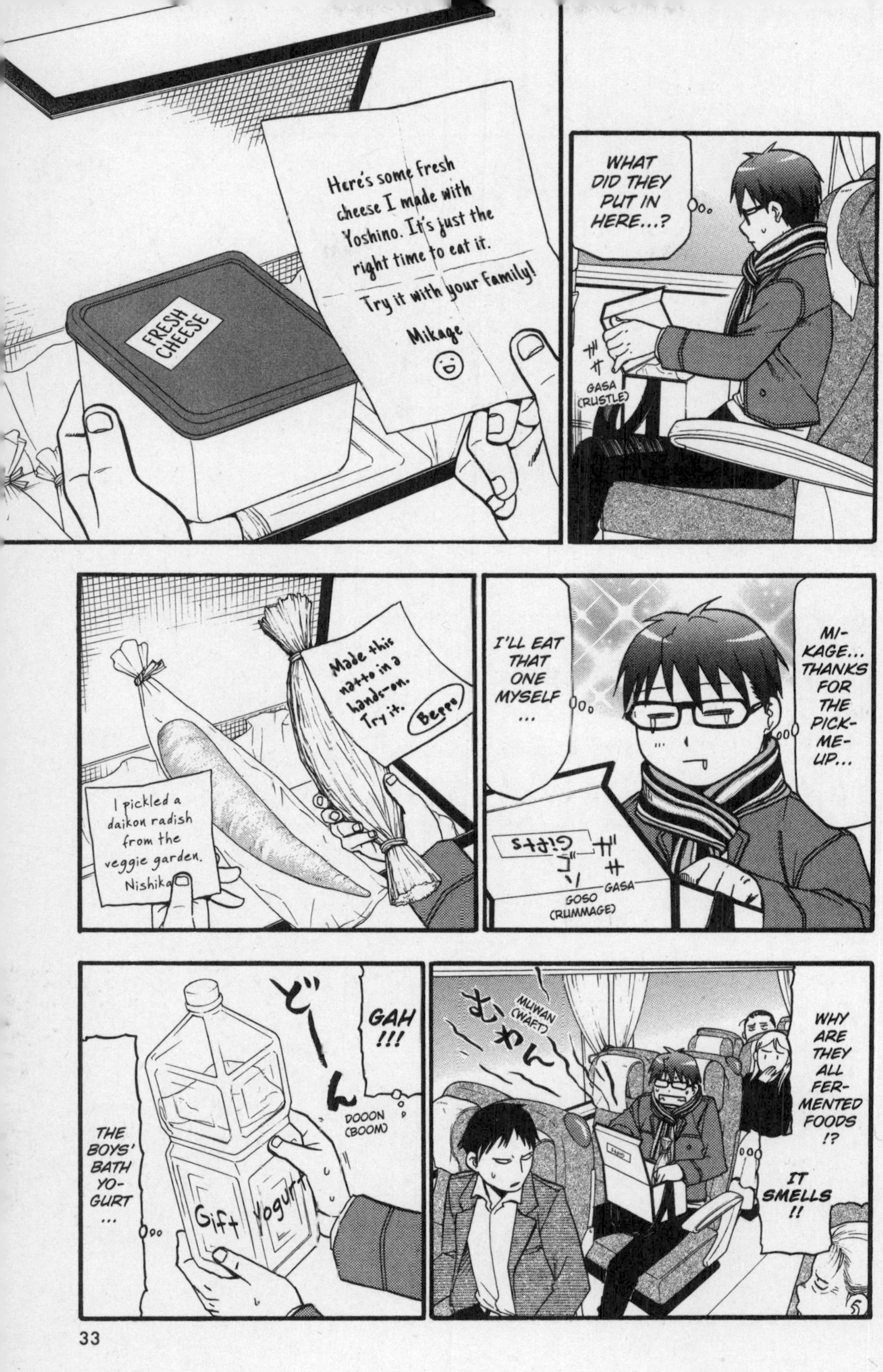

WHAT DID THEY PUT IN HERE...?
GASA (RUSTLE)
FRESH CHEESE
Here's some fresh cheese I made with Yoshino. It's just the right time to eat it.
Try it with your family!
Mikage
MI-KAGE... THANKS FOR THE PICK-ME-UP...
I'LL EAT THAT ONE MYSELF...
Gifts
GOSO (RUMMAGE)
GASA
Made this natto in a hands-on. Try it.
Beppu
I pickled a daikon radish from the veggie garden.
Nishika
MUWAN (WAFT)
WHY ARE THEY ALL FER-MENTED FOODS!?
IT SMELLS!!
GAH!!!
DOOON (BOOM)
THE BOYS' BATH YO-GURT...
Gift Yogurt

I'LL ...
...FEED THIS ONE TO MY PAR-ENTS ......
GO (WHOOSH)
札幌駅
SAPPORO STATION

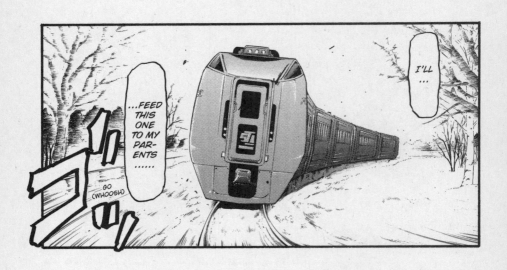

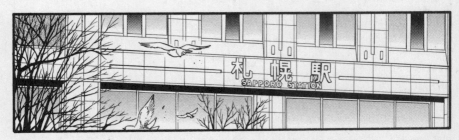

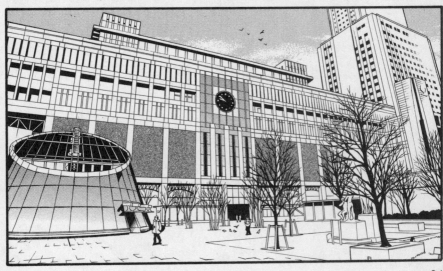

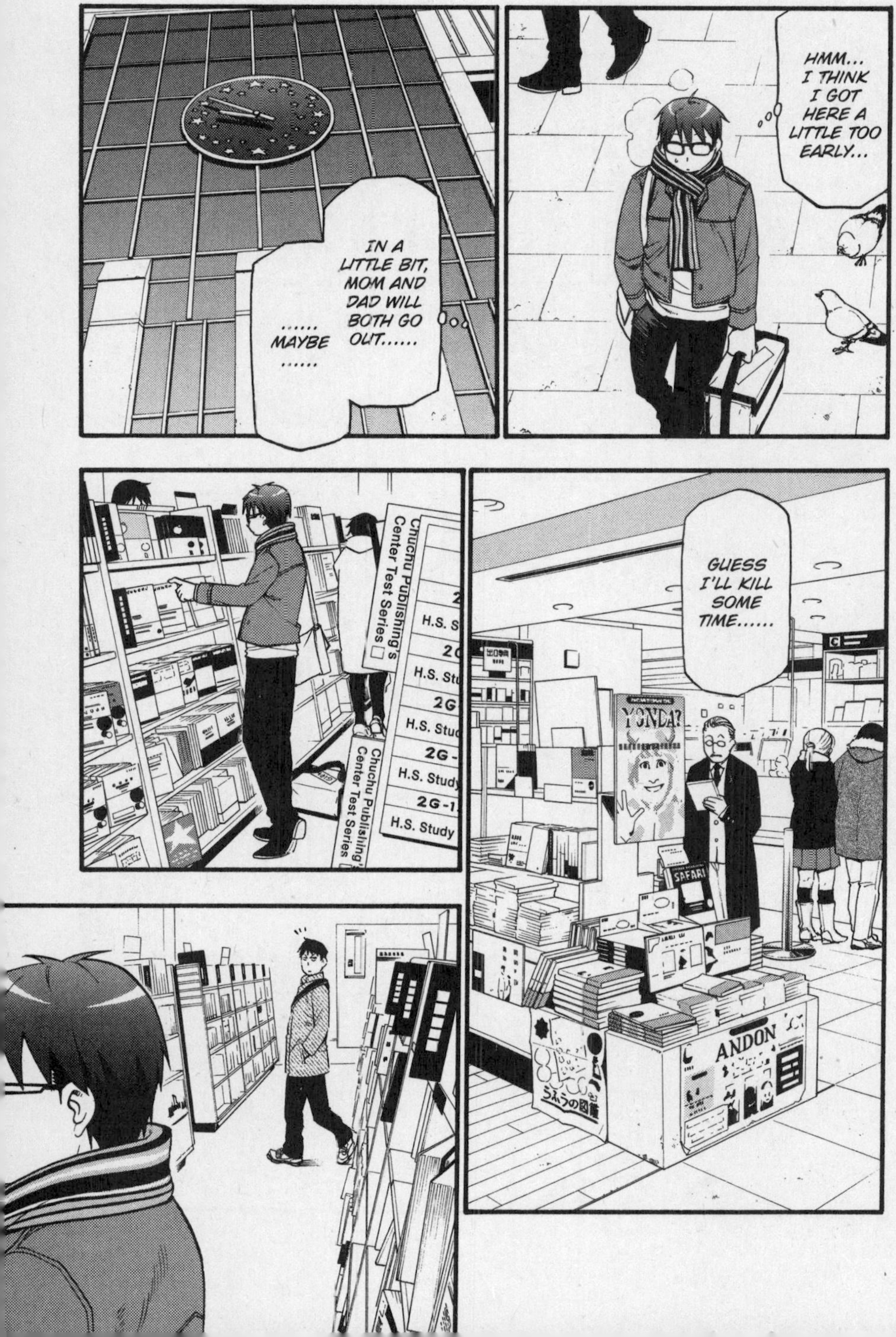

HMM... I THINK I GOT HERE A LITTLE TOO EARLY...
IN A LITTLE BIT, MOM AND DAD WILL BOTH GO OUT......
......MAYBE......
GUESS I'LL KILL SOME TIME......
YONDA?
SAFARI
ANDON
Chuchu Publishing's Center Test Series
H.S. Study

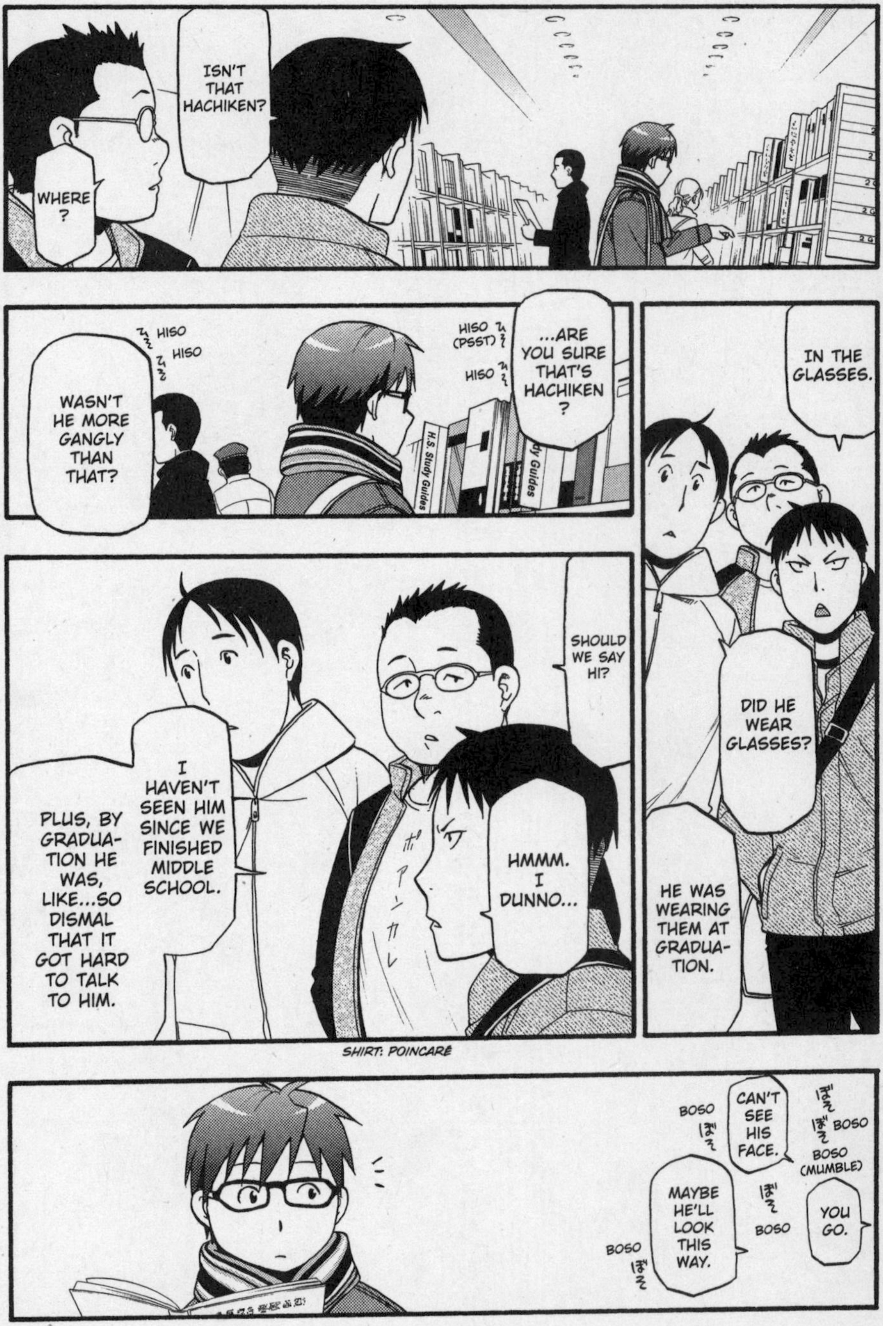
ISN'T THAT HACHIKEN?
WHERE?
IN THE GLASSES.
DID HE WEAR GLASSES?
HE WAS WEARING THEM AT GRADUATION.
HISO (PSST) HISO
...ARE YOU SURE THAT'S HACHIKEN?
H.S. Study Guides
HISO HISO
WASN'T HE MORE GANGLY THAN THAT?
SHOULD WE SAY HI?
HMMM. I DUNNO...
ポアンカレ
I HAVEN'T SEEN HIM SINCE WE FINISHED MIDDLE SCHOOL.
PLUS, BY GRADUATION HE WAS, LIKE...SO DISMAL THAT IT GOT HARD TO TALK TO HIM.
SHIRT: POINCARÉ
ぼそ BOSO
ぼそ BOSO
BOSO (MUMBLE)
YOU GO.
CAN'T SEE HIS FACE.
BOSO ぼそ
ぼそ BOSO
MAYBE HE'LL LOOK THIS WAY.
BOSO ぼそ

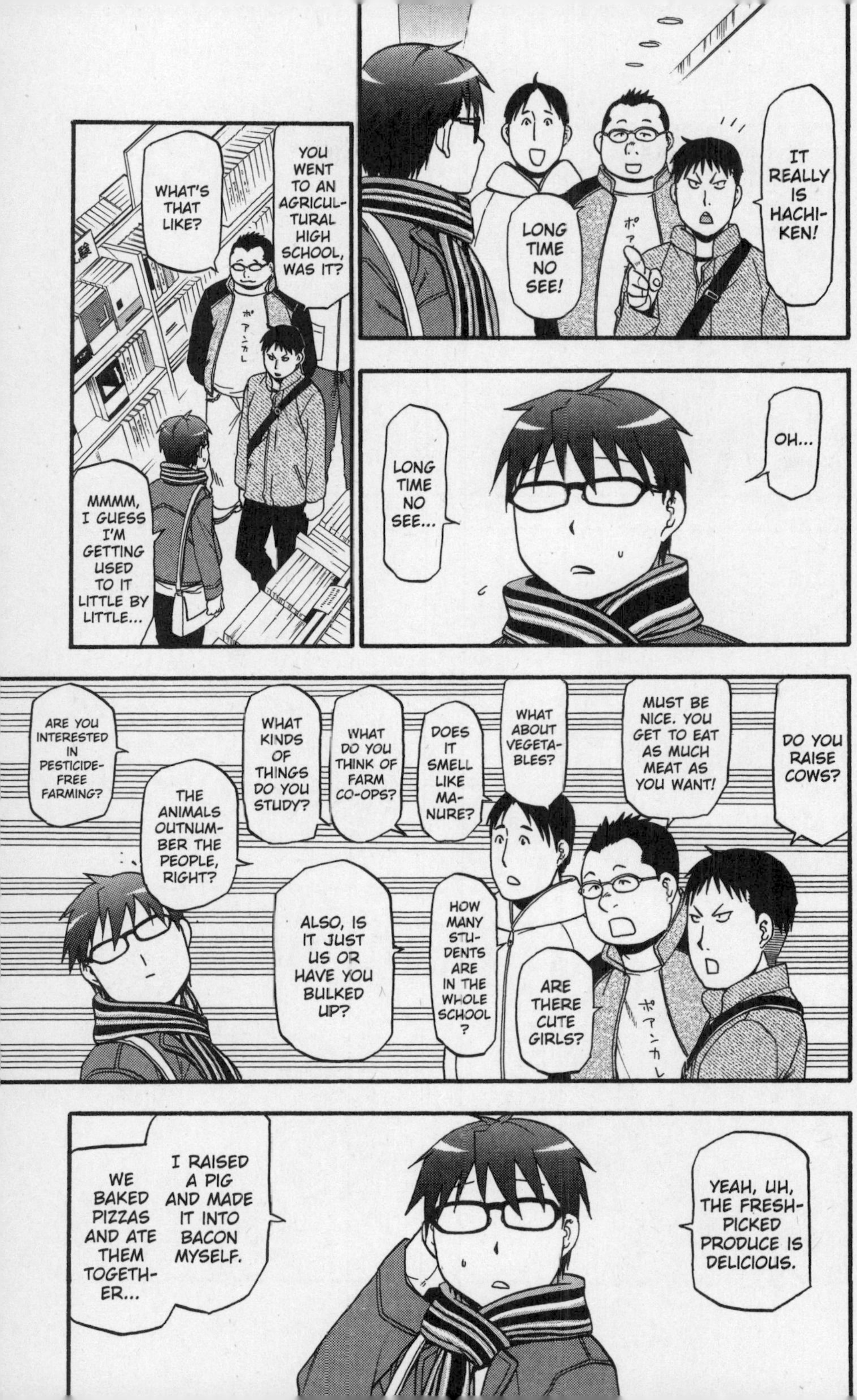
IT REALLY IS HACHIKEN!
LONG TIME NO SEE!
OH...
LONG TIME NO SEE...
YOU WENT TO AN AGRICULTURAL HIGH SCHOOL, WAS IT?
WHAT'S THAT LIKE?
MMMM, I GUESS I'M GETTING USED TO IT LITTLE BY LITTLE...
DO YOU RAISE COWS?
MUST BE NICE. YOU GET TO EAT AS MUCH MEAT AS YOU WANT!
WHAT ABOUT VEGETABLES?
DOES IT SMELL LIKE MANURE?
WHAT DO YOU THINK OF FARM CO-OPS?
WHAT KINDS OF THINGS DO YOU STUDY?
ARE YOU INTERESTED IN PESTICIDE-FREE FARMING?
THE ANIMALS OUTNUMBER THE PEOPLE, RIGHT?
ARE THERE CUTE GIRLS?
HOW MANY STUDENTS ARE IN THE WHOLE SCHOOL?
ALSO, IS IT JUST US OR HAVE YOU BULKED UP?
YEAH, UH, THE FRESH-PICKED PRODUCE IS DELICIOUS.
I RAISED A PIG AND MADE IT INTO BACON MYSELF.
WE BAKED PIZZAS AND ATE THEM TOGETHER...

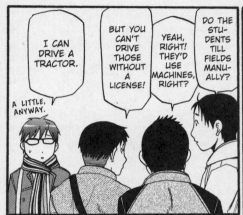

DO THE STUDENTS TILL FIELDS MANUALLY?
YEAH, RIGHT! THEY'D USE MACHINES, RIGHT?
BUT YOU CAN'T DRIVE THOSE WITHOUT A LICENSE!
I CAN DRIVE A TRACTOR.
A LITTLE, ANYWAY.
COOL!!!
YEAH, OF COURSE THEY WOULDN'T DO IT MANUALLY!
I WAS IMAGINING THIS PASTORAL SCENE!
GUESS THERE'D BE NO HORSES EITHER!
YEAH, NO WAY! WITH MODERN FARMING EQUIPMENT, NOBODY WOULD RIDE HORSES!
I... CAN RIDE A HORSE TOO, ACTUALLY.
COOOOL!!!
ポアンカレ
COOOOOOOOL!!!

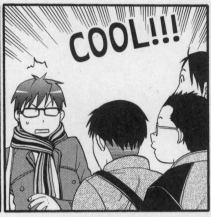

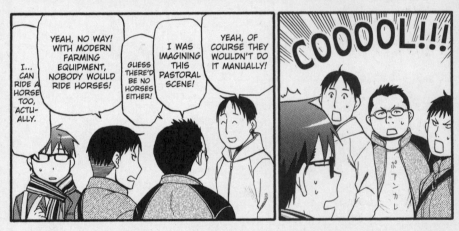

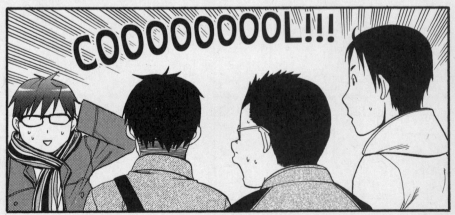

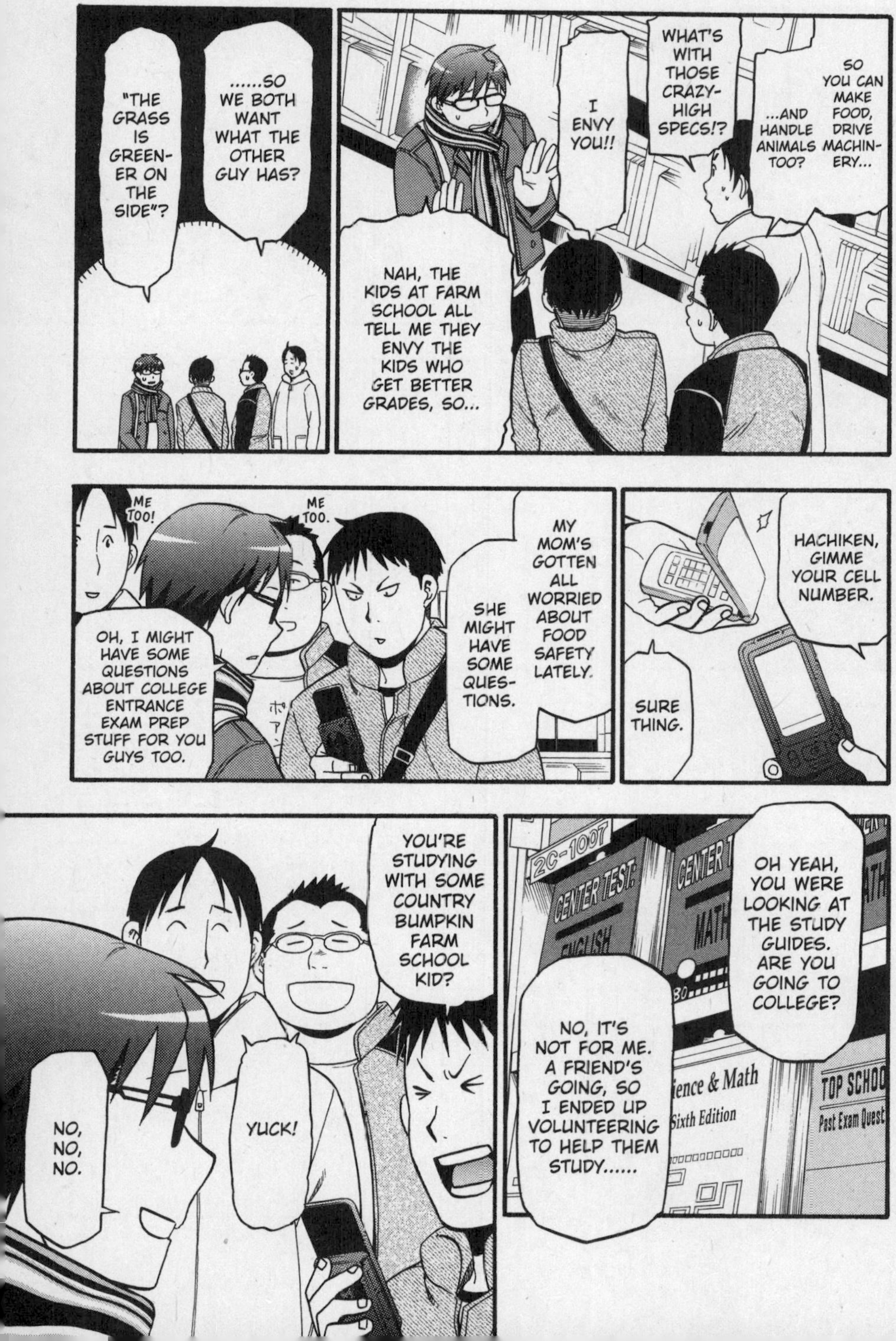
SO YOU CAN MAKE FOOD, DRIVE MACHINERY...
...AND HANDLE ANIMALS TOO?
WHAT'S WITH THOSE CRAZY-HIGH SPECS!?
I ENVY YOU!!
NAH, THE KIDS AT FARM SCHOOL ALL TELL ME THEY ENVY THE KIDS WHO GET BETTER GRADES, SO...
......SO WE BOTH WANT WHAT THE OTHER GUY HAS?
"THE GRASS IS GREENER ON THE SIDE"?
HACHIKEN, GIMME YOUR CELL NUMBER.
SURE THING.
MY MOM'S GOTTEN ALL WORRIED ABOUT FOOD SAFETY LATELY.
SHE MIGHT HAVE SOME QUESTIONS.
ME TOO.
ME TOO!
ポアン
OH, I MIGHT HAVE SOME QUESTIONS ABOUT COLLEGE ENTRANCE EXAM PREP STUFF FOR YOU GUYS TOO.
2C-1007
CENTER TEST
ENGLISH
MATH
Sixth Edition
OH YEAH, YOU WERE LOOKING AT THE STUDY GUIDES. ARE YOU GOING TO COLLEGE?
NO, IT'S NOT FOR ME. A FRIEND'S GOING, SO I ENDED UP VOLUNTEERING TO HELP THEM STUDY......
YOU'RE STUDYING WITH SOME COUNTRY BUMPKIN FARM SCHOOL KID?
YUCK!
NO, NO, NO.

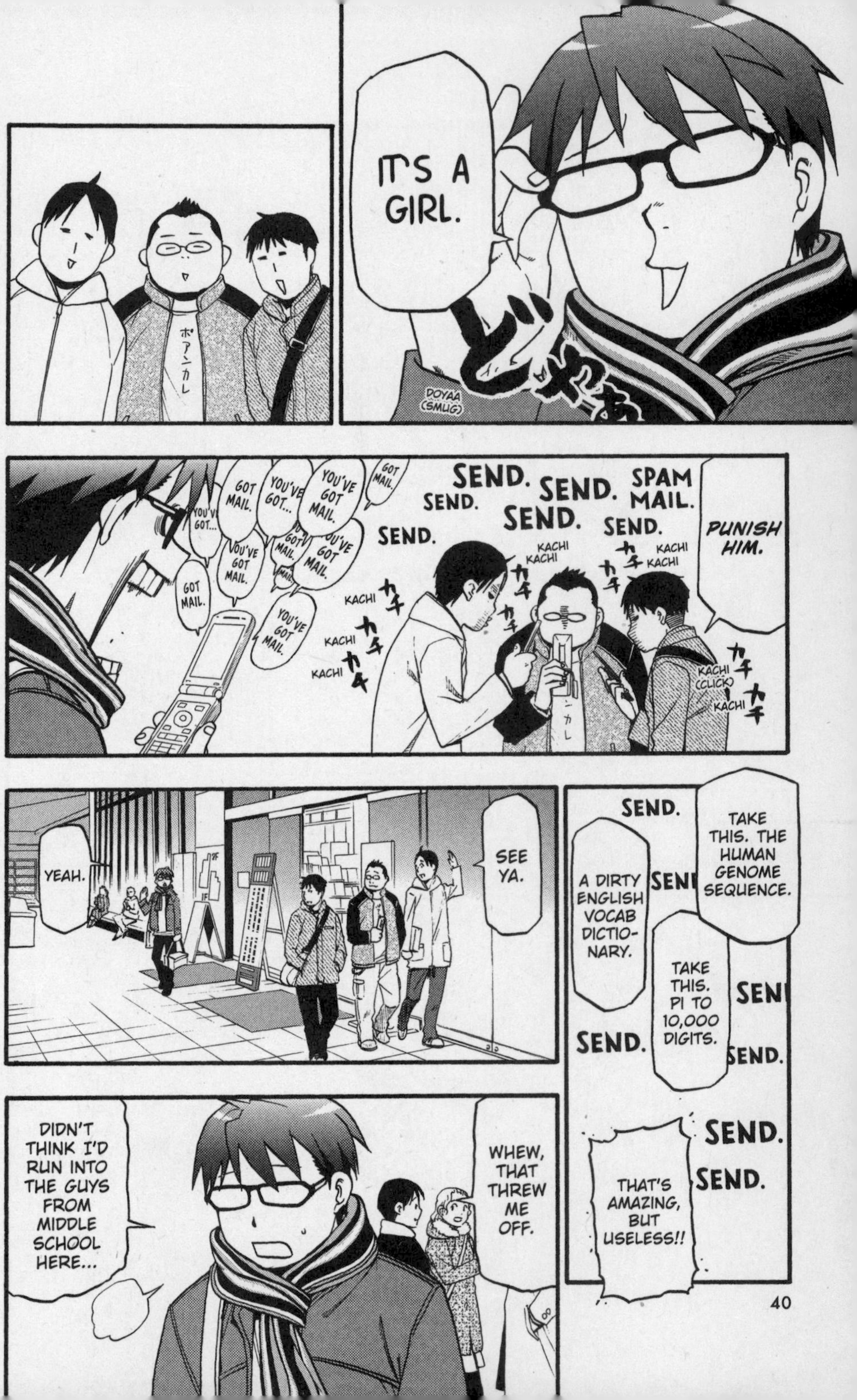
IT'S A GIRL.
DOYAA (SMUG)
ポアンカレ
PUNISH HIM.
SPAM MAIL.
SEND.
SEND.
SEND.
SEND.
SEND.
SEND.
KACHI KACHI
KACHI KACHI
KACHI (CLICK) KACHI
KACHI
KACHI
KACHI
GOT MAIL.
YOU'VE GOT MAIL.
YOU'VE GOT...
GOT MAIL.
YOU'VE GOT...
YOU'VE GOT MAIL.
YOU'VE GOT MAIL.
YOU'VE GOT MAIL.
GOT MAIL.
SEND.
TAKE THIS. THE HUMAN GENOME SEQUENCE.
A DIRTY ENGLISH VOCAB DICTIONARY.
TAKE THIS. PI TO 10,000 DIGITS.
SEND.
SEND.
SEND.
SEND.
THAT'S AMAZING, BUT USELESS!!
SEE YA.
YEAH.
WHEW, THAT THREW ME OFF.
DIDN'T THINK I'D RUN INTO THE GUYS FROM MIDDLE SCHOOL HERE...

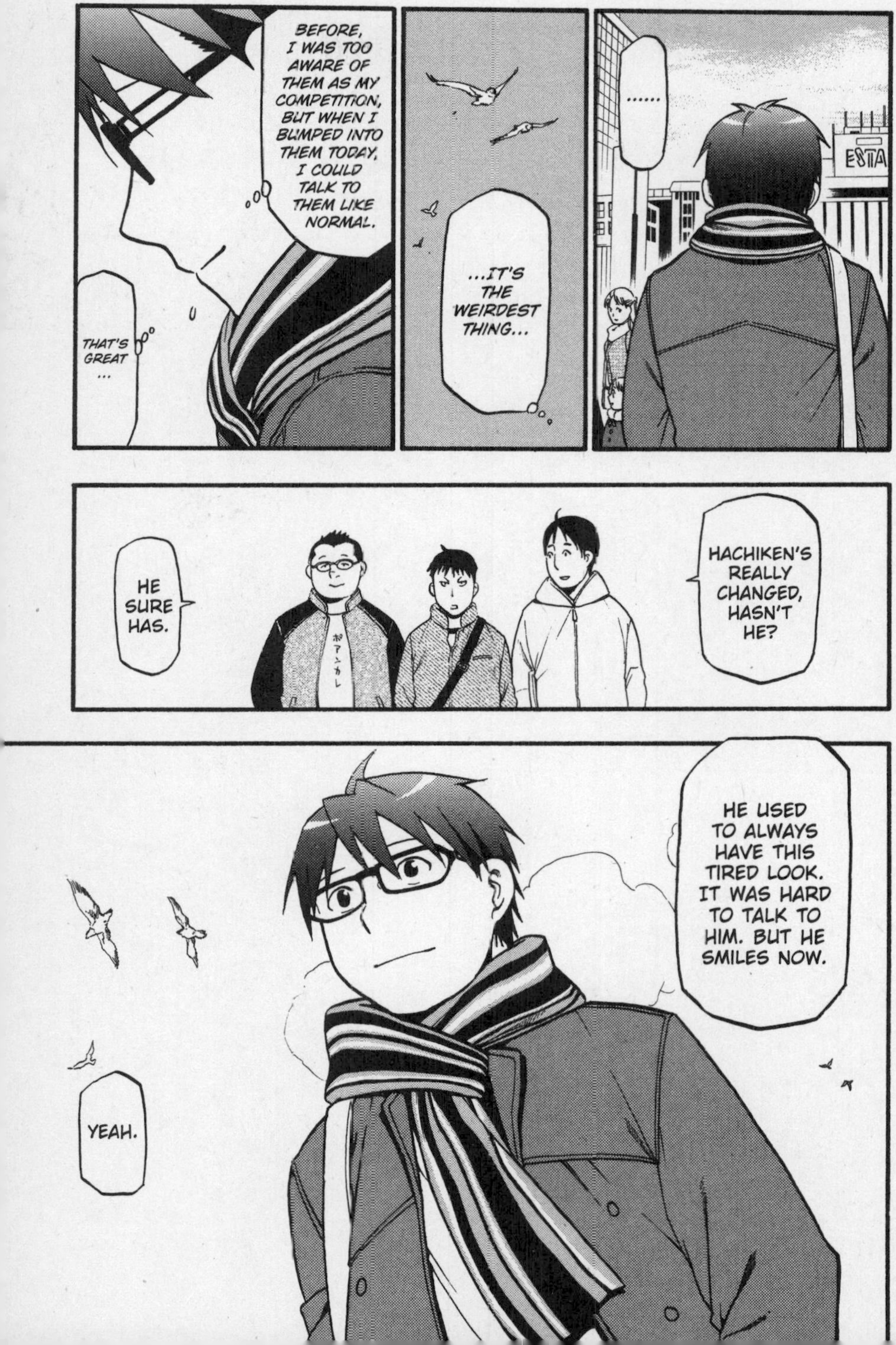
......
...IT'S THE WEIRDEST THING...
BEFORE, I WAS TOO AWARE OF THEM AS MY COMPETITION, BUT WHEN I BUMPED INTO THEM TODAY, I COULD TALK TO THEM LIKE NORMAL.
THAT'S GREAT ...
HACHIKEN'S REALLY CHANGED, HASN'T HE?
HE SURE HAS.
HE USED TO ALWAYS HAVE THIS TIRED LOOK. IT WAS HARD TO TALK TO HIM. BUT HE SMILES NOW.
YEAH.

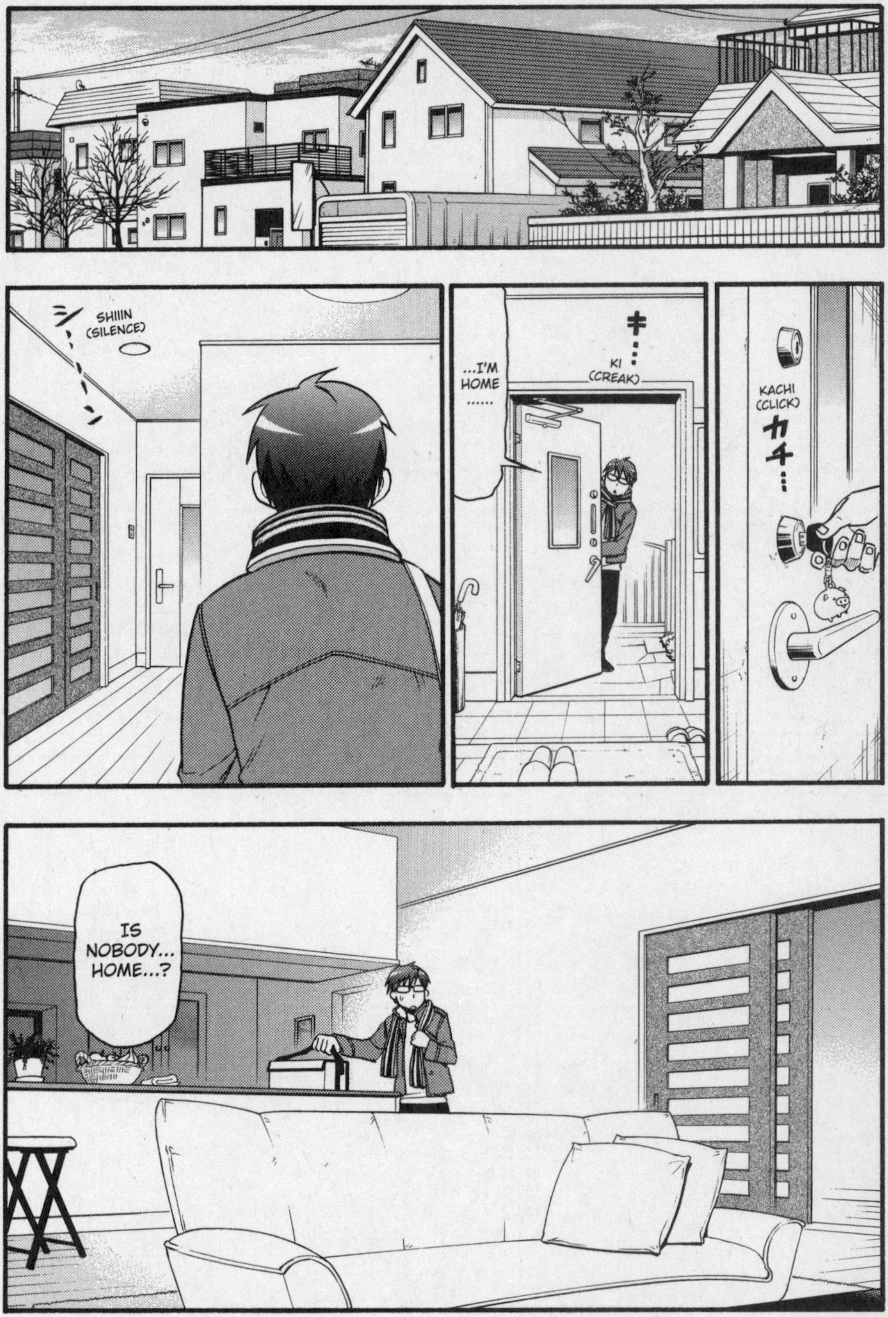
KACHI (CLICK)
カチ…
キ…
KI (CREAK)
...I'M HOME ......
シーン
SHIIIN (SILENCE)
IS NOBODY... HOME...?

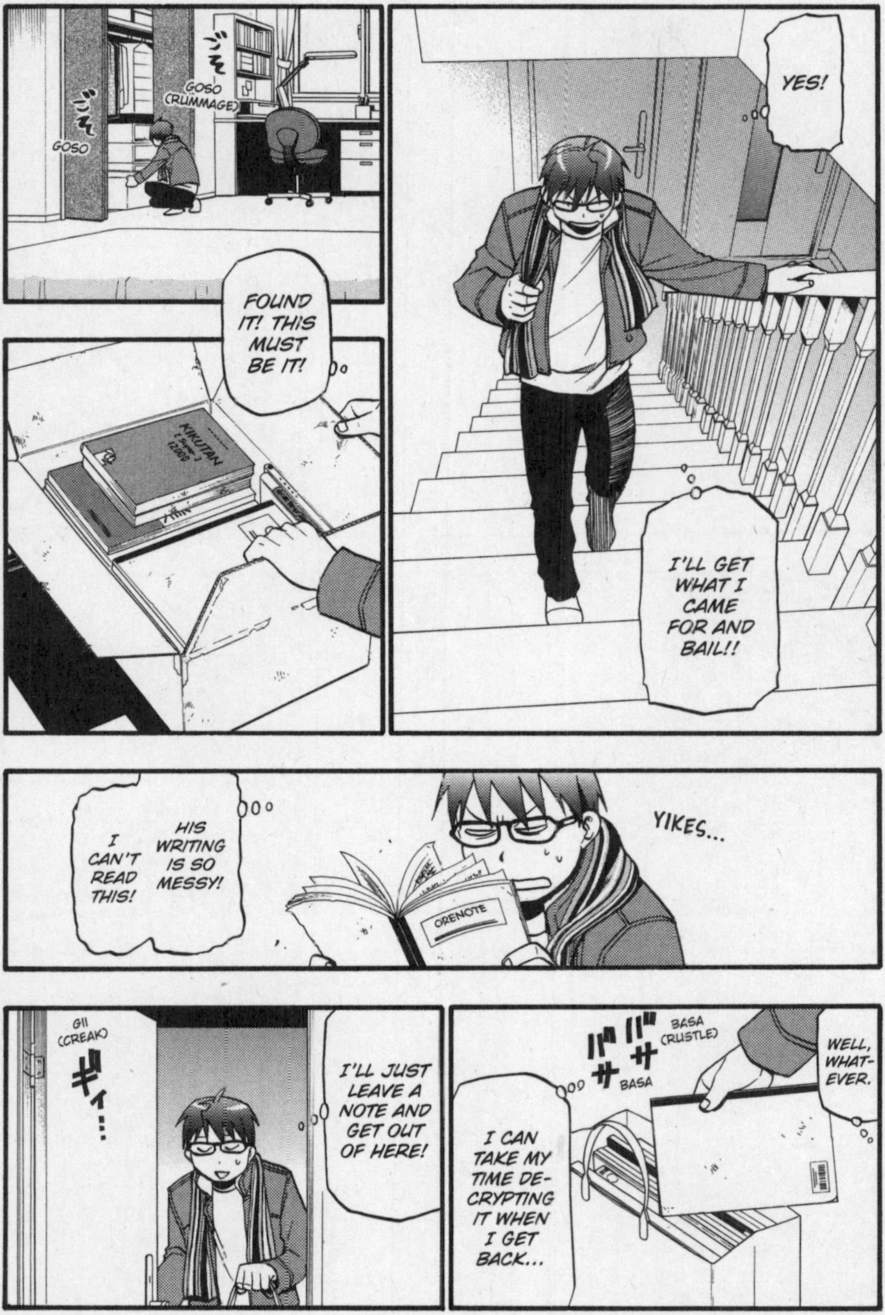
YES!
I'LL GET WHAT I CAME FOR AND BAIL!!
ごそ
GOSO (RUMMAGE)
ごそ
GOSO
FOUND IT! THIS MUST BE IT!
KIKUTAN
YIKES...
HIS WRITING IS SO MESSY!
I CAN'T READ THIS!
ORENOTE
BASA (RUSTLE)
BASA
WELL, WHATEVER.
I CAN TAKE MY TIME DE-CRYPTING IT WHEN I GET BACK...
GII (CREAK)
I'LL JUST LEAVE A NOTE AND GET OUT OF HERE!

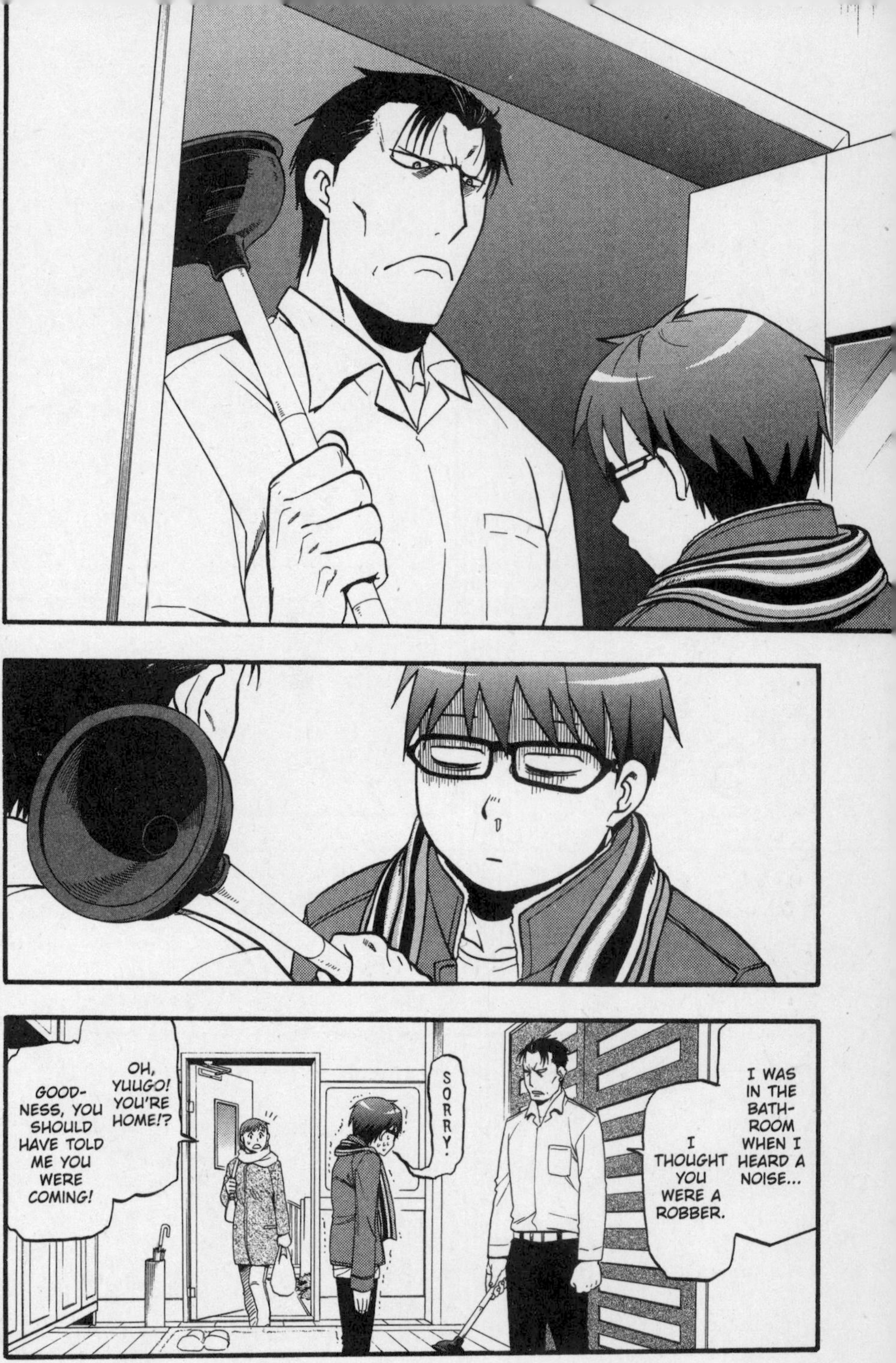
I WAS IN THE BATHROOM WHEN I HEARD A NOISE...
I THOUGHT YOU WERE A ROBBER.
SORRY.
OH, YUUGO! YOU'RE HOME!?
GOODNESS, YOU SHOULD HAVE TOLD ME YOU WERE COMING!

Chapter 73:

Tale of Winter ⑩

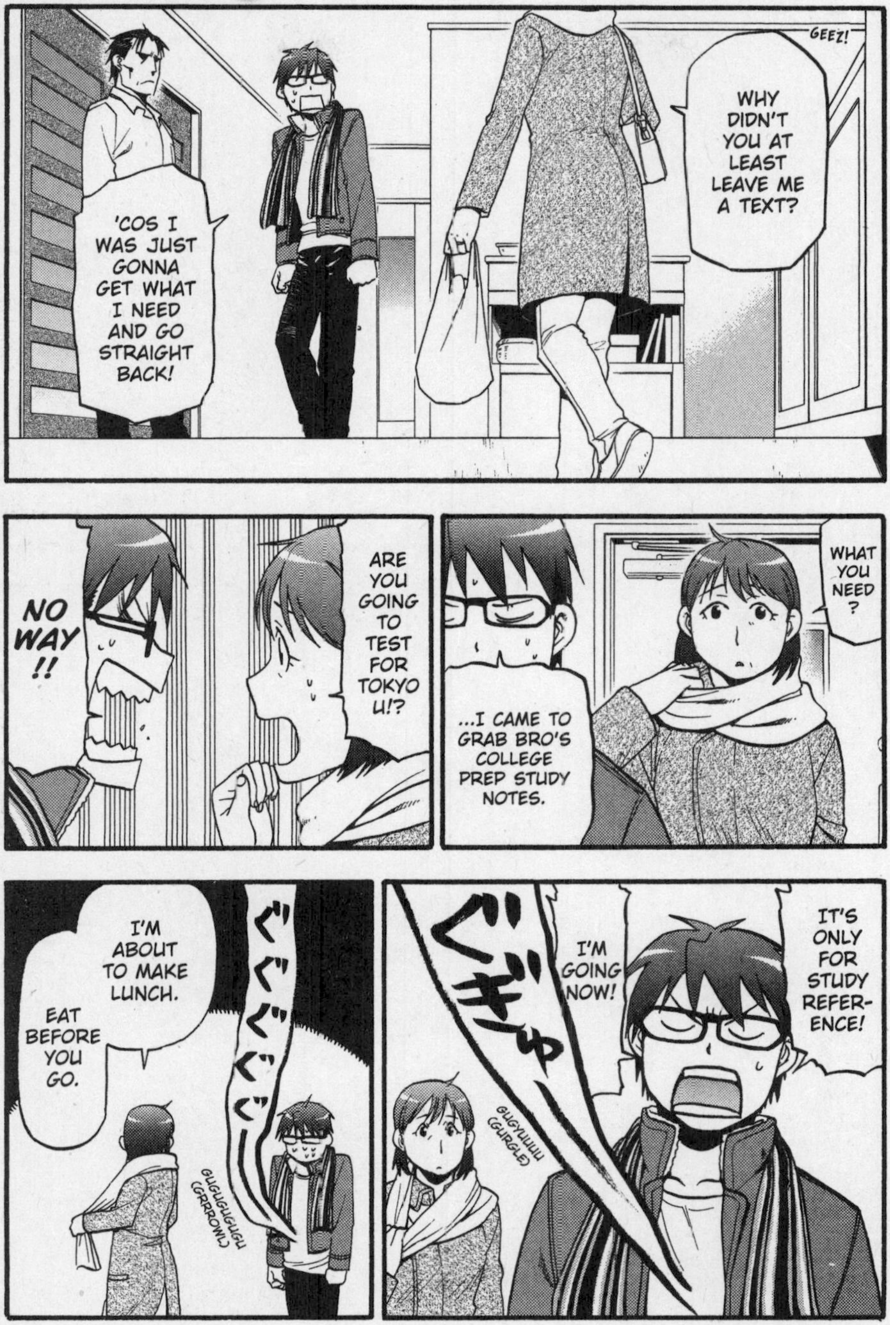
GEEZ!
WHY DIDN'T YOU AT LEAST LEAVE ME A TEXT?
'COS I WAS JUST GONNA GET WHAT I NEED AND GO STRAIGHT BACK!
WHAT YOU NEED?
...I CAME TO GRAB BRO'S COLLEGE PREP STUDY NOTES.
ARE YOU GOING TO TEST FOR TOKYO U!?
NO WAY!!
IT'S ONLY FOR STUDY REFERENCE!
I'M GOING NOW!
ぐぎゅー
GUGYUUUU (GURGLE)
ぐぐぐぐぐー
I'M ABOUT TO MAKE LUNCH.
EAT BEFORE YOU GO.
GUGUGUGUGU (GRRROWL)

Chapter 73:

Tale of Winter ⑩

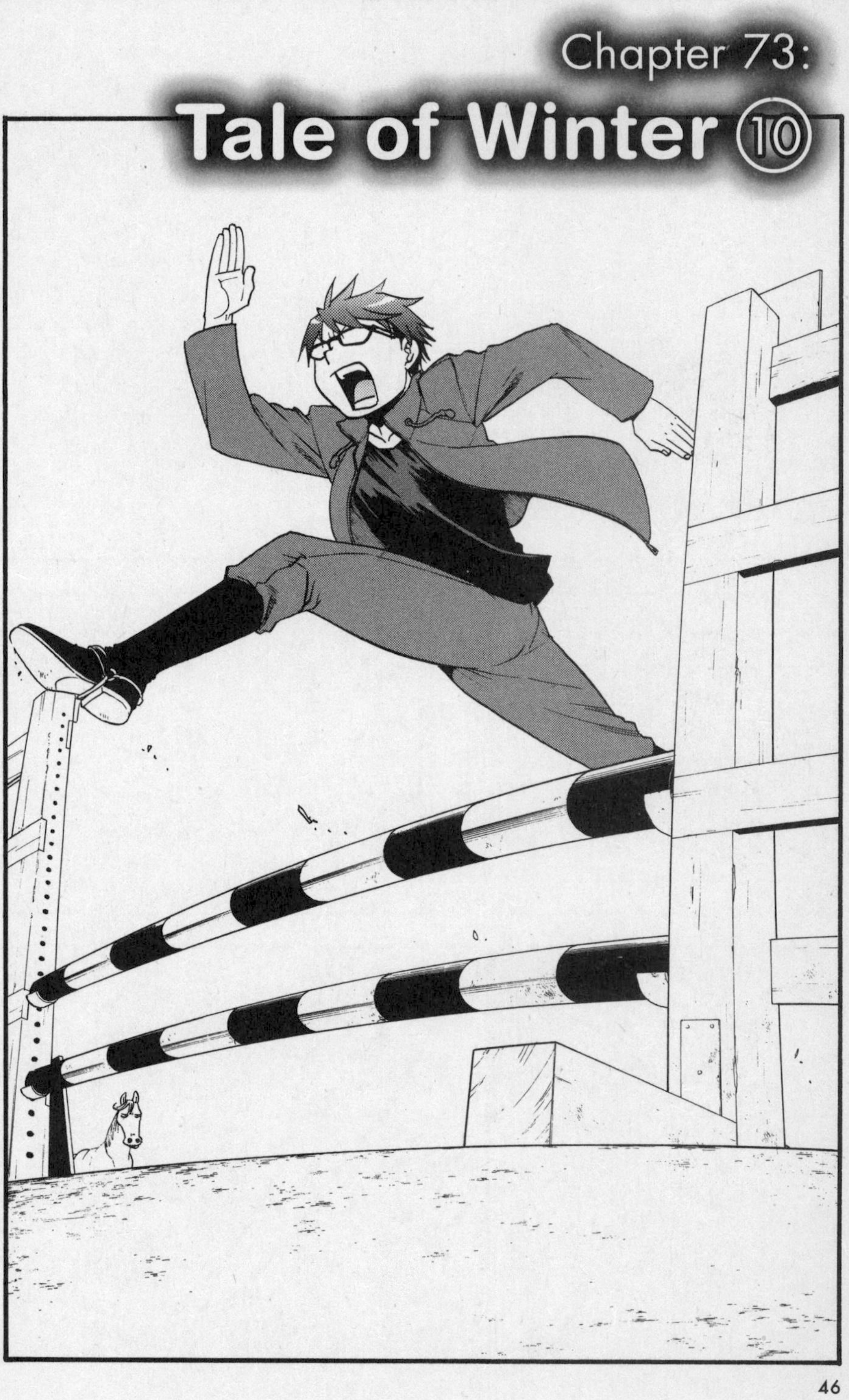

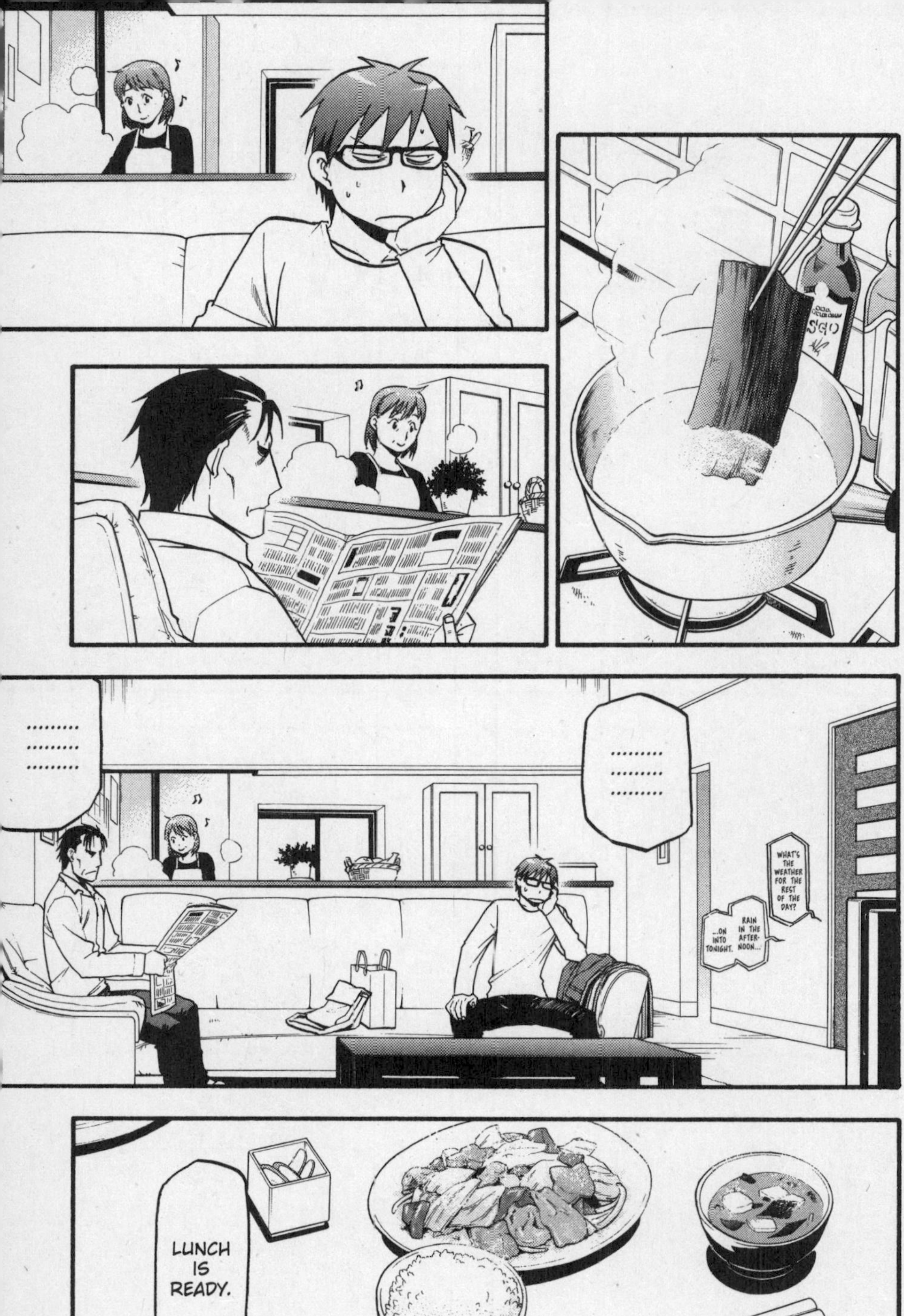
WHAT'S THE WEATHER FOR THE REST OF THE DAY?
RAIN IN THE AFTER-NOON...
...ON INTO TONIGHT.
....
....
....
....
....
....
LUNCH IS READY.

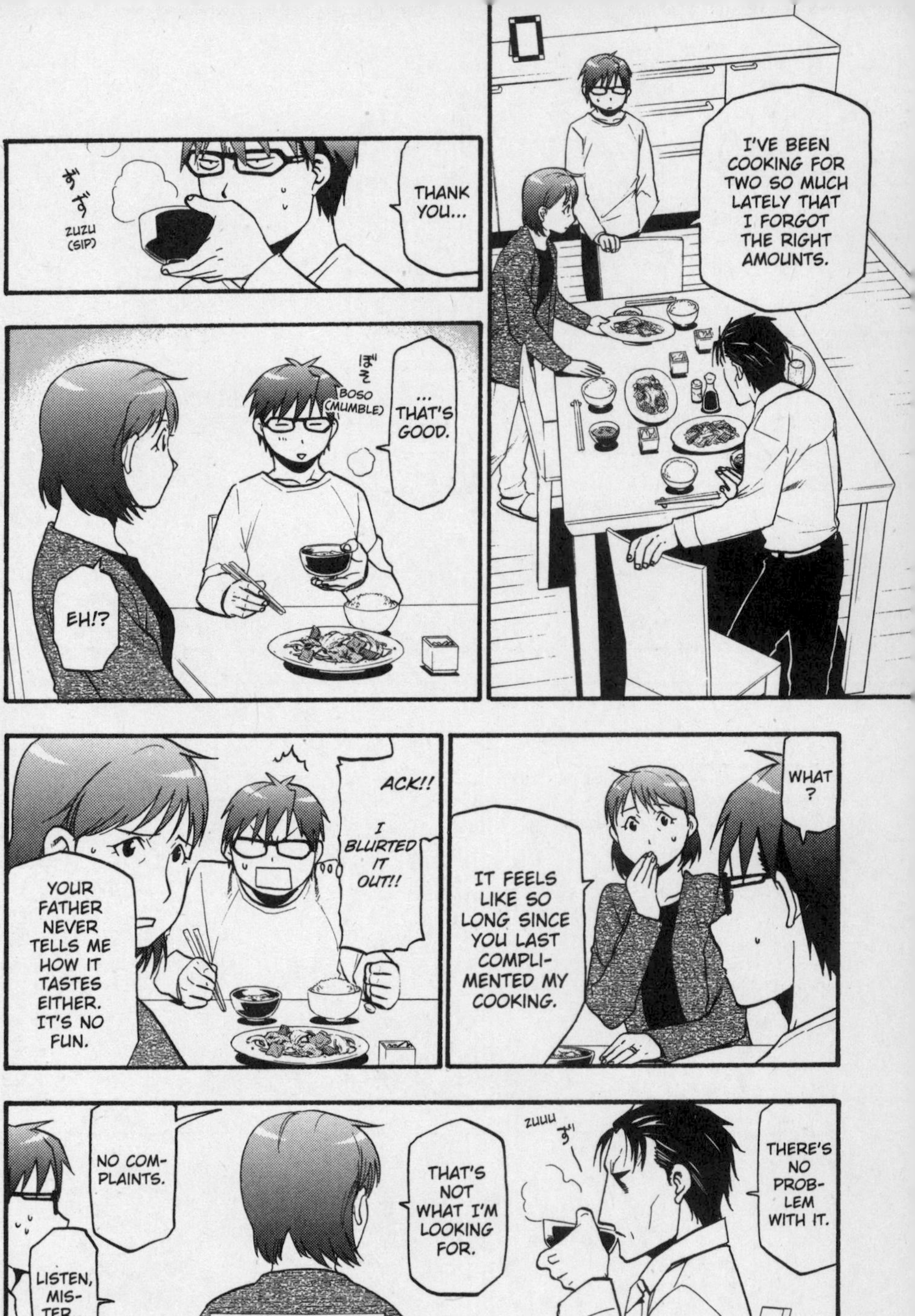
I'VE BEEN COOKING FOR TWO SO MUCH LATELY THAT I FORGOT THE RIGHT AMOUNTS.
ずず
ZUZU (SIP)
THANK YOU...
... THAT'S GOOD.
ぼそ
BOSO (MUMBLE)
EH!?
WHAT?
IT FEELS LIKE SO LONG SINCE YOU LAST COMPLIMENTED MY COOKING.
ACK!!
I BLURTED IT OUT!!
YOUR FATHER NEVER TELLS ME HOW IT TASTES EITHER. IT'S NO FUN.
THERE'S NO PROBLEM WITH IT.
ず
ZUUU
THAT'S NOT WHAT I'M LOOKING FOR.
NO COMPLAINTS.
LISTEN, MISTER...

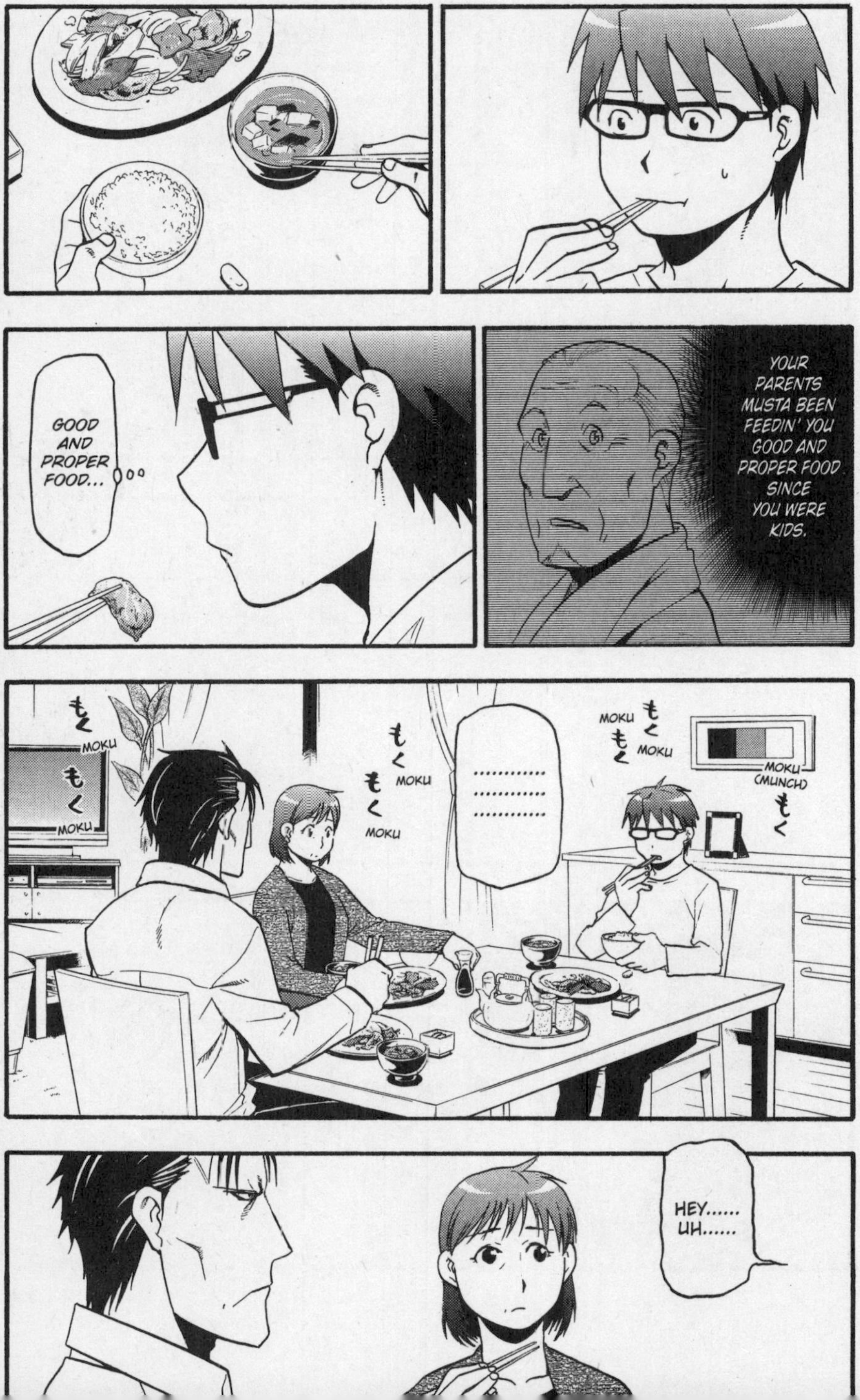

YOUR PARENTS MUSTA BEEN FEEDIN' YOU GOOD AND PROPER FOOD SINCE YOU WERE KIDS.
GOOD AND PROPER FOOD...
MOKU (MUNCH) もく
MOKU もく もく MOKU
....
....
....
もく MOKU もく MOKU
もく MOKU もく MOKU
HEY...... UH......

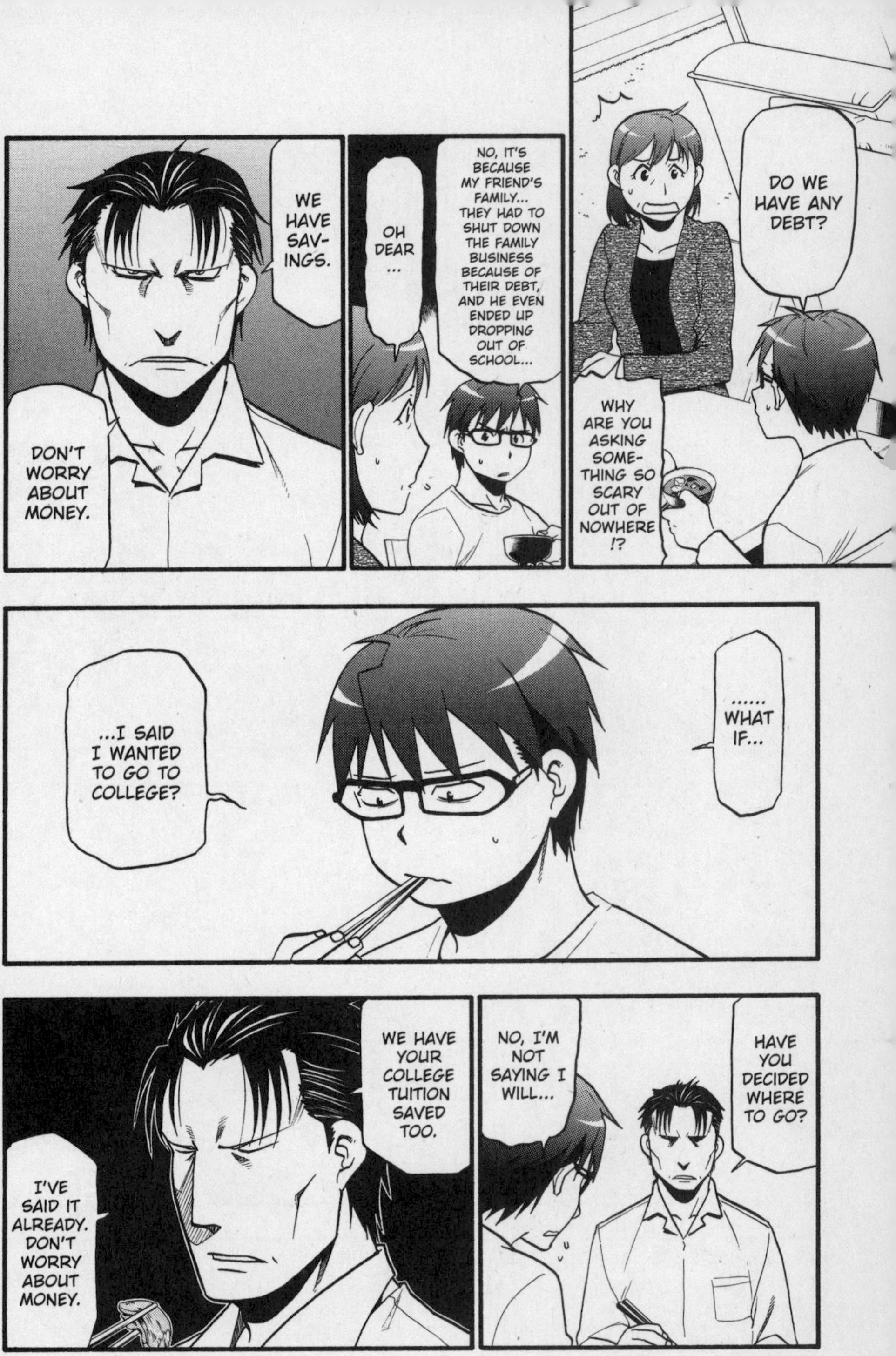
DO WE HAVE ANY DEBT?
WHY ARE YOU ASKING SOMETHING SO SCARY OUT OF NOWHERE!?
NO, IT'S BECAUSE MY FRIEND'S FAMILY... THEY HAD TO SHUT DOWN THE FAMILY BUSINESS BECAUSE OF THEIR DEBT, AND HE EVEN ENDED UP DROPPING OUT OF SCHOOL...
OH DEAR ...
WE HAVE SAV-INGS.
DON'T WORRY ABOUT MONEY.
......WHAT IF...
...I SAID I WANTED TO GO TO COLLEGE?
HAVE YOU DECIDED WHERE TO GO?
NO, I'M NOT SAYING I WILL...
WE HAVE YOUR COLLEGE TUITION SAVED TOO.
I'VE SAID IT ALREADY. DON'T WORRY ABOUT MONEY.

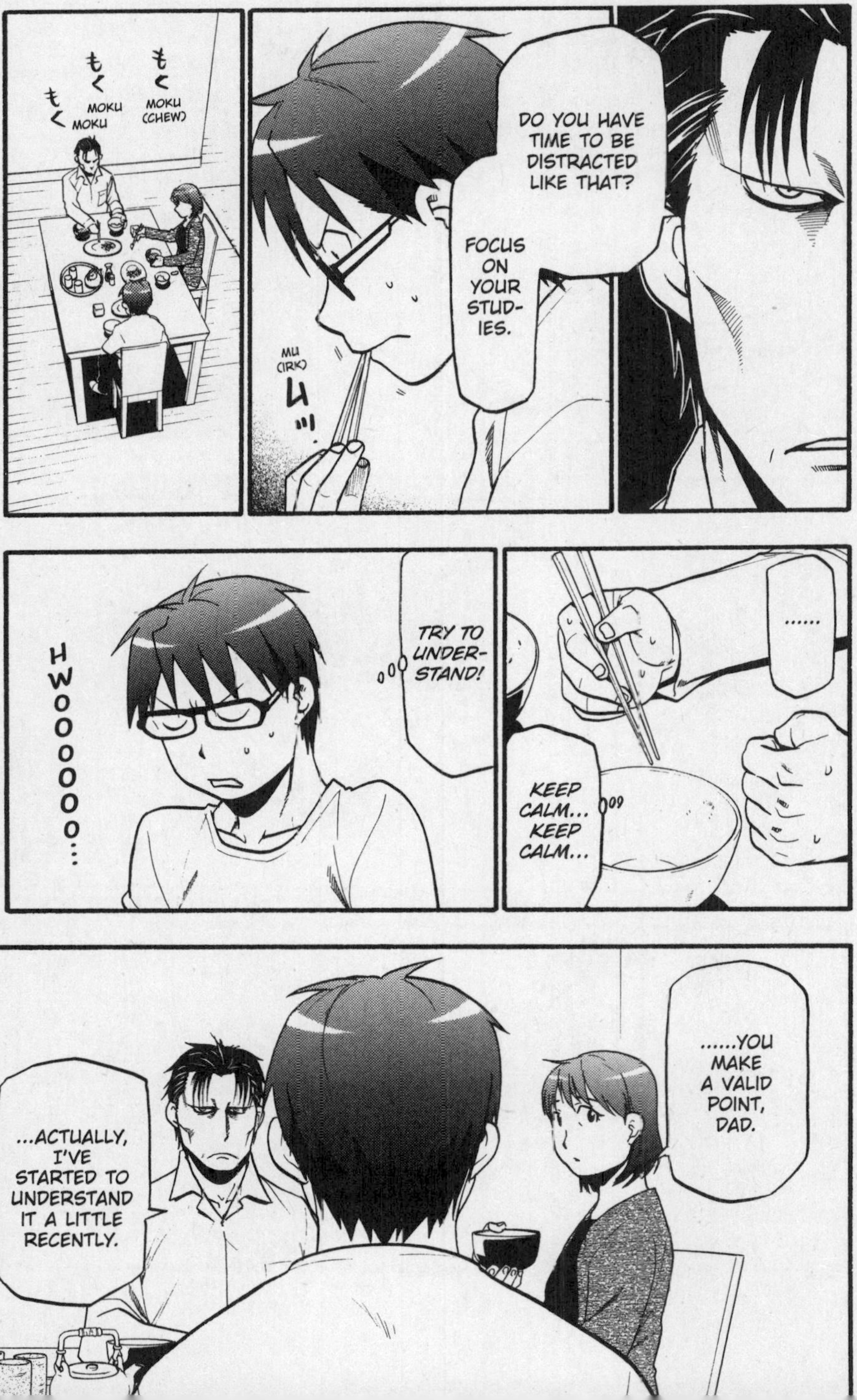

DO YOU HAVE TIME TO BE DISTRACTED LIKE THAT?
FOCUS ON YOUR STUDIES.
MU (IRK)
ムッ
もく
MOKU (CHEW)
もく
MOKU
もく
MOKU
......
KEEP CALM... KEEP CALM...
TRY TO UNDERSTAND!
HWOOOOOOO...
......YOU MAKE A VALID POINT, DAD.
...ACTUALLY, I'VE STARTED TO UNDERSTAND IT A LITTLE RECENTLY.

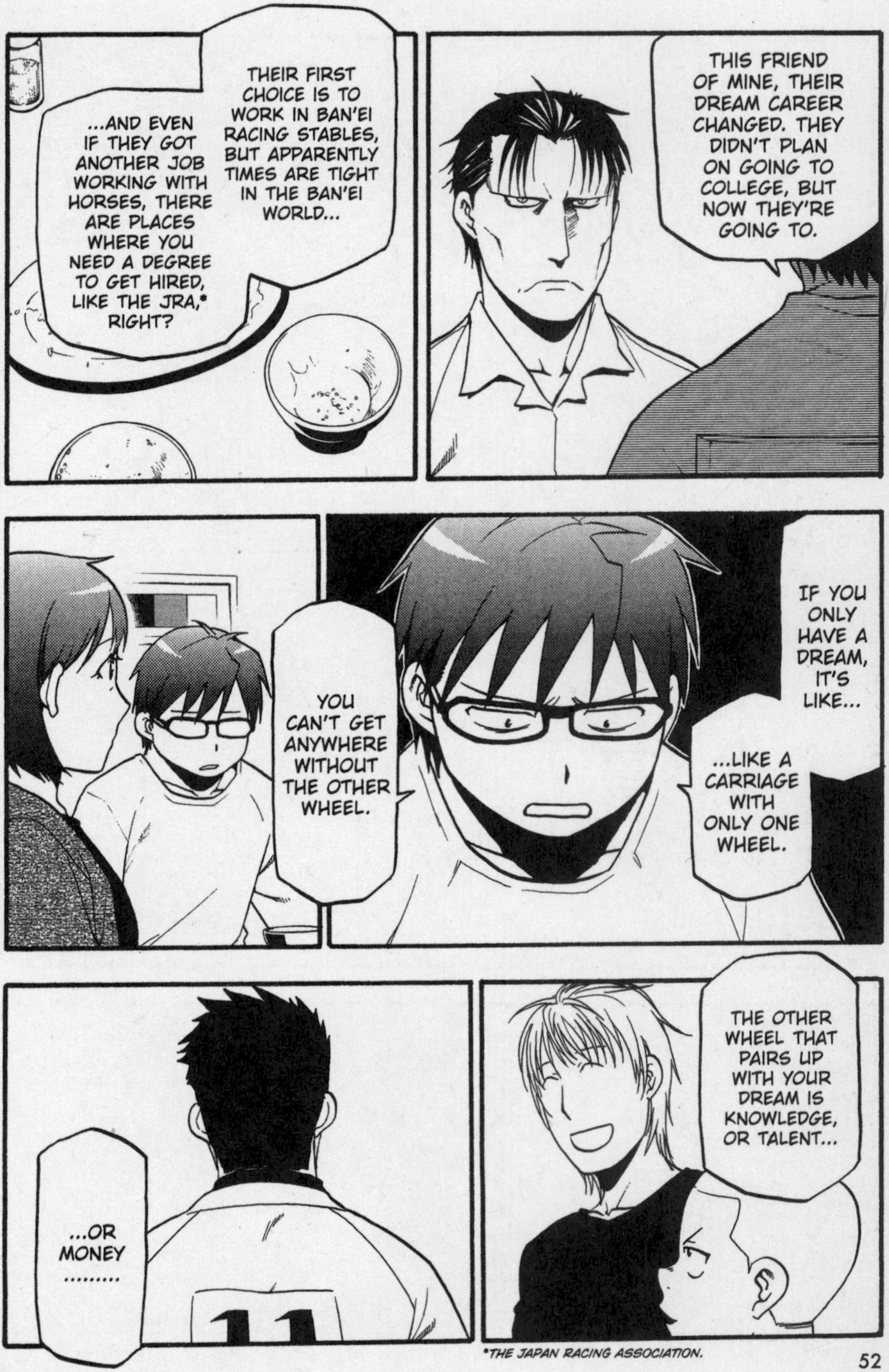
THIS FRIEND OF MINE, THEIR DREAM CAREER CHANGED. THEY DIDN'T PLAN ON GOING TO COLLEGE, BUT NOW THEY'RE GOING TO.
THEIR FIRST CHOICE IS TO WORK IN BAN'EI RACING STABLES, BUT APPARENTLY TIMES ARE TIGHT IN THE BAN'EI WORLD...
...AND EVEN IF THEY GOT ANOTHER JOB WORKING WITH HORSES, THERE ARE PLACES WHERE YOU NEED A DEGREE TO GET HIRED, LIKE THE JRA,* RIGHT?
IF YOU ONLY HAVE A DREAM, IT'S LIKE...
...LIKE A CARRIAGE WITH ONLY ONE WHEEL.
YOU CAN'T GET ANYWHERE WITHOUT THE OTHER WHEEL.
THE OTHER WHEEL THAT PAIRS UP WITH YOUR DREAM IS KNOWLEDGE, OR TALENT...
...OR MONEY ....

*THE JAPAN RACING ASSOCIATION.

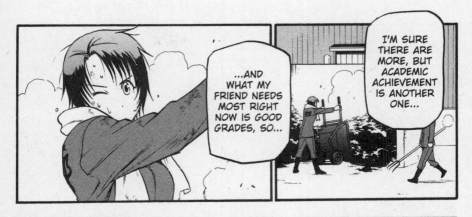

I'M SURE THERE ARE MORE, BUT ACADEMIC ACHIEVEMENT IS ANOTHER ONE...
...AND WHAT MY FRIEND NEEDS MOST RIGHT NOW IS GOOD GRADES, SO...
YOU CAME TO GET SHINGO'S COLLEGE PREP NOTES FOR THIS FRIEND?
YEAH... MY FRIEND WANTS TO GO TO A SCHOOL THAT WILL BE LITTLE DIFFICULT AT THEIR CURRENT LEVEL, SO THAT'S THE PLAN.
I'M HELPING WITH THEIR STUDIES RIGHT NOW...
...AND I THOUGHT... IF THERE'S ANYTHING I CAN TEACH THEM......

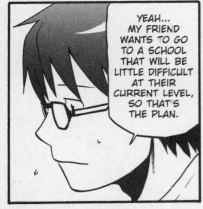

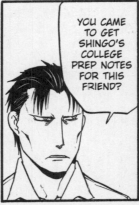

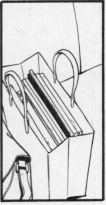

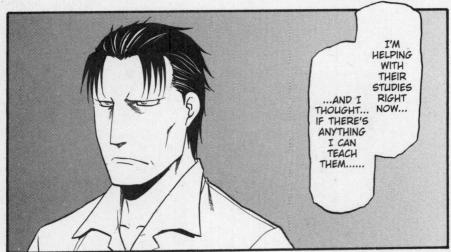

ARE YOU TELLING ME SOMEONE WHO DROPPED OUT OF THE ACADEMIC RACE IS GOING TO TEACH ANOTHER PERSON HOW TO STUDY?

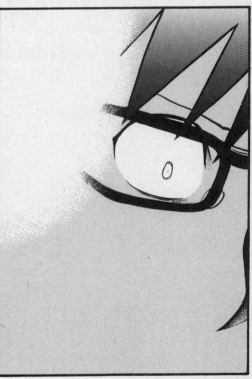

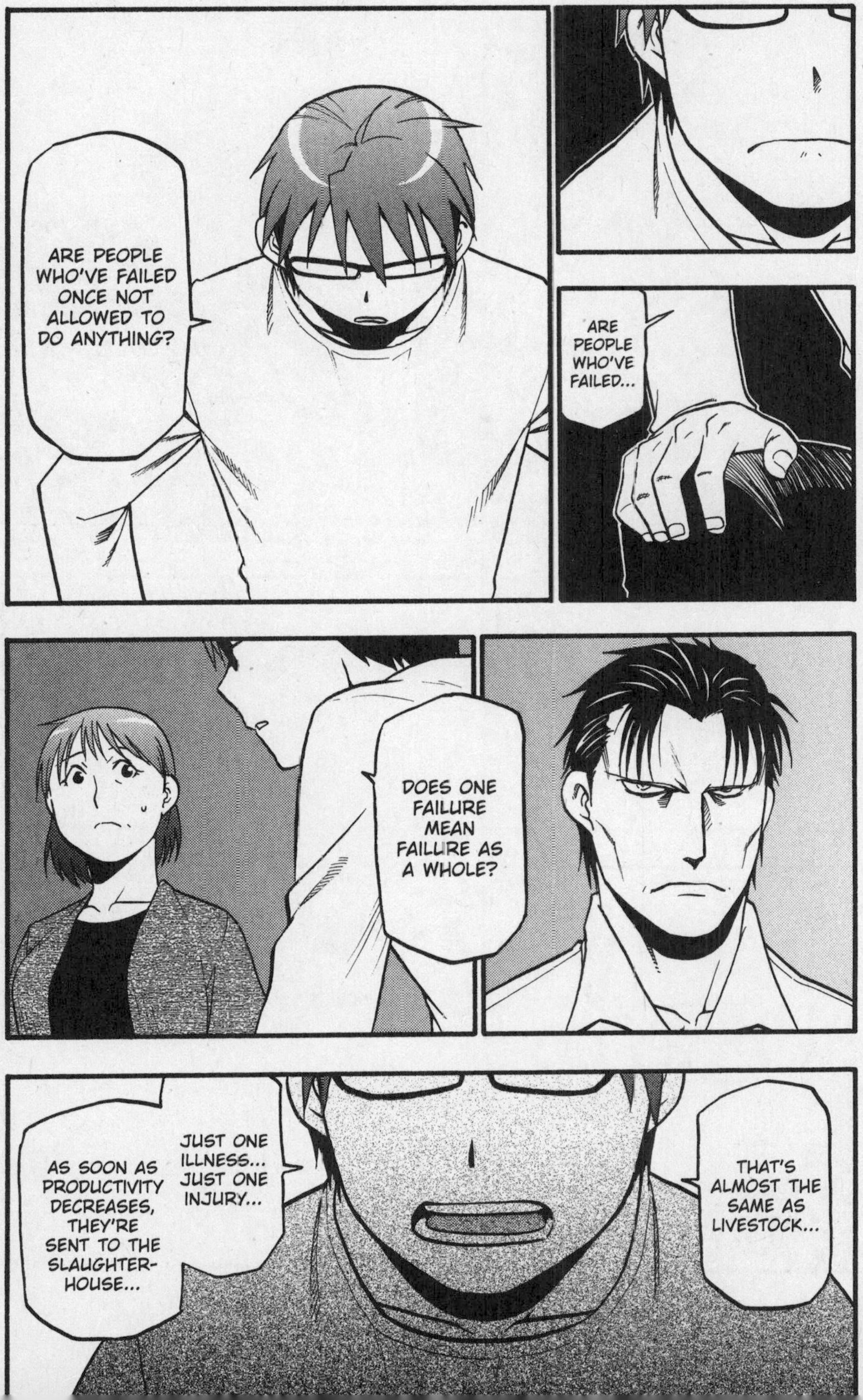
ARE PEOPLE WHO'VE FAILED...
ARE PEOPLE WHO'VE FAILED ONCE NOT ALLOWED TO DO ANYTHING?
DOES ONE FAILURE MEAN FAILURE AS A WHOLE?
THAT'S ALMOST THE SAME AS LIVESTOCK...
JUST ONE ILLNESS... JUST ONE INJURY...
AS SOON AS PRODUCTIVITY DECREASES, THEY'RE SENT TO THE SLAUGHTER-HOUSE...

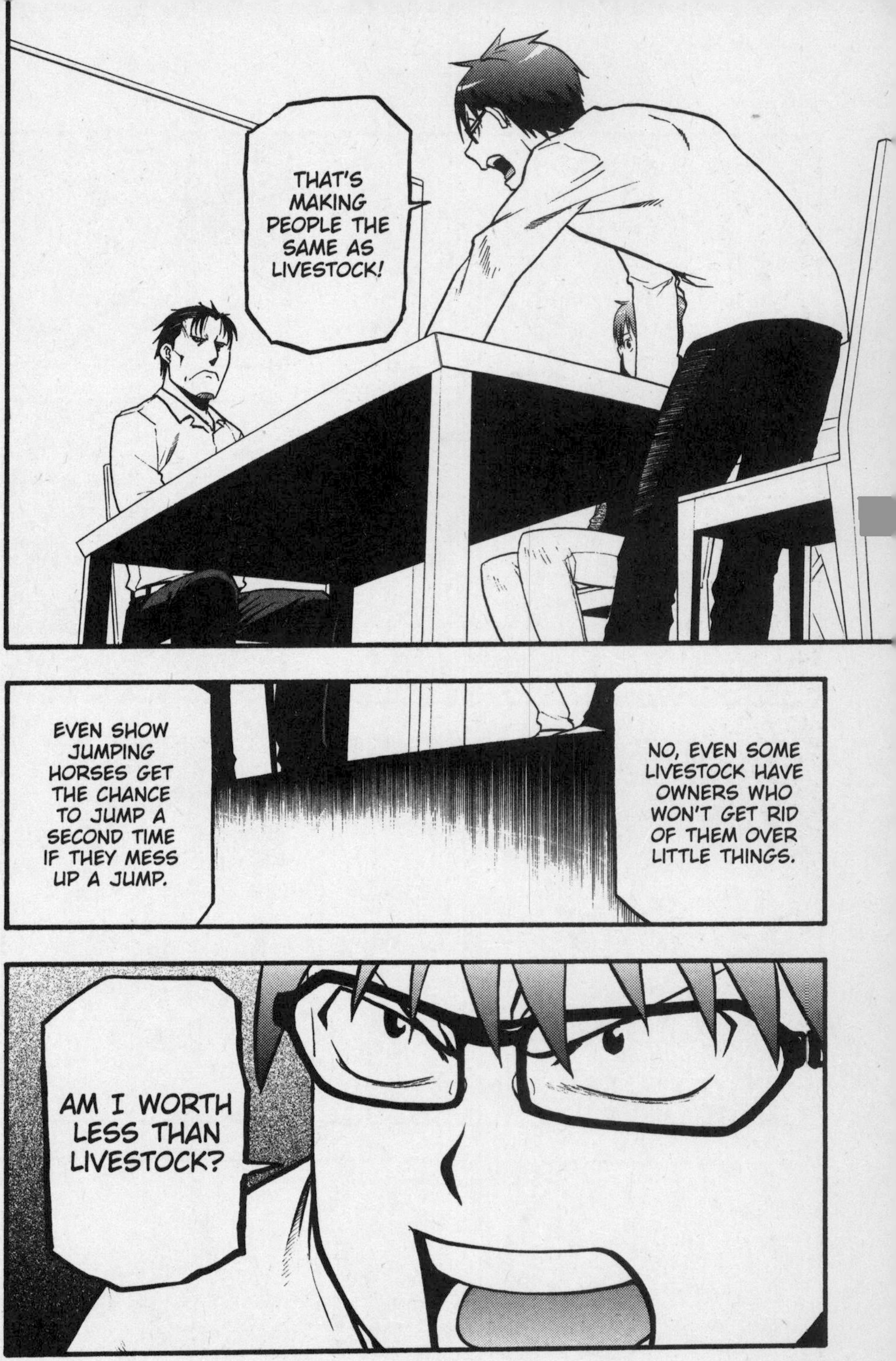
THAT'S MAKING PEOPLE THE SAME AS LIVESTOCK!
NO, EVEN SOME LIVESTOCK HAVE OWNERS WHO WON'T GET RID OF THEM OVER LITTLE THINGS.
EVEN SHOW JUMPING HORSES GET THE CHANCE TO JUMP A SECOND TIME IF THEY MESS UP A JUMP.
AM I WORTH LESS THAN LIVESTOCK?

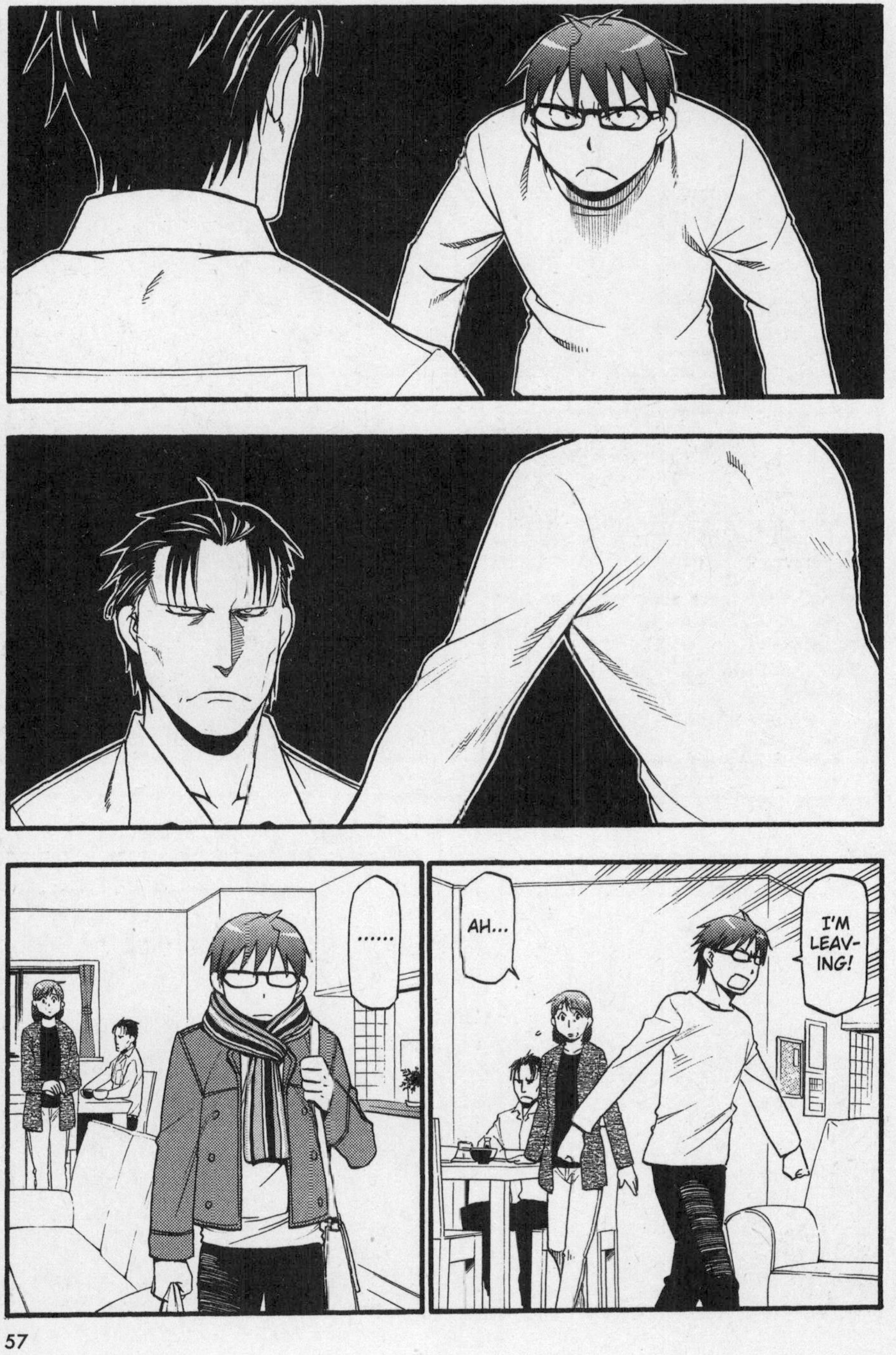
I'M LEAV-ING!
AH...
......

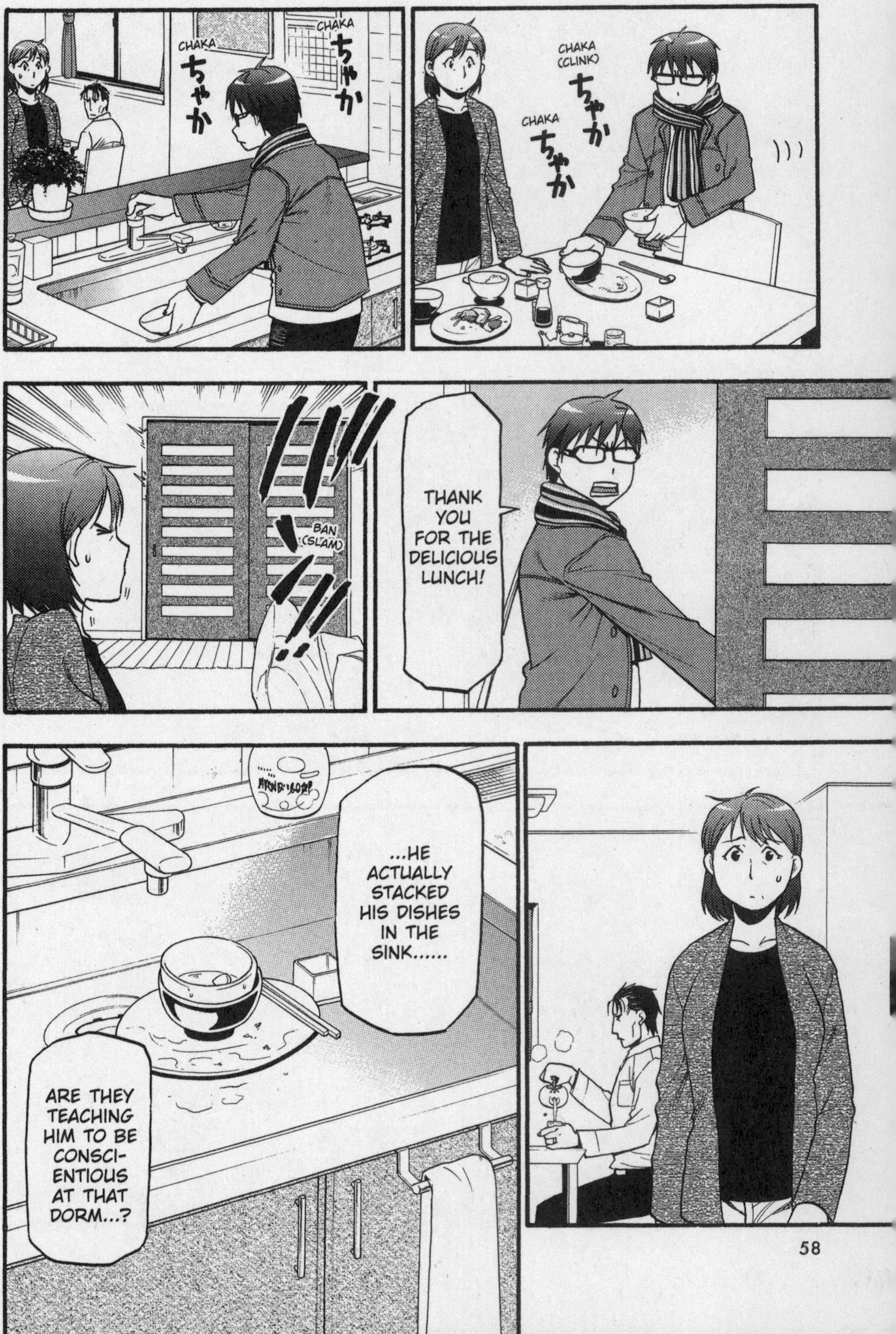
CHAKA (CLINK)
ちゃか
CHAKA
ちゃか
CHAKA
ちゃか
CHAKA
ちゃか
THANK YOU FOR THE DELICIOUS LUNCH!
BAN (SLAM)
...HE ACTUALLY STACKED HIS DISHES IN THE SINK......
ARE THEY TEACHING HIM TO BE CONSCI-ENTIOUS AT THAT DORM...?

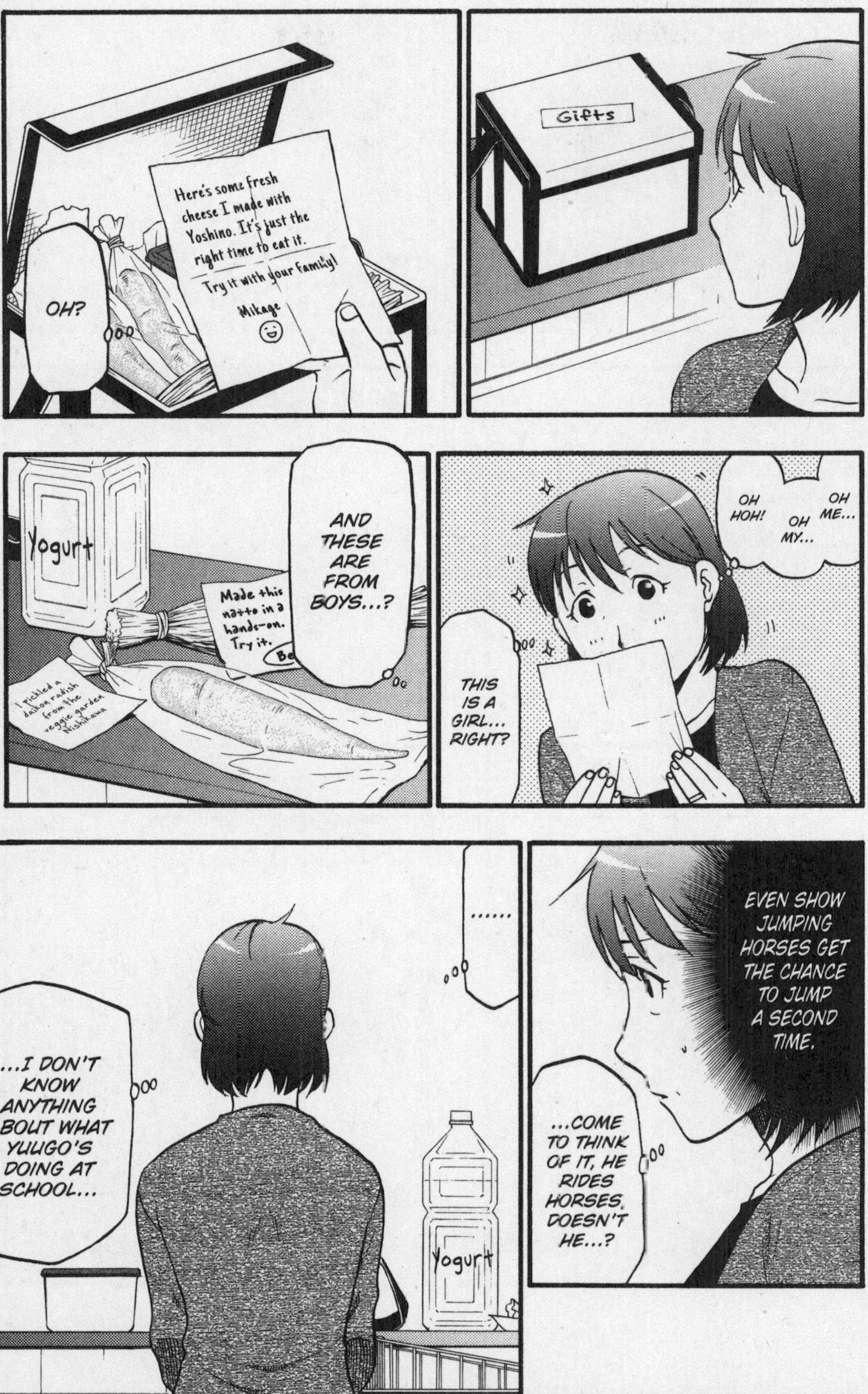
Gifts
Here's some fresh cheese I made with Yoshino. It's just the right time to eat it.
Try it with your family!
Mikage
OH?
OH HOH!
OH MY...
OH ME...
THIS IS A GIRL... RIGHT?
AND THESE ARE FROM BOYS...?
Yogurt
Made this natto in a hands-on. Try it.
I pickled a daikon radish from the veggie garden Nishikawa
EVEN SHOW JUMPING HORSES GET THE CHANCE TO JUMP A SECOND TIME.
...COME TO THINK OF IT, HE RIDES HORSES, DOESN'T HE...?
......
...I DON'T KNOW ANYTHING ABOUT WHAT YUUGO'S DOING AT SCHOOL...
Yogurt

...I UP AND FORGOT ALL OF THE GIFTS BACK THERE...

I WANTED TO EAT THAT FRESH CHEESE...!!

HRnnnGH!

ZU (SIP)

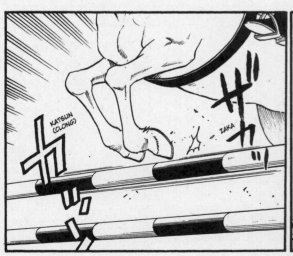

KATSUN (CLONG)

ZAKA

I'M GOING IIIN!

ZAKA

ZAKA

ZAKA (CLOP)

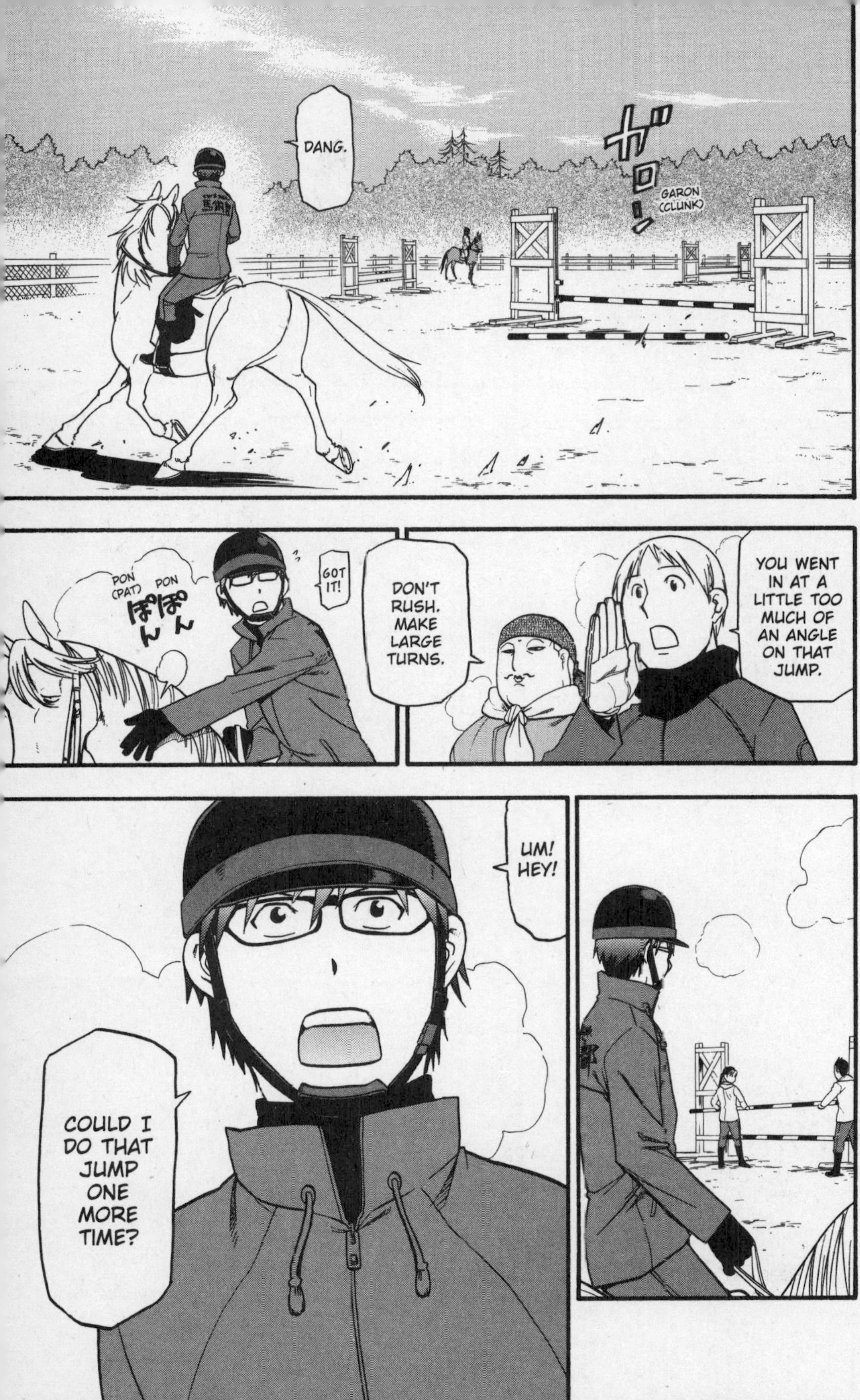
GARON (CLUNK)
DANG.
YOU WENT IN AT A LITTLE TOO MUCH OF AN ANGLE ON THAT JUMP.
DON'T RUSH. MAKE LARGE TURNS.
GOT IT!
PON (PAT) PON
ぽぽん
UM! HEY!
COULD I DO THAT JUMP ONE MORE TIME?

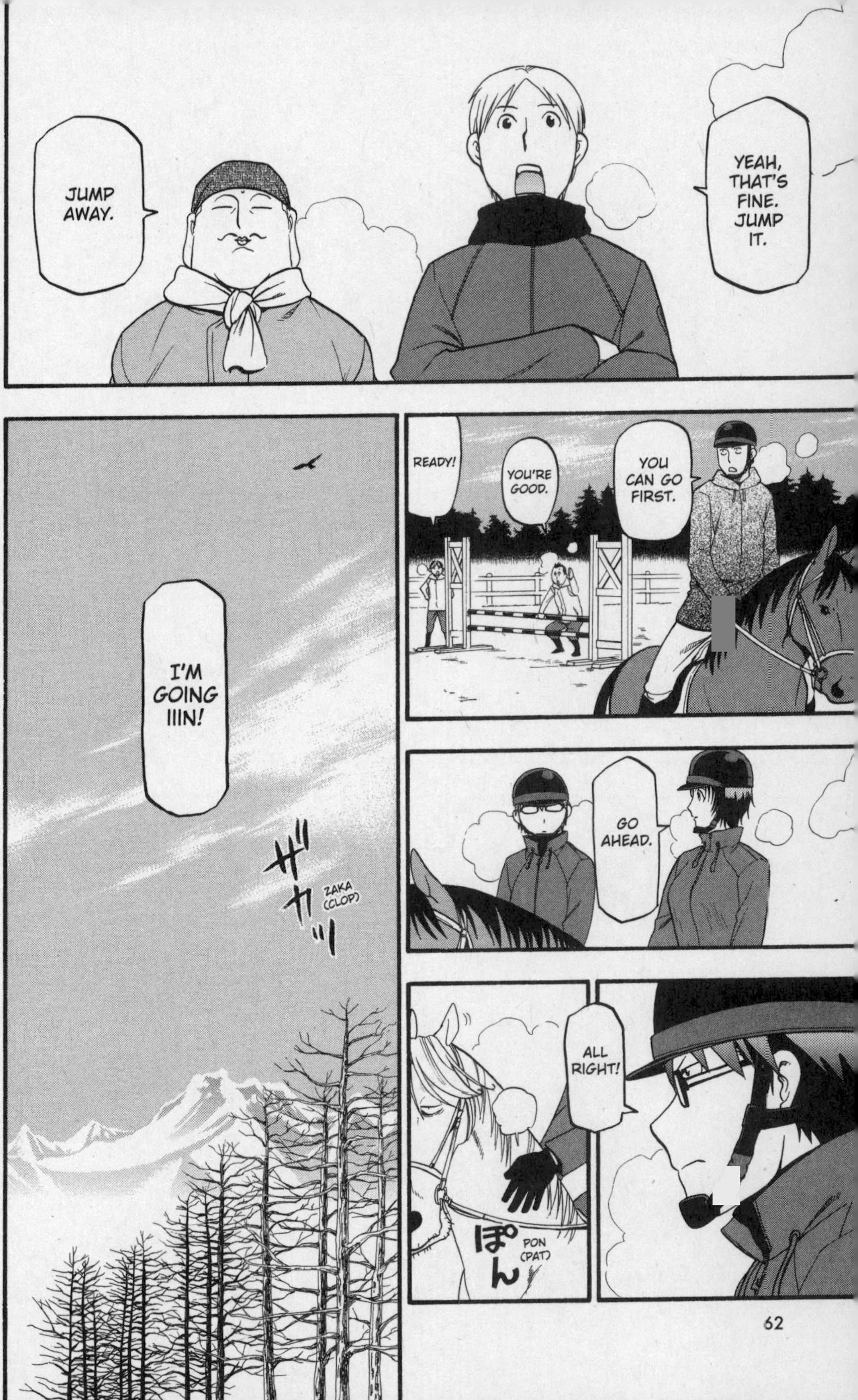
YEAH, THAT'S FINE. JUMP IT.
JUMP AWAY.
YOU CAN GO FIRST.
YOU'RE GOOD.
READY!
GO AHEAD.
ALL RIGHT!
ぽん
PON (PAT)
I'M GOING IIIN!
ザカッ
ZAKA (CLOP)

Silver Spoon

DORM HEAD

SHOUICHI
FUYUSHIMA

Chapter 74:

Tale of Winter ⑪

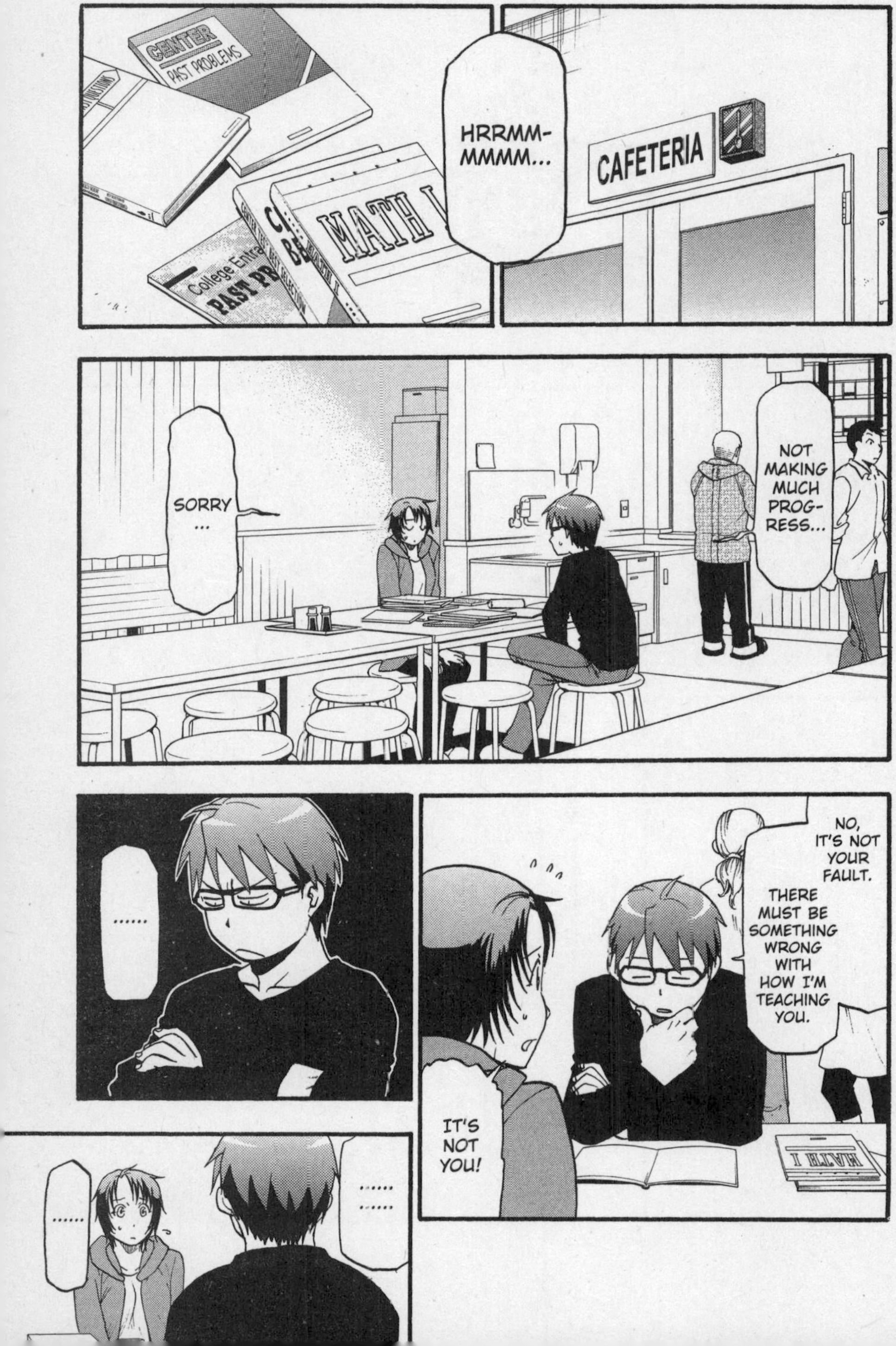
CAFETERIA
HRRMM-MMMM...
CENTER
PAST PROBLEMS
MATH I
NOT MAKING MUCH PROGRESS...
SORRY...
NO, IT'S NOT YOUR FAULT. THERE MUST BE SOMETHING WRONG WITH HOW I'M TEACHING YOU.
IT'S NOT YOU!
MATH I
......
....
......

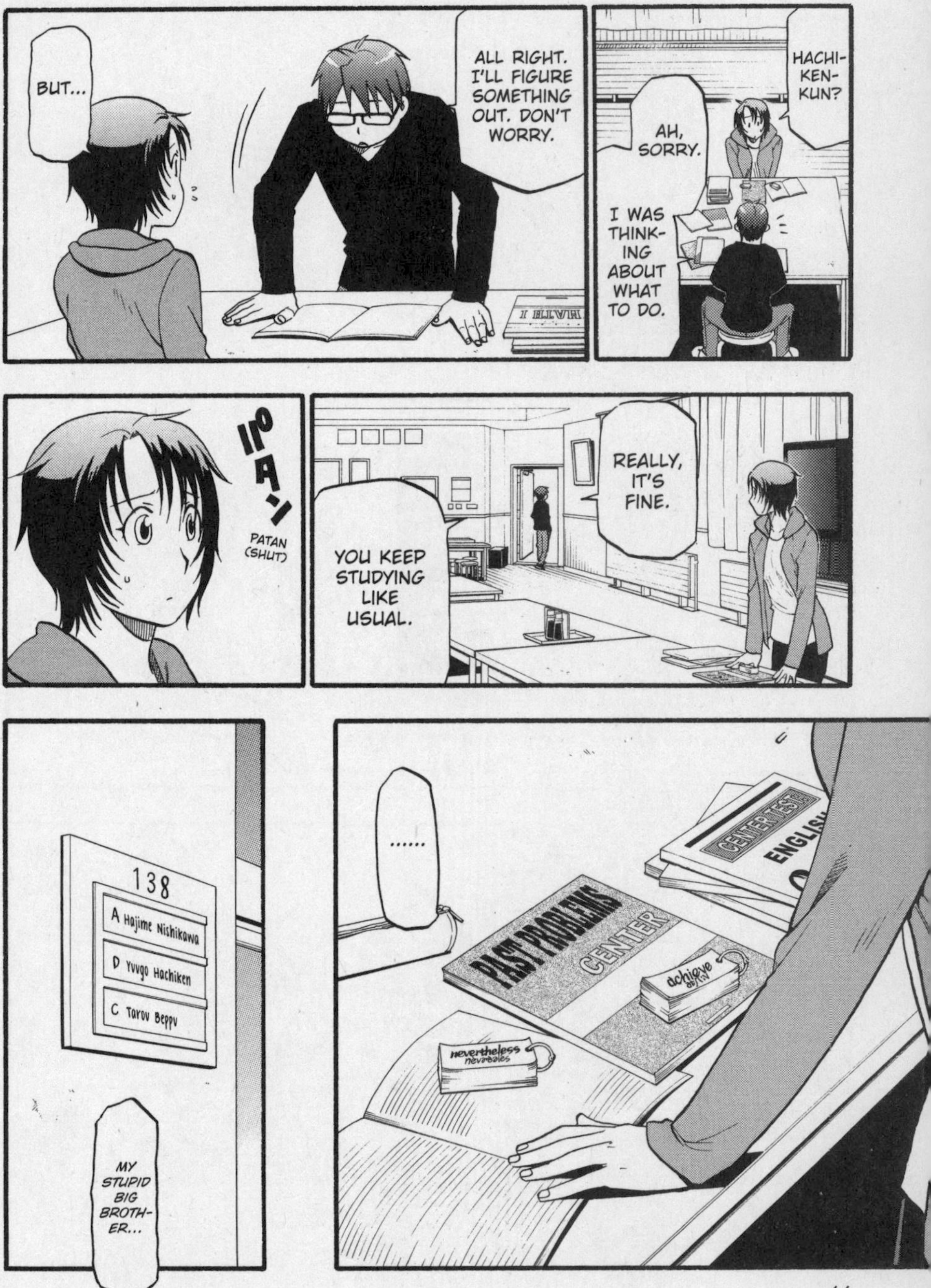
HACHI-KEN-KUN?
AH, SORRY.
I WAS THINKING ABOUT WHAT TO DO.
ALL RIGHT. I'LL FIGURE SOMETHING OUT. DON'T WORRY.
BUT...
REALLY, IT'S FINE.
YOU KEEP STUDYING LIKE USUAL.
パタン
PATAN (SHUT)
......
CENTER TEST
ENGLISH
PAST PROBLEMS
CENTER
achieve
nevertheless
138
A Hajime Nishikawa
D Yuugo Hachiken
C Tarou Beppu
MY STUPID BIG BROTHER...

...AND HIS STUPID MESSY HAND-WRITING ...
IT TAKES WAY TOO MUCH TIME TO DECIPHER THIS!!
CRAP...AT THIS RATE, I WON'T GET MIKAGE INTO HER FIRST CHOICE OF SCHOOL...
ARE YOU TELLING ME SOMEONE WHO DROPPED OUT OF THE ACADEMIC RACE IS GOING TO TEACH ANOTHER PERSON HOW TO STUDY?
DAMN IT...!
I'LL SHOW YOU...

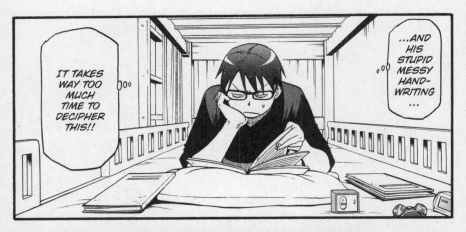

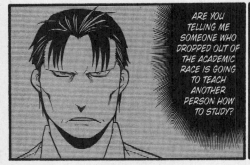

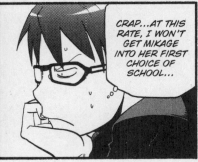

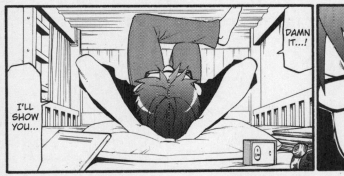

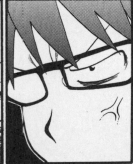

Chapter 74:
Tale of Winter ⑪

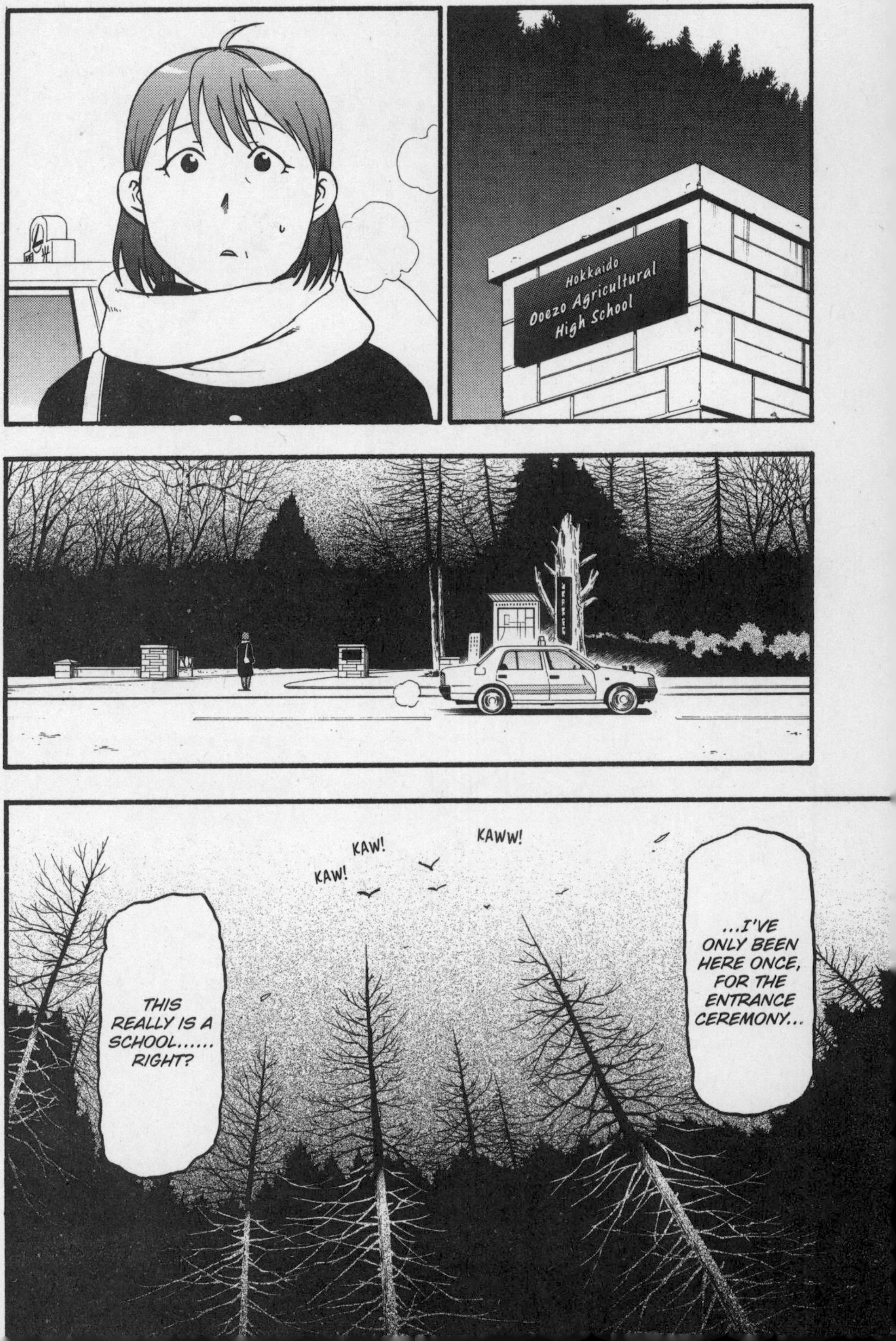
Hokkaido
Ooezo Agricultural
High School
KAWW!
...I'VE ONLY BEEN HERE ONCE, FOR THE ENTRANCE CEREMONY...
KAW!
KAW!
THIS REALLY IS A SCHOOL...... RIGHT?

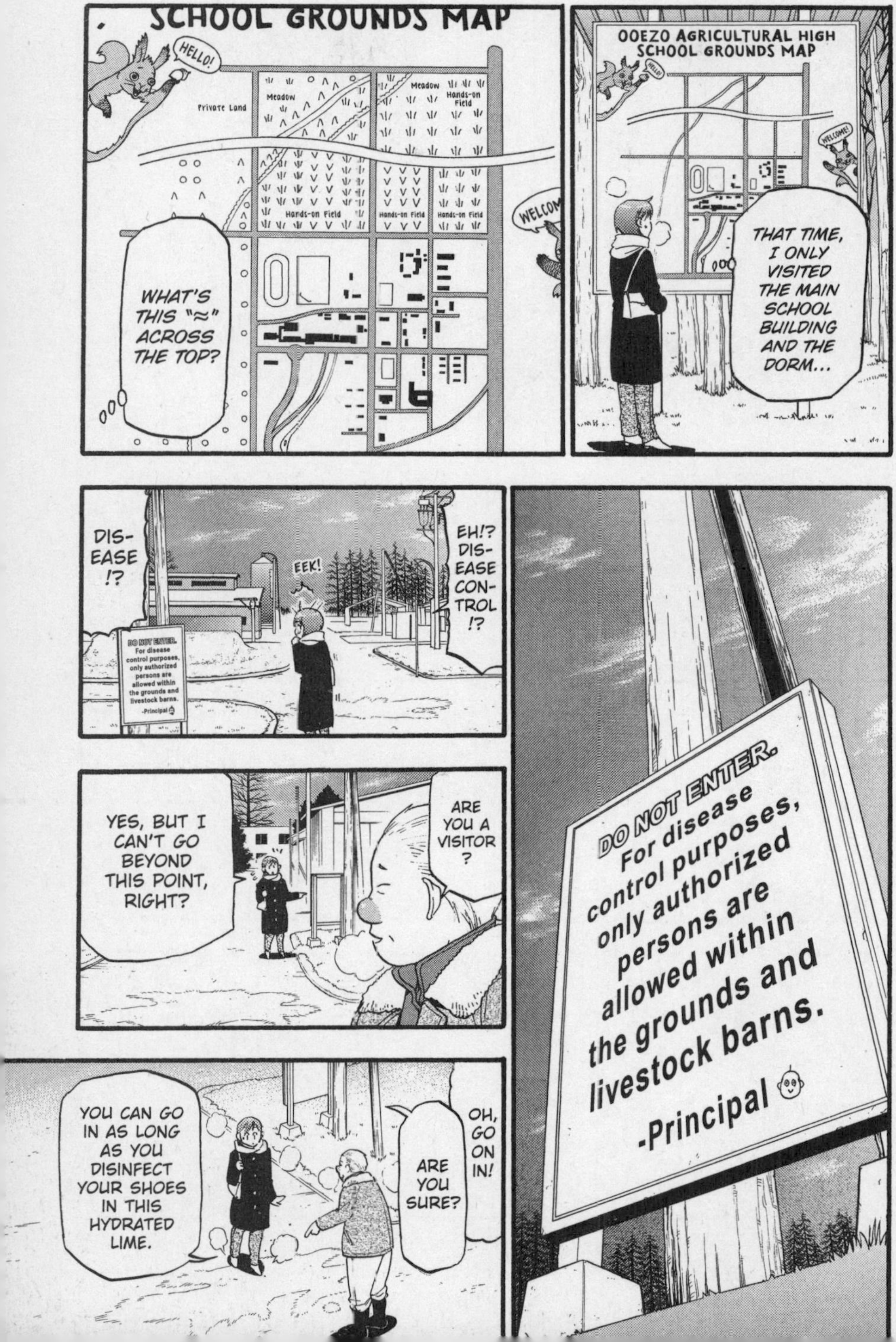
OOEZO AGRICULTURAL HIGH SCHOOL GROUNDS MAP
HELLO!
WELCOME!
THAT TIME, I ONLY VISITED THE MAIN SCHOOL BUILDING AND THE DORM...
SCHOOL GROUNDS MAP
HELLO!
Private Land
Meadow
Meadow
Hands-on Field
Hands-on Field
Hands-on Field
Hands-on Field
WELCOM
WHAT'S THIS "≈" ACROSS THE TOP?
DO NOT ENTER. For disease control purposes, only authorized persons are allowed within the grounds and livestock barns. -Principal
EH!? DIS-EASE CON-TROL!?
EEK!
DO NOT ENTER. For disease control purposes, only authorized persons are allowed within the grounds and livestock barns. -Principal
DIS-EASE!?
ARE YOU A VISITOR?
YES, BUT I CAN'T GO BEYOND THIS POINT, RIGHT?
OH, GO ON IN!
ARE YOU SURE?
YOU CAN GO IN AS LONG AS YOU DISINFECT YOUR SHOES IN THIS HYDRATED LIME.

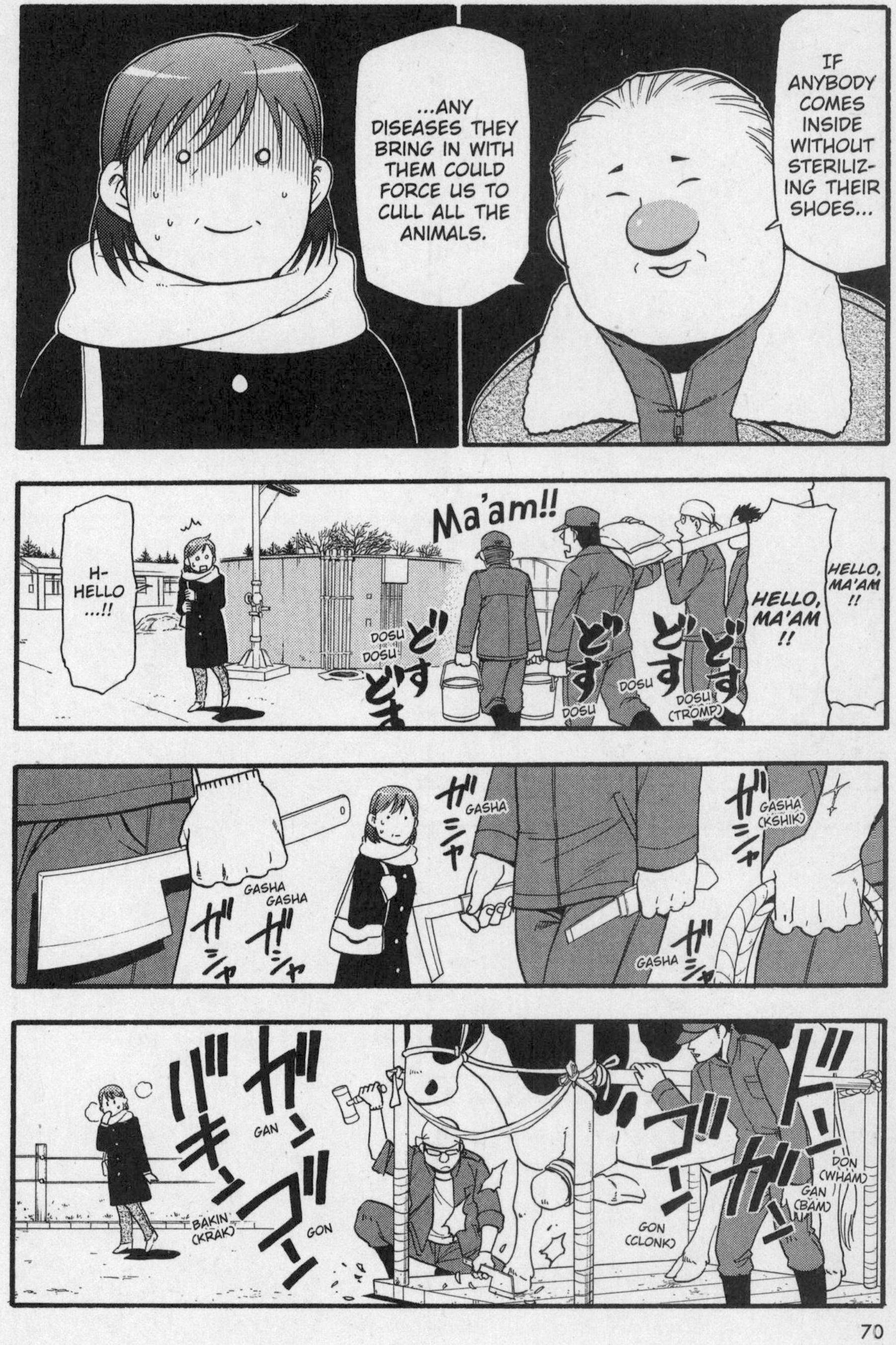
IF ANYBODY COMES INSIDE WITHOUT STERILIZ-ING THEIR SHOES...
...ANY DISEASES THEY BRING IN WITH THEM COULD FORCE US TO CULL ALL THE ANIMALS.
HELLO, MA'AM!!
HELLO, MA'AM!!
Ma'am!!
どす
DOSU (TROMP)
どす
DOSU
どす
DOSU
どす
どす
DOSU DOSU
H-HELLO...!!
ガシャ
GASHA (KSHIK)
ガシャ
GASHA
ガシャ
GASHA
ガシャ
ガシャ
GASHA GASHA
ドン
DON (WHAM)
ガン
GAN (BAM)
ゴン
GON (CLONK)
ガン
GAN
ゴン
GON
バキン
BAKIN (KRAK)

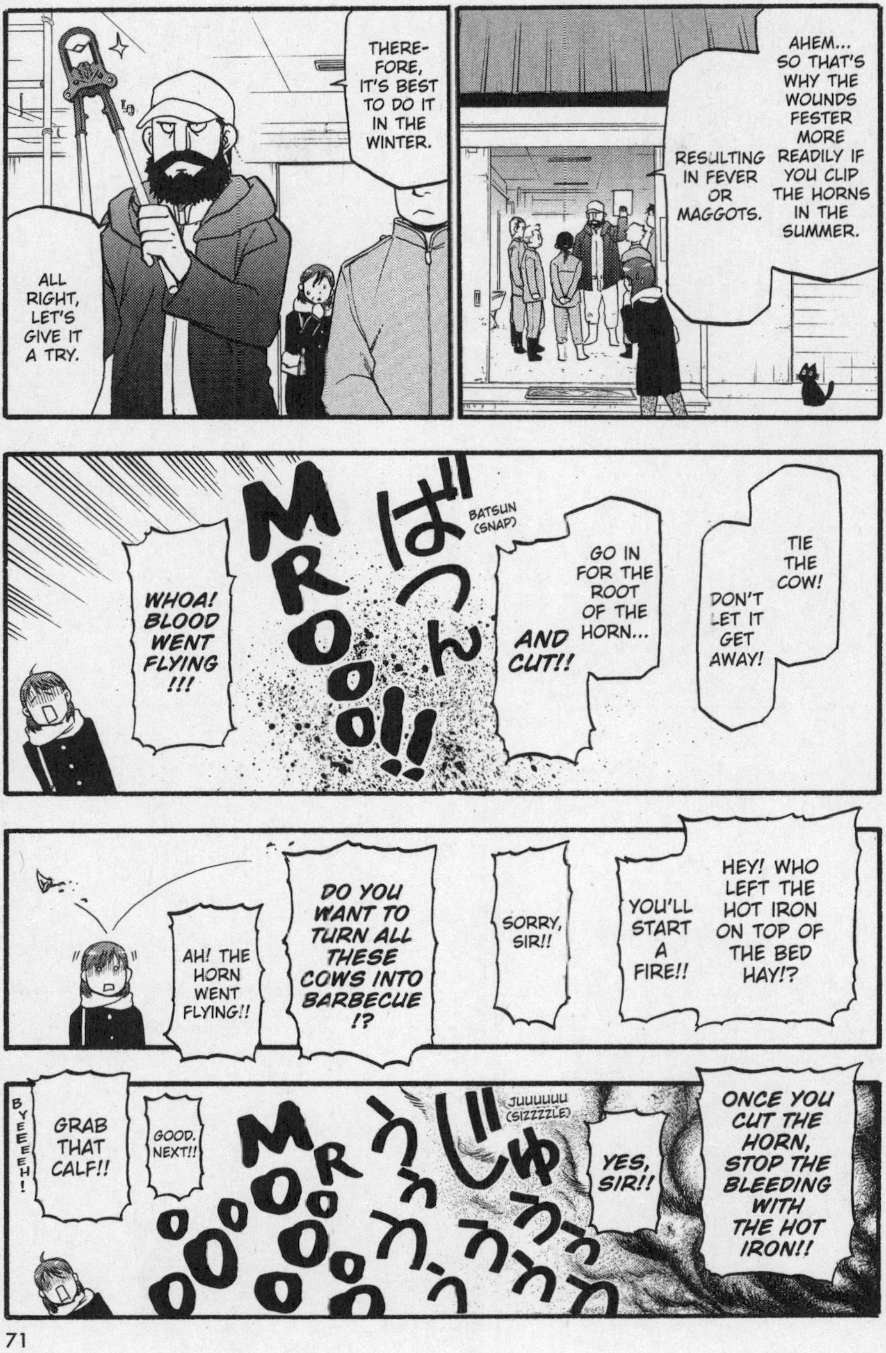
AHEM... SO THAT'S WHY THE WOUNDS FESTER MORE READILY IF YOU CLIP THE HORNS IN THE SUMMER.
RESULTING IN FEVER OR MAGGOTS.
THERE-FORE, IT'S BEST TO DO IT IN THE WINTER.
ALL RIGHT, LET'S GIVE IT A TRY.
TIE THE COW!
DON'T LET IT GET AWAY!
GO IN FOR THE ROOT OF THE HORN...
AND CUT!!
ばつん
BATSUN (SNAP)
MROOOO!!
WHOA! BLOOD WENT FLYING!!!
HEY! WHO LEFT THE HOT IRON ON TOP OF THE BED HAY!?
YOU'LL START A FIRE!!
SORRY, SIR!!
DO YOU WANT TO TURN ALL THESE COWS INTO BARBECUE!?
AH! THE HORN WENT FLYING!!
ONCE YOU CUT THE HORN, STOP THE BLEEDING WITH THE HOT IRON!!
YES, SIR!!
じゅうううう
JUUUUUU (SIZZZZLE)
うううう
MROOOOO
GOOD. NEXT!!
GRAB THAT CALF!!
BYEEEEH!

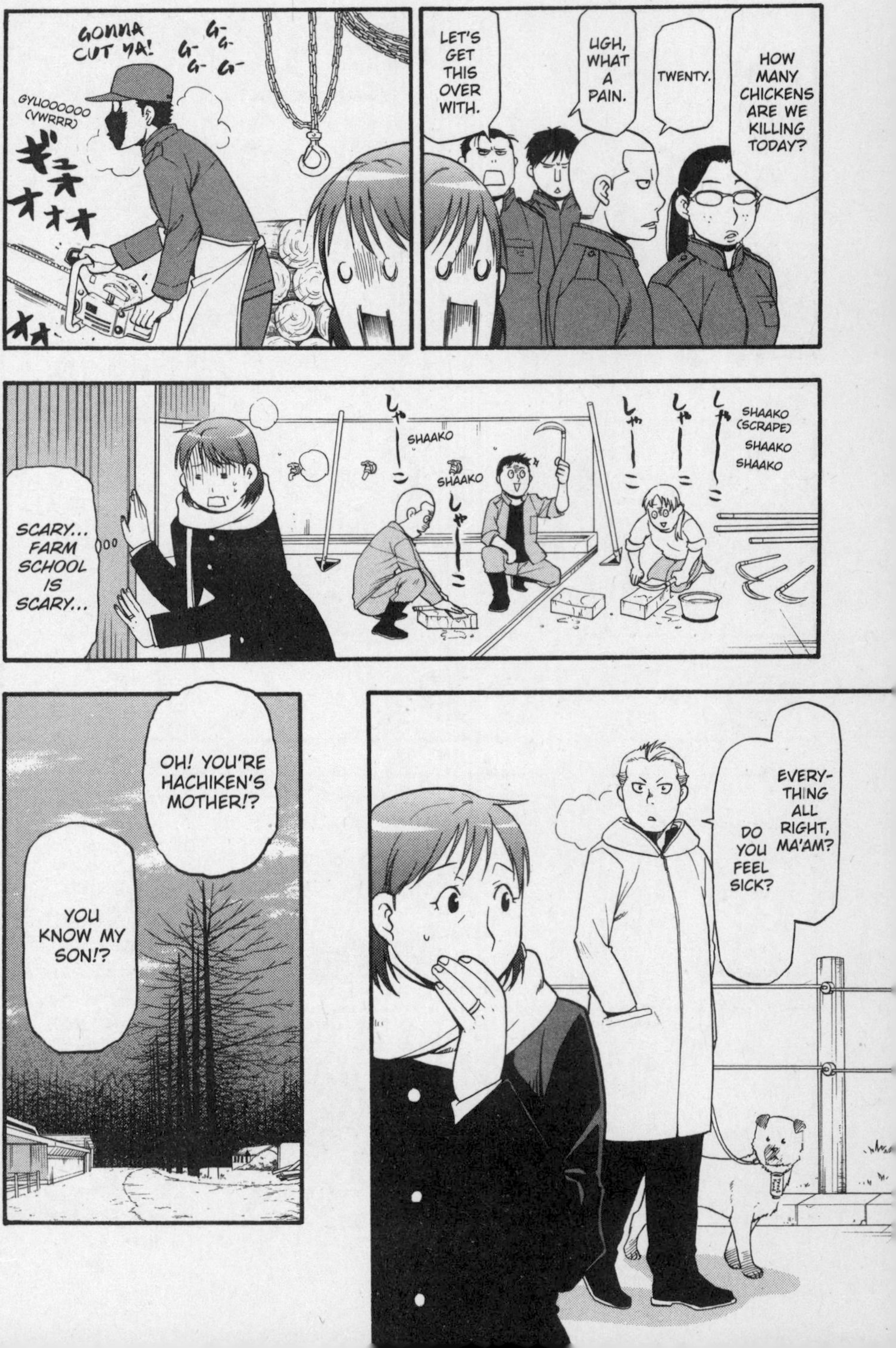
HOW MANY CHICKENS ARE WE KILLING TODAY?
TWENTY.
UGH, WHAT A PAIN.
LET'S GET THIS OVER WITH.
GONNA CUT YA!
G-G-G-G-G-G
GYUOOOOOO (VWRRR)
ギュオオオオオ
SHAAKO (SCRAPE) SHAAKO SHAAKO
しゃーこ しゃーこ しゃーこ
SHAAKO
しゃーこ
SHAAKO
しゃーこ
SCARY... FARM SCHOOL IS SCARY...
EVERYTHING ALL RIGHT, MA'AM?
DO YOU FEEL SICK?
OH! YOU'RE HACHIKEN'S MOTHER!?
YOU KNOW MY SON!?

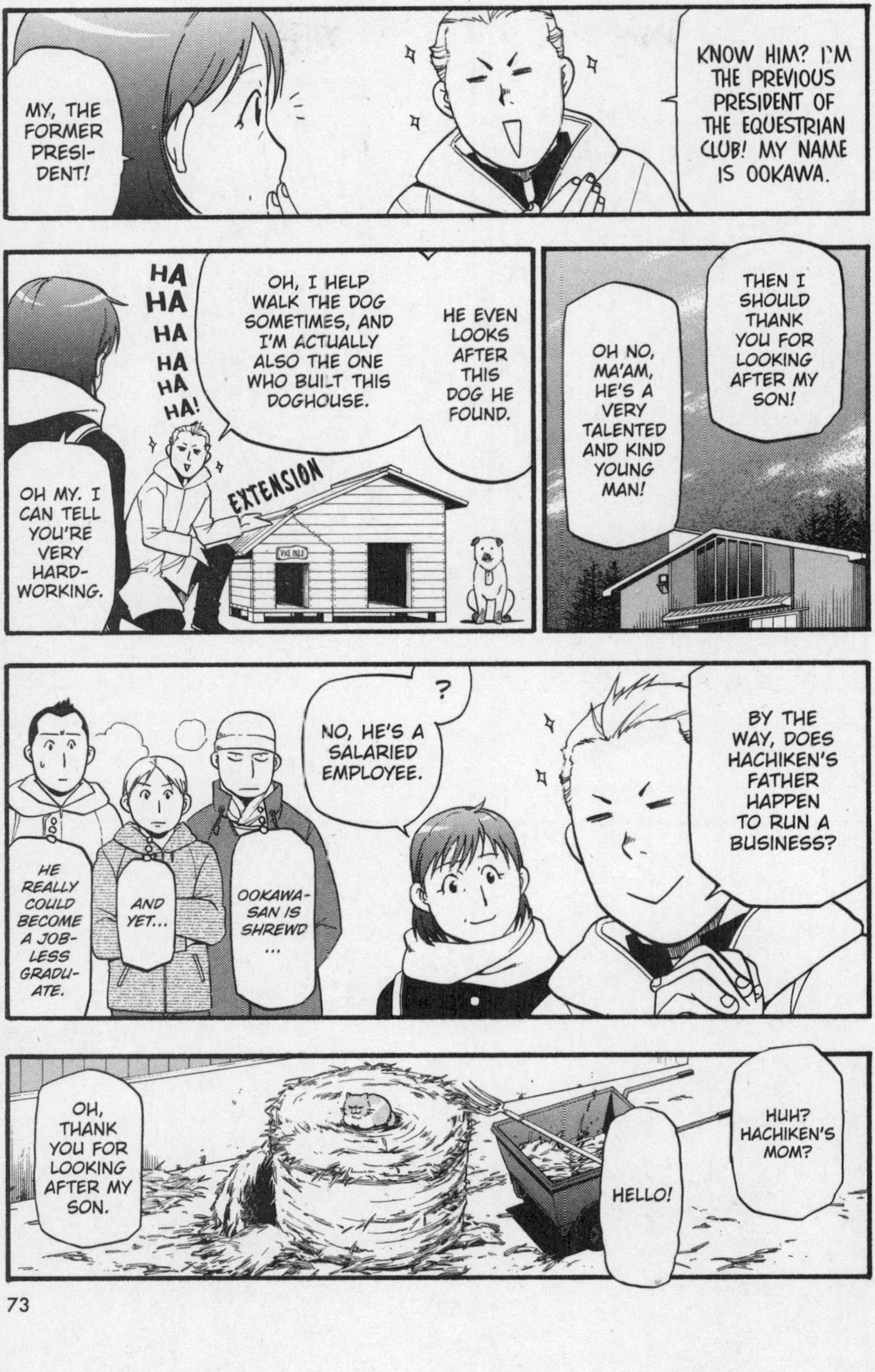
KNOW HIM? I'M THE PREVIOUS PRESIDENT OF THE EQUESTRIAN CLUB! MY NAME IS OOKAWA.
MY, THE FORMER PRESI-DENT!
THEN I SHOULD THANK YOU FOR LOOKING AFTER MY SON!
OH NO, MA'AM, HE'S A VERY TALENTED AND KIND YOUNG MAN!
HE EVEN LOOKS AFTER THIS DOG HE FOUND.
OH, I HELP WALK THE DOG SOMETIMES, AND I'M ACTUALLY ALSO THE ONE WHO BUILT THIS DOGHOUSE.
HA HA HA HA HA HA!
EXTENSION
OH MY. I CAN TELL YOU'RE VERY HARD-WORKING.
BY THE WAY, DOES HACHIKEN'S FATHER HAPPEN TO RUN A BUSINESS?
?
NO, HE'S A SALARIED EMPLOYEE.
OOKAWA-SAN IS SHREWD ...
AND YET...
HE REALLY COULD BECOME A JOB-LESS GRADU-ATE.
HUH? HACHIKEN'S MOM?
HELLO!
OH, THANK YOU FOR LOOKING AFTER MY SON.

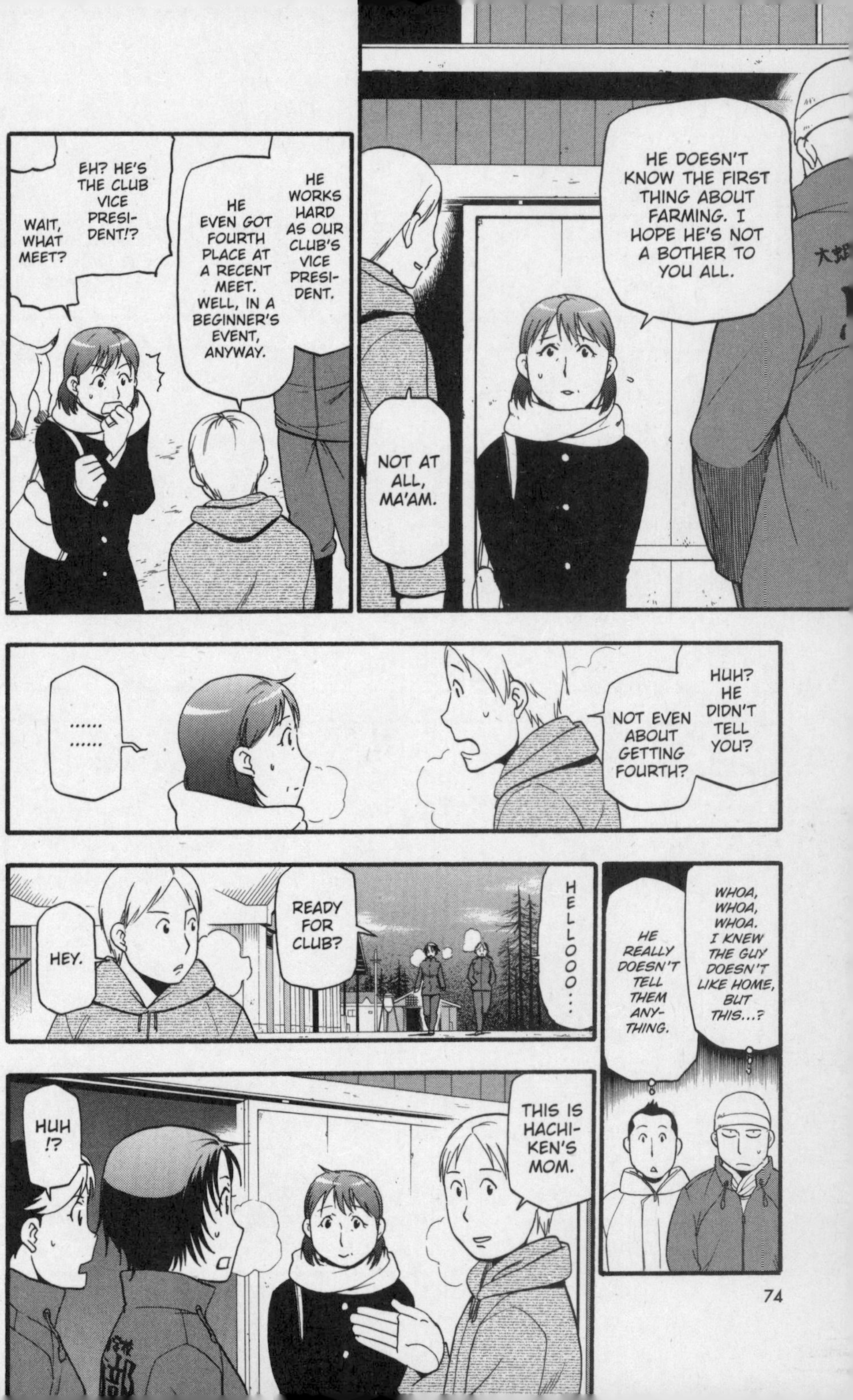
HE DOESN'T KNOW THE FIRST THING ABOUT FARMING. I HOPE HE'S NOT A BOTHER TO YOU ALL.
NOT AT ALL, MA'AM.
HE WORKS HARD AS OUR CLUB'S VICE PRESI-DENT.
HE EVEN GOT FOURTH PLACE AT A RECENT MEET. WELL, IN A BEGINNER'S EVENT, ANYWAY.
EH? HE'S THE CLUB VICE PRESI-DENT!?
WAIT, WHAT MEET?
HUH? HE DIDN'T TELL YOU?
NOT EVEN ABOUT GETTING FOURTH?
......
......
WHOA, WHOA, WHOA. I KNEW THE GUY DOESN'T LIKE HOME, BUT THIS...?
HE REALLY DOESN'T TELL THEM ANY-THING.
HELLOOO...
READY FOR CLUB?
HEY.
THIS IS HACHI-KEN'S MOM.
HUH!?

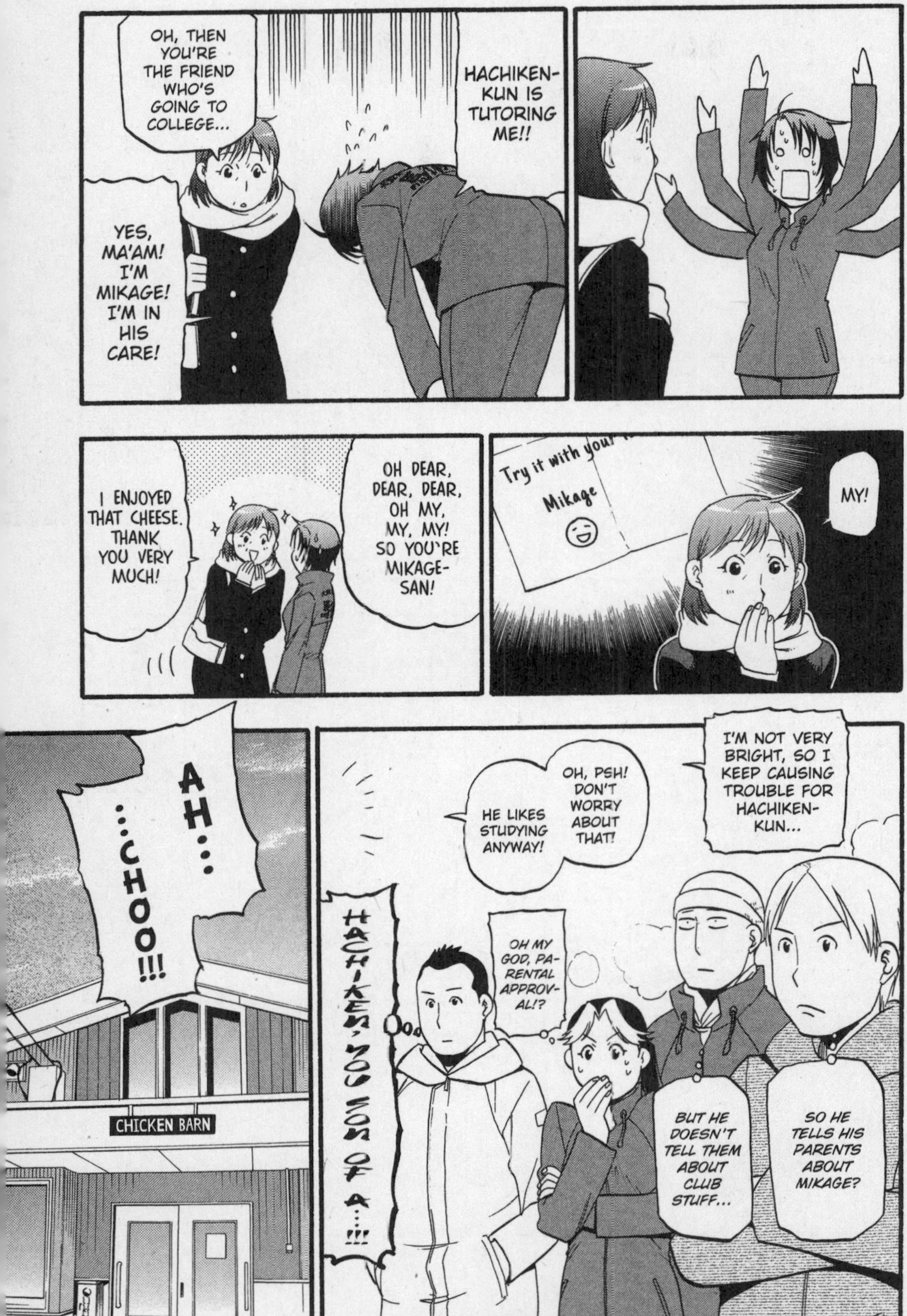
HACHIKEN-KUN IS TUTORING ME!!
OH, THEN YOU'RE THE FRIEND WHO'S GOING TO COLLEGE...
YES, MA'AM! I'M MIKAGE! I'M IN HIS CARE!
Try it with you
Mikage
MY!
OH DEAR, DEAR, DEAR, OH MY, MY, MY! SO YOU'RE MIKAGE-SAN!
I ENJOYED THAT CHEESE. THANK YOU VERY MUCH!
I'M NOT VERY BRIGHT, SO I KEEP CAUSING TROUBLE FOR HACHIKEN-KUN...
OH, PSH! DON'T WORRY ABOUT THAT!
HE LIKES STUDYING ANYWAY!
SO HE TELLS HIS PARENTS ABOUT MIKAGE?
BUT HE DOESN'T TELL THEM ABOUT CLUB STUFF...
OH MY GOD, PA-RENTAL APPROV-AL!?
HACHIKEN, YOU SON OF A...!!!
AH... ...CHOO!!!
CHICKEN BARN

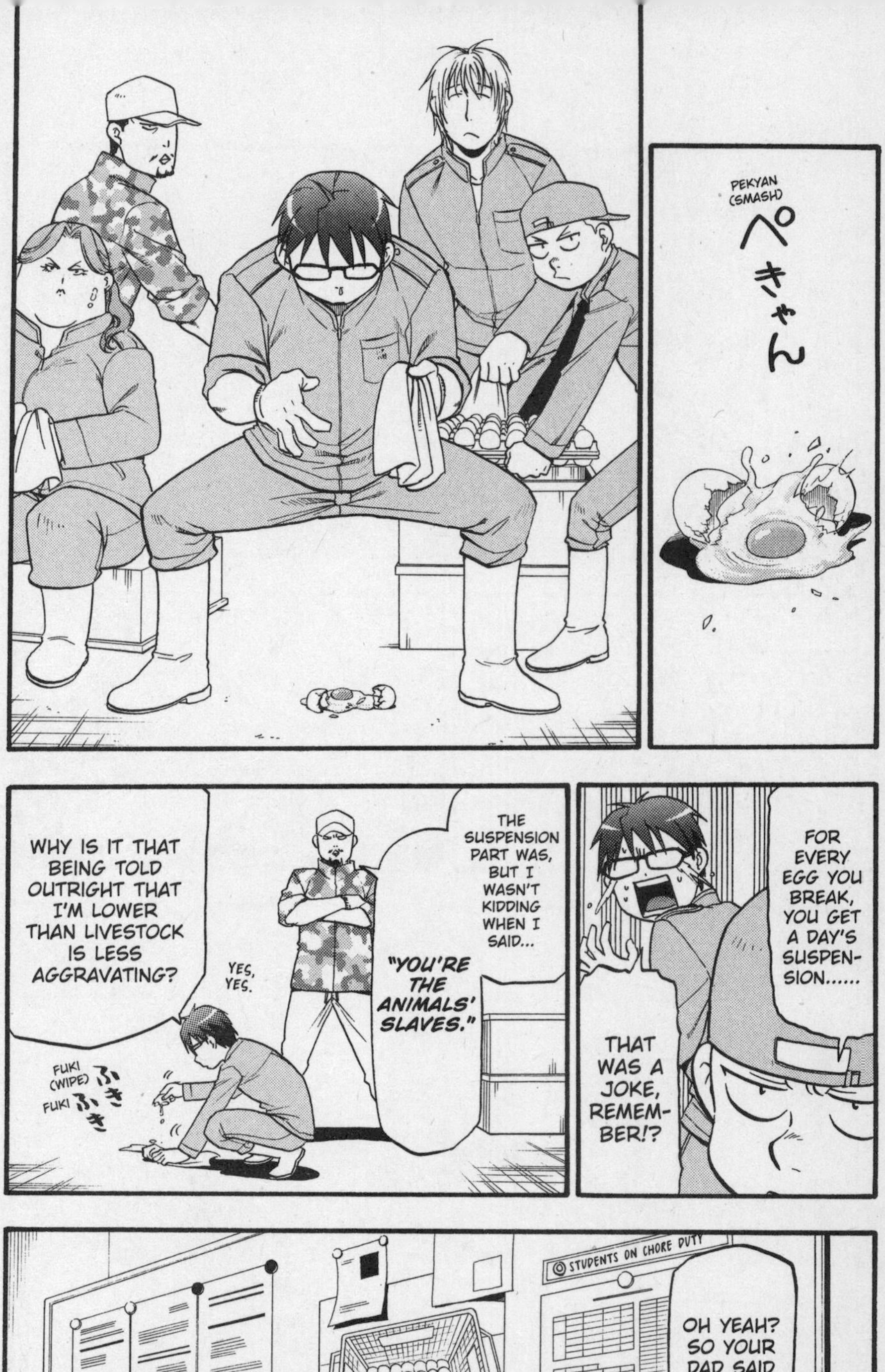
PEKYAN (SMASH)
ぺきゃん
FOR EVERY EGG YOU BREAK, YOU GET A DAY'S SUSPENSION......
THAT WAS A JOKE, REMEMBER!?
THE SUSPENSION PART WAS, BUT I WASN'T KIDDING WHEN I SAID...
"YOU'RE THE ANIMALS' SLAVES."
YES, YES.
WHY IS IT THAT BEING TOLD OUTRIGHT THAT I'M LOWER THAN LIVESTOCK IS LESS AGGRAVATING?
FUKI (WIPE) ふき
FUKI ふき
OH YEAH? SO YOUR DAD SAID THAT?
STUDENTS ON CHORE DUTY
5-11

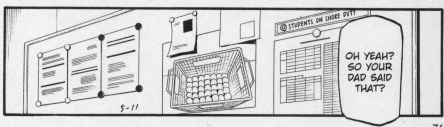

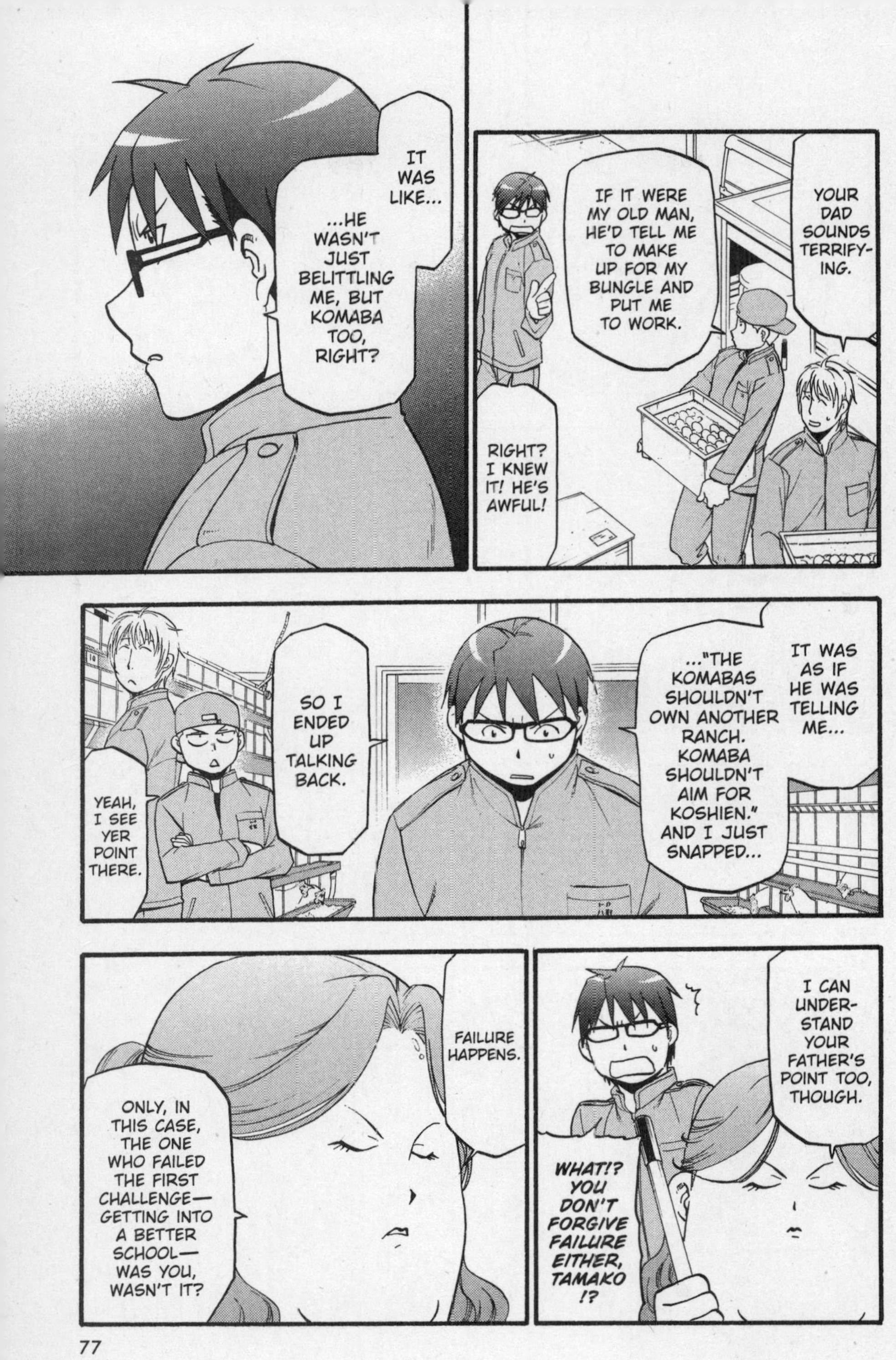
YOUR DAD SOUNDS TERRIFY-ING.
IF IT WERE MY OLD MAN, HE'D TELL ME TO MAKE UP FOR MY BUNGLE AND PUT ME TO WORK.
RIGHT? I KNEW IT! HE'S AWFUL!
IT WAS LIKE...
...HE WASN'T JUST BELITTLING ME, BUT KOMABA TOO, RIGHT?
IT WAS AS IF HE WAS TELLING ME...
..."THE KOMABAS SHOULDN'T OWN ANOTHER RANCH. KOMABA SHOULDN'T AIM FOR KOSHIEN." AND I JUST SNAPPED...
SO I ENDED UP TALKING BACK.
YEAH, I SEE YER POINT THERE.
I CAN UNDER-STAND YOUR FATHER'S POINT TOO, THOUGH.
WHAT!? YOU DON'T FORGIVE FAILURE EITHER, TAMAKO!?
FAILURE HAPPENS.
ONLY, IN THIS CASE, THE ONE WHO FAILED THE FIRST CHALLENGE—GETTING INTO A BETTER SCHOOL—WAS YOU, WASN'T IT?

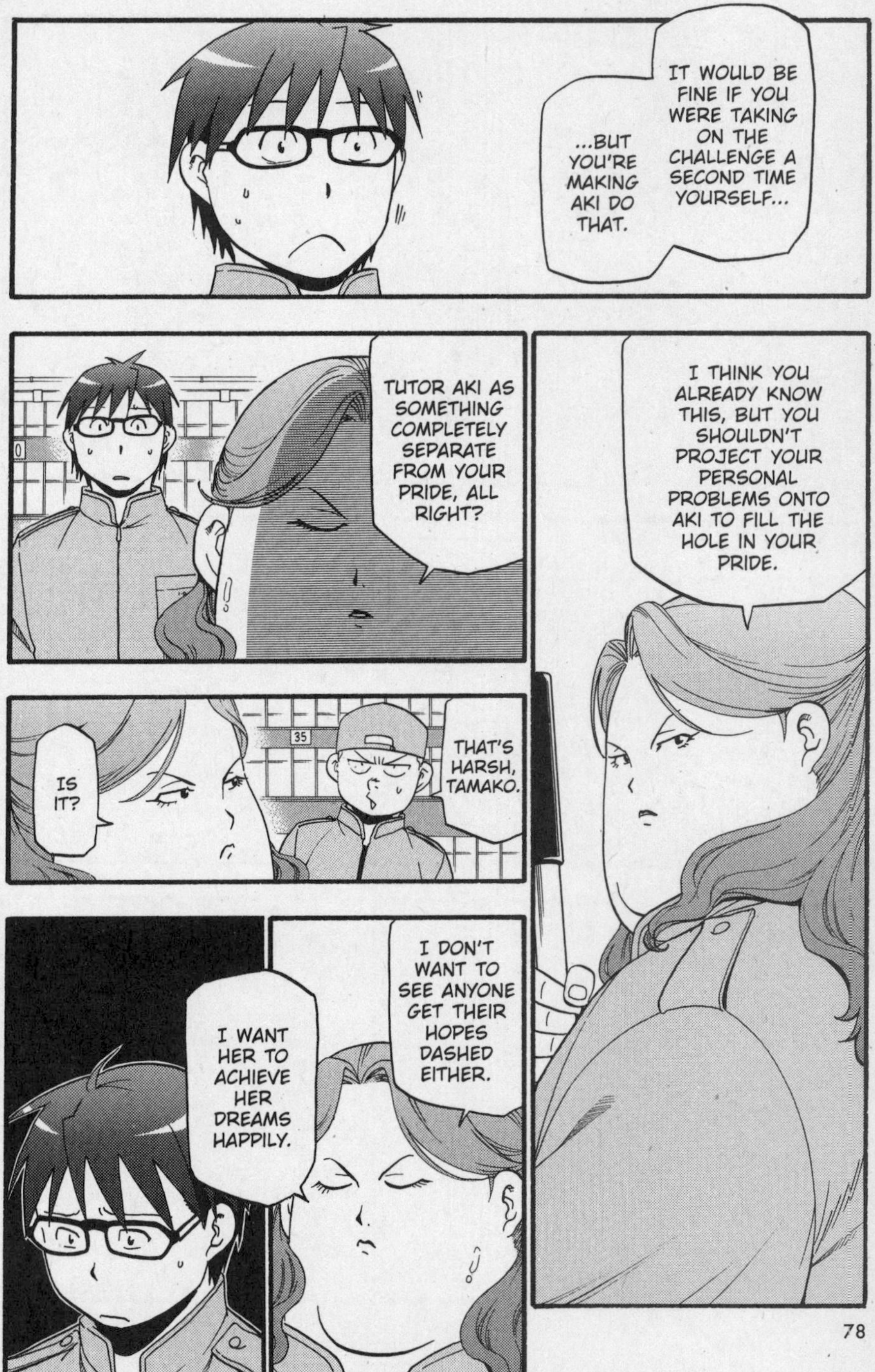

IT WOULD BE FINE IF YOU WERE TAKING ON THE CHALLENGE A SECOND TIME YOURSELF...
...BUT YOU'RE MAKING AKI DO THAT.
I THINK YOU ALREADY KNOW THIS, BUT YOU SHOULDN'T PROJECT YOUR PERSONAL PROBLEMS ONTO AKI TO FILL THE HOLE IN YOUR PRIDE.
TUTOR AKI AS SOMETHING COMPLETELY SEPARATE FROM YOUR PRIDE, ALL RIGHT?
THAT'S HARSH, TAMAKO.
IS IT?
I DON'T WANT TO SEE ANYONE GET THEIR HOPES DASHED EITHER.
I WANT HER TO ACHIEVE HER DREAMS HAPPILY.

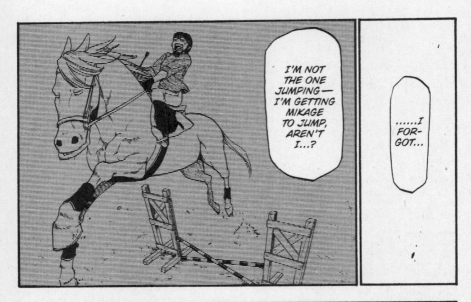

I'M NOT THE ONE JUMPING— I'M GETTING MIKAGE TO JUMP, AREN'T I...?

.......I FORGOT...

TAMAKO!!!

I'M SUCH AN IDIOT!! I WAS SUPPOSED TO HAVE UNDERSTOOD THAT FROM RISKING MY OWN NECK, BUT I......

WITH PLEASURE.

HIT M—

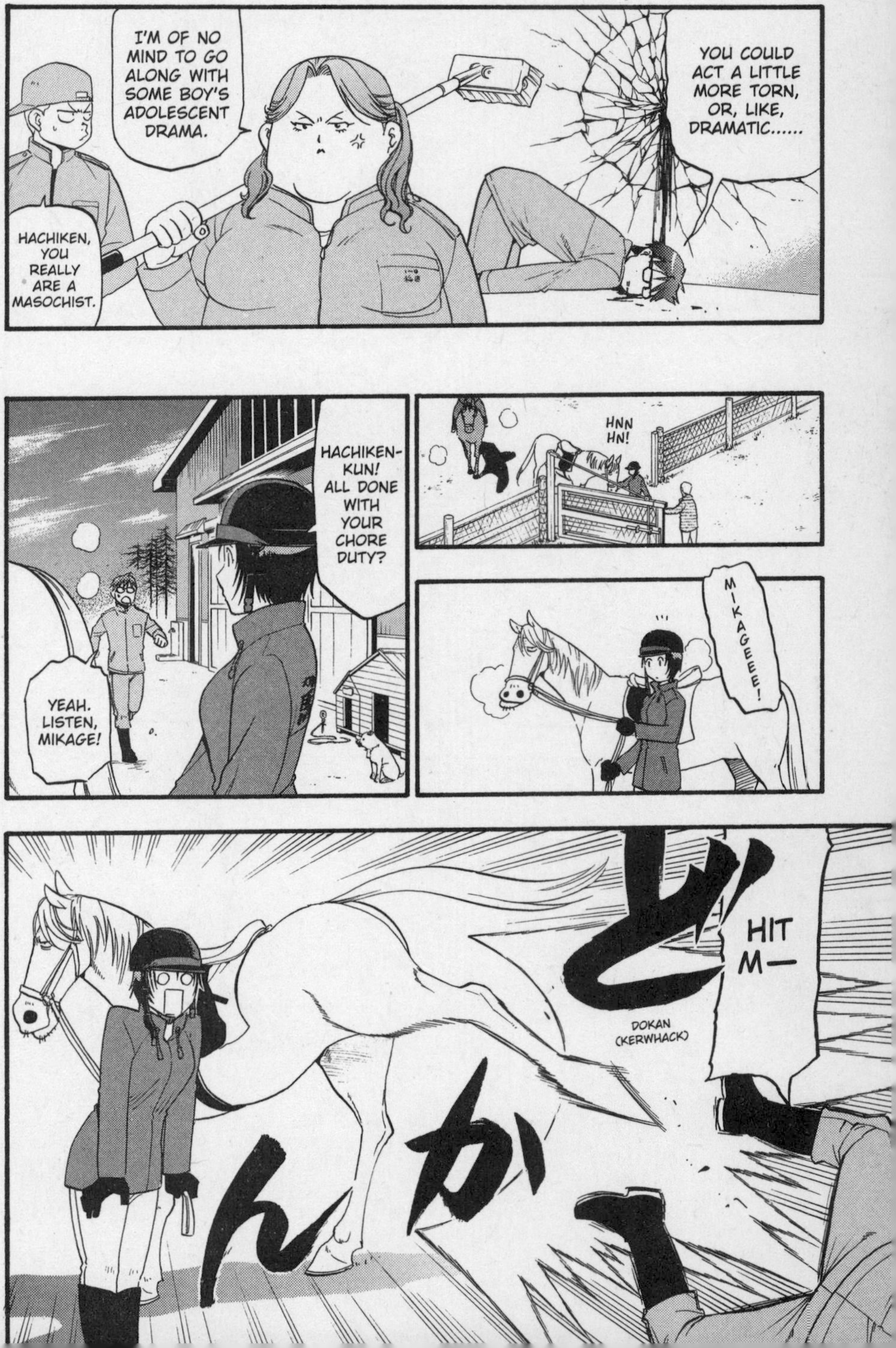
YOU COULD ACT A LITTLE MORE TORN, OR, LIKE, DRAMATIC......
I'M OF NO MIND TO GO ALONG WITH SOME BOY'S ADOLESCENT DRAMA.
HACHIKEN, YOU REALLY ARE A MASOCHIST.
HNN HN!
MIKAGEEE!
HACHIKEN-KUN! ALL DONE WITH YOUR CHORE DUTY?
YEAH. LISTEN, MIKAGE!
HIT M—
DOKAN (KERWHACK)

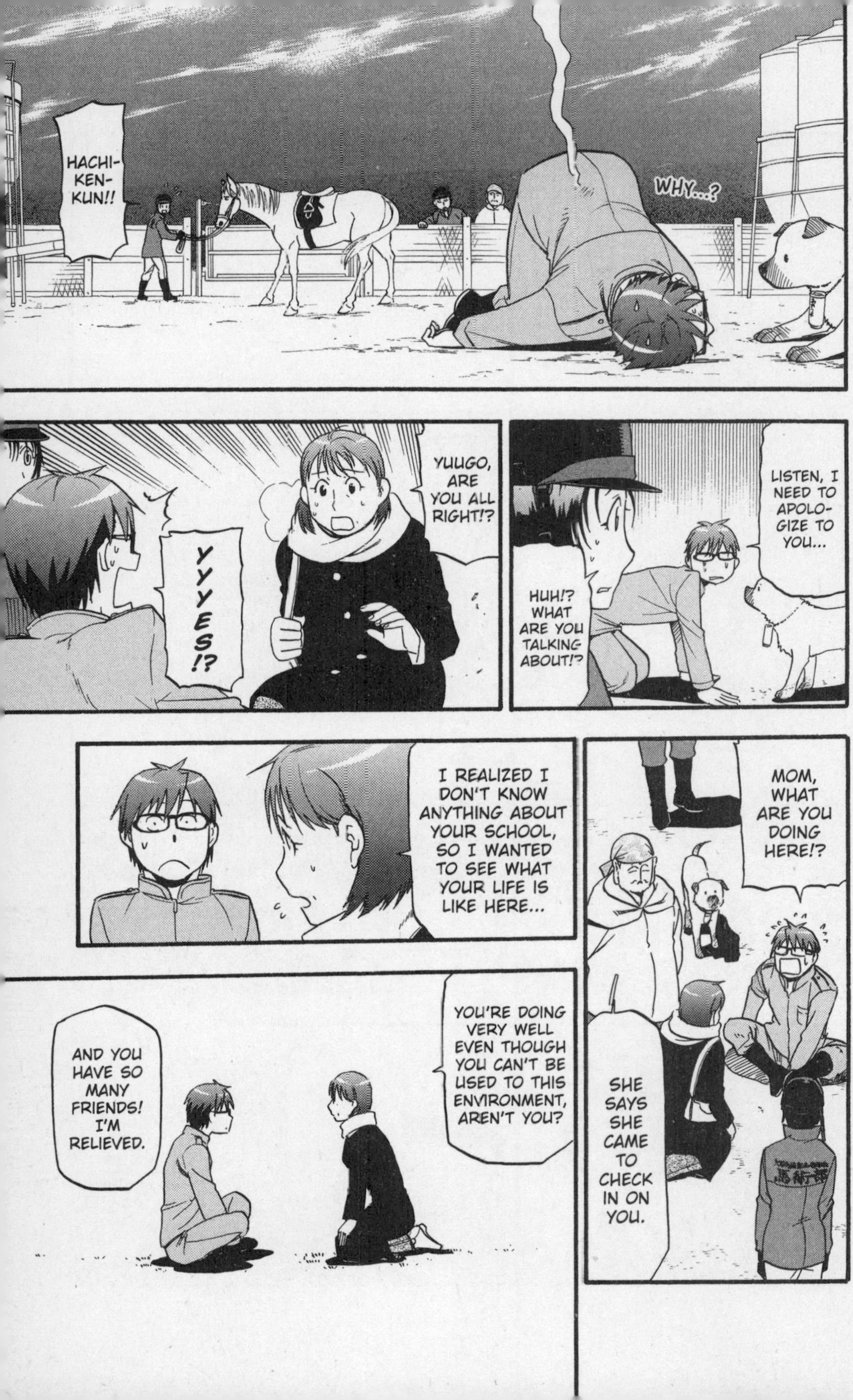
WHY...?
HACHI-KEN-KUN!!
LISTEN, I NEED TO APOLO-GIZE TO YOU...
HUH!? WHAT ARE YOU TALKING ABOUT!?
YUUGO, ARE YOU ALL RIGHT!?
YYYES!?
MOM, WHAT ARE YOU DOING HERE!?
SHE SAYS SHE CAME TO CHECK IN ON YOU.
I REALIZED I DON'T KNOW ANYTHING ABOUT YOUR SCHOOL, SO I WANTED TO SEE WHAT YOUR LIFE IS LIKE HERE...
YOU'RE DOING VERY WELL EVEN THOUGH YOU CAN'T BE USED TO THIS ENVIRONMENT, AREN'T YOU?
AND YOU HAVE SO MANY FRIENDS! I'M RELIEVED.

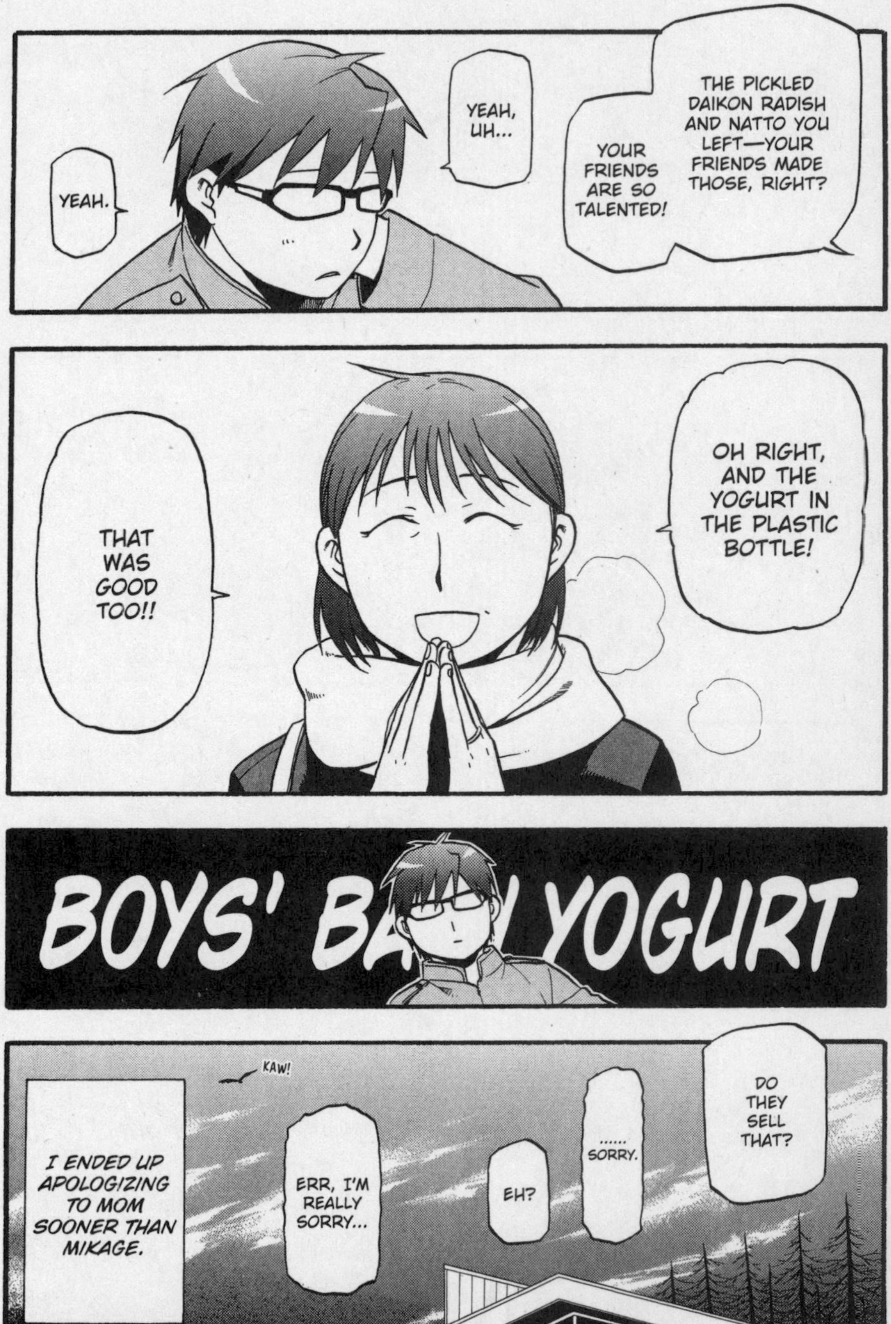
THE PICKLED DAIKON RADISH AND NATTO YOU LEFT—YOUR FRIENDS MADE THOSE, RIGHT?
YOUR FRIENDS ARE SO TALENTED!
YEAH, UH...
YEAH.
OH RIGHT, AND THE YOGURT IN THE PLASTIC BOTTLE!
THAT WAS GOOD TOO!!
BOYS' BA
YOGURT
DO THEY SELL THAT?
......SORRY.
EH?
KAW!
ERR, I'M REALLY SORRY...
I ENDED UP APOLOGIZING TO MOM SOONER THAN MIKAGE.

Silver Spoon

NEW SAPPORO
MIDDLE SCHOOL

SOU SHIROISHI

HACHIKEN'S MIDDLE
SCHOOL TEACHER

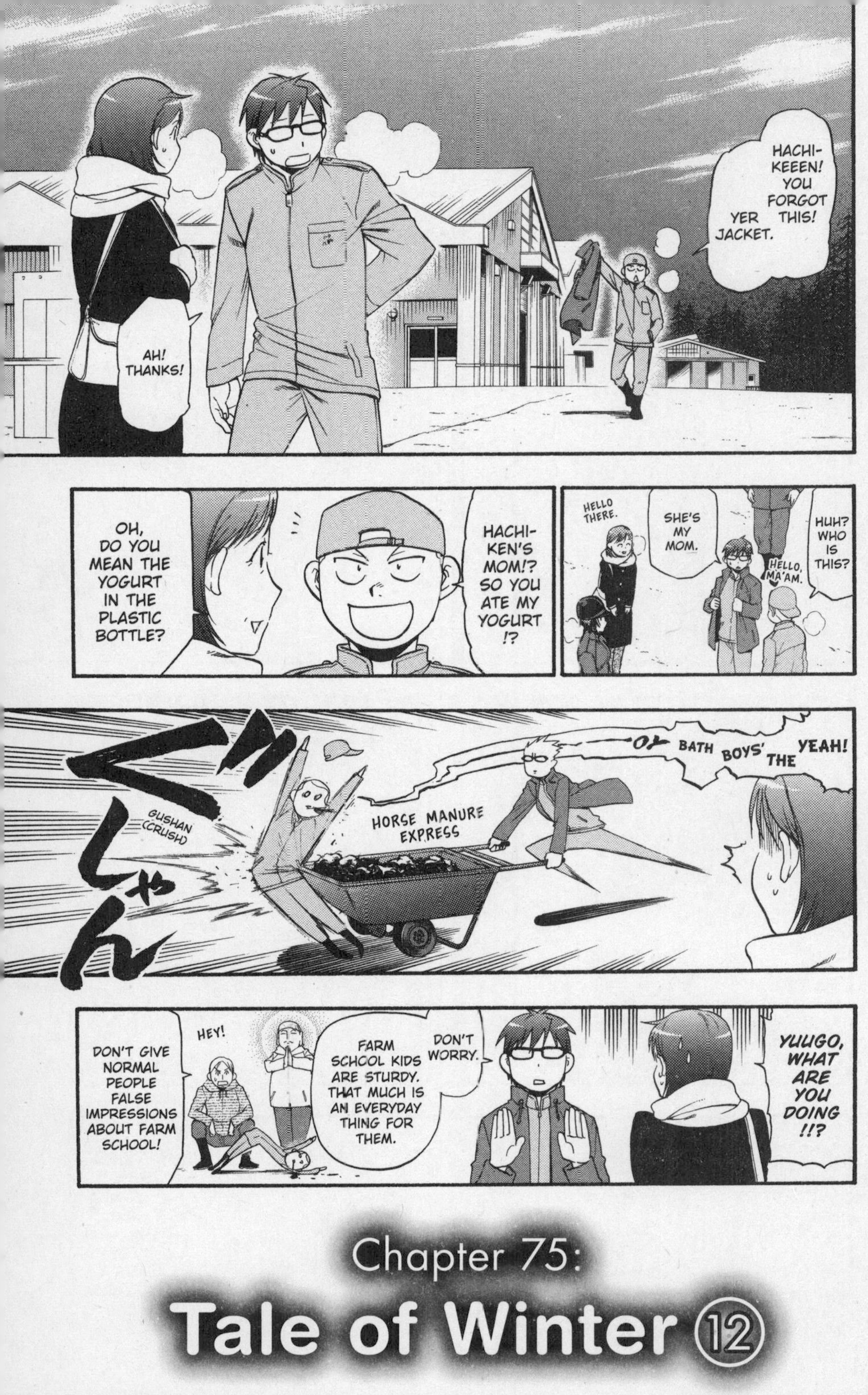
HACHI-KEEEN! YOU FORGOT THIS!
YER JACKET.
AH! THANKS!
HUH? WHO IS THIS?
SHE'S MY MOM.
HELLO, MA'AM.
HELLO THERE.
HACHI-KEN'S MOM!? SO YOU ATE MY YOGURT !?
OH, DO YOU MEAN THE YOGURT IN THE PLASTIC BOTTLE?
-OY BATH BOYS' THE YEAH!
HORSE MANURE EXPRESS
ぐしゃん
GUSHAN (CRUSH)
YUUGO, WHAT ARE YOU DOING !!?
DON'T WORRY.
FARM SCHOOL KIDS ARE STURDY. THAT MUCH IS AN EVERYDAY THING FOR THEM.
HEY!
DON'T GIVE NORMAL PEOPLE FALSE IMPRESSIONS ABOUT FARM SCHOOL!

Chapter 75:
Tale of Winter ⑫

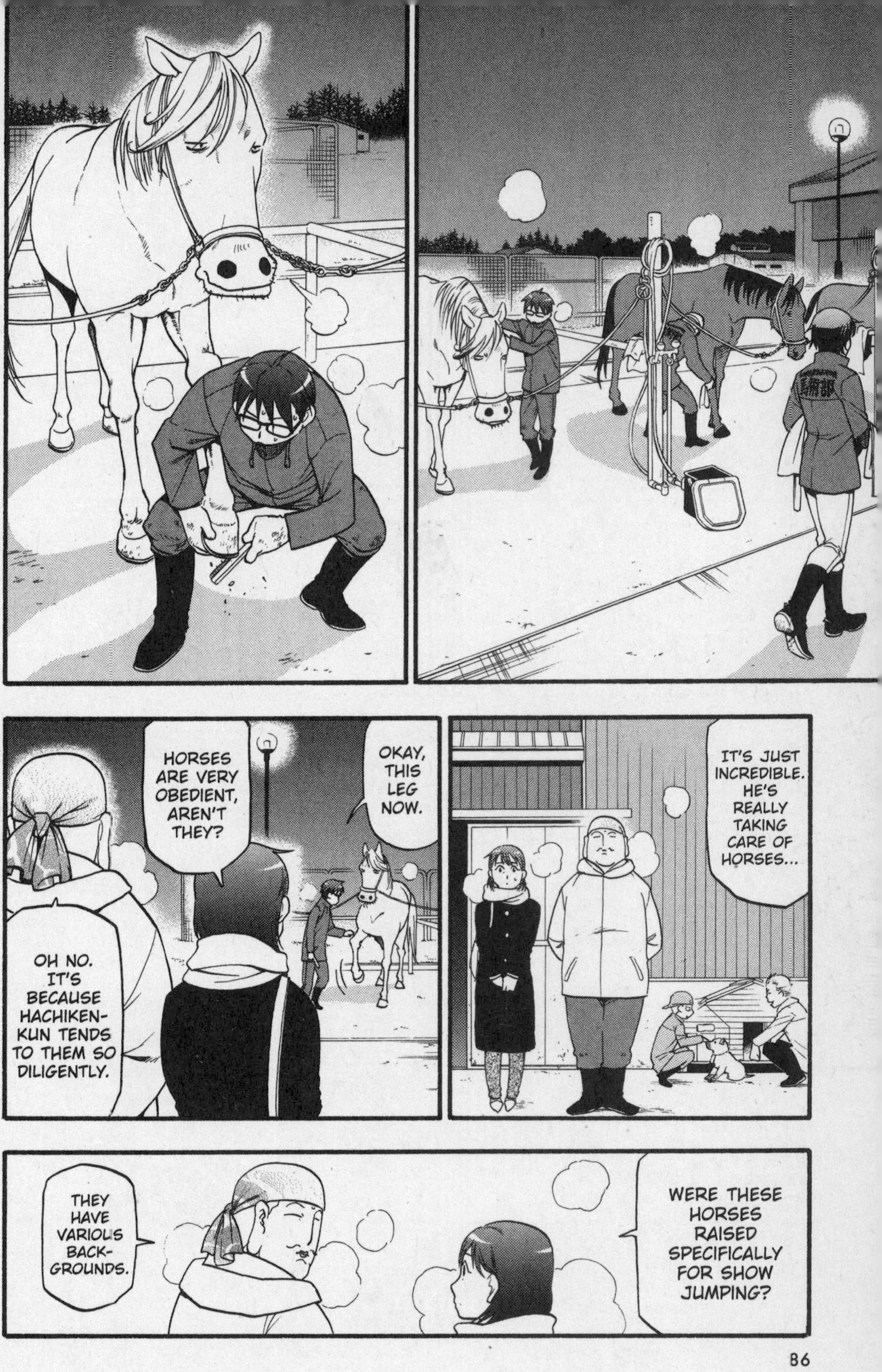
IT'S JUST INCREDIBLE. HE'S REALLY TAKING CARE OF HORSES...
OKAY, THIS LEG NOW.
HORSES ARE VERY OBEDIENT, AREN'T THEY?
OH NO. IT'S BECAUSE HACHIKEN-KUN TENDS TO THEM SO DILIGENTLY.
WERE THESE HORSES RAISED SPECIFICALLY FOR SHOW JUMPING?
THEY HAVE VARIOUS BACK-GROUNDS.

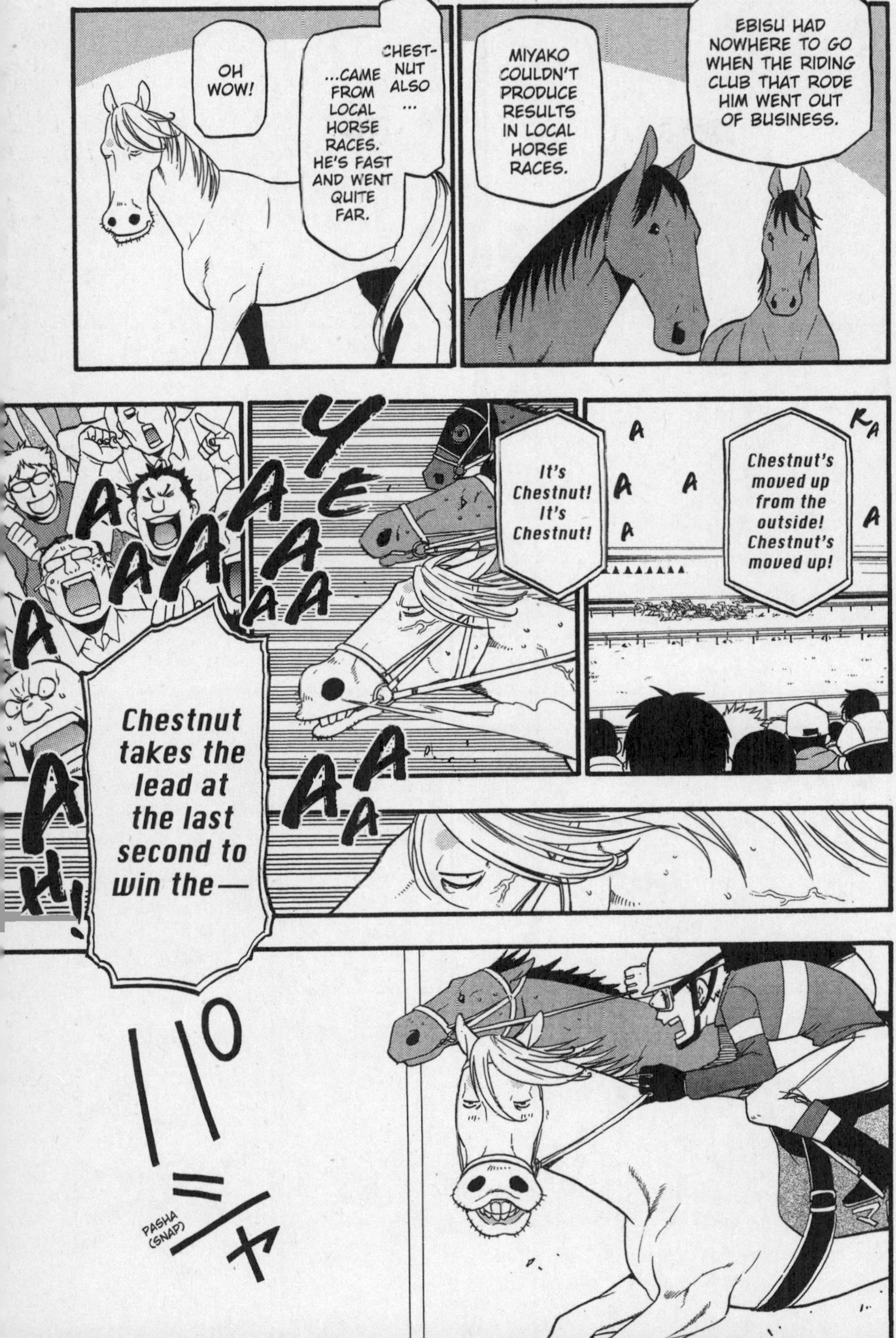
EBISU HAD NOWHERE TO GO WHEN THE RIDING CLUB THAT RODE HIM WENT OUT OF BUSINESS.
MIYAKO COULDN'T PRODUCE RESULTS IN LOCAL HORSE RACES.
CHESTNUT ALSO...
...CAME FROM LOCAL HORSE RACES. HE'S FAST AND WENT QUITE FAR.
OH WOW!
KA A A A A A A
Chestnut's moved up from the outside! Chestnut's moved up!
It's Chestnut! It's Chestnut!
YEAAAAAAAA
AAAAAAAAH!
Chestnut takes the lead at the last second to win the—
PASHA (SNAP)

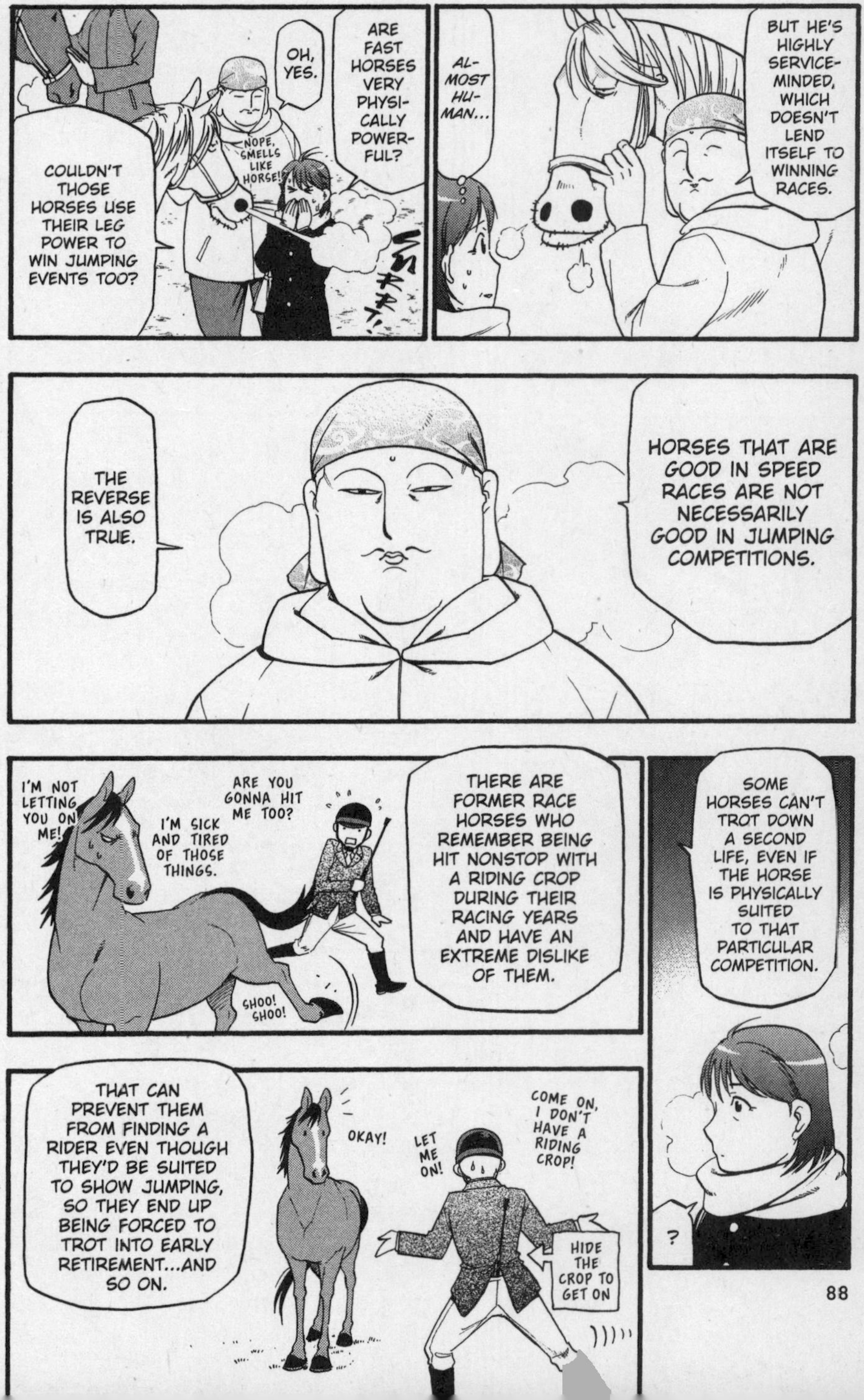
BUT HE'S HIGHLY SERVICE-MINDED, WHICH DOESN'T LEND ITSELF TO WINNING RACES.
AL-MOST HU-MAN...
ARE FAST HORSES VERY PHYSI-CALLY POWER-FUL?
OH, YES.
NOPE, SMELLS LIKE HORSE!
COULDN'T THOSE HORSES USE THEIR LEG POWER TO WIN JUMPING EVENTS TOO?
SNRRT!
HORSES THAT ARE GOOD IN SPEED RACES ARE NOT NECESSARILY GOOD IN JUMPING COMPETITIONS.
THE REVERSE IS ALSO TRUE.
SOME HORSES CAN'T TROT DOWN A SECOND LIFE, EVEN IF THE HORSE IS PHYSICALLY SUITED TO THAT PARTICULAR COMPETITION.
?
THERE ARE FORMER RACE HORSES WHO REMEMBER BEING HIT NONSTOP WITH A RIDING CROP DURING THEIR RACING YEARS AND HAVE AN EXTREME DISLIKE OF THEM.
ARE YOU GONNA HIT ME TOO?
I'M SICK AND TIRED OF THOSE THINGS.
I'M NOT LETTING YOU ON ME!
SHOO! SHOO!
COME ON, I DON'T HAVE A RIDING CROP!
LET ME ON!
OKAY!
THAT CAN PREVENT THEM FROM FINDING A RIDER EVEN THOUGH THEY'D BE SUITED TO SHOW JUMPING, SO THEY END UP BEING FORCED TO TROT INTO EARLY RETIREMENT...AND SO ON.
HIDE THE CROP TO GET ON

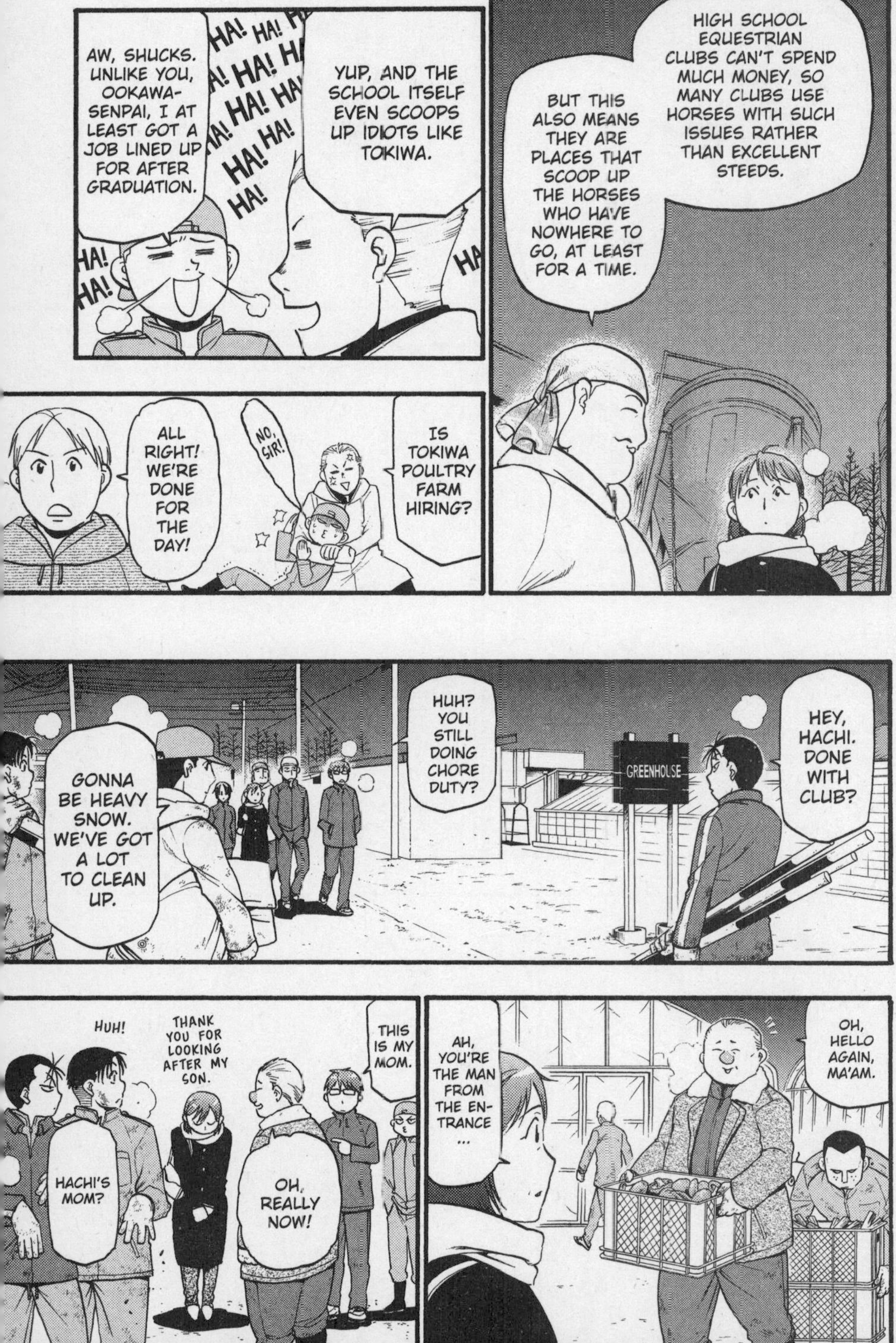
HIGH SCHOOL EQUESTRIAN CLUBS CAN'T SPEND MUCH MONEY, SO MANY CLUBS USE HORSES WITH SUCH ISSUES RATHER THAN EXCELLENT STEEDS.
BUT THIS ALSO MEANS THEY ARE PLACES THAT SCOOP UP THE HORSES WHO HAVE NOWHERE TO GO, AT LEAST FOR A TIME.
YUP, AND THE SCHOOL ITSELF EVEN SCOOPS UP IDIOTS LIKE TOKIWA.
HA! HA! HA! HA! HA! HA! HA! HA! HA! HA!
AW, SHUCKS. UNLIKE YOU, OOKAWA-SENPAI, I AT LEAST GOT A JOB LINED UP FOR AFTER GRADUATION.
HA! HA! HA
IS TOKIWA POULTRY FARM HIRING?
NO, SIR!
ALL RIGHT! WE'RE DONE FOR THE DAY!
HEY, HACHI. DONE WITH CLUB?
GREENHOUSE
HUH? YOU STILL DOING CHORE DUTY?
GONNA BE HEAVY SNOW. WE'VE GOT A LOT TO CLEAN UP.
OH, HELLO AGAIN, MA'AM.
AH, YOU'RE THE MAN FROM THE EN-TRANCE ...
THIS IS MY MOM.
THANK YOU FOR LOOKING AFTER MY SON.
HUH!
OH, REALLY NOW!
HACHI'S MOM?

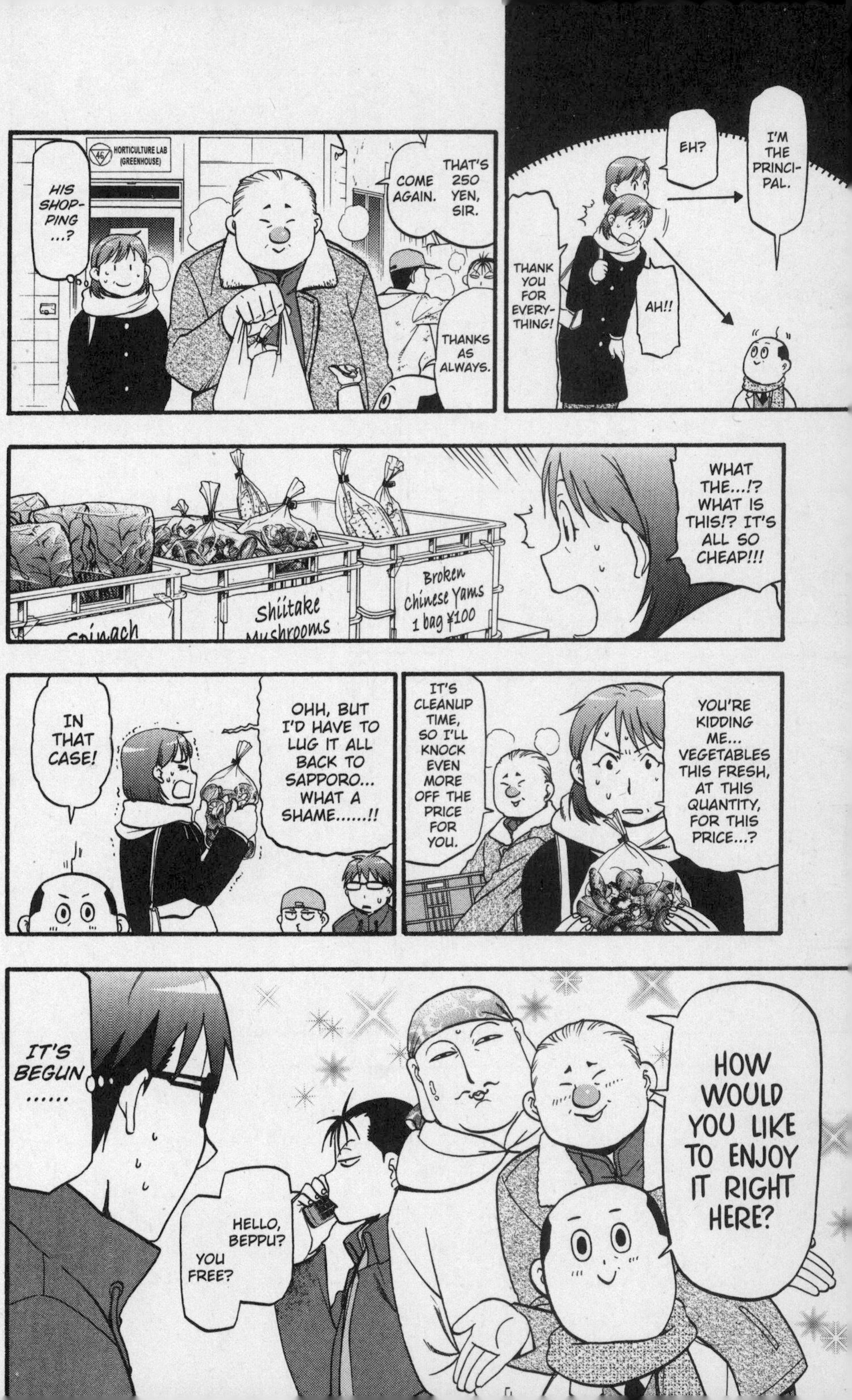
I'M THE PRINCIPAL.
EH?
AH!!
THANK YOU FOR EVERYTHING!
THAT'S 250 YEN, SIR.
COME AGAIN.
THANKS AS ALWAYS.
46
HORTICULTURE LAB (GREENHOUSE)
HIS SHOPPING...?
WHAT THE...!? WHAT IS THIS!? IT'S ALL SO CHEAP!!!
Broken Chinese Yams 1 bag ¥100
Shiitake Mushrooms
YOU'RE KIDDING ME... VEGETABLES THIS FRESH, AT THIS QUANTITY, FOR THIS PRICE...?
IT'S CLEANUP TIME, SO I'LL KNOCK EVEN MORE OFF THE PRICE FOR YOU.
OHH, BUT I'D HAVE TO LUG IT ALL BACK TO SAPPORO... WHAT A SHAME......!!
IN THAT CASE!
HOW WOULD YOU LIKE TO ENJOY IT RIGHT HERE?
HELLO, BEPPU?
YOU FREE?
IT'S BEGUN......

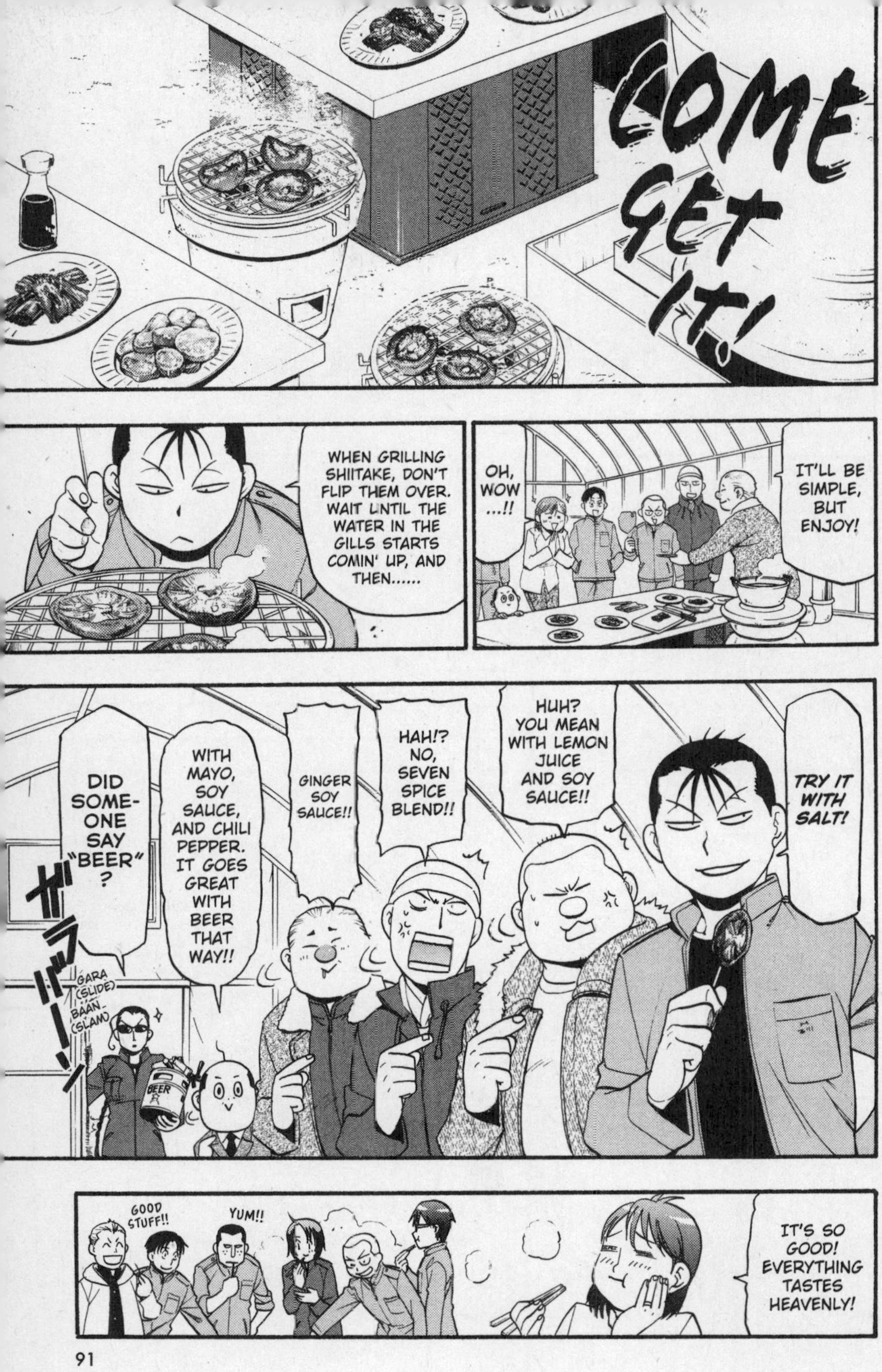
COME GET IT!
IT'LL BE SIMPLE, BUT ENJOY!
OH, WOW ...!!
WHEN GRILLING SHIITAKE, DON'T FLIP THEM OVER. WAIT UNTIL THE WATER IN THE GILLS STARTS COMIN' UP, AND THEN......
TRY IT WITH SALT!
HUH? YOU MEAN WITH LEMON JUICE AND SOY SAUCE!!
HAH!? NO, SEVEN SPICE BLEND!!
GINGER SOY SAUCE!!
WITH MAYO, SOY SAUCE, AND CHILI PEPPER. IT GOES GREAT WITH BEER THAT WAY!!
DID SOME-ONE SAY "BEER"?
GARA (SLIDE)
BAAN (SLAM)
BEER
IT'S SO GOOD! EVERYTHING TASTES HEAVENLY!
YUM!!
GOOD STUFF!!

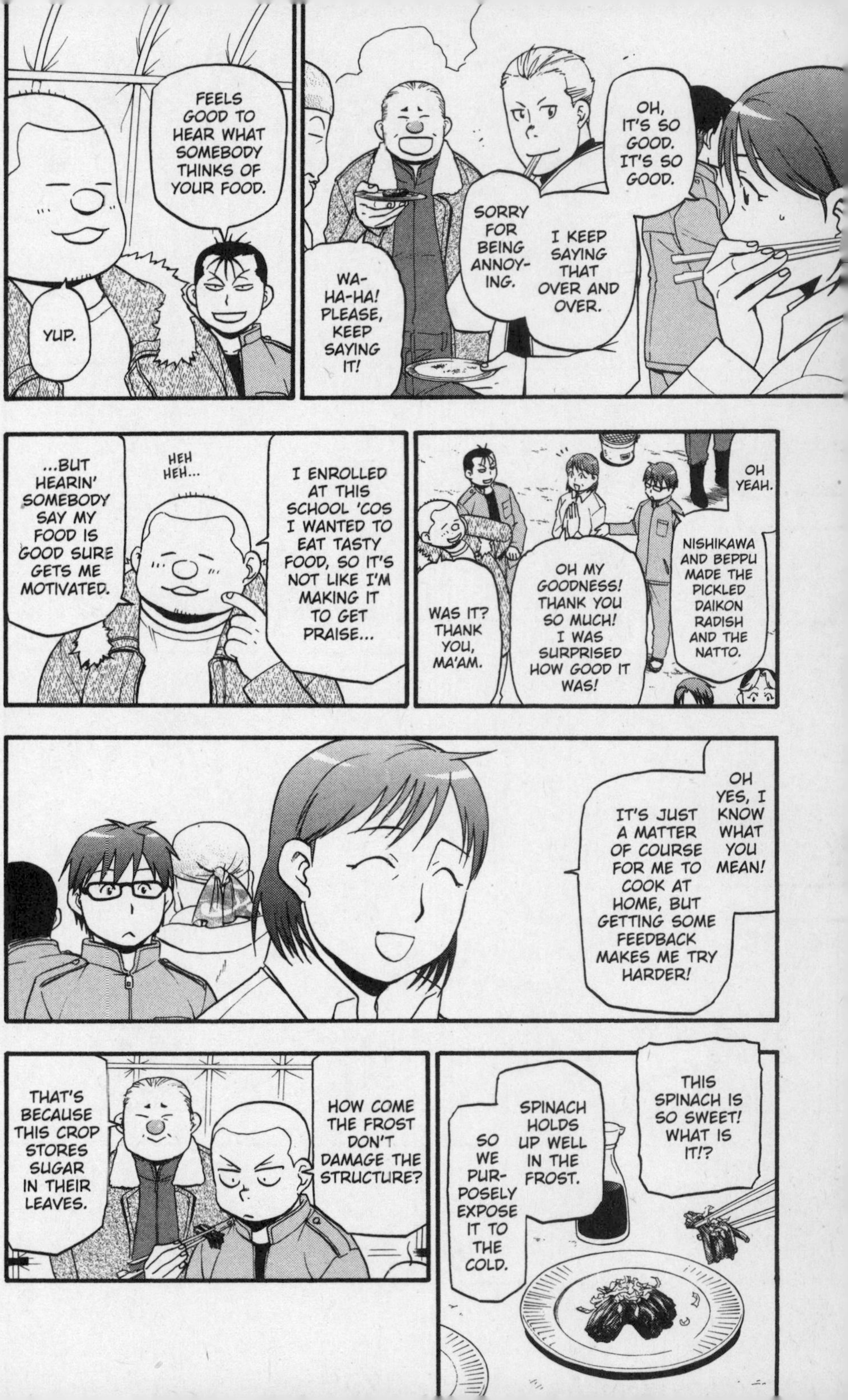
OH, IT'S SO GOOD. IT'S SO GOOD.
I KEEP SAYING THAT OVER AND OVER.
SORRY FOR BEING ANNOY-ING.
WA-HA-HA! PLEASE, KEEP SAYING IT!
FEELS GOOD TO HEAR WHAT SOMEBODY THINKS OF YOUR FOOD.
YUP.
OH YEAH.
NISHIKAWA AND BEPPU MADE THE PICKLED DAIKON RADISH AND THE NATTO.
OH MY GOODNESS! THANK YOU SO MUCH! I WAS SURPRISED HOW GOOD IT WAS!
WAS IT? THANK YOU, MA'AM.
I ENROLLED AT THIS SCHOOL 'COS I WANTED TO EAT TASTY FOOD, SO IT'S NOT LIKE I'M MAKING IT TO GET PRAISE...
HEH HEH...
...BUT HEARIN' SOMEBODY SAY MY FOOD IS GOOD SURE GETS ME MOTIVATED.
OH YES, I KNOW WHAT YOU MEAN!
IT'S JUST A MATTER OF COURSE FOR ME TO COOK AT HOME, BUT GETTING SOME FEEDBACK MAKES ME TRY HARDER!
THIS SPINACH IS SO SWEET! WHAT IS IT!?
SPINACH HOLDS UP WELL IN THE FROST.
SO WE PURPOSELY EXPOSE IT TO THE COLD.
HOW COME THE FROST DON'T DAMAGE THE STRUCTURE?
THAT'S BECAUSE THIS CROP STORES SUGAR IN THEIR LEAVES.

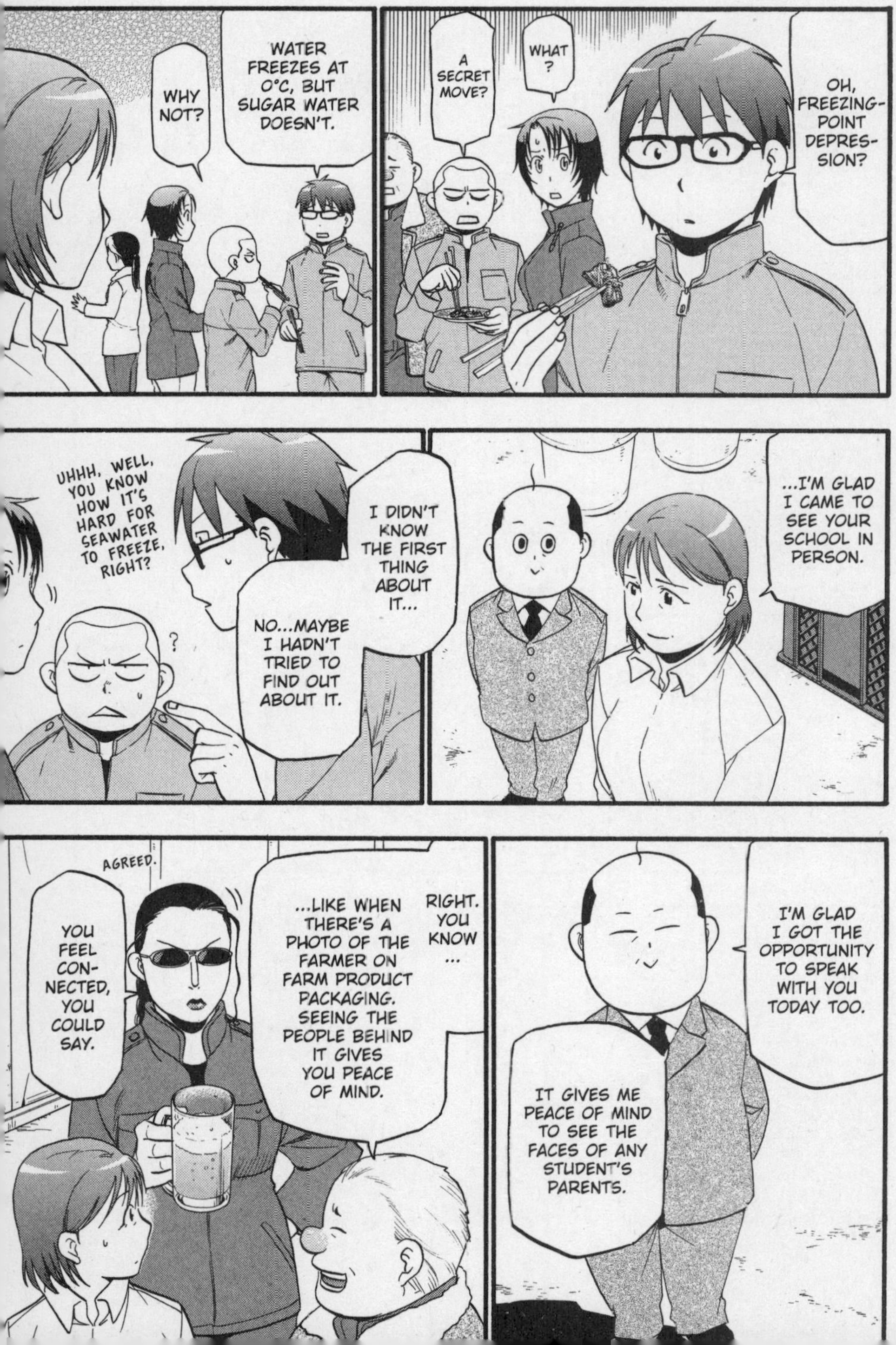
OH, FREEZING-POINT DEPRESSION?
WHAT ?
A SECRET MOVE?
WATER FREEZES AT 0°C, BUT SUGAR WATER DOESN'T.
WHY NOT?
...I'M GLAD I CAME TO SEE YOUR SCHOOL IN PERSON.
I DIDN'T KNOW THE FIRST THING ABOUT IT...
NO...MAYBE I HADN'T TRIED TO FIND OUT ABOUT IT.
UHHH, WELL, YOU KNOW HOW IT'S HARD FOR SEAWATER TO FREEZE, RIGHT?
?
I'M GLAD I GOT THE OPPORTUNITY TO SPEAK WITH YOU TODAY TOO.
IT GIVES ME PEACE OF MIND TO SEE THE FACES OF ANY STUDENT'S PARENTS.
RIGHT. YOU KNOW ...
...LIKE WHEN THERE'S A PHOTO OF THE FARMER ON FARM PRODUCT PACKAGING. SEEING THE PEOPLE BEHIND IT GIVES YOU PEACE OF MIND.
AGREED.
YOU FEEL CONNECTED, YOU COULD SAY.

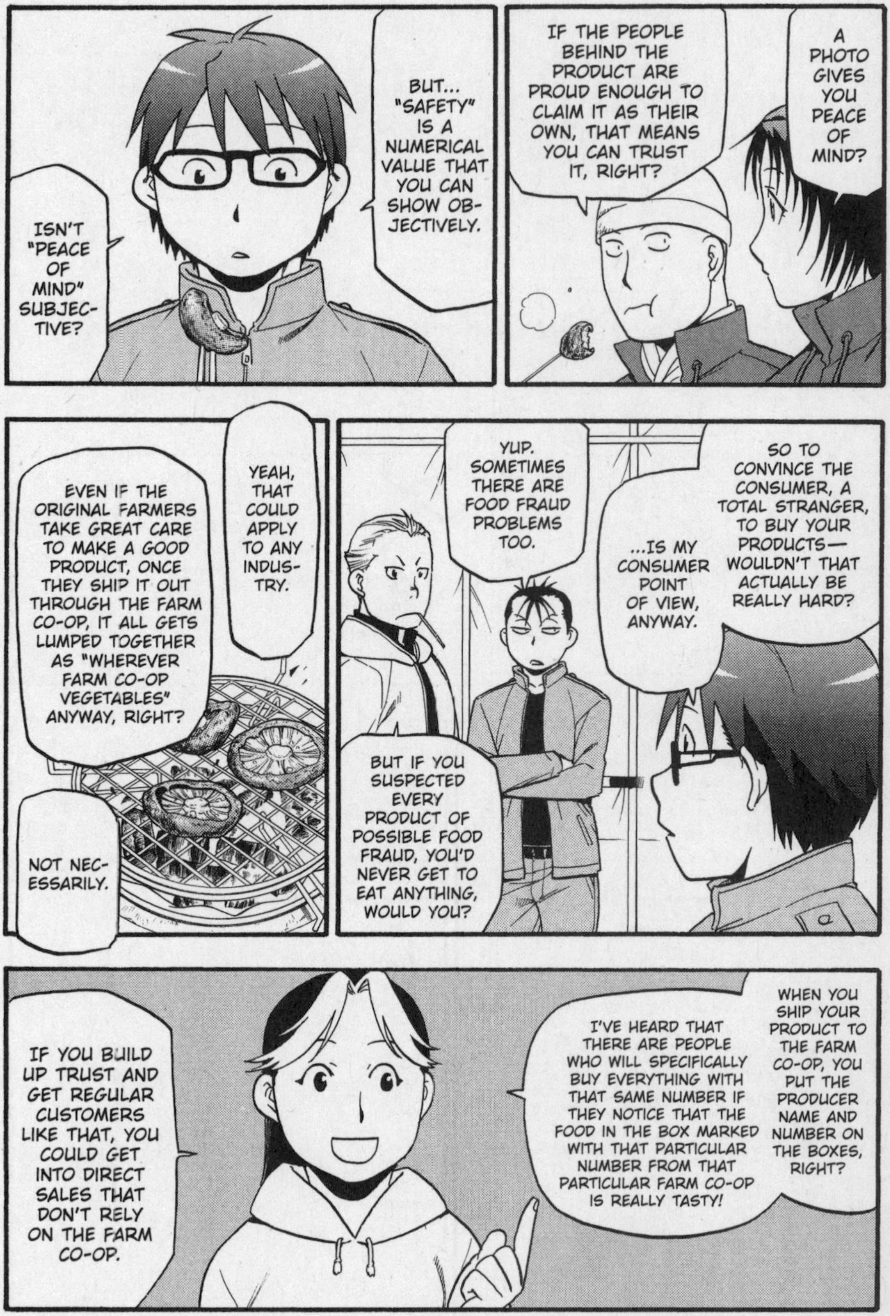
A PHOTO GIVES YOU PEACE OF MIND?
IF THE PEOPLE BEHIND THE PRODUCT ARE PROUD ENOUGH TO CLAIM IT AS THEIR OWN, THAT MEANS YOU CAN TRUST IT, RIGHT?
BUT... "SAFETY" IS A NUMERICAL VALUE THAT YOU CAN SHOW OBJECTIVELY.
ISN'T "PEACE OF MIND" SUBJECTIVE?
SO TO CONVINCE THE CONSUMER, A TOTAL STRANGER, TO BUY YOUR PRODUCTS—WOULDN'T THAT ACTUALLY BE REALLY HARD?
...IS MY CONSUMER POINT OF VIEW, ANYWAY.
YUP. SOMETIMES THERE ARE FOOD FRAUD PROBLEMS TOO.
BUT IF YOU SUSPECTED EVERY PRODUCT OF POSSIBLE FOOD FRAUD, YOU'D NEVER GET TO EAT ANYTHING, WOULD YOU?
YEAH, THAT COULD APPLY TO ANY INDUSTRY.
EVEN IF THE ORIGINAL FARMERS TAKE GREAT CARE TO MAKE A GOOD PRODUCT, ONCE THEY SHIP IT OUT THROUGH THE FARM CO-OP, IT ALL GETS LUMPED TOGETHER AS "WHEREVER FARM CO-OP VEGETABLES" ANYWAY, RIGHT?
NOT NECESSARILY.
WHEN YOU SHIP YOUR PRODUCT TO THE FARM CO-OP, YOU PUT THE PRODUCER NAME AND NUMBER ON THE BOXES, RIGHT?
I'VE HEARD THAT THERE ARE PEOPLE WHO WILL SPECIFICALLY BUY EVERYTHING WITH THAT SAME NUMBER IF THEY NOTICE THAT THE FOOD IN THE BOX MARKED WITH THAT PARTICULAR NUMBER FROM THAT PARTICULAR FARM CO-OP IS REALLY TASTY!
IF YOU BUILD UP TRUST AND GET REGULAR CUSTOMERS LIKE THAT, YOU COULD GET INTO DIRECT SALES THAT DON'T RELY ON THE FARM CO-OP.

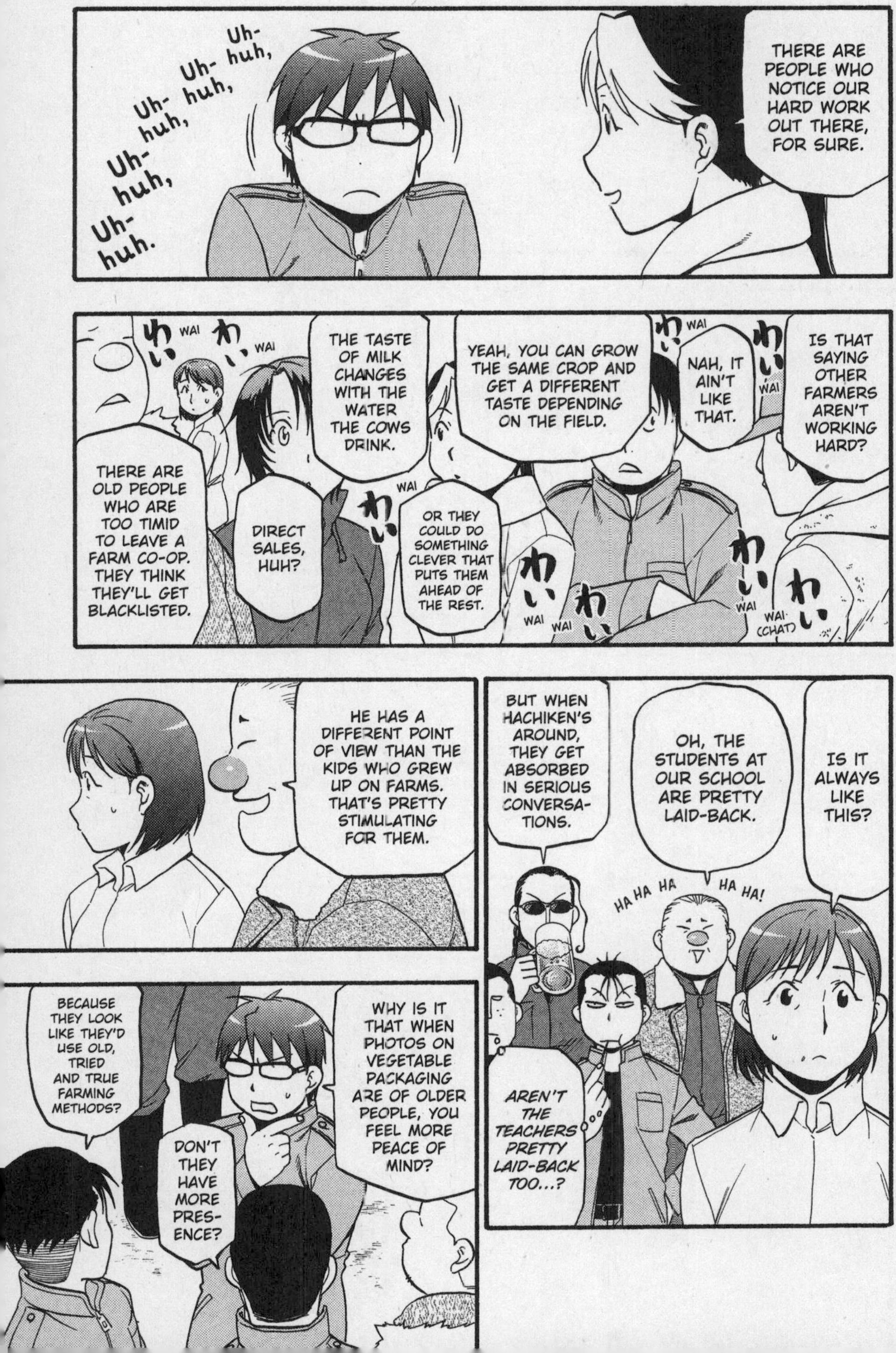
THERE ARE PEOPLE WHO NOTICE OUR HARD WORK OUT THERE, FOR SURE.
Uh-huh, Uh-huh, Uh-huh, Uh-huh, Uh-huh.
IS THAT SAYING OTHER FARMERS AREN'T WORKING HARD?
わい WAI
NAH, IT AIN'T LIKE THAT.
わい WAI
YEAH, YOU CAN GROW THE SAME CROP AND GET A DIFFERENT TASTE DEPENDING ON THE FIELD.
THE TASTE OF MILK CHANGES WITH THE WATER THE COWS DRINK.
わい WAI
わい WAI
わい WAI
OR THEY COULD DO SOMETHING CLEVER THAT PUTS THEM AHEAD OF THE REST.
DIRECT SALES, HUH?
THERE ARE OLD PEOPLE WHO ARE TOO TIMID TO LEAVE A FARM CO-OP. THEY THINK THEY'LL GET BLACKLISTED.
わい WAI (CHAT)
わい WAI
わい WAI
わい WAI
IS IT ALWAYS LIKE THIS?
OH, THE STUDENTS AT OUR SCHOOL ARE PRETTY LAID-BACK.
HA HA HA HA HA!
BUT WHEN HACHIKEN'S AROUND, THEY GET ABSORBED IN SERIOUS CONVERSA-TIONS.
AREN'T THE TEACHERS PRETTY LAID-BACK TOO...?
HE HAS A DIFFERENT POINT OF VIEW THAN THE KIDS WHO GREW UP ON FARMS. THAT'S PRETTY STIMULATING FOR THEM.
WHY IS IT THAT WHEN PHOTOS ON VEGETABLE PACKAGING ARE OF OLDER PEOPLE, YOU FEEL MORE PEACE OF MIND?
BECAUSE THEY LOOK LIKE THEY'D USE OLD, TRIED AND TRUE FARMING METHODS?
DON'T THEY HAVE MORE PRES-ENCE?

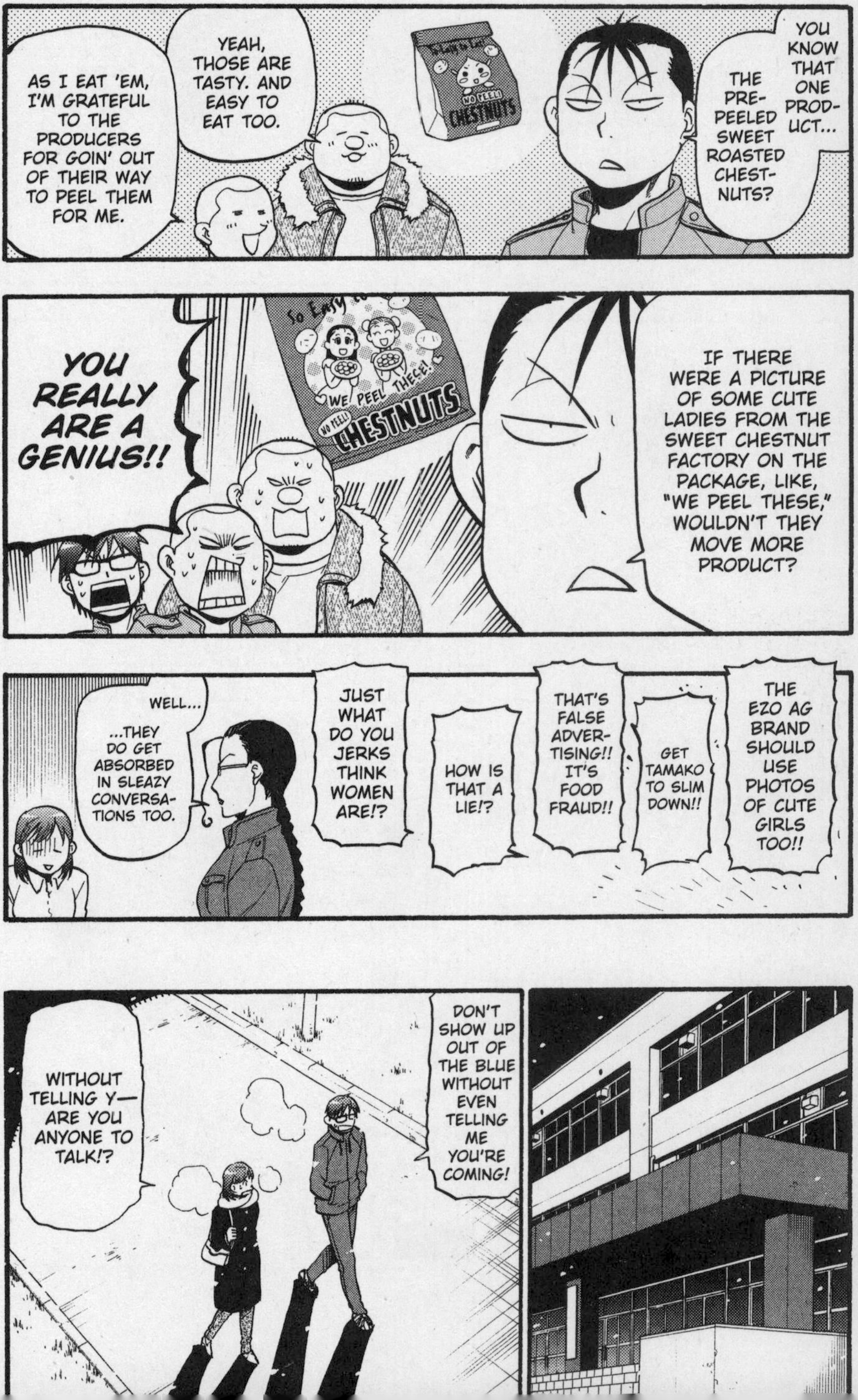
YOU KNOW THAT ONE PRODUCT...
THE PRE-PEELED SWEET ROASTED CHESTNUTS?
NO PEEL! CHESTNUTS
YEAH, THOSE ARE TASTY. AND EASY TO EAT TOO.
AS I EAT 'EM, I'M GRATEFUL TO THE PRODUCERS FOR GOIN' OUT OF THEIR WAY TO PEEL THEM FOR ME.
IF THERE WERE A PICTURE OF SOME CUTE LADIES FROM THE SWEET CHESTNUT FACTORY ON THE PACKAGE, LIKE, "WE PEEL THESE," WOULDN'T THEY MOVE MORE PRODUCT?
WE PEEL THESE!
NO PEEL! CHESTNUTS
YOU REALLY ARE A GENIUS!!
THE EZO AG BRAND SHOULD USE PHOTOS OF CUTE GIRLS TOO!!
GET TAMAKO TO SLIM DOWN!!
THAT'S FALSE ADVERTISING!! IT'S FOOD FRAUD!!
HOW IS THAT A LIE!?
JUST WHAT DO YOU JERKS THINK WOMEN ARE!?
WELL...
...THEY DO GET ABSORBED IN SLEAZY CONVERSATIONS TOO.
DON'T SHOW UP OUT OF THE BLUE WITHOUT EVEN TELLING ME YOU'RE COMING!
WITHOUT TELLING Y— ARE YOU ANYONE TO TALK!?

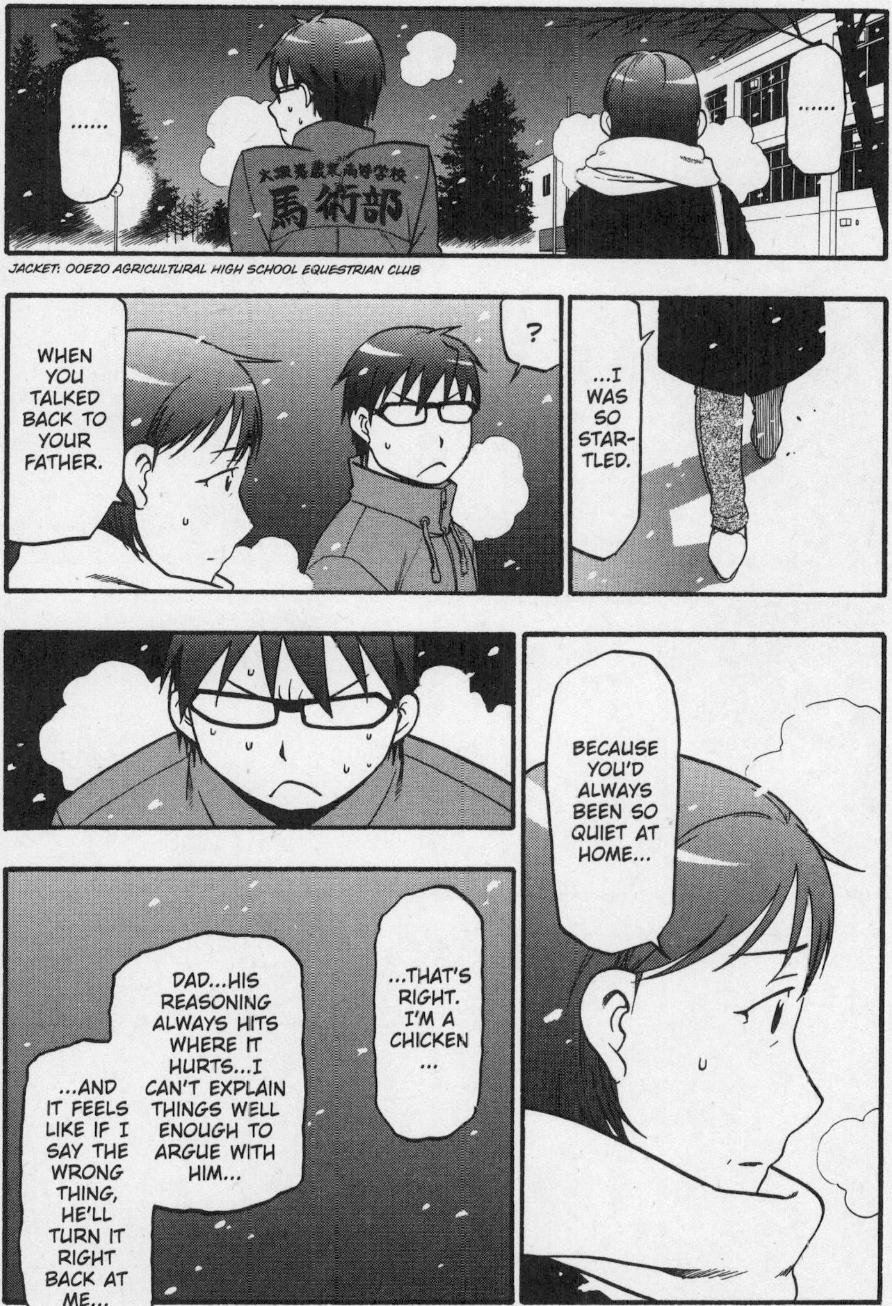
......
......
JACKET: OOEZO AGRICULTURAL HIGH SCHOOL EQUESTRIAN CLUB
...I WAS SO STARTLED.
?
WHEN YOU TALKED BACK TO YOUR FATHER.
BECAUSE YOU'D ALWAYS BEEN SO QUIET AT HOME...
...THAT'S RIGHT. I'M A CHICKEN...
DAD...HIS REASONING ALWAYS HITS WHERE IT HURTS...I CAN'T EXPLAIN THINGS WELL ENOUGH TO ARGUE WITH HIM...
...AND IT FEELS LIKE IF I SAY THE WRONG THING, HE'LL TURN IT RIGHT BACK AT ME...

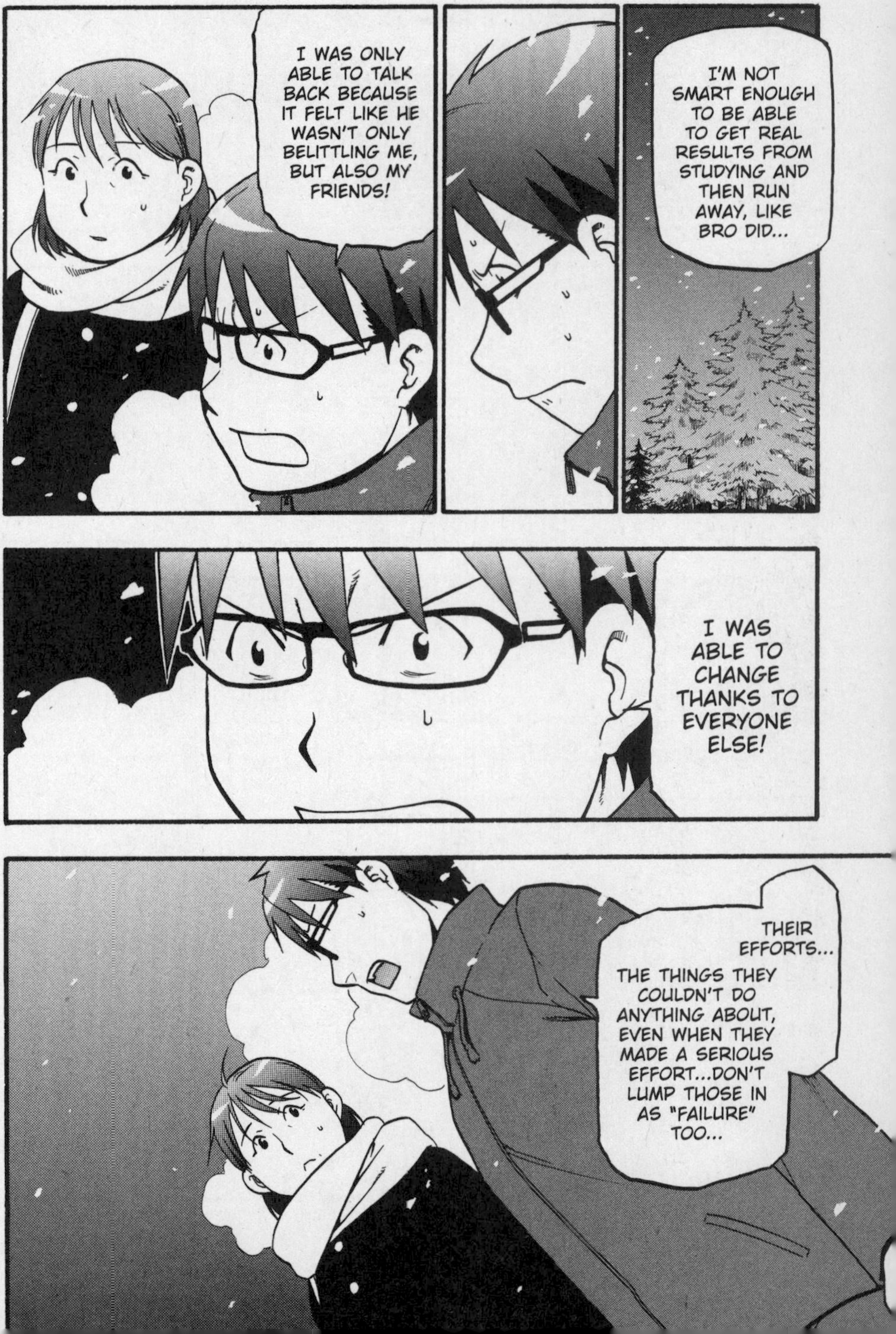
I'M NOT SMART ENOUGH TO BE ABLE TO GET REAL RESULTS FROM STUDYING AND THEN RUN AWAY, LIKE BRO DID...
I WAS ONLY ABLE TO TALK BACK BECAUSE IT FELT LIKE HE WASN'T ONLY BELITTLING ME, BUT ALSO MY FRIENDS!
I WAS ABLE TO CHANGE THANKS TO EVERYONE ELSE!
THEIR EFFORTS...
THE THINGS THEY COULDN'T DO ANYTHING ABOUT, EVEN WHEN THEY MADE A SERIOUS EFFORT...DON'T LUMP THOSE IN AS "FAILURE" TOO...

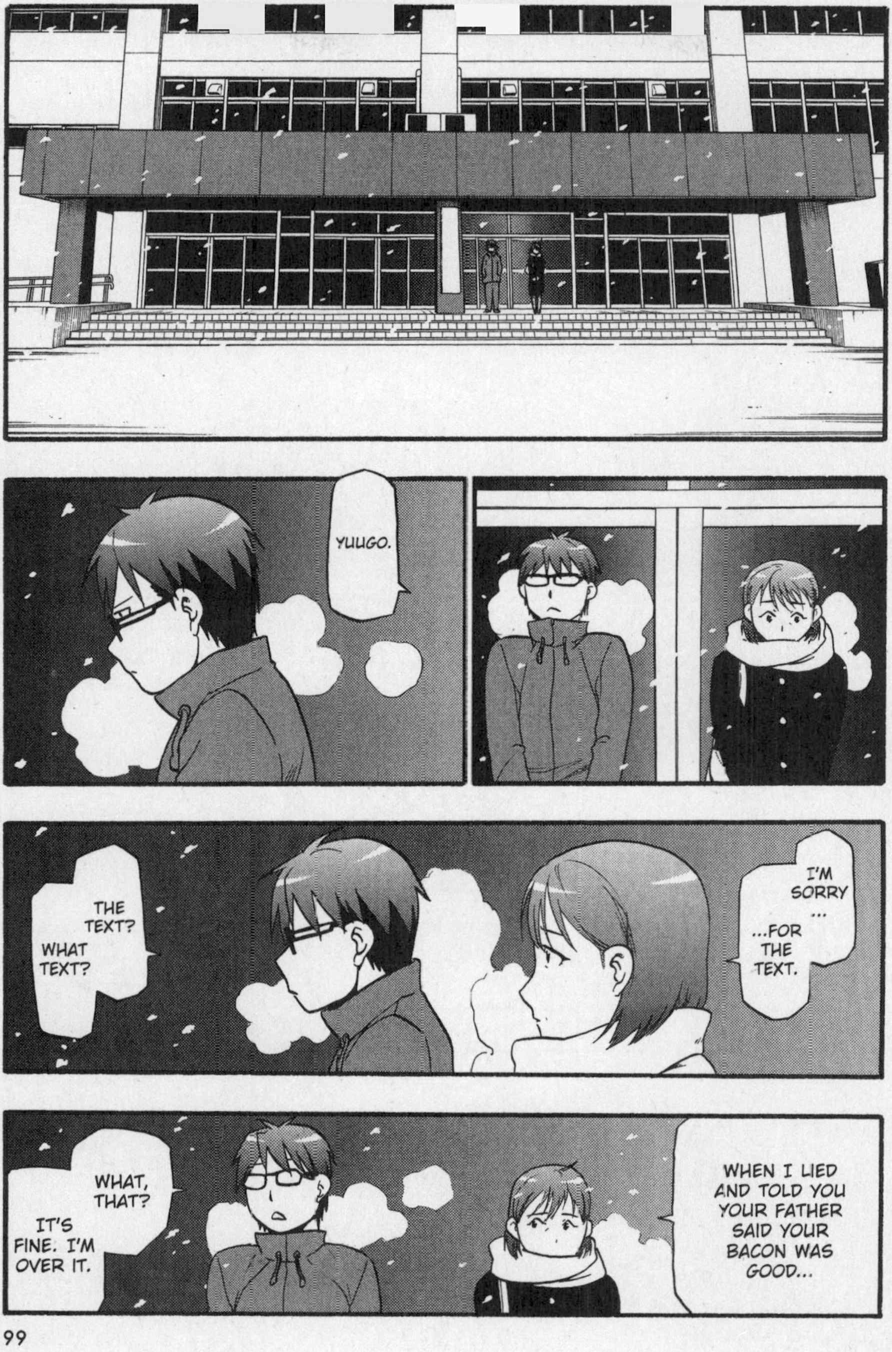
YUUGO.
I'M SORRY ... ...FOR THE TEXT.
THE TEXT? WHAT TEXT?
WHEN I LIED AND TOLD YOU YOUR FATHER SAID YOUR BACON WAS GOOD...
WHAT, THAT?
IT'S FINE. I'M OVER IT.

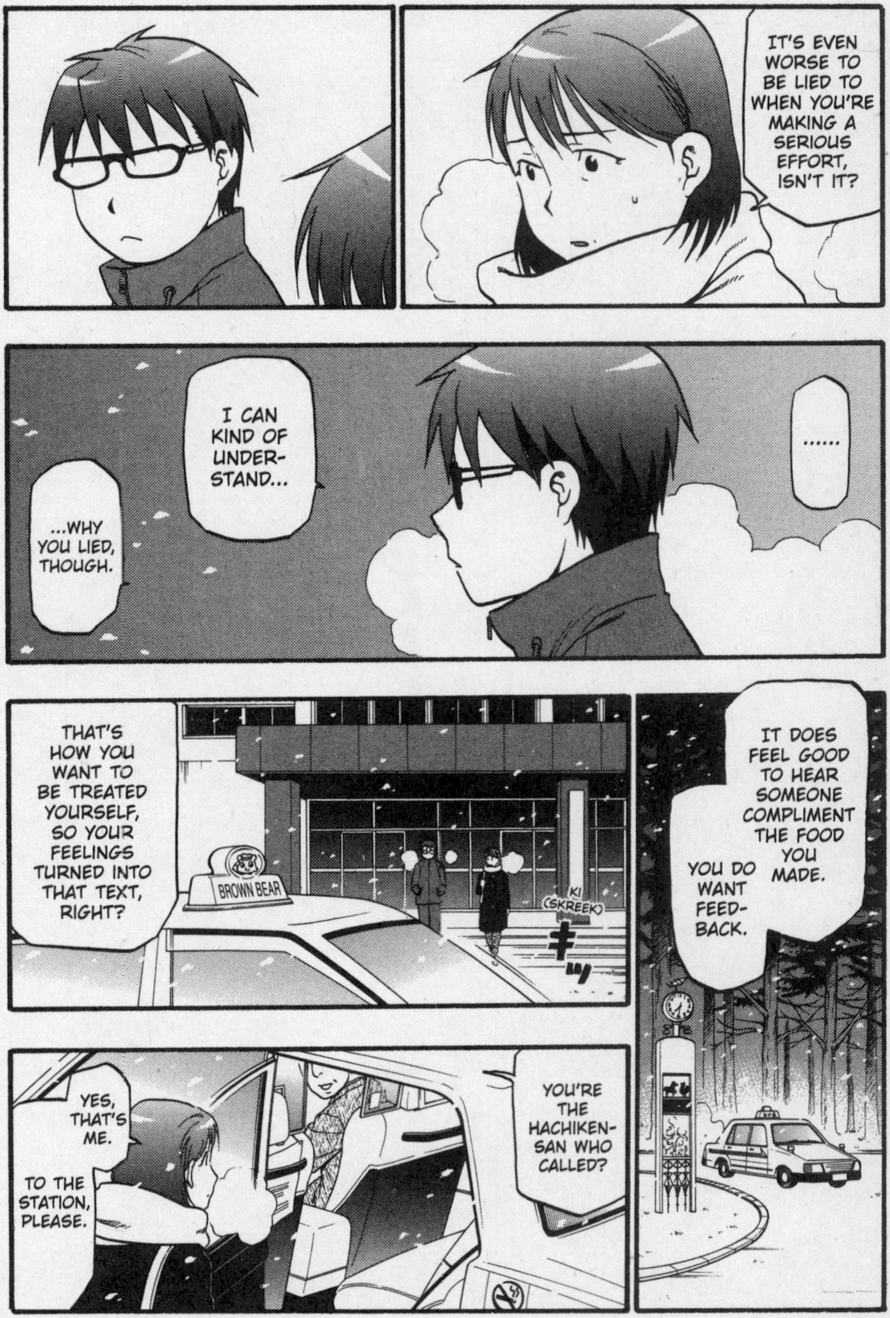
IT'S EVEN WORSE TO BE LIED TO WHEN YOU'RE MAKING A SERIOUS EFFORT, ISN'T IT?
......
I CAN KIND OF UNDER-STAND...
...WHY YOU LIED, THOUGH.
IT DOES FEEL GOOD TO HEAR SOMEONE COMPLIMENT THE FOOD YOU MADE.
YOU DO WANT FEED-BACK.
THAT'S HOW YOU WANT TO BE TREATED YOURSELF, SO YOUR FEELINGS TURNED INTO THAT TEXT, RIGHT?
BROWN BEAR
KI (SKREEK)
YOU'RE THE HACHIKEN-SAN WHO CALLED?
YES, THAT'S ME.
TO THE STATION, PLEASE.

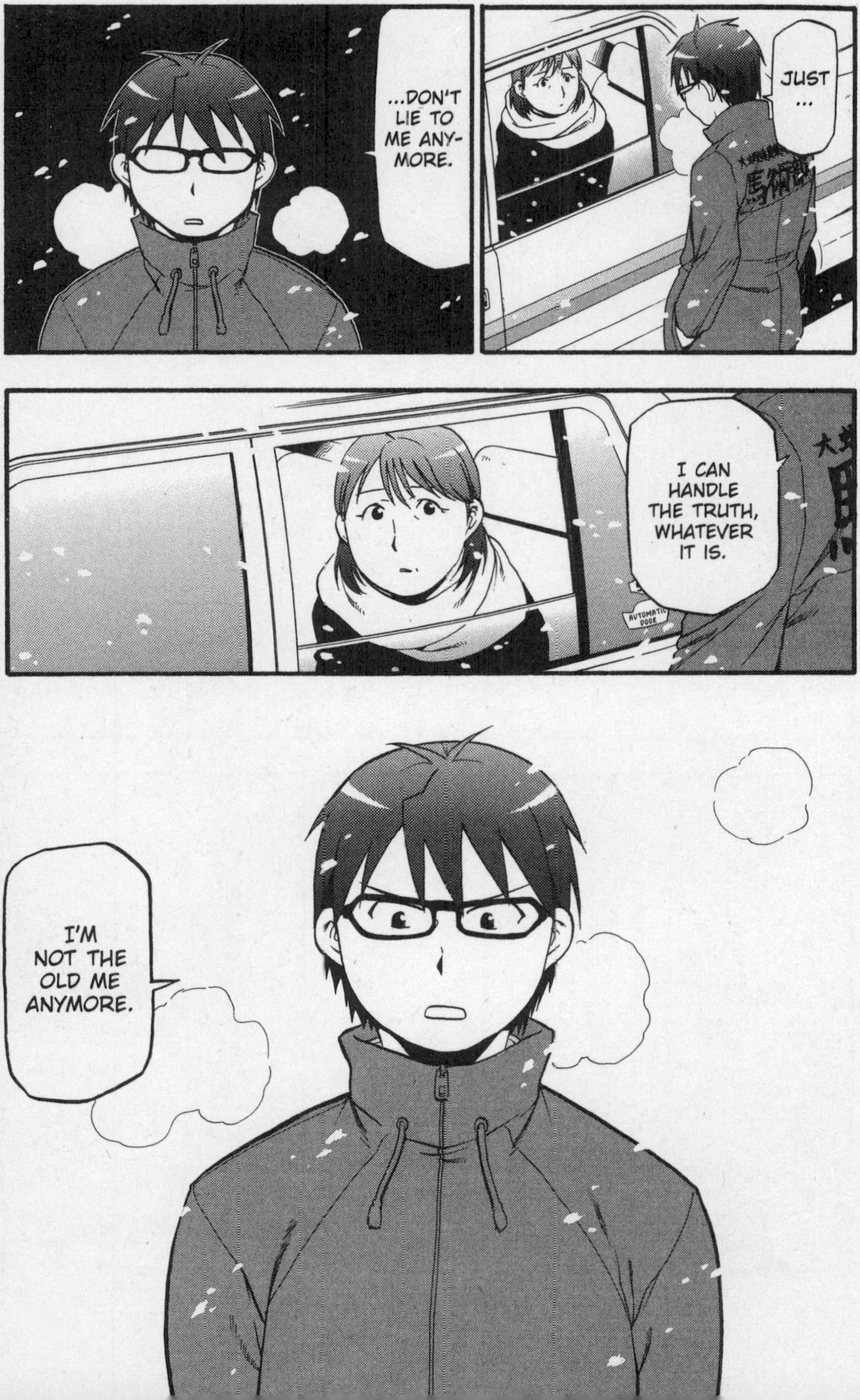
JUST ...
...DON'T LIE TO ME ANY-MORE.
I CAN HANDLE THE TRUTH, WHATEVER IT IS.
AUTOMATIC DOOR
I'M NOT THE OLD ME ANYMORE.

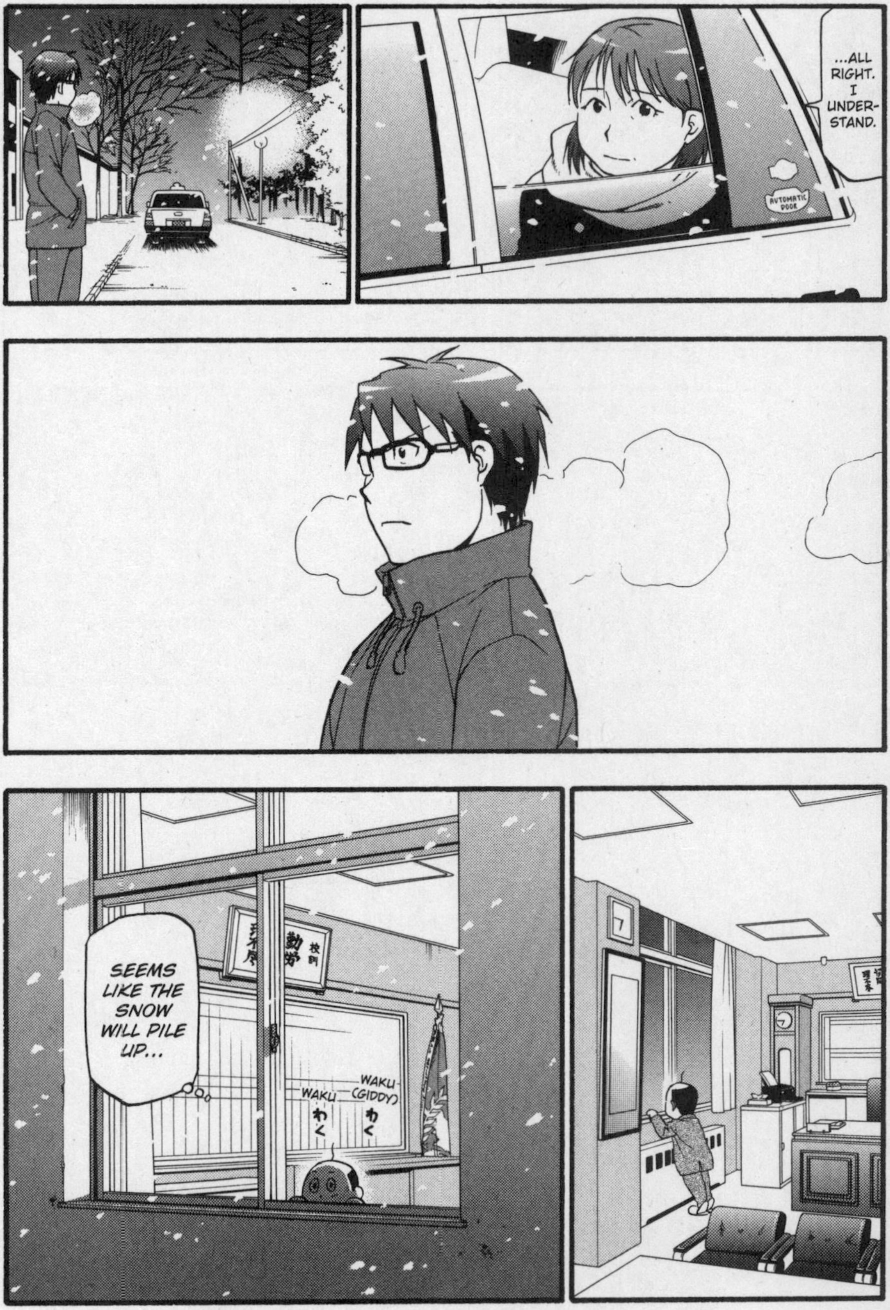
...ALL RIGHT. I UNDERSTAND.
AUTOMATIC DOOR
SEEMS LIKE THE SNOW WILL PILE UP...
WAKU (GIDDY) わく
WAKU わく

Silver Spoon

YOSHINOBU
SAKURAGI

DAIRY SCIENCE PROGRAM
YEAR 1 HOMEROOM TEACHER

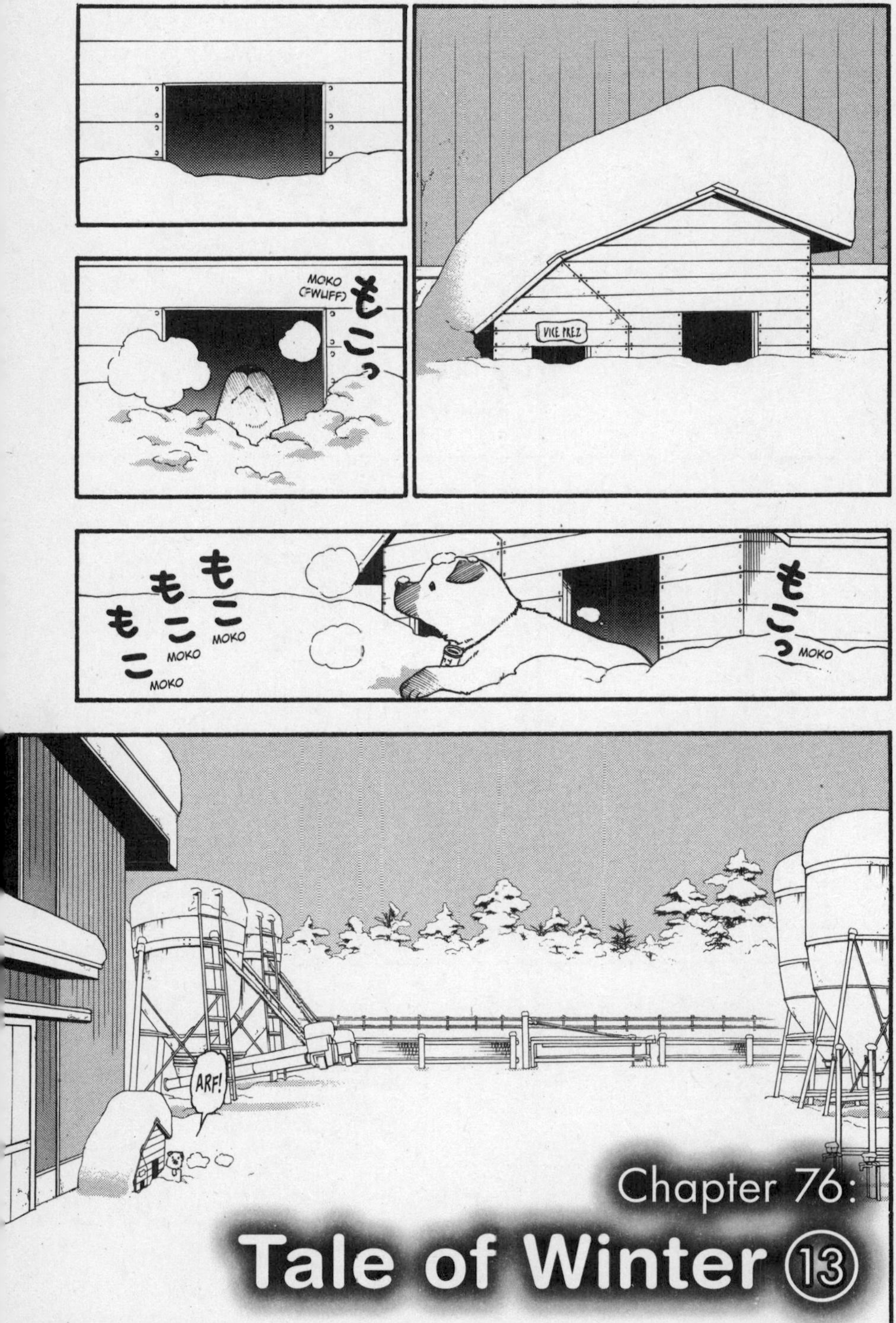
VICE PREZ
もこっ
MOKO (FWUFF)
もこっ
MOKO
もこ
MOKO
もこ
MOKO
もこ
MOKO
ARF!

Chapter 76:
Tale of Winter ⑬

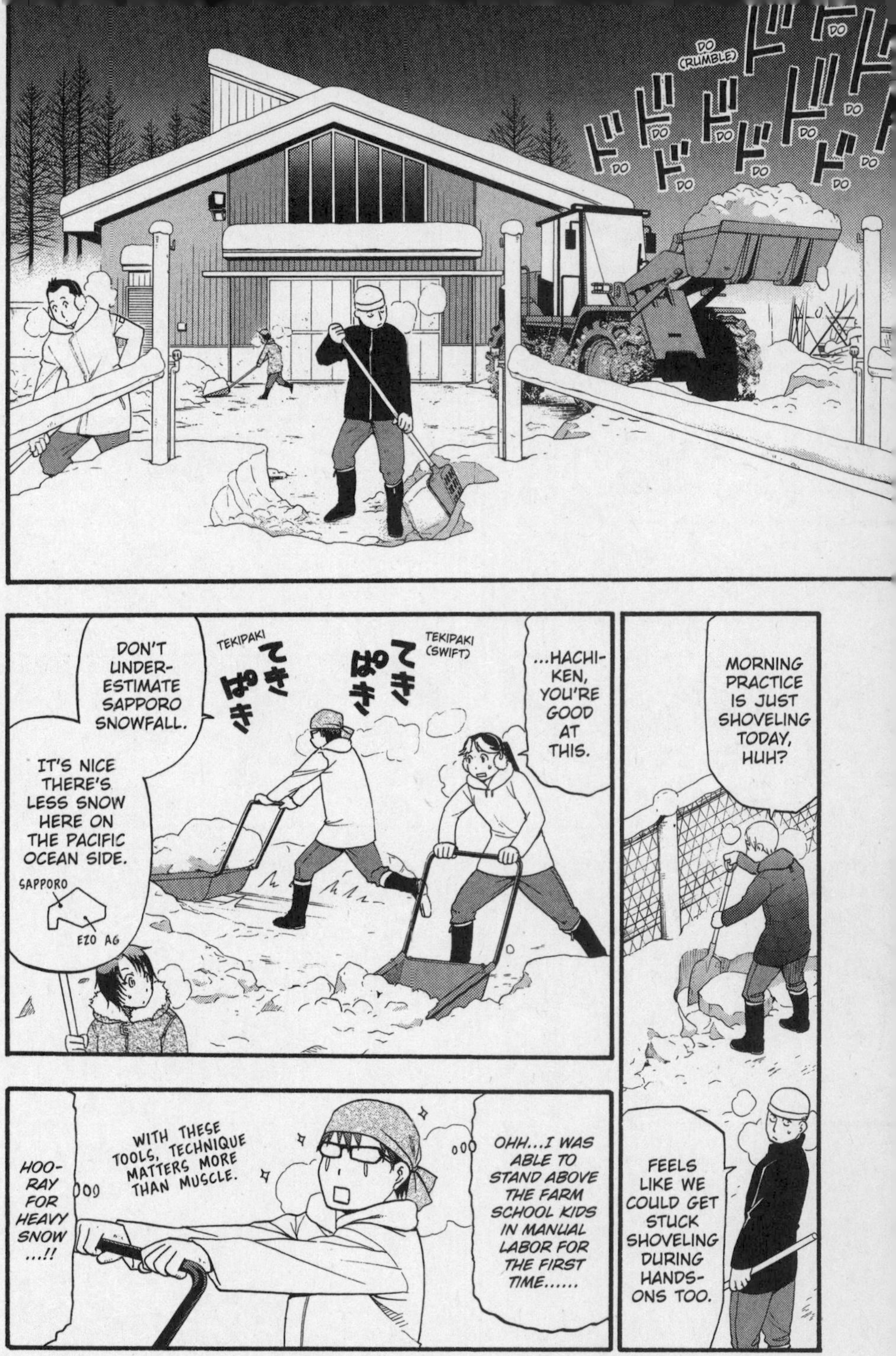
ドドドドドドドドドドド
DO (RUMBLE)
DO DO DO DO DO DO DO DO DO DO
MORNING PRACTICE IS JUST SHOVELING TODAY, HUH?
FEELS LIKE WE COULD GET STUCK SHOVELING DURING HANDS-ONS TOO.
...HACHIKEN, YOU'RE GOOD AT THIS.
てきぱき
TEKIPAKI (SWIFT)
てきぱき
TEKIPAKI
DON'T UNDER-ESTIMATE SAPPORO SNOWFALL.
IT'S NICE THERE'S LESS SNOW HERE ON THE PACIFIC OCEAN SIDE.
SAPPORO
EZO AG
OHH...I WAS ABLE TO STAND ABOVE THE FARM SCHOOL KIDS IN MANUAL LABOR FOR THE FIRST TIME......
WITH THESE TOOLS, TECHNIQUE MATTERS MORE THAN MUSCLE.
HOO-RAY FOR HEAVY SNOW ...!!

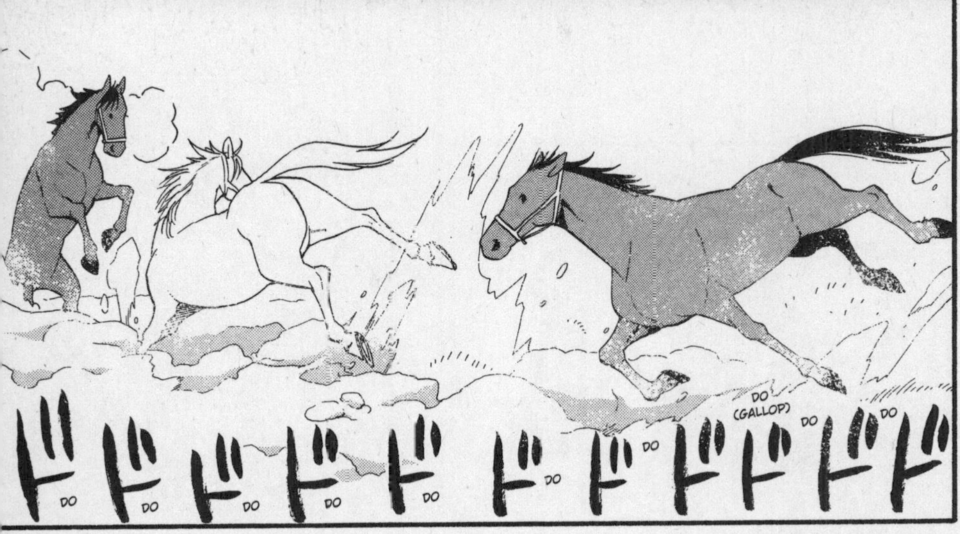
DO
DO
DO
DO
DO
DO
DO
DO (GALLOP)
DO
DO
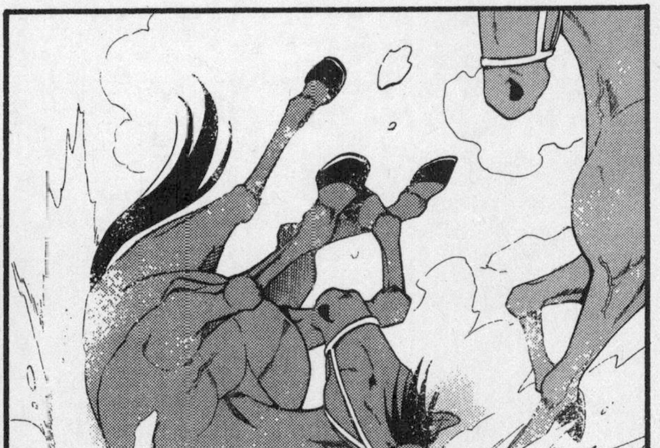
BRR HIIHNN!
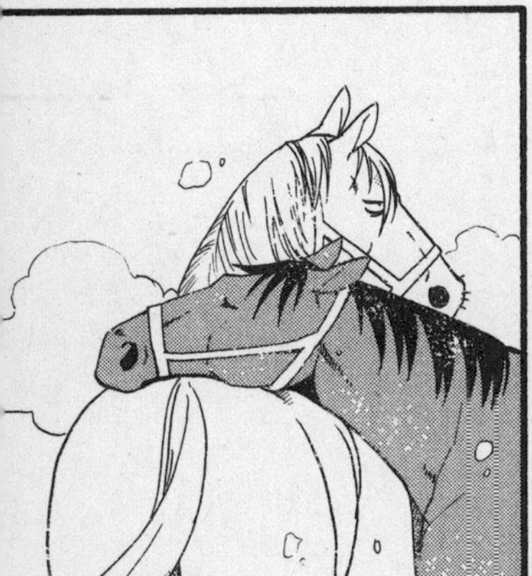
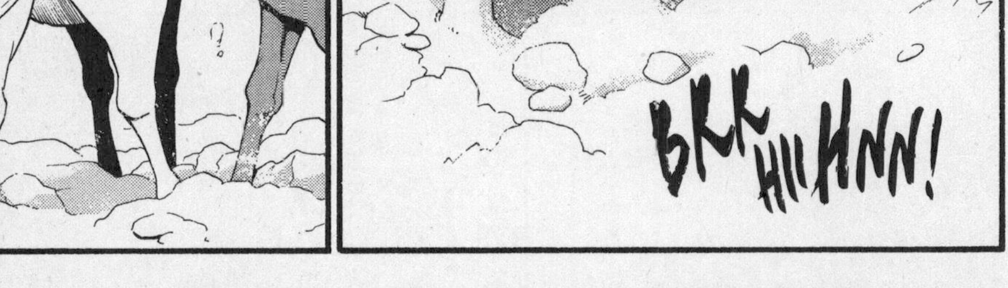
HUH. SO HORSES PLAY IN THE SNOW?

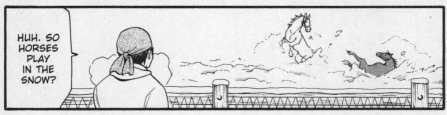

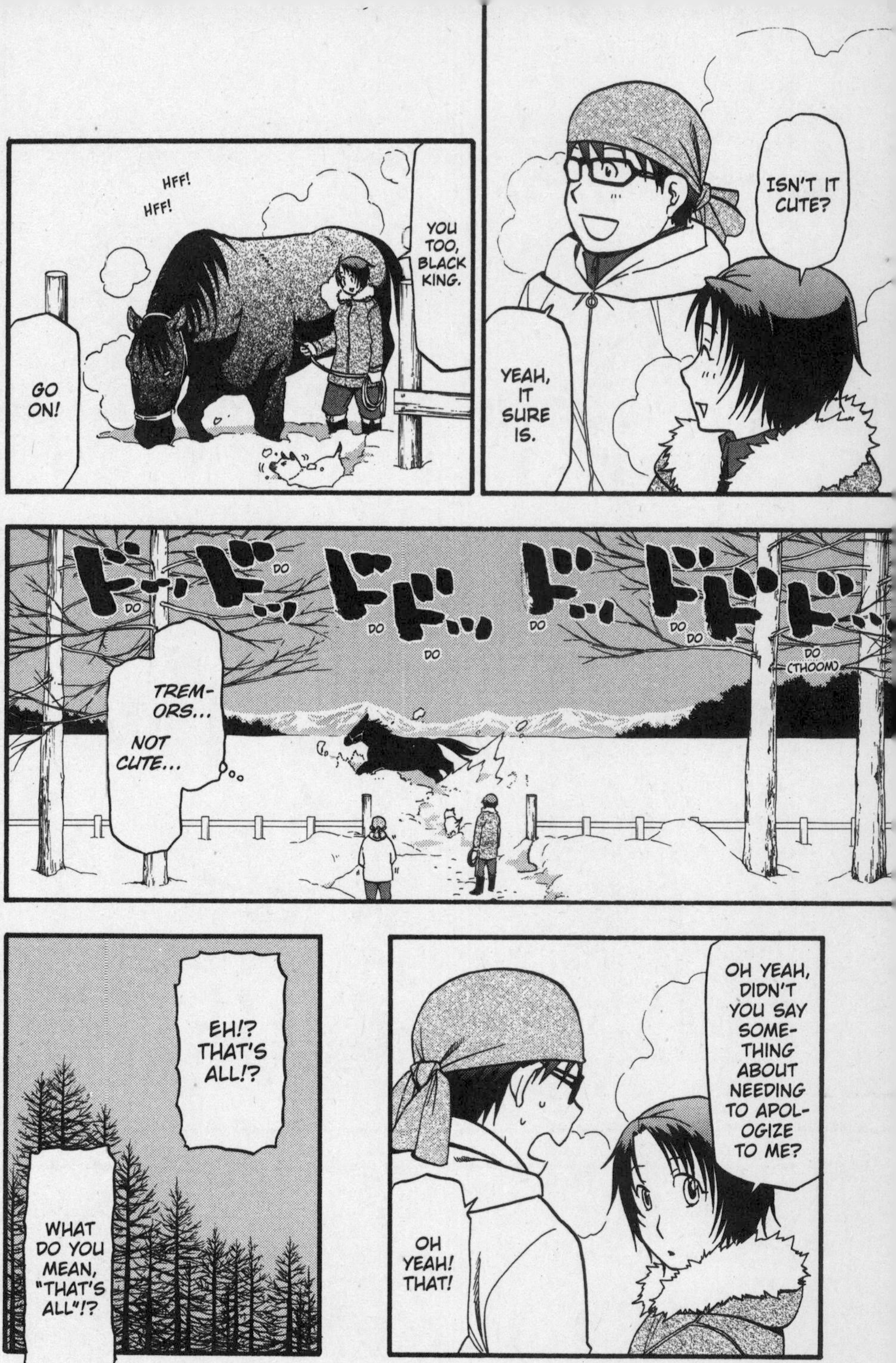
ISN'T IT CUTE?
YEAH, IT SURE IS.
YOU TOO, BLACK KING.
HFF!
HFF!
GO ON!
DO DO DO DO DO DO DO DO (THOOM)
TREMORS... NOT CUTE...
OH YEAH, DIDN'T YOU SAY SOMETHING ABOUT NEEDING TO APOLOGIZE TO ME?
OH YEAH! THAT!
EH!? THAT'S ALL!?
WHAT DO YOU MEAN, "THAT'S ALL"!?

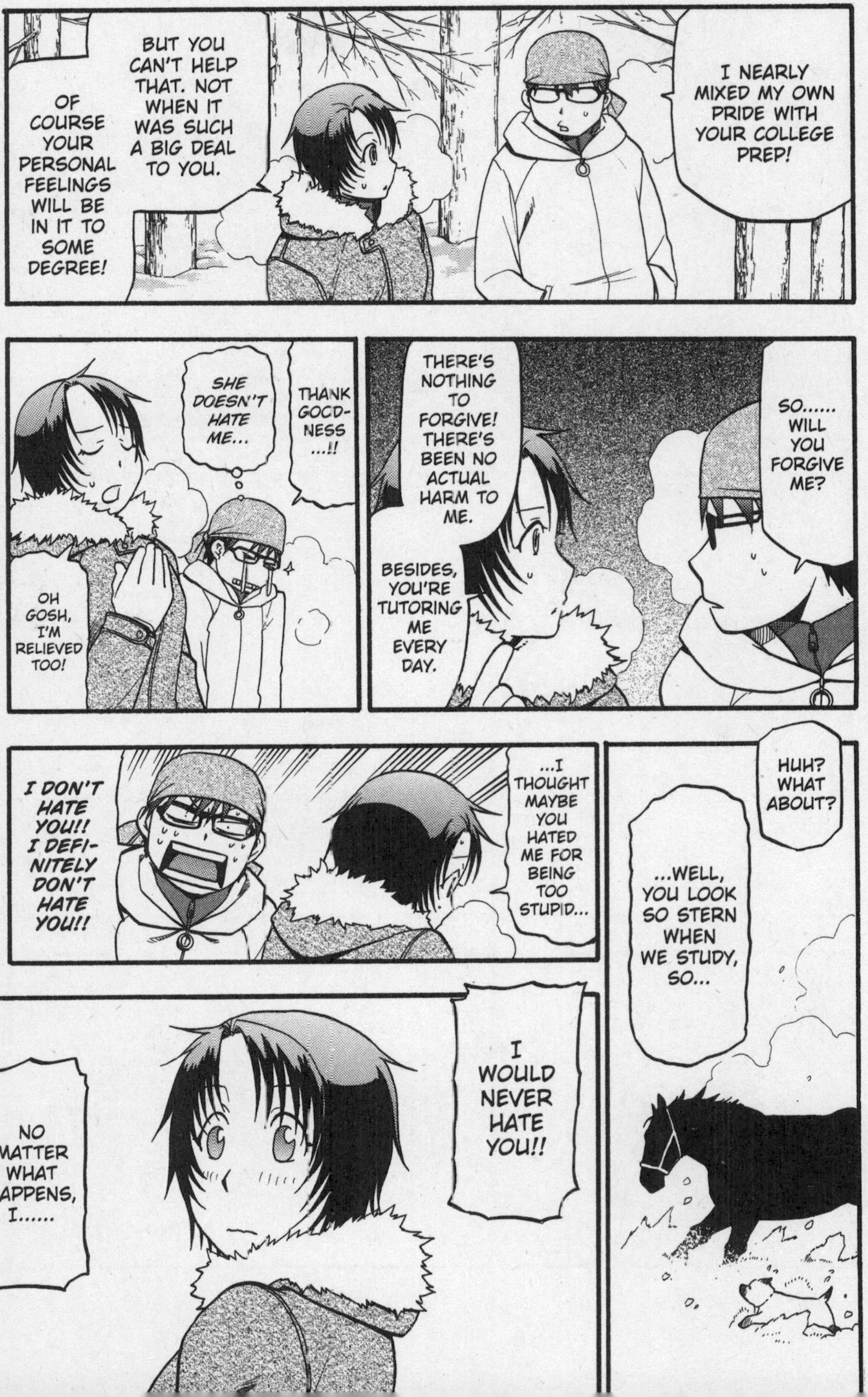
I NEARLY MIXED MY OWN PRIDE WITH YOUR COLLEGE PREP!
BUT YOU CAN'T HELP THAT. NOT WHEN IT WAS SUCH A BIG DEAL TO YOU.
OF COURSE YOUR PERSONAL FEELINGS WILL BE IN IT TO SOME DEGREE!
SO...... WILL YOU FORGIVE ME?
THERE'S NOTHING TO FORGIVE! THERE'S BEEN NO ACTUAL HARM TO ME.
BESIDES, YOU'RE TUTORING ME EVERY DAY.
THANK GOOD-NESS ...!!
SHE DOESN'T HATE ME...
OH GOSH, I'M RELIEVED TOO!
HUH? WHAT ABOUT?
...WELL, YOU LOOK SO STERN WHEN WE STUDY, SO...
...I THOUGHT MAYBE YOU HATED ME FOR BEING TOO STUPID...
I DON'T HATE YOU!! I DEFI-NITELY DON'T HATE YOU!!
I WOULD NEVER HATE YOU!!
NO MATTER WHAT HAPPENS, I......

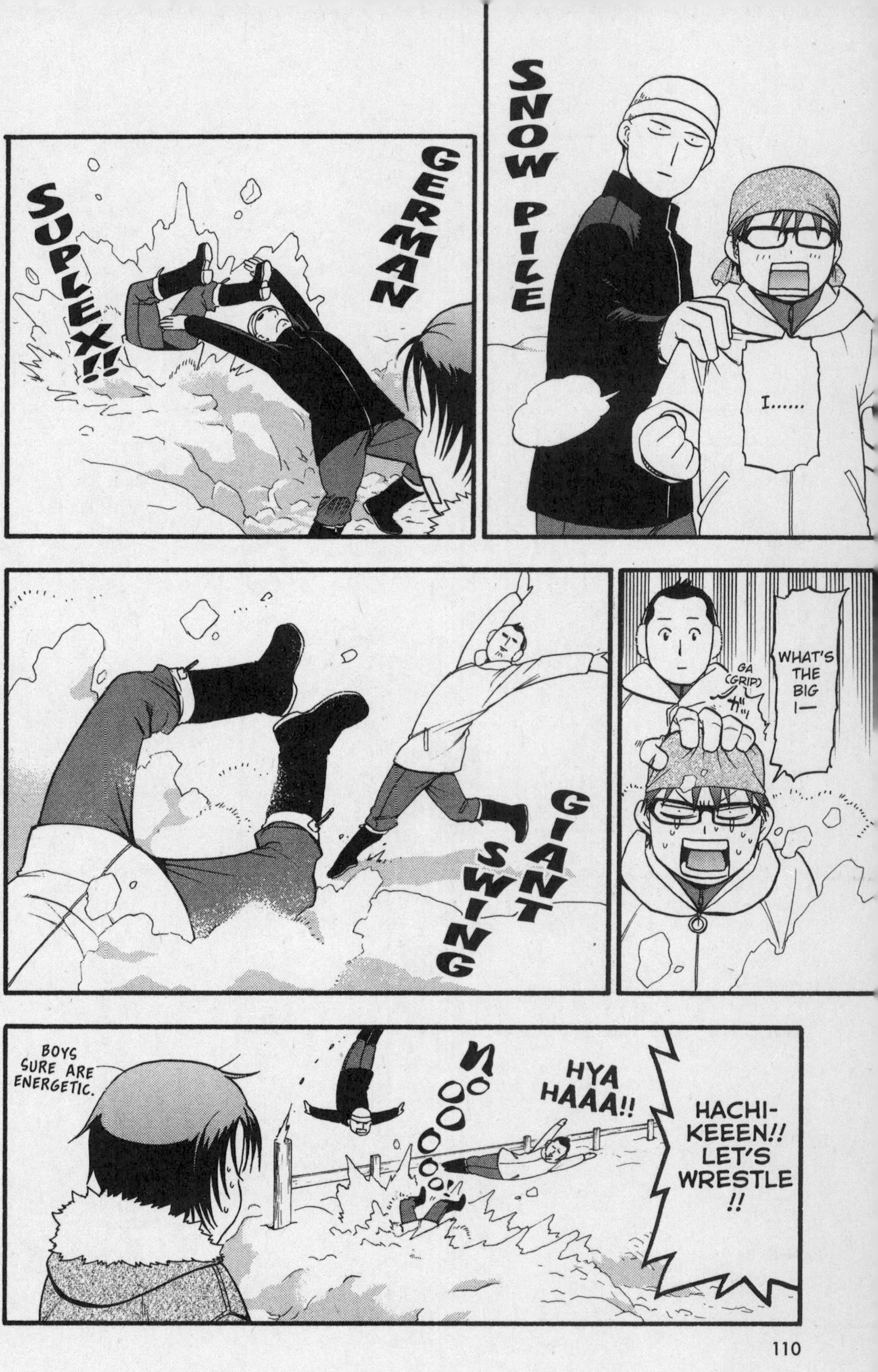
SNOW PILE
I......
GERMAN SUPLEX!!
WHAT'S THE BIG I—
GA (GRIP)
GIANT SWING
HACHI-KEEEN!! LET'S WRESTLE!!
HYA HAAAA!!
NOOOOOOO!!
BOYS SURE ARE ENERGETIC.

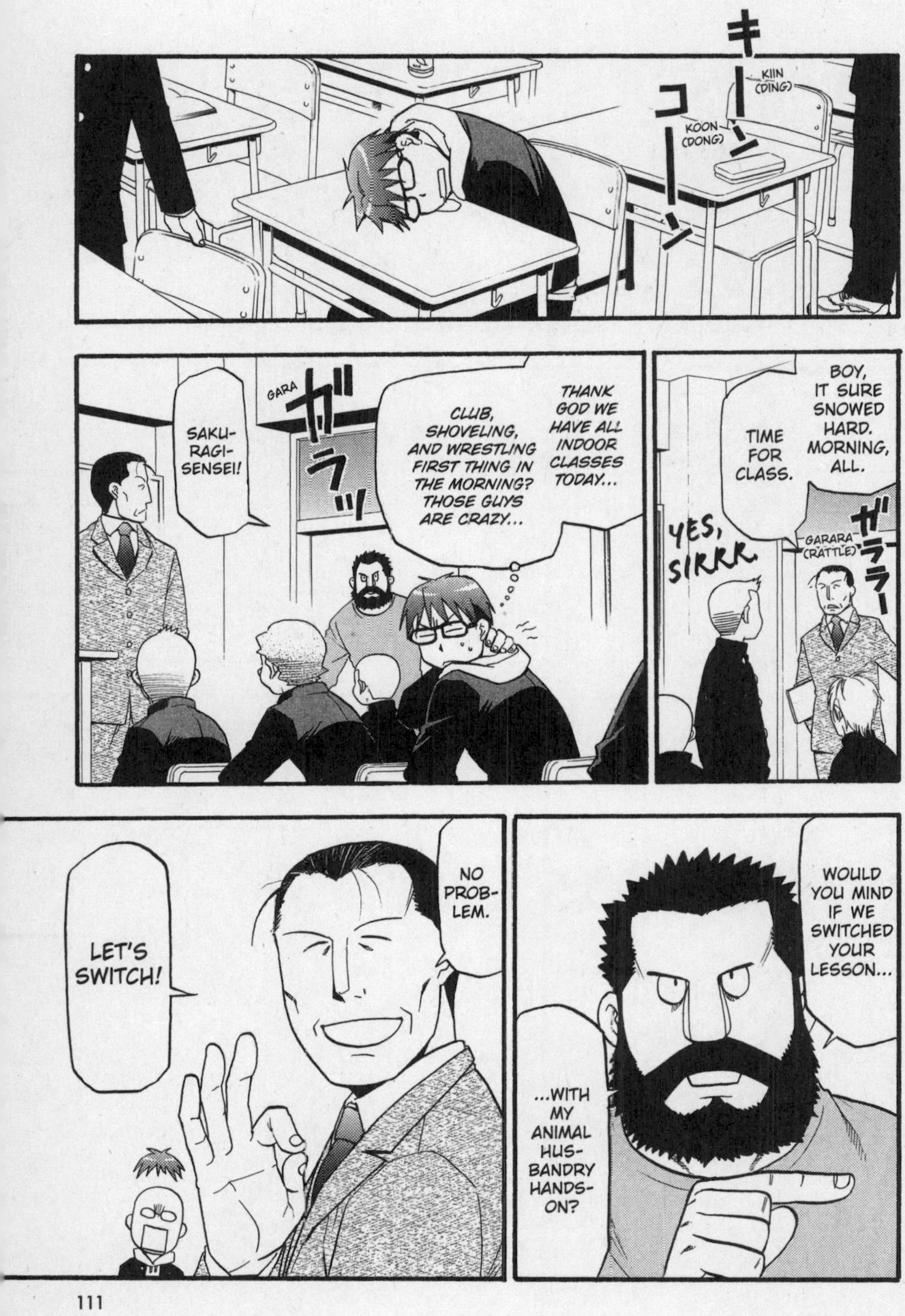
キーン
KIIN (DING)
コーン
KOON (DONG)
BOY, IT SURE SNOWED HARD. MORNING, ALL.
TIME FOR CLASS.
ガララー
GARARA (RATTLE)
YES, SIRRR.
THANK GOD WE HAVE ALL INDOOR CLASSES TODAY...
CLUB, SHOVELING, AND WRESTLING FIRST THING IN THE MORNING? THOSE GUYS ARE CRAZY...
ガラッ
GARA
SAKURAGI-SENSEI!
WOULD YOU MIND IF WE SWITCHED YOUR LESSON...
...WITH MY ANIMAL HUSBANDRY HANDS-ON?
NO PROBLEM.
LET'S SWITCH!

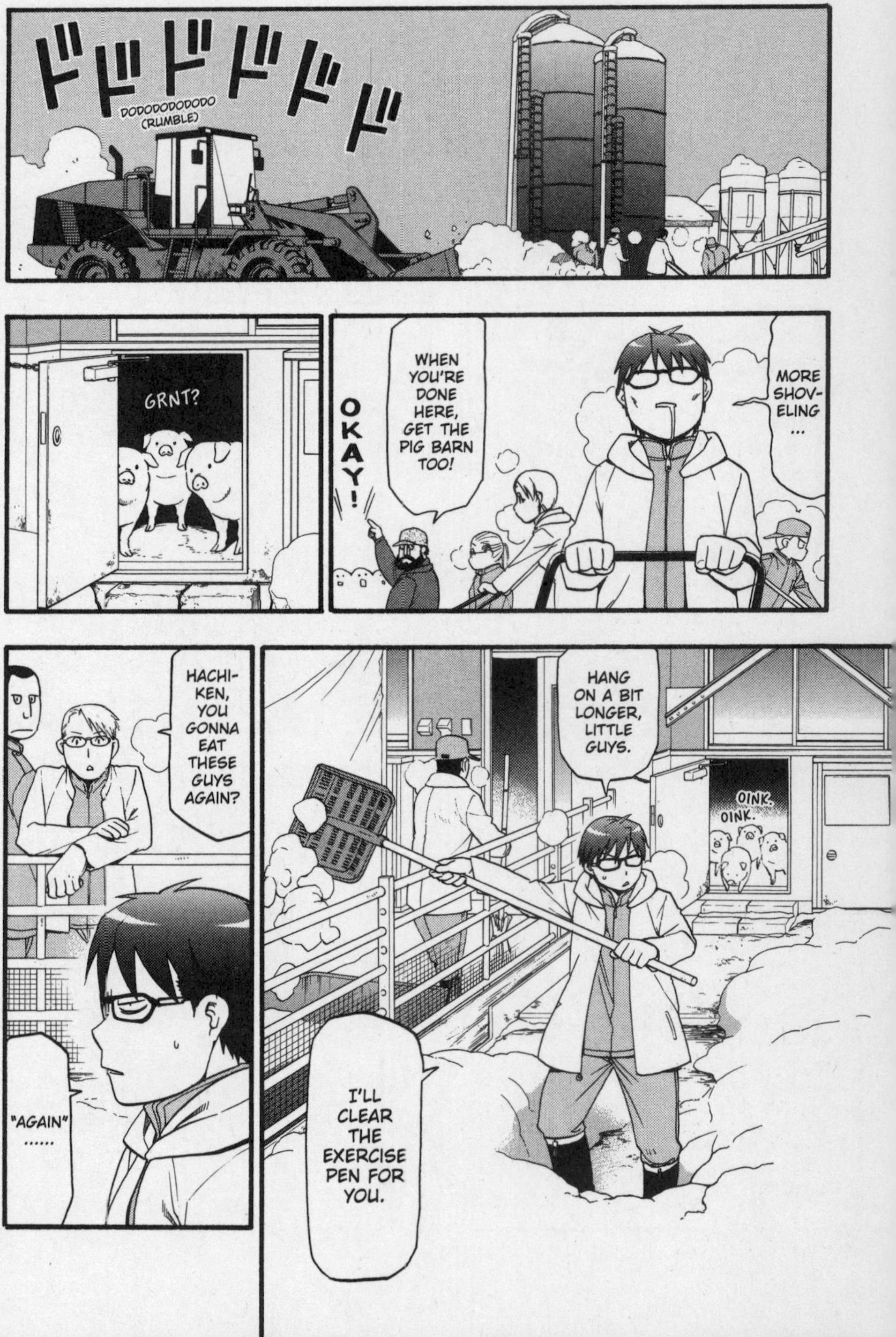
ドドドドドドド
DODODODODODO (RUMBLE)
MORE SHOVELING ...
WHEN YOU'RE DONE HERE, GET THE PIG BARN TOO!
OKAY!
GRNT?
HANG ON A BIT LONGER, LITTLE GUYS.
OINK. OINK.
I'LL CLEAR THE EXERCISE PEN FOR YOU.
HACHIKEN, YOU GONNA EAT THESE GUYS AGAIN?
"AGAIN" ......

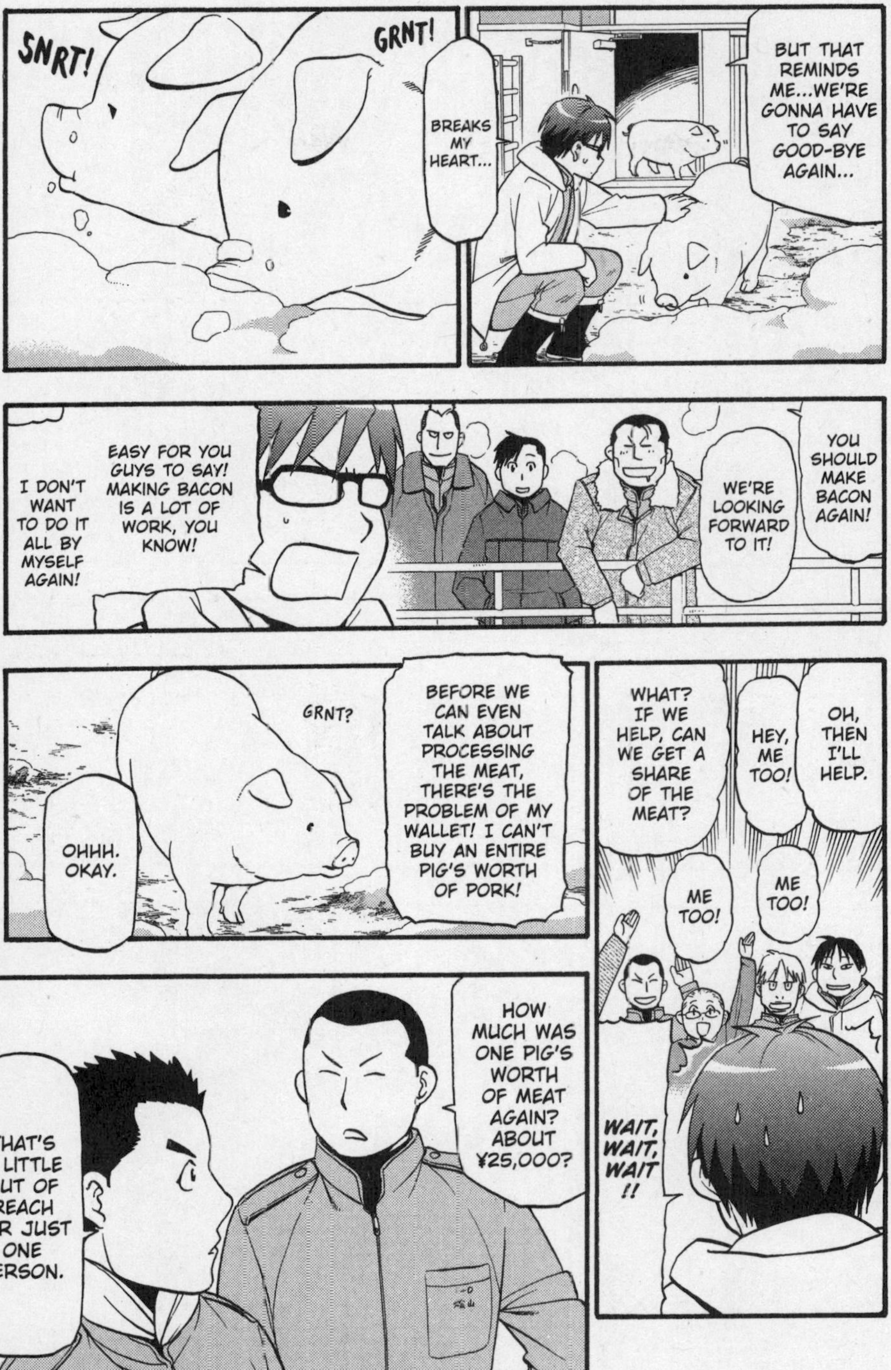
BUT THAT REMINDS ME...WE'RE GONNA HAVE TO SAY GOOD-BYE AGAIN...
BREAKS MY HEART...
GRNT!
SNRT!
YOU SHOULD MAKE BACON AGAIN!
WE'RE LOOKING FORWARD TO IT!
EASY FOR YOU GUYS TO SAY! MAKING BACON IS A LOT OF WORK, YOU KNOW!
I DON'T WANT TO DO IT ALL BY MYSELF AGAIN!
BEFORE WE CAN EVEN TALK ABOUT PROCESSING THE MEAT, THERE'S THE PROBLEM OF MY WALLET! I CAN'T BUY AN ENTIRE PIG'S WORTH OF PORK!
GRNT?
OHHH. OKAY.
HOW MUCH WAS ONE PIG'S WORTH OF MEAT AGAIN? ABOUT ¥25,000?
THAT'S A LITTLE OUT OF REACH FOR JUST ONE PERSON.
OH, THEN I'LL HELP.
HEY, ME TOO!
WHAT? IF WE HELP, CAN WE GET A SHARE OF THE MEAT?
ME TOO!
ME TOO!
WAIT, WAIT, WAIT!!

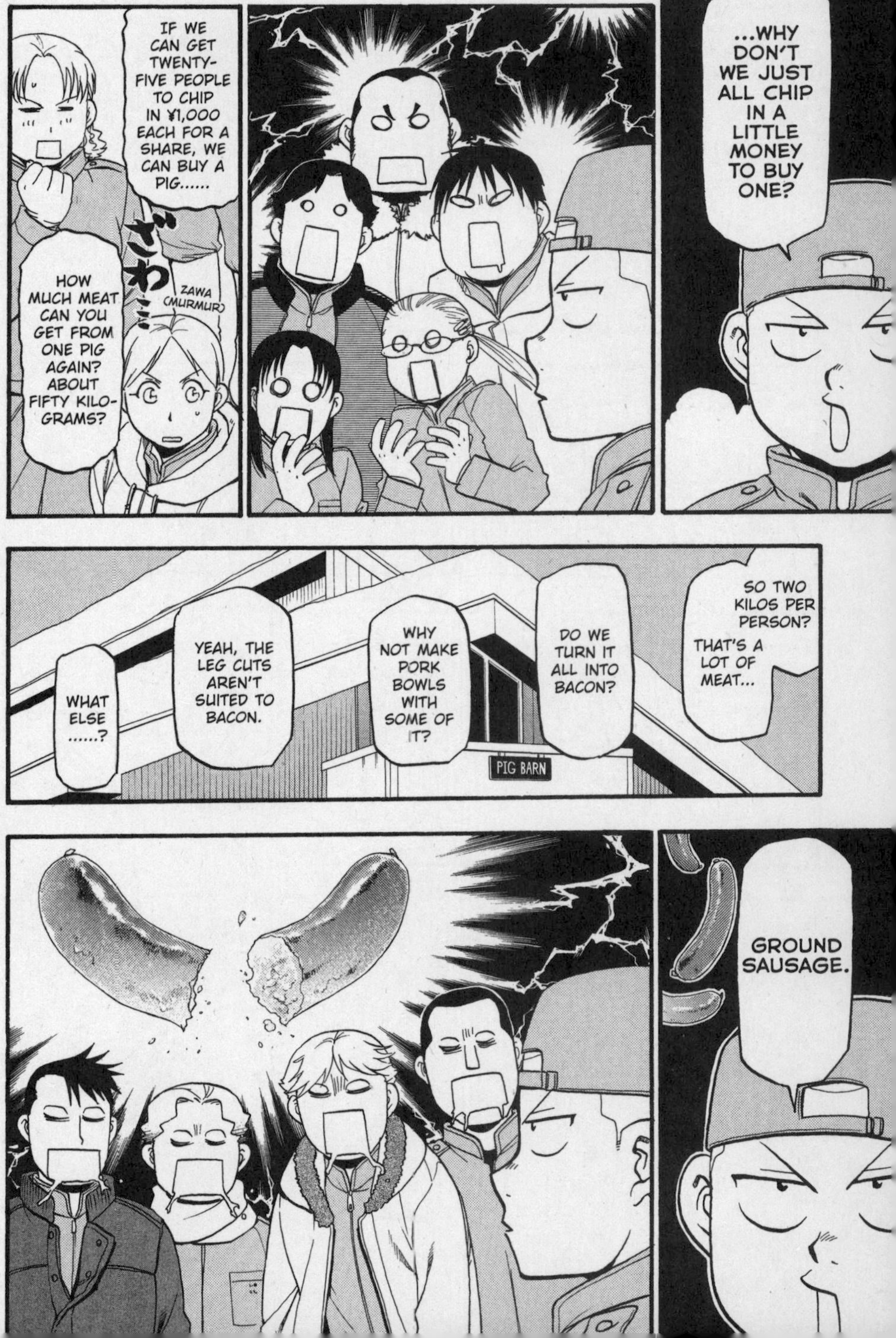
...WHY DON'T WE JUST ALL CHIP IN A LITTLE MONEY TO BUY ONE?
IF WE CAN GET TWENTY-FIVE PEOPLE TO CHIP IN ¥1,000 EACH FOR A SHARE, WE CAN BUY A PIG......
ざわ
ZAWA (MURMUR)
HOW MUCH MEAT CAN YOU GET FROM ONE PIG AGAIN? ABOUT FIFTY KILO-GRAMS?
SO TWO KILOS PER PERSON?
THAT'S A LOT OF MEAT...
DO WE TURN IT ALL INTO BACON?
WHY NOT MAKE PORK BOWLS WITH SOME OF IT?
YEAH, THE LEG CUTS AREN'T SUITED TO BACON.
WHAT ELSE......?
PIG BARN
GROUND SAUSAGE.

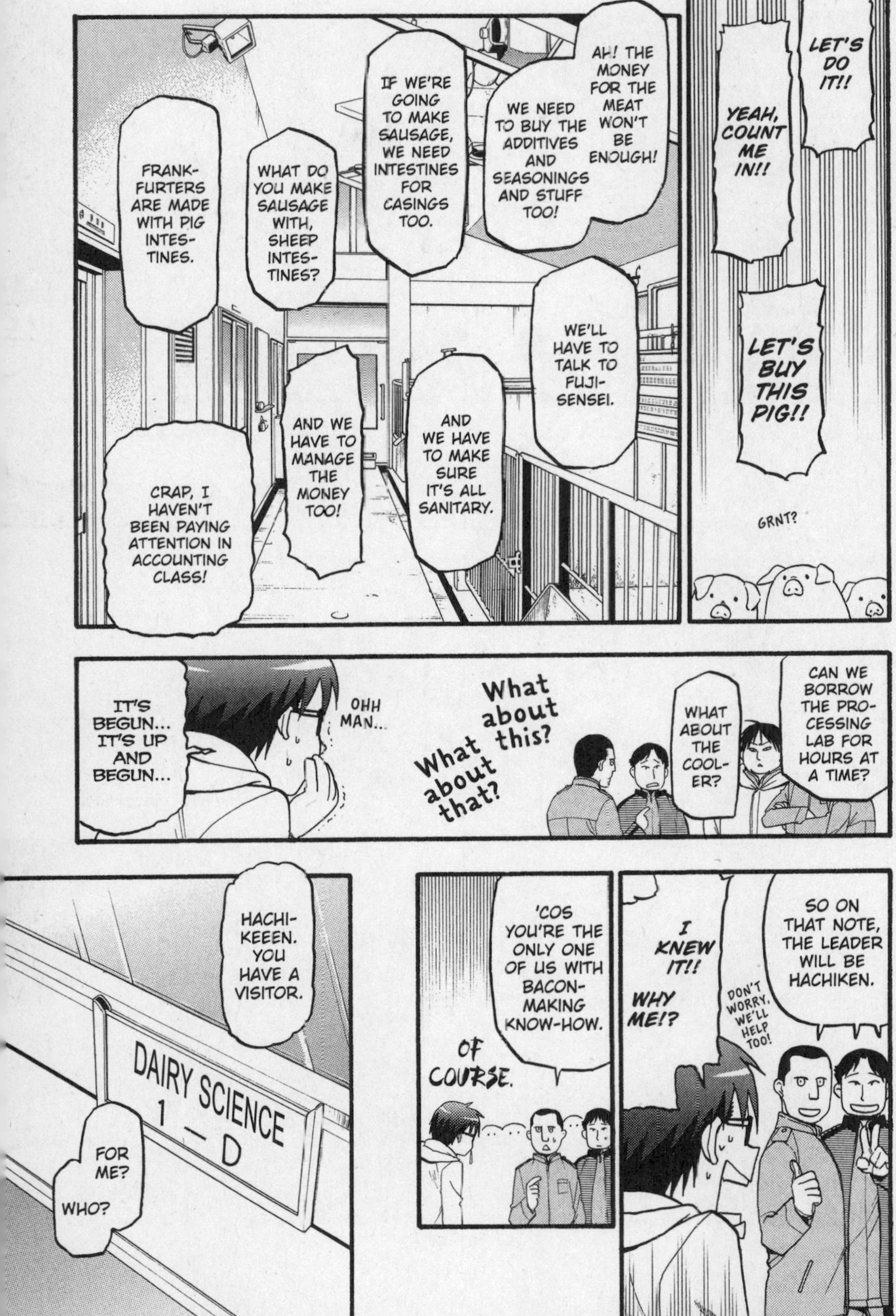
LET'S DO IT!!
YEAH, COUNT ME IN!!
LET'S BUY THIS PIG!!
GRNT?
AH! THE MONEY FOR THE MEAT WON'T BE ENOUGH!
WE NEED TO BUY THE ADDITIVES AND SEASONINGS AND STUFF TOO!
IF WE'RE GOING TO MAKE SAUSAGE, WE NEED INTESTINES FOR CASINGS TOO.
WHAT DO YOU MAKE SAUSAGE WITH, SHEEP INTESTINES?
FRANKFURTERS ARE MADE WITH PIG INTESTINES.
WE'LL HAVE TO TALK TO FUJI-SENSEI.
AND WE HAVE TO MAKE SURE IT'S ALL SANITARY.
AND WE HAVE TO MANAGE THE MONEY TOO!
CRAP, I HAVEN'T BEEN PAYING ATTENTION IN ACCOUNTING CLASS!
CAN WE BORROW THE PROCESSING LAB FOR HOURS AT A TIME?
WHAT ABOUT THE COOLER?
What about this?
What about that?
OHH MAN...
IT'S BEGUN... IT'S UP AND BEGUN...
SO ON THAT NOTE, THE LEADER WILL BE HACHIKEN.
DON'T WORRY, WE'LL HELP TOO!
I KNEW IT!!
WHY ME!?
'COS YOU'RE THE ONLY ONE OF US WITH BACON-MAKING KNOW-HOW.
OF COURSE.
HACHIKEEEN. YOU HAVE A VISITOR.
DAIRY SCIENCE 1 — D
FOR ME?
WHO?

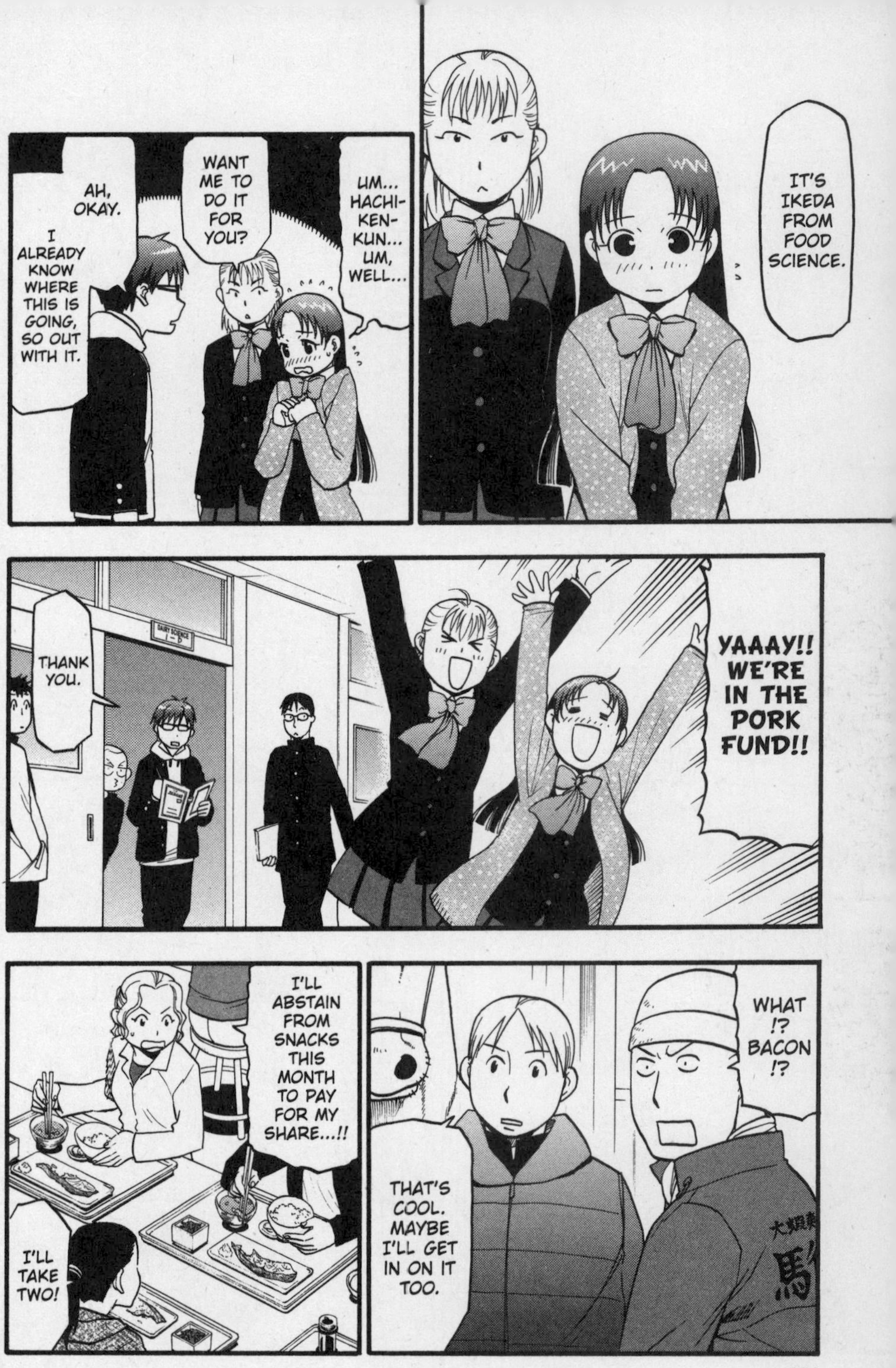
IT'S IKEDA FROM FOOD SCIENCE.
UM... HACHI-KEN-KUN... UM, WELL...
WANT ME TO DO IT FOR YOU?
AH, OKAY. I ALREADY KNOW WHERE THIS IS GOING, SO OUT WITH IT.
YAAAY!! WE'RE IN THE PORK FUND!!
THANK YOU.
WHAT!? BACON!?
THAT'S COOL. MAYBE I'LL GET IN ON IT TOO.
I'LL ABSTAIN FROM SNACKS THIS MONTH TO PAY FOR MY SHARE...!!
I'LL TAKE TWO!

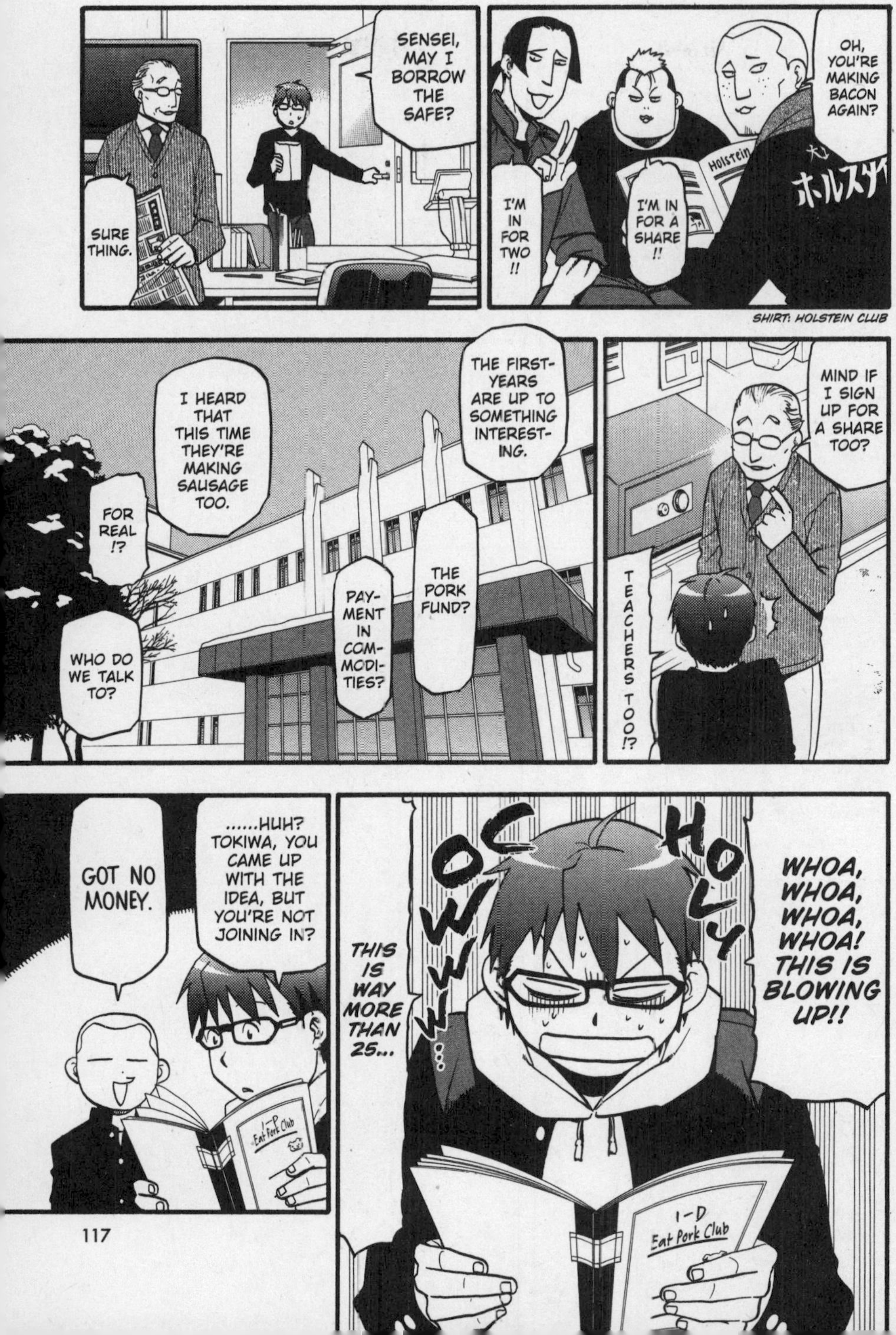
OH, YOU'RE MAKING BACON AGAIN?
Holstein
I'M IN FOR A SHARE!!
I'M IN FOR TWO!!
SHIRT: HOLSTEIN CLUB
SENSEI, MAY I BORROW THE SAFE?
SURE THING.
MIND IF I SIGN UP FOR A SHARE TOO?
TEACHERS TOO!?
THE FIRST-YEARS ARE UP TO SOMETHING INTERESTING.
THE PORK FUND?
I HEARD THAT THIS TIME THEY'RE MAKING SAUSAGE TOO.
PAYMENT IN COMMODITIES?
FOR REAL!?
WHO DO WE TALK TO?
WHOA, WHOA, WHOA, WHOA! THIS IS BLOWING UP!!
HOLY COWWWW...
THIS IS WAY MORE THAN 25...
1-D Eat Pork Club
......HUH? TOKIWA, YOU CAME UP WITH THE IDEA, BUT YOU'RE NOT JOINING IN?
GOT NO MONEY.
1-D Eat Pork Club

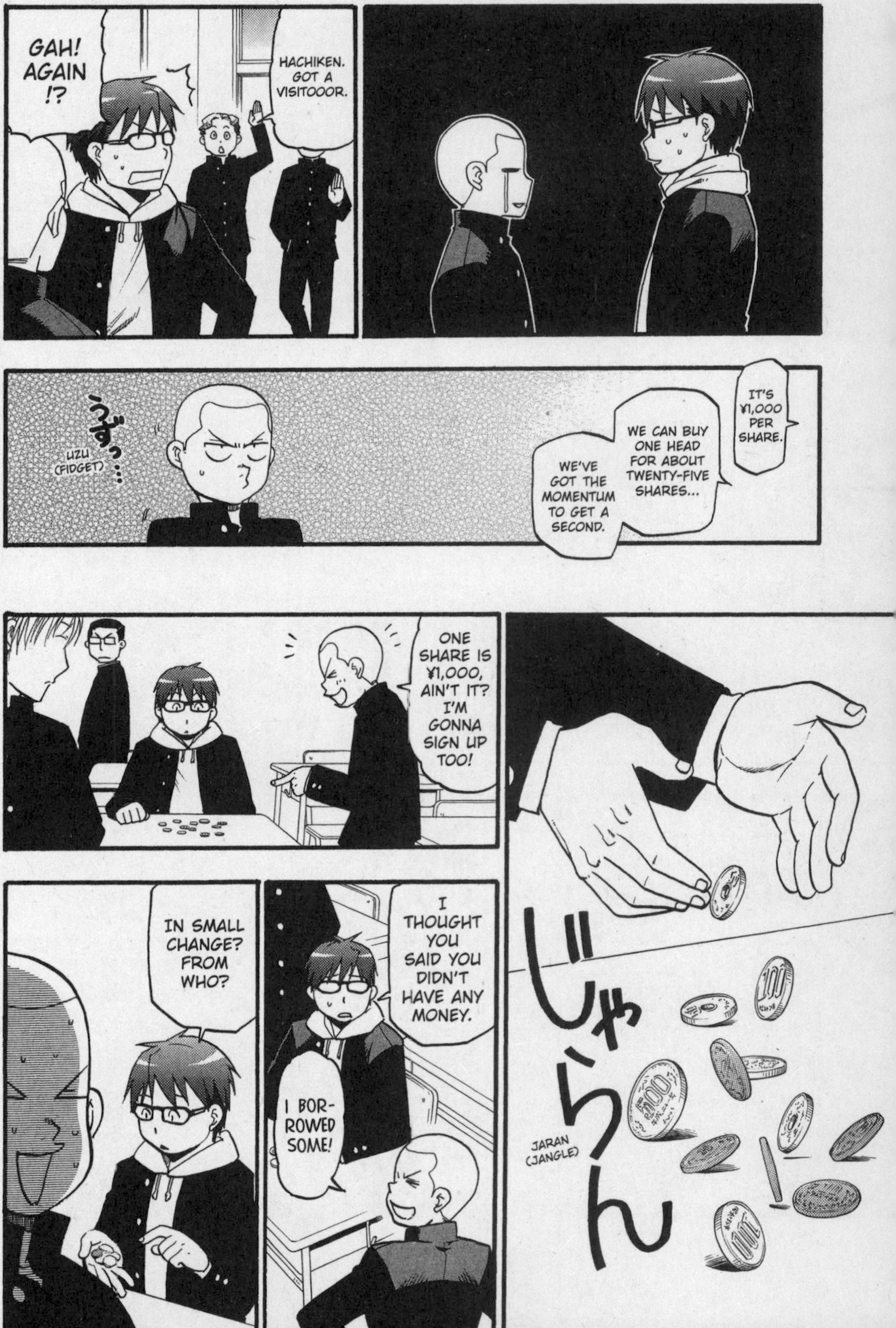
HACHIKEN. GOT A VISITOOOR.
GAH! AGAIN !?
IT'S ¥1,000 PER SHARE.
WE CAN BUY ONE HEAD FOR ABOUT TWENTY-FIVE SHARES...
WE'VE GOT THE MOMENTUM TO GET A SECOND.
うずっ…
UZU (FIDGET)
じゃらん
JARAN (JANGLE)
ONE SHARE IS ¥1,000, AIN'T IT? I'M GONNA SIGN UP TOO!
I THOUGHT YOU SAID YOU DIDN'T HAVE ANY MONEY.
I BOR-ROWED SOME!
IN SMALL CHANGE? FROM WHO?

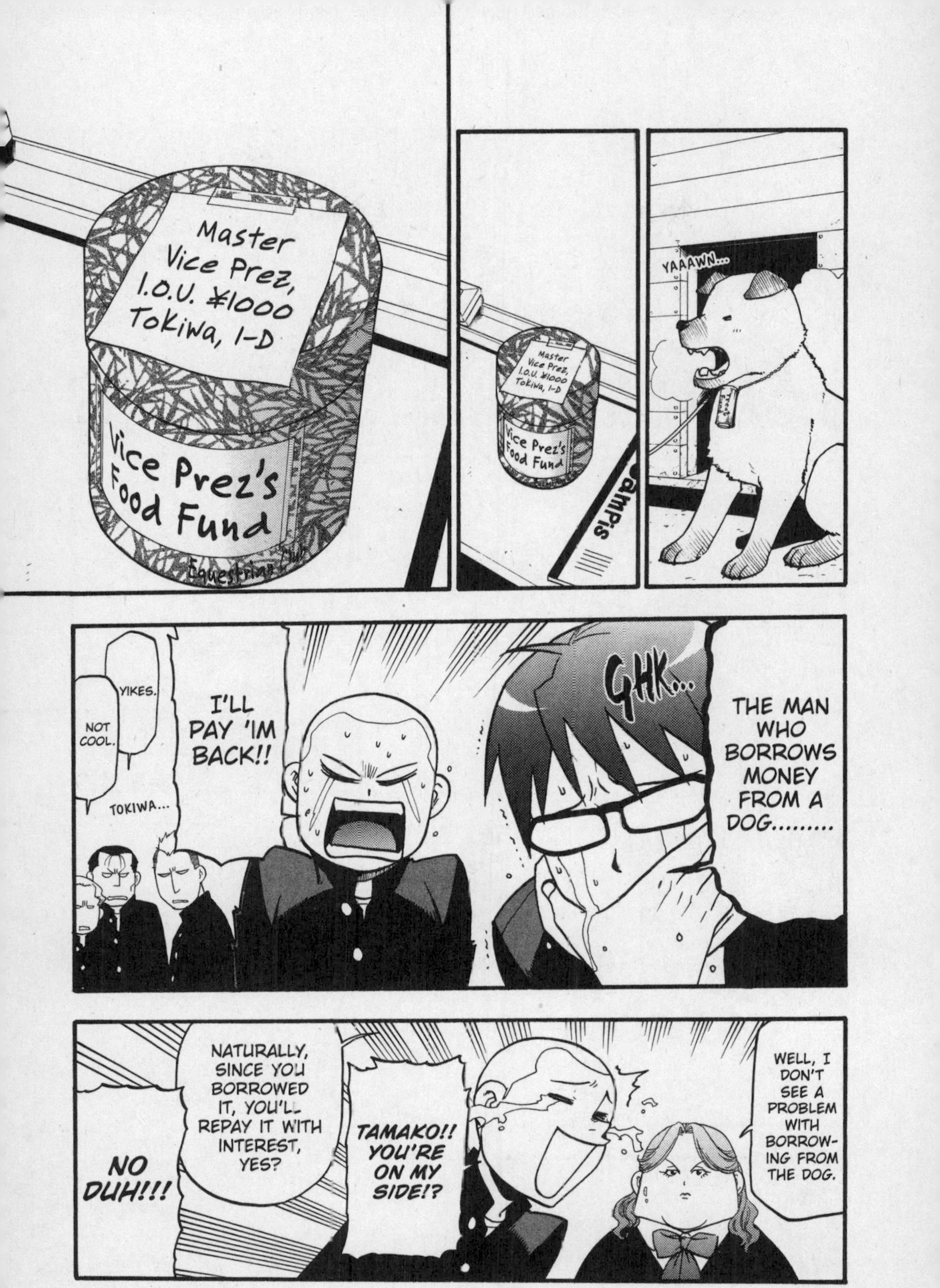
YAAAWN...
Master Vice Prez, I.O.U. ¥1000 Tokiwa, 1-D
Vice Prez's Food Fund
Master Vice Prez, I.O.U. ¥1000 Tokiwa, 1-D
Vice Prez's Food Fund
Equestrian Club
THE MAN WHO BORROWS MONEY FROM A DOG.........
GHK...
I'LL PAY 'IM BACK!!
TOKIWA...
YIKES.
NOT COOL.
WELL, I DON'T SEE A PROBLEM WITH BORROWING FROM THE DOG.
TAMAKO!! YOU'RE ON MY SIDE!?
NATURALLY, SINCE YOU BORROWED IT, YOU'LL REPAY IT WITH INTEREST, YES?
NO DUH!!!

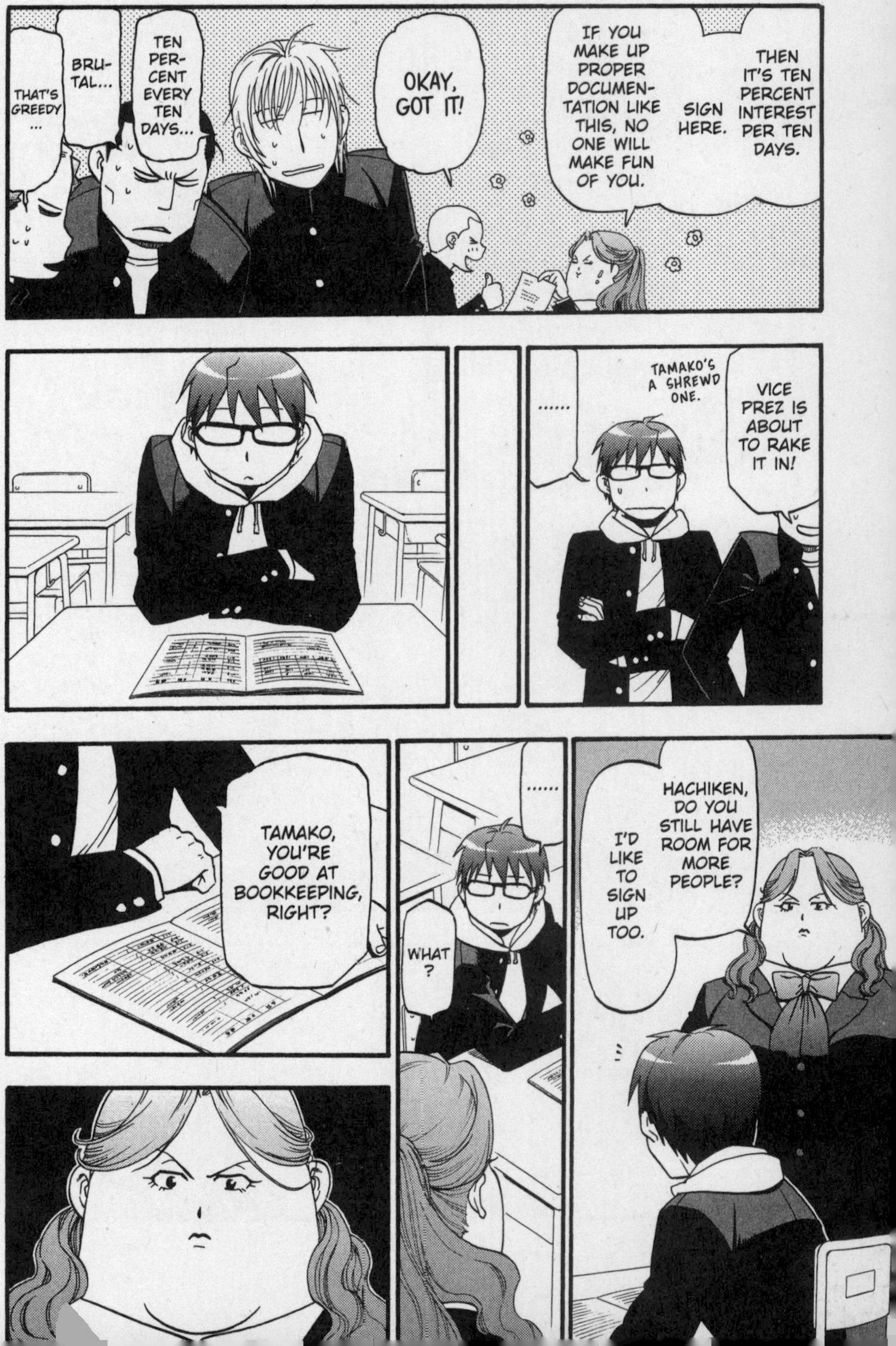
THEN IT'S TEN PERCENT INTEREST PER TEN DAYS.
SIGN HERE.
IF YOU MAKE UP PROPER DOCUMENTATION LIKE THIS, NO ONE WILL MAKE FUN OF YOU.
OKAY, GOT IT!
TEN PER-CENT EVERY TEN DAYS...
BRU-TAL...
THAT'S GREEDY...
VICE PREZ IS ABOUT TO RAKE IT IN!
TAMAKO'S A SHREWD ONE.
......
HACHIKEN, DO YOU STILL HAVE ROOM FOR MORE PEOPLE?
I'D LIKE TO SIGN UP TOO.
......
WHAT?
TAMAKO, YOU'RE GOOD AT BOOKKEEPING, RIGHT?

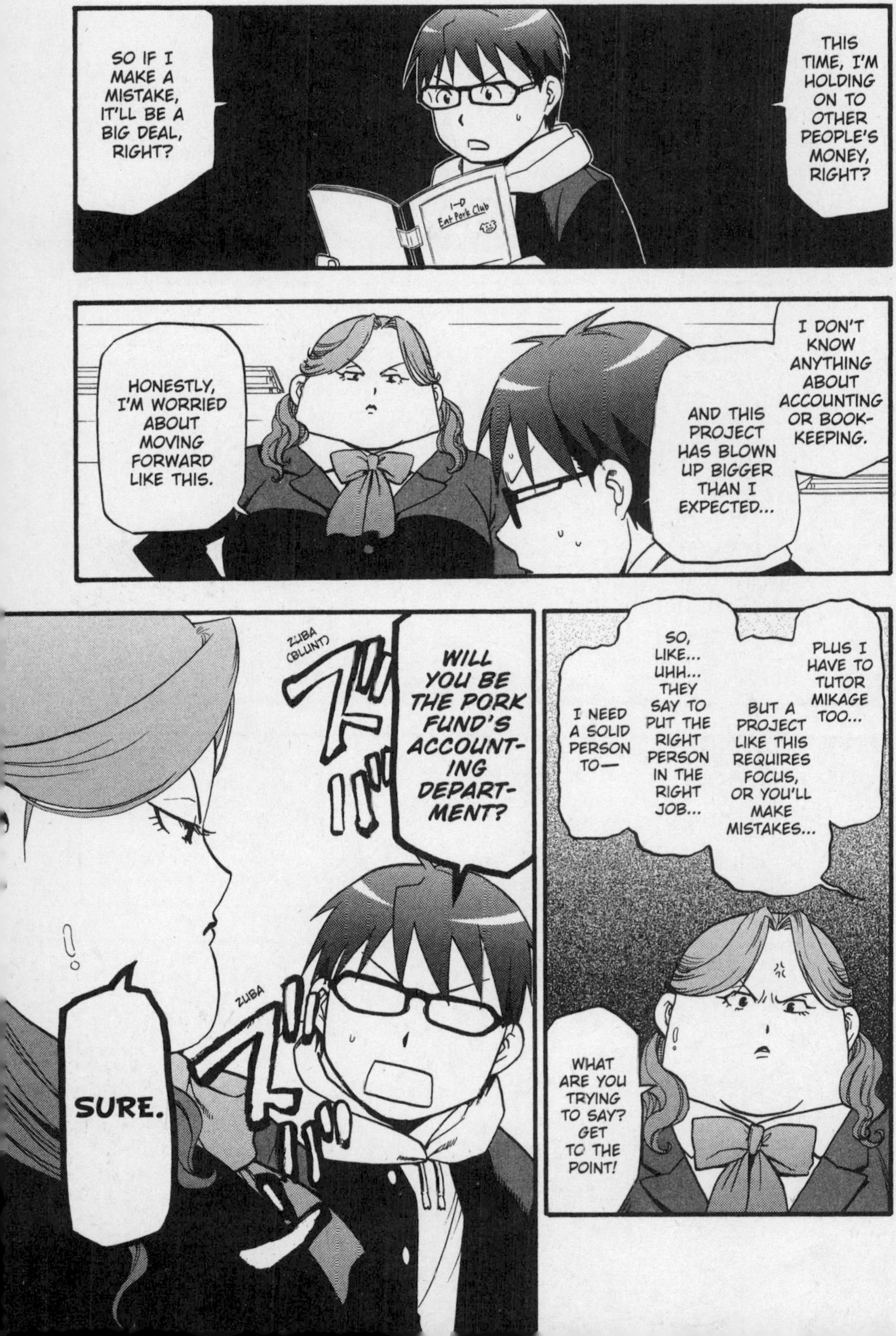
THIS TIME, I'M HOLDING ON TO OTHER PEOPLE'S MONEY, RIGHT?
SO IF I MAKE A MISTAKE, IT'LL BE A BIG DEAL, RIGHT?
I-D Eat Pork Club
I DON'T KNOW ANYTHING ABOUT ACCOUNTING OR BOOK-KEEPING.
AND THIS PROJECT HAS BLOWN UP BIGGER THAN I EXPECTED...
HONESTLY, I'M WORRIED ABOUT MOVING FORWARD LIKE THIS.
PLUS I HAVE TO TUTOR MIKAGE TOO...
BUT A PROJECT LIKE THIS REQUIRES FOCUS, OR YOU'LL MAKE MISTAKES...
SO, LIKE... UHH... THEY SAY TO PUT THE RIGHT PERSON IN THE RIGHT JOB...
I NEED A SOLID PERSON TO—
WHAT ARE YOU TRYING TO SAY? GET TO THE POINT!
ZUBA (BLUNT)
WILL YOU BE THE PORK FUND'S ACCOUNT-ING DEPART-MENT?
ZUBA
SURE.

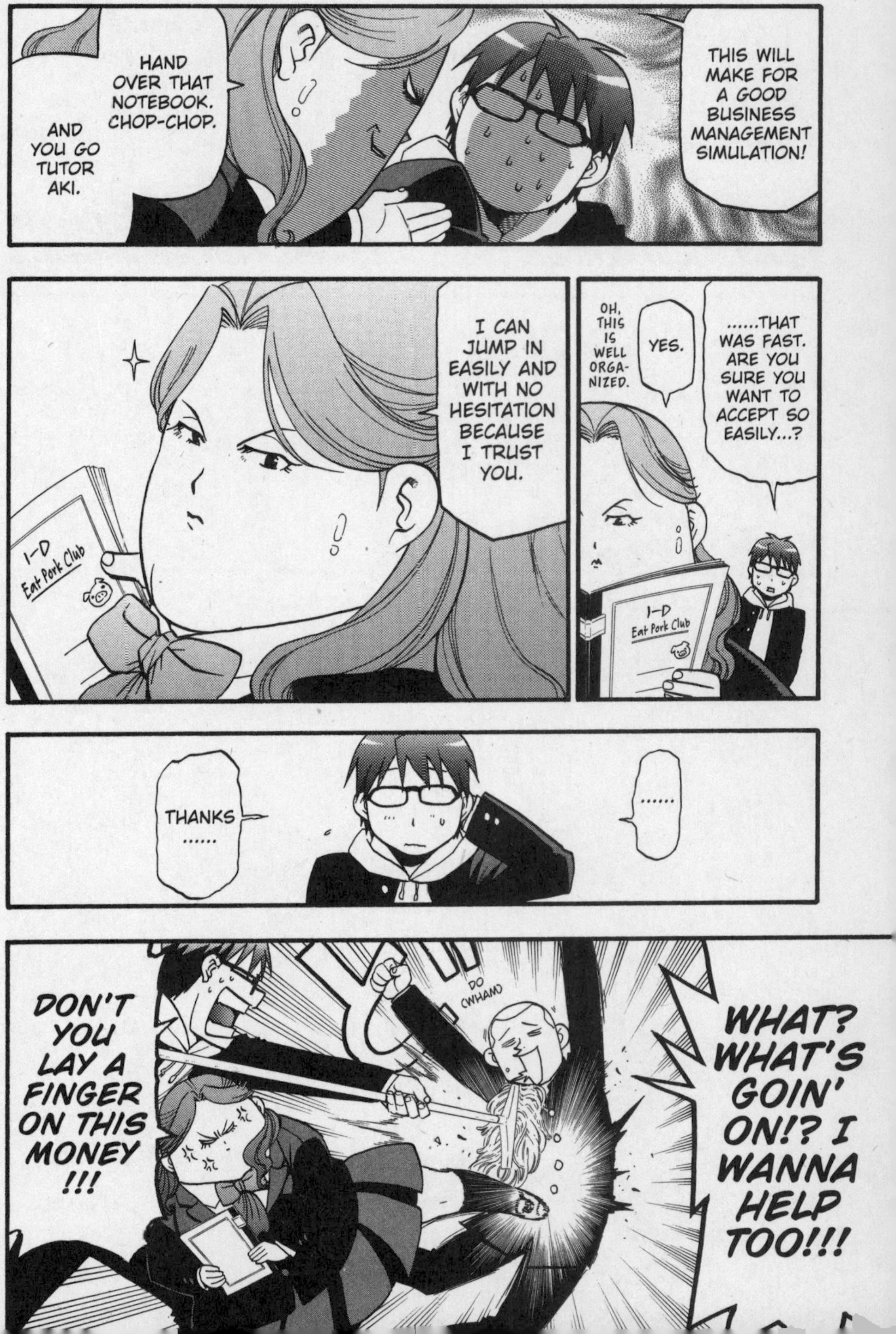
THIS WILL MAKE FOR A GOOD BUSINESS MANAGEMENT SIMULATION!
HAND OVER THAT NOTEBOOK. CHOP-CHOP.
AND YOU GO TUTOR AKI.
......THAT WAS FAST. ARE YOU SURE YOU WANT TO ACCEPT SO EASILY...?
YES.
OH, THIS IS WELL ORGA-NIZED.
I-D Eat Pork Club
I CAN JUMP IN EASILY AND WITH NO HESITATION BECAUSE I TRUST YOU.
I-D Eat Pork Club
......
THANKS ......
WHAT? WHAT'S GOIN' ON!? I WANNA HELP TOO!!!
DO (WHAM)
DON'T YOU LAY A FINGER ON THIS MONEY!!!

Silver Spoon

HACHIKEN'S FATHER

HIS ANCESTORS
WERE MILITARY
SETTLER COLONISTS.

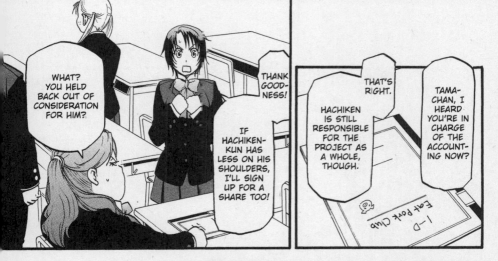

TAMA-CHAN, I HEARD YOU'RE IN CHARGE OF THE ACCOUNTING NOW?
THAT'S RIGHT.
HACHIKEN IS STILL RESPONSIBLE FOR THE PROJECT AS A WHOLE, THOUGH.
I-D Eat Pork Club
THANK GOODNESS!
IF HACHIKEN-KUN HAS LESS ON HIS SHOULDERS, I'LL SIGN UP FOR A SHARE TOO!
WHAT? YOU HELD BACK OUT OF CONSIDERATION FOR HIM?
HACHIKEN'S LIGHTENED HIS LOAD?
IF YOU'RE THE ACCOUNTANT, INADA-SAN, THEN I'LL SIGN UP TOO!
ME TOO, THEN.
IS THAT TRUE, TAMAKO?
WHAT IS WITH YOU PEOPLE!? YOU WERE HOLDING BACK THAT MUCH FOR HACHIKEN!?
ME TOO.
ME TOO!
WELL, THAT'S PART OF IT, BUT ALSO...
...BECAUSE YOU SEEM LIKE YOU'D MANAGE OUR MONEY TO A DEVIOUSLY PERFECT DEGREE!
IT FEELS SUPER SAFE!!
I'M FLATTERED.
¥1,000 IS A LOT OF MONEY!!

Chapter 77:
Tale of Winter ⑭

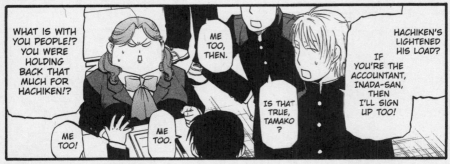

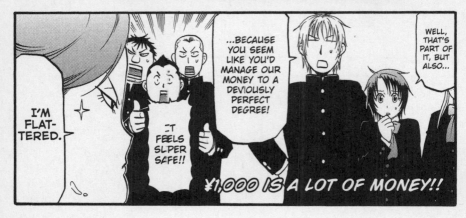

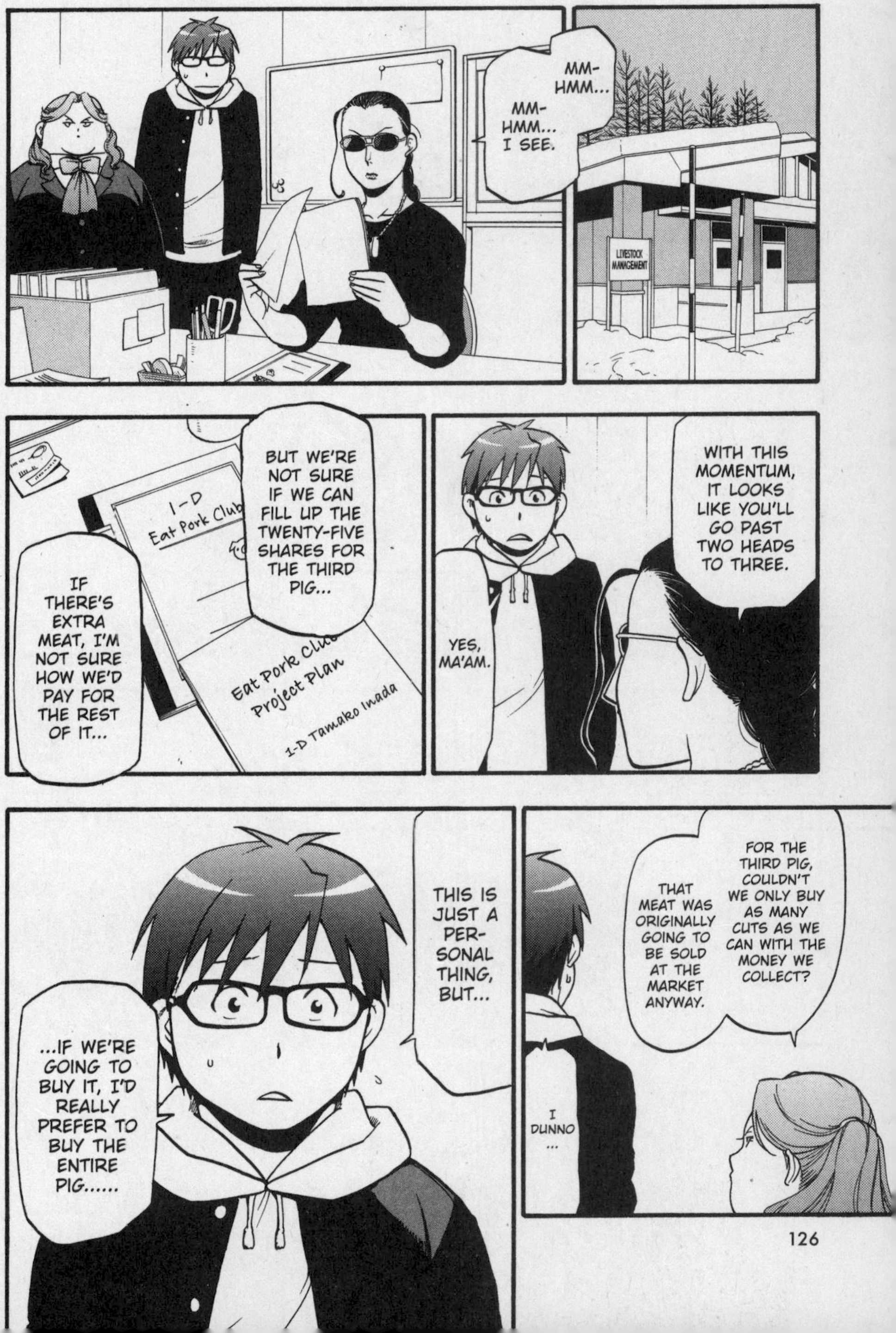
LIVESTOCK MANAGEMENT
MM-HMM... MM-HMM... I SEE.
WITH THIS MOMENTUM, IT LOOKS LIKE YOU'LL GO PAST TWO HEADS TO THREE.
YES, MA'AM.
BUT WE'RE NOT SURE IF WE CAN FILL UP THE TWENTY-FIVE SHARES FOR THE THIRD PIG...
IF THERE'S EXTRA MEAT, I'M NOT SURE HOW WE'D PAY FOR THE REST OF IT...
1-D
Eat Pork Club
Project Plan
1-D Tamako Inada
FOR THE THIRD PIG, COULDN'T WE ONLY BUY AS MANY CUTS AS WE CAN WITH THE MONEY WE COLLECT?
THAT MEAT WAS ORIGINALLY GOING TO BE SOLD AT THE MARKET ANYWAY.
I DUNNO...
THIS IS JUST A PER-SONAL THING, BUT...
...IF WE'RE GOING TO BUY IT, I'D REALLY PREFER TO BUY THE ENTIRE PIG......

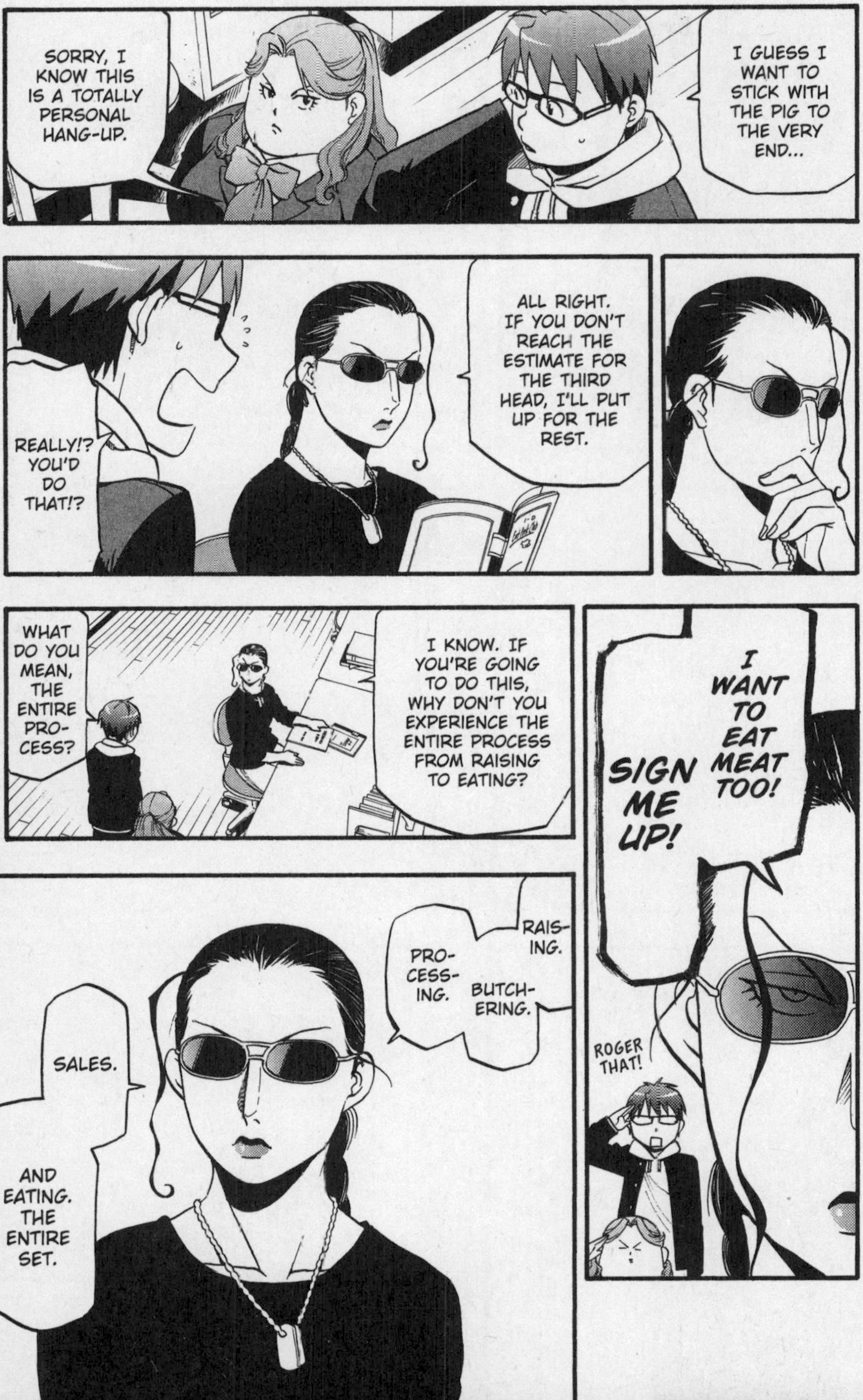
I GUESS I WANT TO STICK WITH THE PIG TO THE VERY END...
SORRY, I KNOW THIS IS A TOTALLY PERSONAL HANG-UP.
ALL RIGHT. IF YOU DON'T REACH THE ESTIMATE FOR THE THIRD HEAD, I'LL PUT UP FOR THE REST.
REALLY!? YOU'D DO THAT!?
I WANT TO EAT MEAT TOO!
SIGN ME UP!
ROGER THAT!
I KNOW. IF YOU'RE GOING TO DO THIS, WHY DON'T YOU EXPERIENCE THE ENTIRE PROCESS FROM RAISING TO EATING?
WHAT DO YOU MEAN, THE ENTIRE PRO-CESS?
RAIS-ING.
BUTCH-ERING.
PRO-CESS-ING.
SALES.
AND EATING. THE ENTIRE SET.

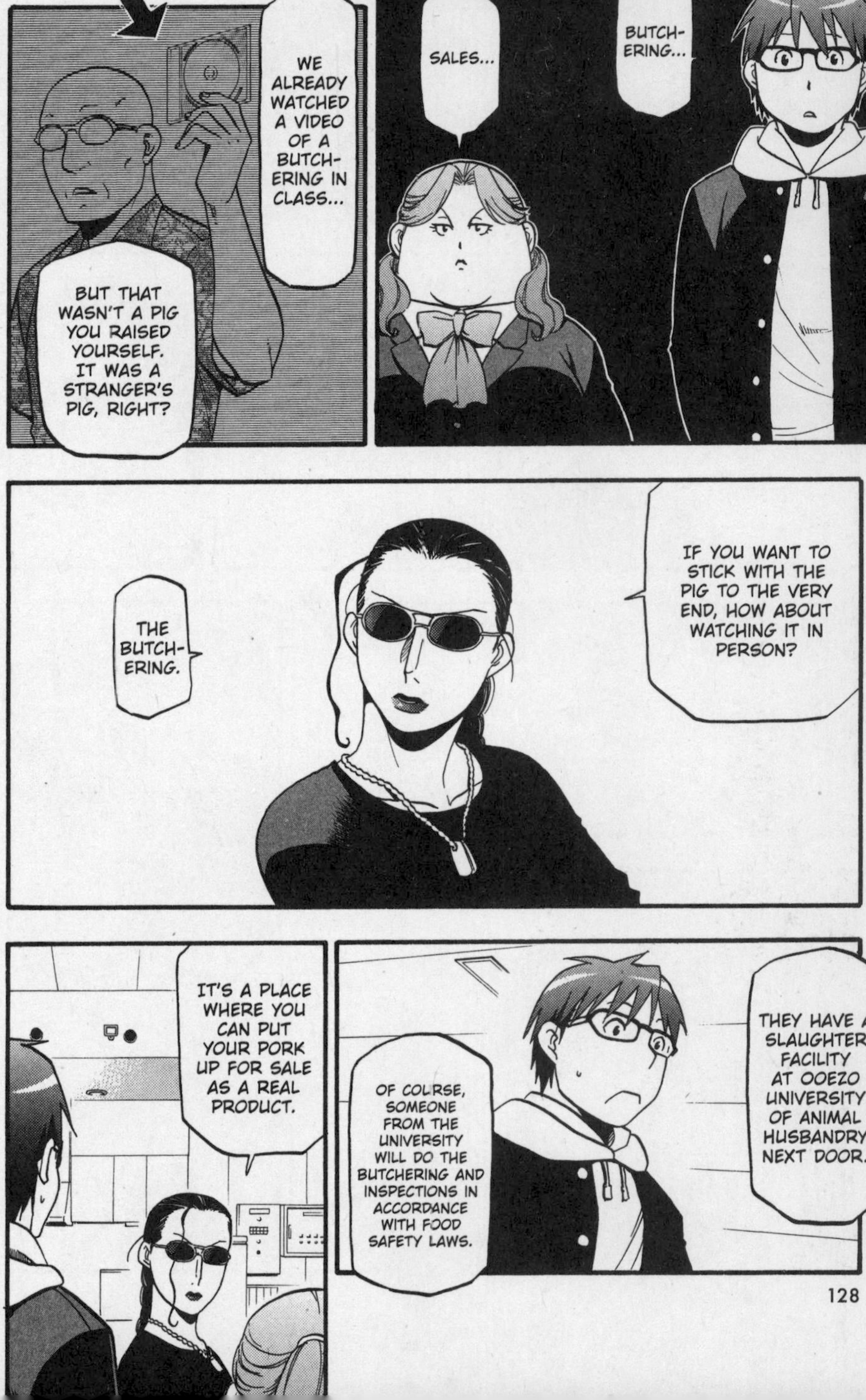
BUTCHERING...
SALES...
WE ALREADY WATCHED A VIDEO OF A BUTCHERING IN CLASS...
BUT THAT WASN'T A PIG YOU RAISED YOURSELF. IT WAS A STRANGER'S PIG, RIGHT?
IF YOU WANT TO STICK WITH THE PIG TO THE VERY END, HOW ABOUT WATCHING IT IN PERSON?
THE BUTCHERING.
THEY HAVE A SLAUGHTER FACILITY AT OOEZO UNIVERSITY OF ANIMAL HUSBANDRY NEXT DOOR.
OF COURSE, SOMEONE FROM THE UNIVERSITY WILL DO THE BUTCHERING AND INSPECTIONS IN ACCORDANCE WITH FOOD SAFETY LAWS.
IT'S A PLACE WHERE YOU CAN PUT YOUR PORK UP FOR SALE AS A REAL PRODUCT.

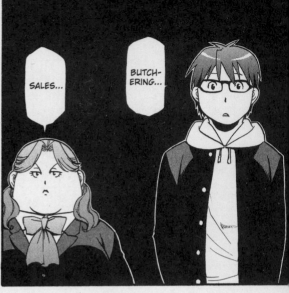

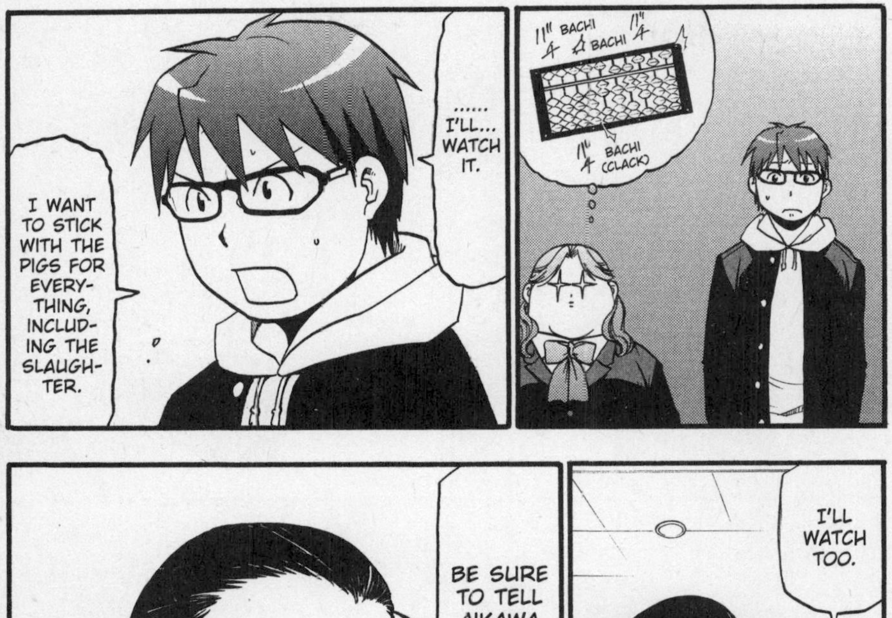
BACHI
BACHI
BACHI (CLACK)
......I'LL... WATCH IT.
I WANT TO STICK WITH THE PIGS FOR EVERYTHING, INCLUDING THE SLAUGHTER.
I'LL WATCH TOO.
ALL RIGHT. FIND OUT WHO ELSE FROM YOUR PORK FUND WANTS TO PARTICIPATE IN THIS FIELD TRIP.
BE SURE TO TELL AIKAWA TOO.

SIGN: OOEZO AGRICULTURAL HIGH SCHOOL STUDENT DORMS

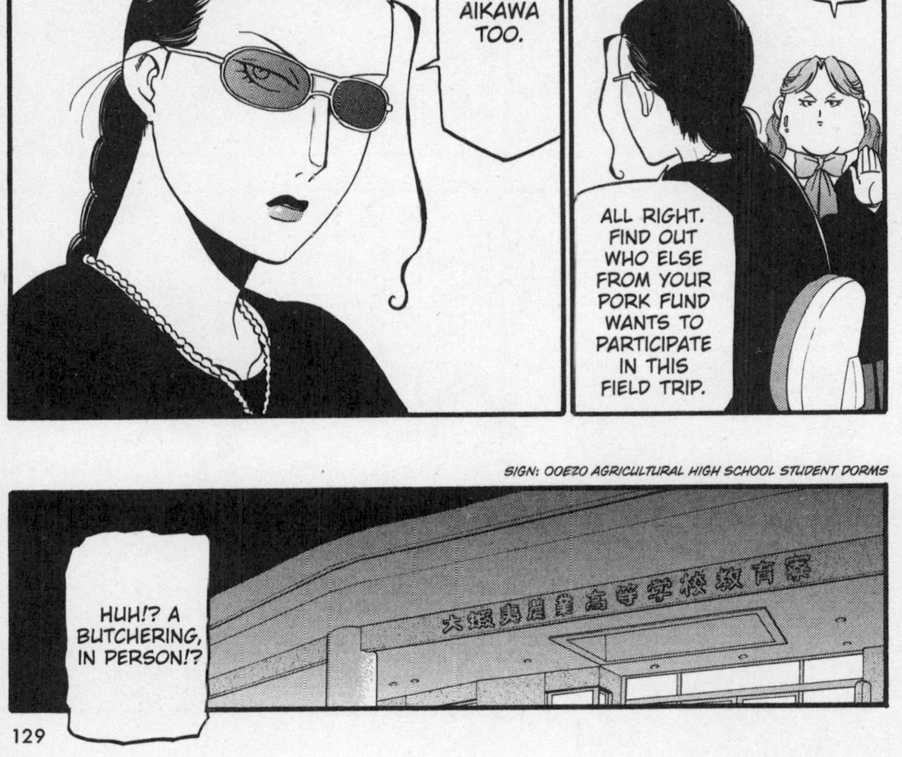
HUH!? A BUTCHERING, IN PERSON!?

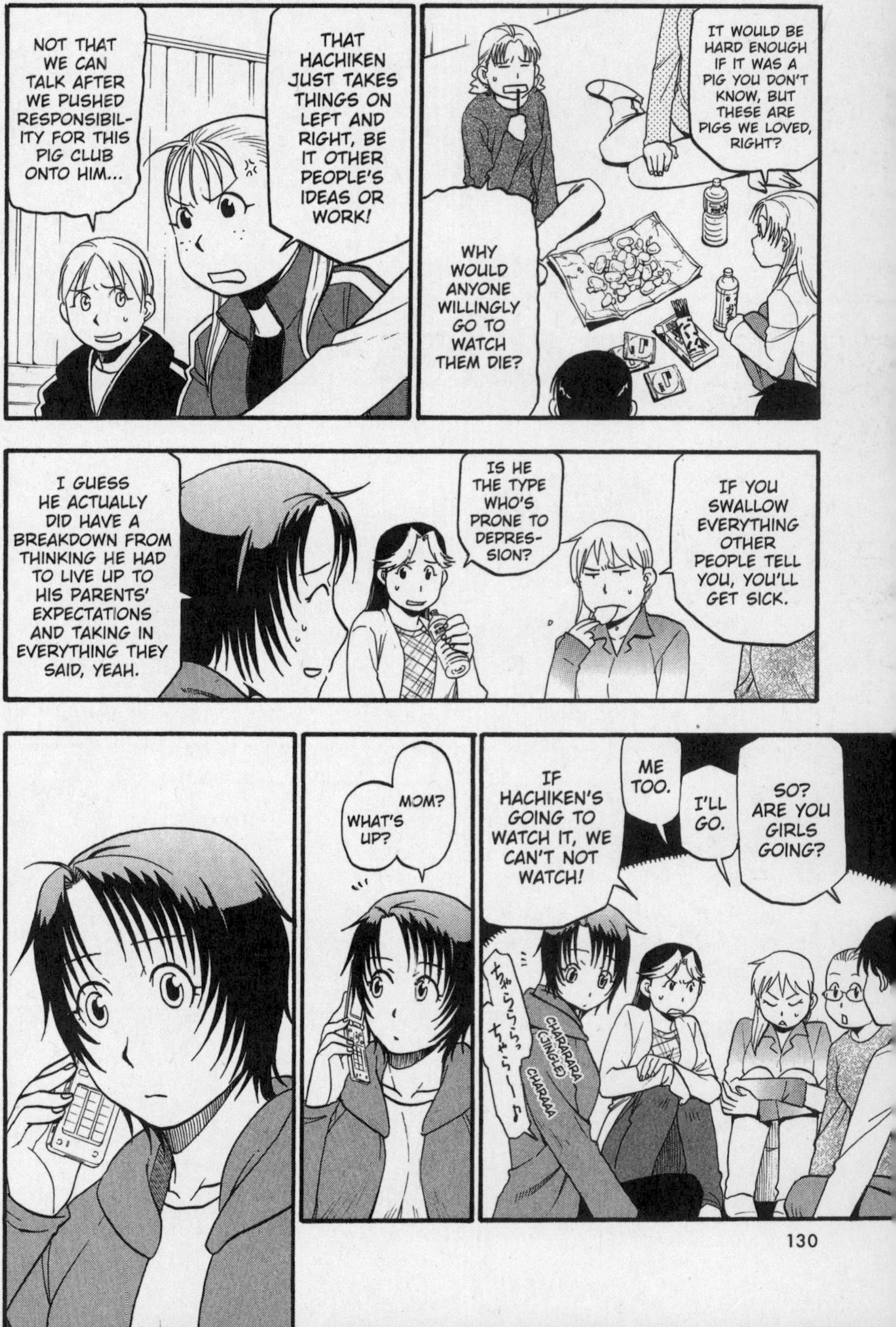
IT WOULD BE HARD ENOUGH IF IT WAS A PIG YOU DON'T KNOW, BUT THESE ARE PIGS WE LOVED, RIGHT?
WHY WOULD ANYONE WILLINGLY GO TO WATCH THEM DIE?
THAT HACHIKEN JUST TAKES THINGS ON LEFT AND RIGHT, BE IT OTHER PEOPLE'S IDEAS OR WORK!
NOT THAT WE CAN TALK AFTER WE PUSHED RESPONSIBILITY FOR THIS PIG CLUB ONTO HIM...
IF YOU SWALLOW EVERYTHING OTHER PEOPLE TELL YOU, YOU'LL GET SICK.
IS HE THE TYPE WHO'S PRONE TO DEPRESSION?
I GUESS HE ACTUALLY DID HAVE A BREAKDOWN FROM THINKING HE HAD TO LIVE UP TO HIS PARENTS' EXPECTATIONS AND TAKING IN EVERYTHING THEY SAID, YEAH.
SO? ARE YOU GIRLS GOING?
I'LL GO.
ME TOO.
IF HACHIKEN'S GOING TO WATCH IT, WE CAN'T NOT WATCH!
CHARARARA (JINGLE) CHARAAA
MOM? WHAT'S UP?

...COWS, HORSES, PIGS, SHEEP, AND GOATS... ARE TREATED SO THEY CAN BE OFFERED FOR CONSUMPTION.

THIS IS WHERE "LIVE-STOCK"...

SANITIZA-TION IS STRICTLY MANAGED BASED ON SLAUGH-TERHOUSE LAWS.

WE ASK THAT YOU ALSO BE CONSIDERATE OF THE FREQUENT SANITIZATION, AND THE SAFETY OF THE WORKERS.

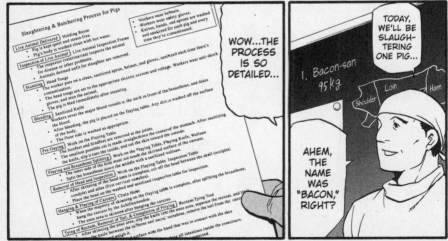

Slaughtering & Butchering Process for Pigs

Live Animal Delivered | Holding Room
· Pig is kept quiet and stress-free.
· Pig's body is washed clean with hot water.

Inspection of Live Animal | Live Animal Inspection Frame
· The inspector (veterinarian) inspects the animal for disease or other problems.
· Animals deemed unfit for slaughter are removed.

Stunning | Head Tongs
· The worker puts on a clean, sanitized apron, helmet, and gloves, sanitized each time there's contamination.
· The head tongs are set to the appropriate electric current and voltage. Workers wear anti-shock gloves, and stun the animal.
· The pig is bled immediately after stunning.

Bleeding | Sanitized Knife
· Workers sever the major blood vessels at the neck in front of the breastbone, and drain the blood.
· After bleeding, the pig is placed on the flaying table. Any dirt is washed off the surface of the body.
· The floor side is washed as appropriate.

Pre-flaying | Work on the Flaying Table
· The forefeet and hindfeet are removed at the joints.
· The smallest possible cut is made straight down the center of the stomach. After sanitizing the knife, slip it into the inside, and cut the skin toward the outside.

Flaying and Breastbone Splitting | Work on the Flaying Table. Flaying Knife. Wellsaw
· The outer side of the hide must not touch the skinned surface of the carcass.
· Split the breastbone down the middle with a sanitized Flaying Table Inspection Table

Removal of Head and Inspection | Work on the Flaying Table Inspection Table
· After skinning of the head area is complete, cut off the head between the skull (occipital condyle) and atlas (first cervical vertebra).
· Place the head on the washed and sanitized inspection table for inspection.

Hanging & Flaying of Carcass | Chain Hoist
· When the majority of skinning on the flaying table is complete, after splitting the breastbone, hang the carcass by the Achilles tendon.

Tying of Rectum, Removal of Tail, & Completion of Flaying | Rectum-Tying Tool
· The anus area is skinned after banging the carcass.
· The anus area is skinned after banging the carcass, separate the rectum, and tie the knife between the tailbone and sacra, vertabrae, remove the tail from the carcass. After skinning the anus area, slip the knife into the anus area, remove the tail from the carcass.

· Workers wear helmets.
· Workers wear safety gloves.
· Knives, boards, and aprons are washed and sanitized for each pig and every time they're contaminated.

WOW...THE PROCESS IS SO DETAILED...

TODAY, WE'LL BE SLAUGH-TERING ONE PIG...

1. Bacon-san 95 kg

Shoulder   Loin   Ham

AHEM, THE NAME WAS "BACON," RIGHT?

131

CONSULTING: HOKKAIDO OBIHIRO AGRICULTURAL HIGH SCHOOL DAIRY SCIENCE PROGRAM LED BY HISASHI ORII

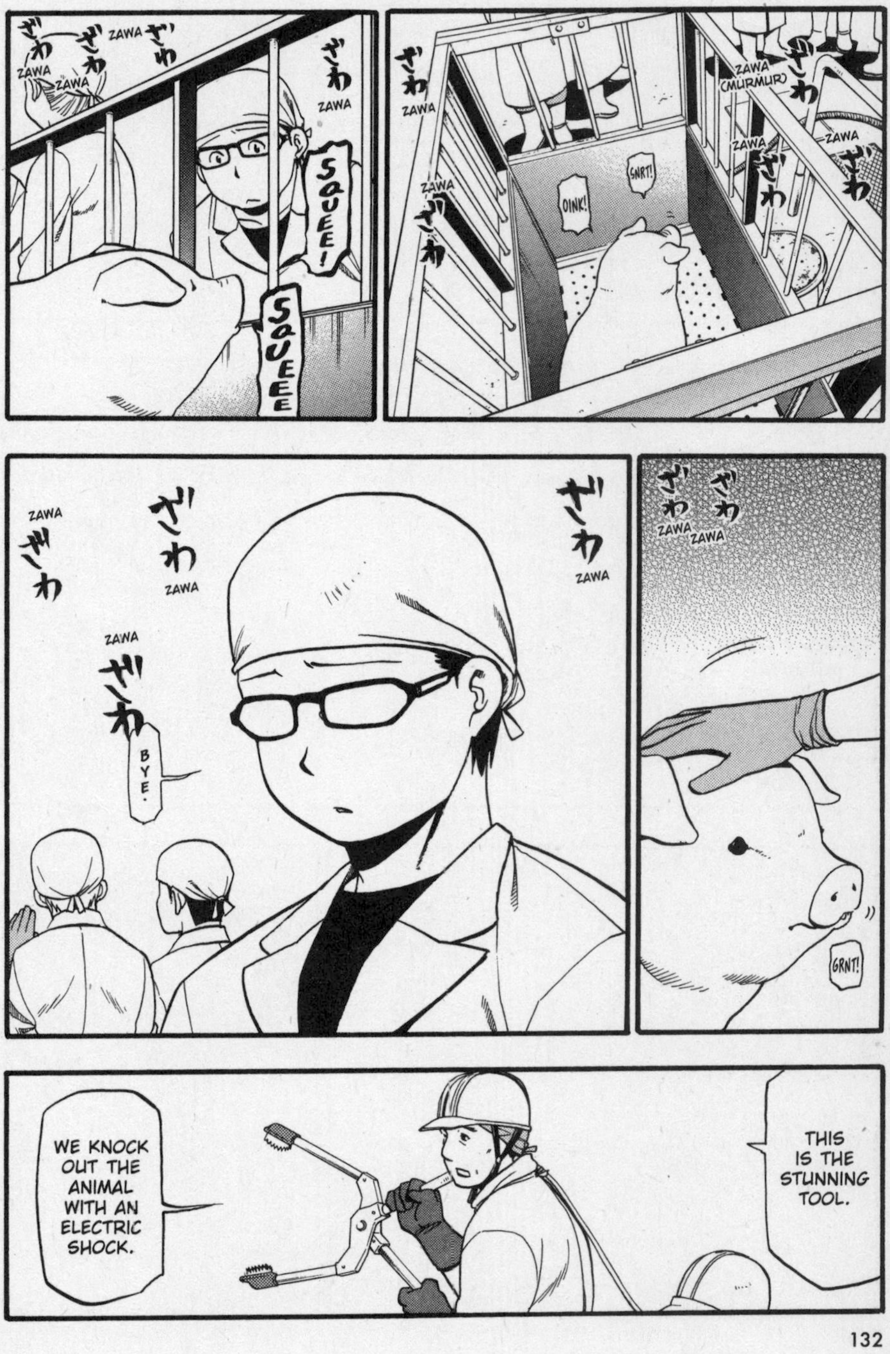
ZAWA (MURMUR) ざわ
ZAWA ざわ
ZAWA ざわ
SNRT!
OINK!
ざわ ZAWA
ZAWA ざわ
ざわ ZAWA
SQUEEE!
SQUEEE
ざわ ZAWA
ざわ ZAWA
ざわ ZAWA
ざわ ZAWA
ざわ ざわ ZAWA ZAWA
GRNT!
ざわ ZAWA
ざわ ZAWA
ZAWA ざわ
ZAWA ざわ
BYE.
THIS IS THE STUNNING TOOL.
WE KNOCK OUT THE ANIMAL WITH AN ELECTRIC SHOCK.

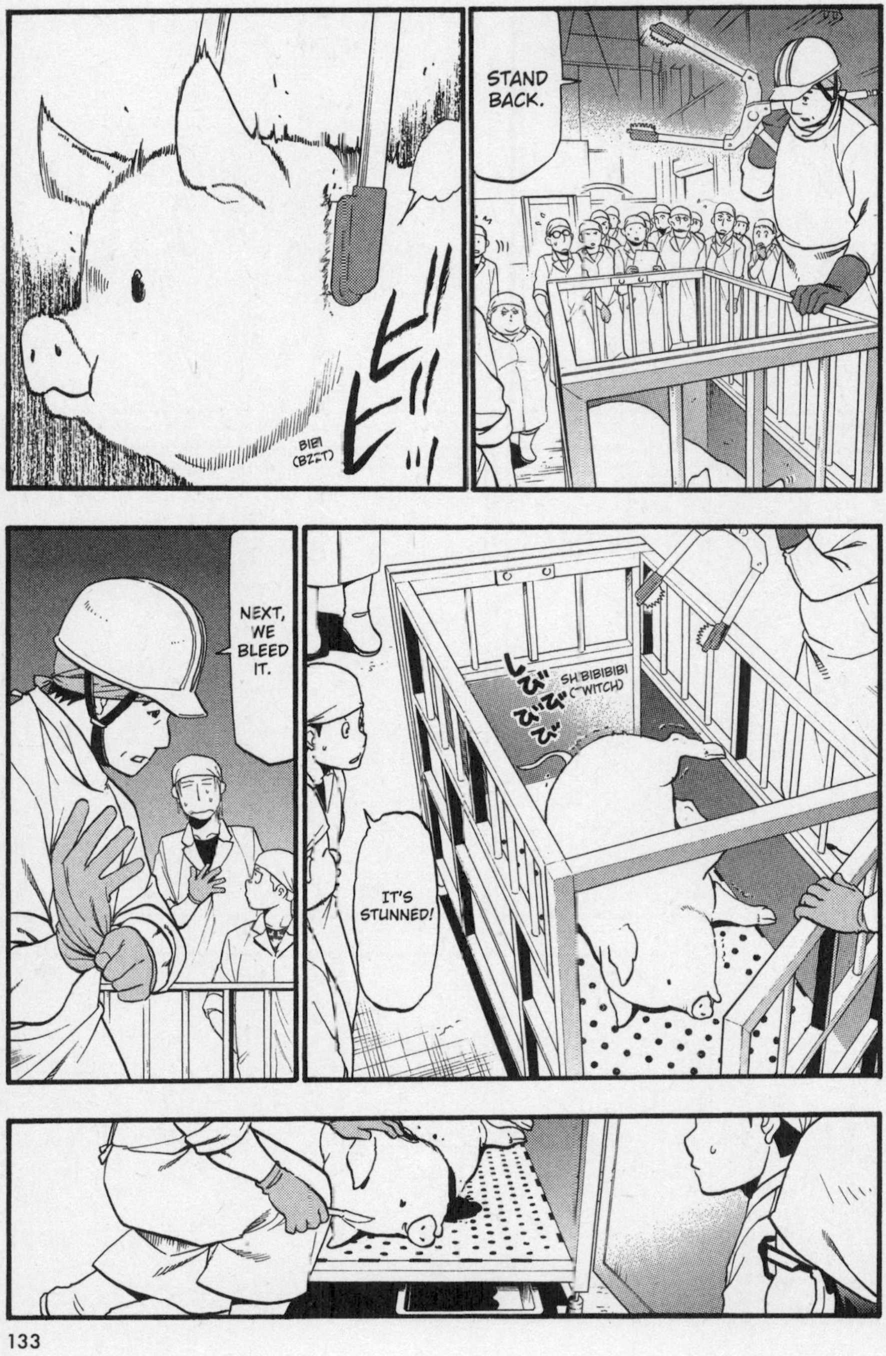
STAND BACK.
BIBI (BZZT)
SHIBIBIBI (TWITCH)
IT'S STUNNED!
NEXT, WE BLEED IT.

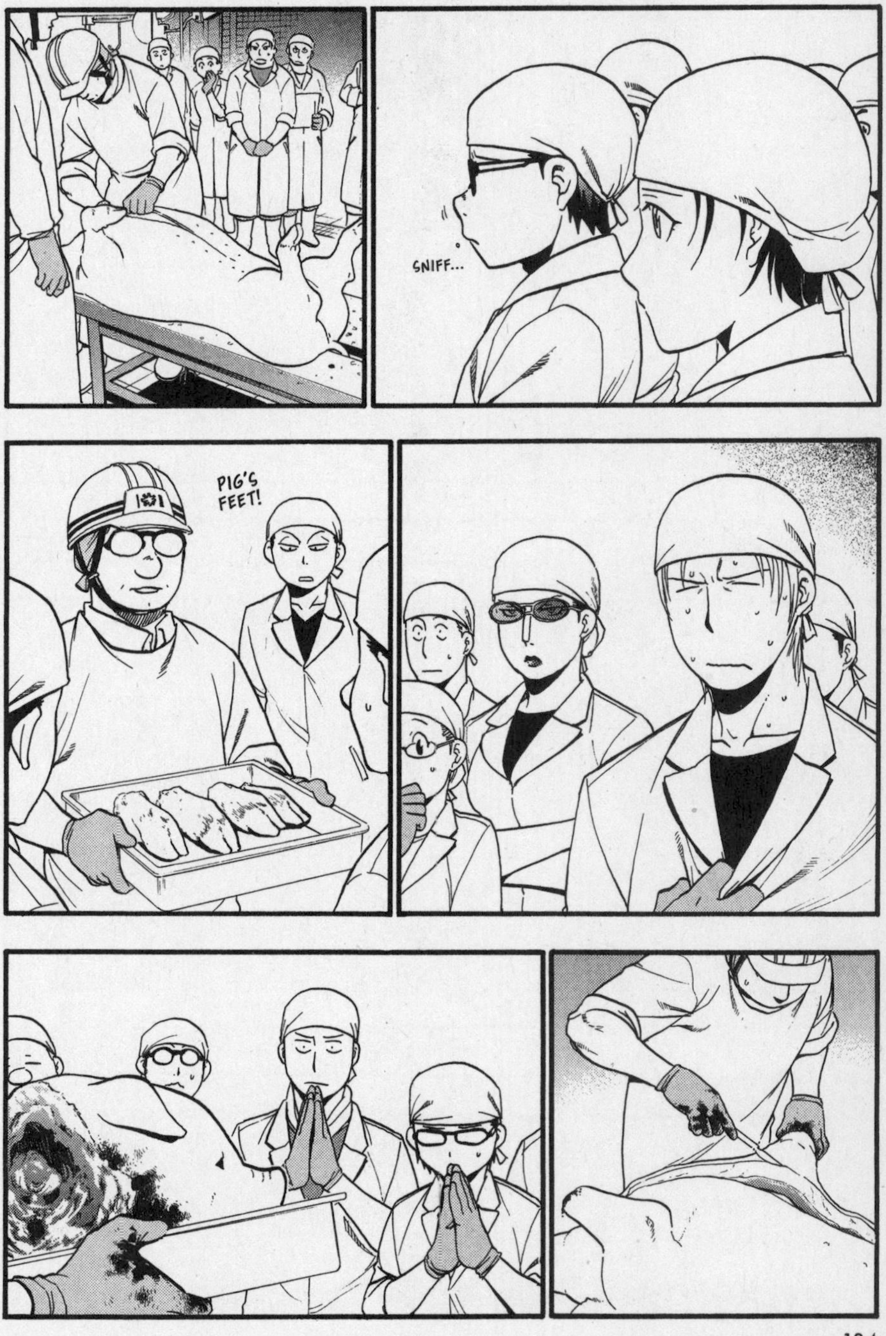
SNIFF...
PIG'S FEET!

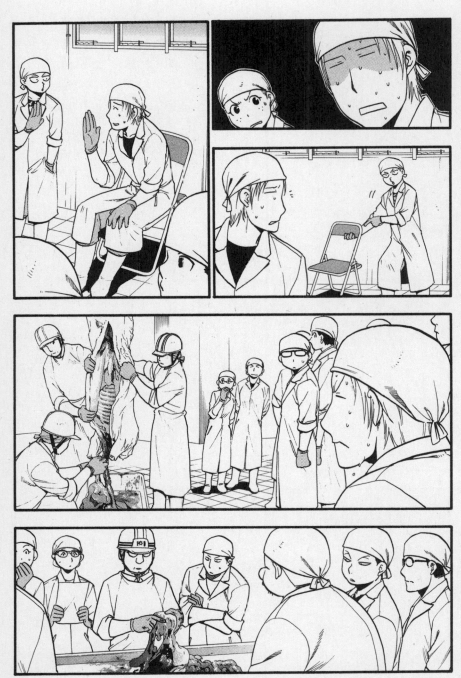

135

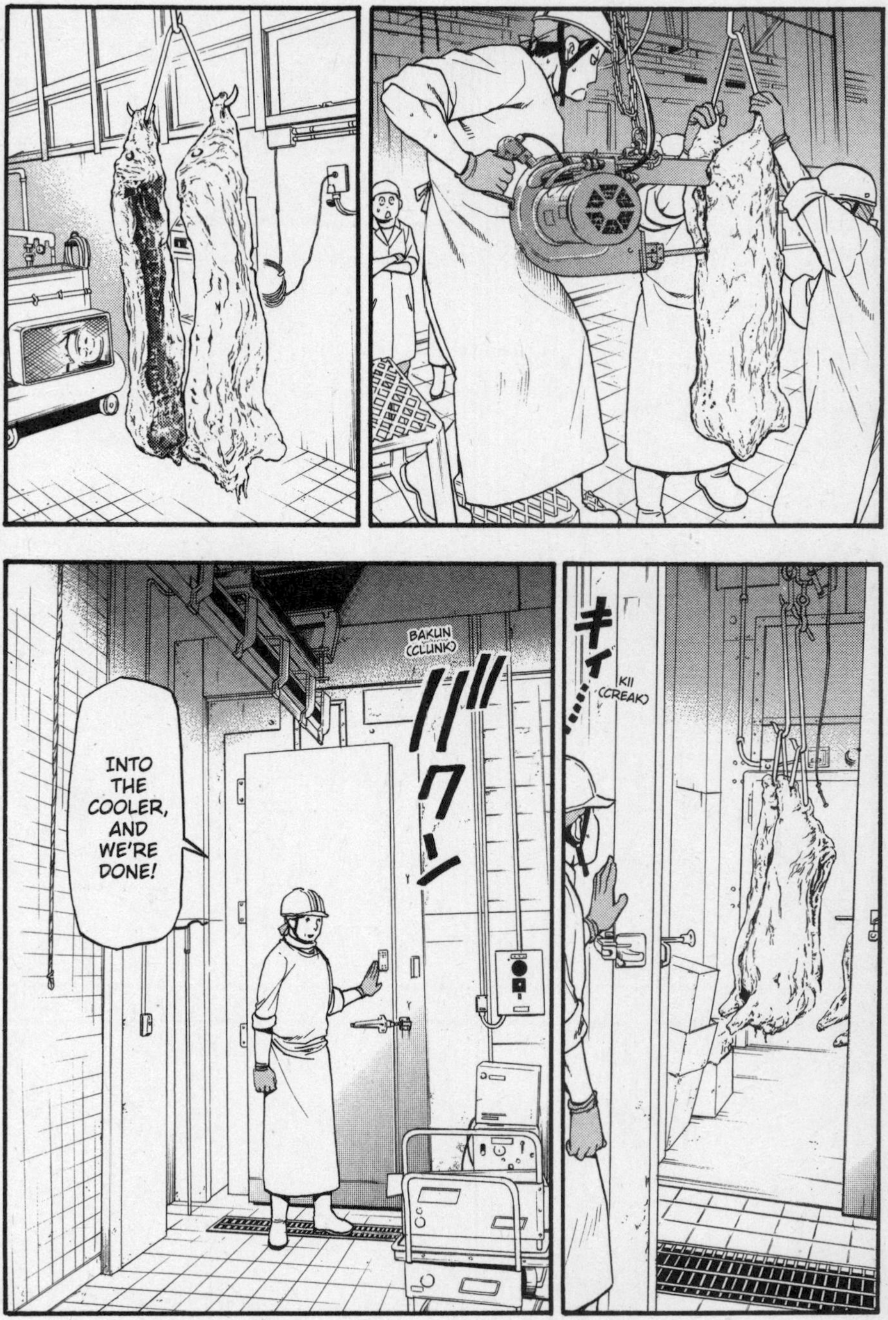
キィ…
KII (CREAK)
バクン
BAKUN (CLUNK)
INTO THE COOLER, AND WE'RE DONE!

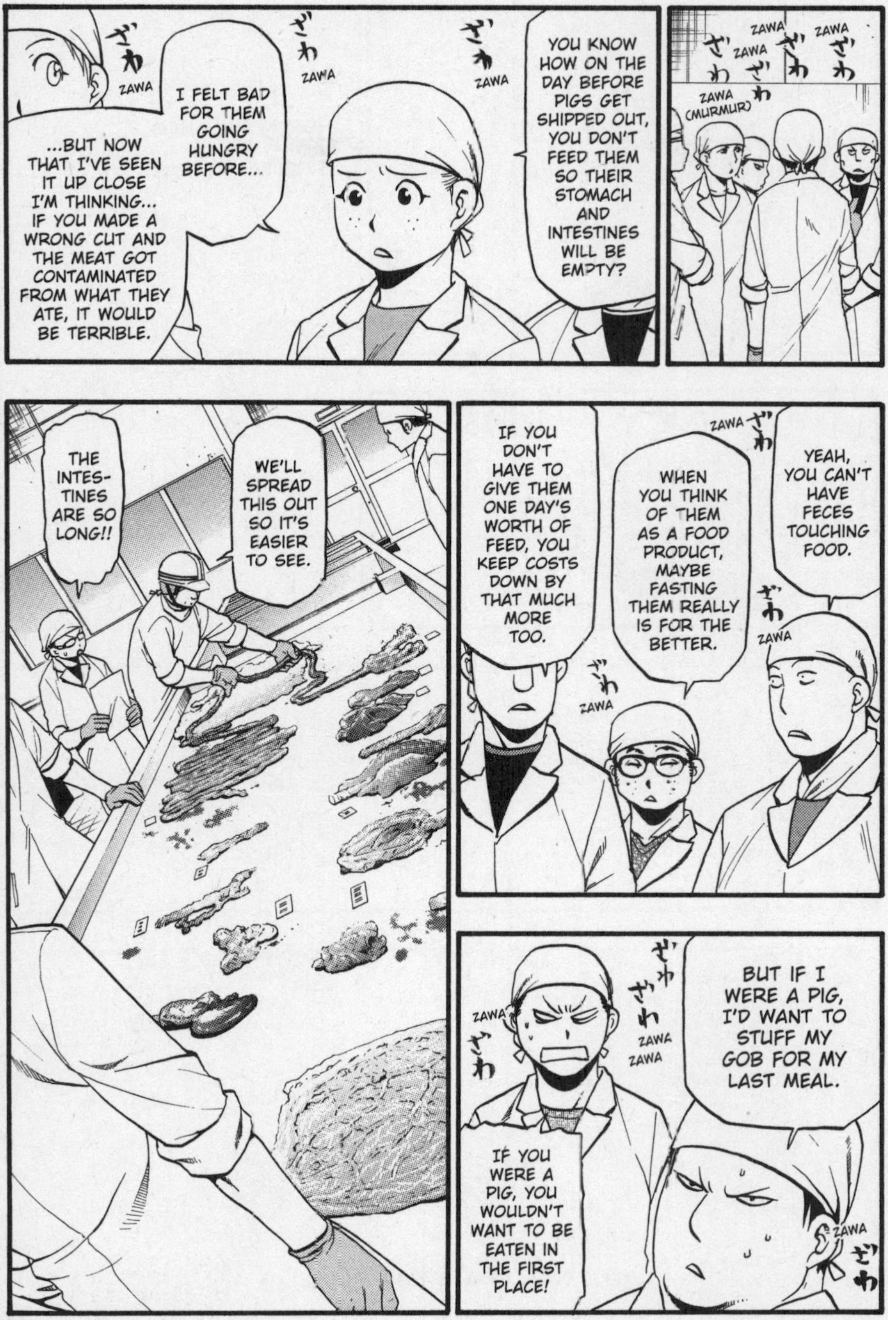

ZAWA
ZAWA
ZAWA
ZAWA (MURMUR)
YOU KNOW HOW ON THE DAY BEFORE PIGS GET SHIPPED OUT, YOU DON'T FEED THEM SO THEIR STOMACH AND INTESTINES WILL BE EMPTY?
ZAWA
ZAWA
I FELT BAD FOR THEM GOING HUNGRY BEFORE...
ZAWA
...BUT NOW THAT I'VE SEEN IT UP CLOSE I'M THINKING... IF YOU MADE A WRONG CUT AND THE MEAT GOT CONTAMINATED FROM WHAT THEY ATE, IT WOULD BE TERRIBLE.
ZAWA
YEAH, YOU CAN'T HAVE FECES TOUCHING FOOD.
ZAWA
WHEN YOU THINK OF THEM AS A FOOD PRODUCT, MAYBE FASTING THEM REALLY IS FOR THE BETTER.
ZAWA
IF YOU DON'T HAVE TO GIVE THEM ONE DAY'S WORTH OF FEED, YOU KEEP COSTS DOWN BY THAT MUCH MORE TOO.
BUT IF I WERE A PIG, I'D WANT TO STUFF MY GOB FOR MY LAST MEAL.
ZAWA
ZAWA
ZAWA
ZAWA
IF YOU WERE A PIG, YOU WOULDN'T WANT TO BE EATEN IN THE FIRST PLACE!
WE'LL SPREAD THIS OUT SO IT'S EASIER TO SEE.
THE INTES-TINES ARE SO LONG!!

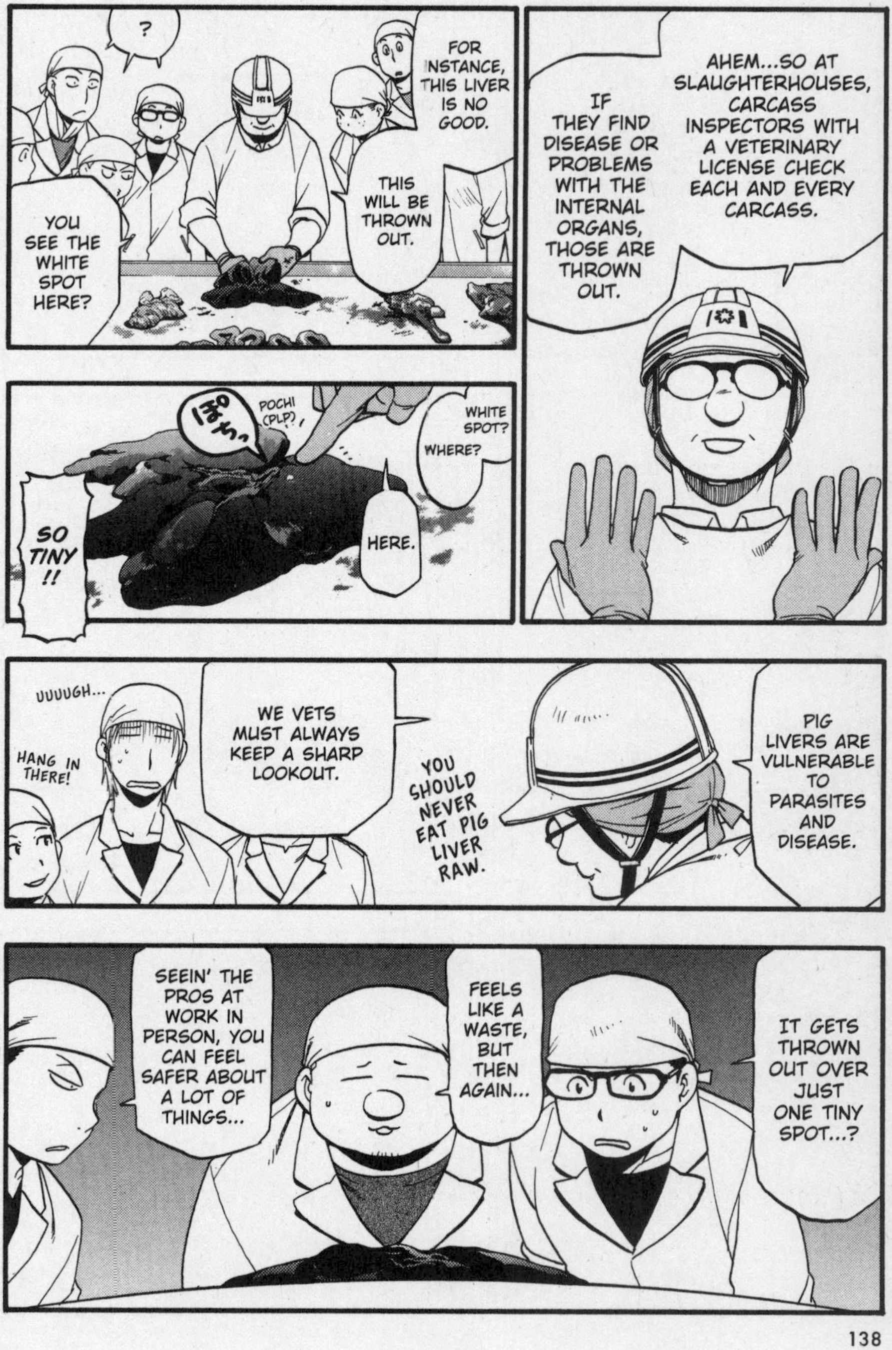
AHEM...SO AT SLAUGHTERHOUSES, CARCASS INSPECTORS WITH A VETERINARY LICENSE CHECK EACH AND EVERY CARCASS.
IF THEY FIND DISEASE OR PROBLEMS WITH THE INTERNAL ORGANS, THOSE ARE THROWN OUT.
FOR INSTANCE, THIS LIVER IS NO GOOD.
?
THIS WILL BE THROWN OUT.
YOU SEE THE WHITE SPOT HERE?
WHITE SPOT?
WHERE?
ぽちっ
POCHI (PLP)
HERE.
SO TINY!!
PIG LIVERS ARE VULNERABLE TO PARASITES AND DISEASE.
YOU SHOULD NEVER EAT PIG LIVER RAW.
WE VETS MUST ALWAYS KEEP A SHARP LOOKOUT.
UUUUGH...
HANG IN THERE!
IT GETS THROWN OUT OVER JUST ONE TINY SPOT...?
FEELS LIKE A WASTE, BUT THEN AGAIN...
SEEIN' THE PROS AT WORK IN PERSON, YOU CAN FEEL SAFER ABOUT A LOT OF THINGS...

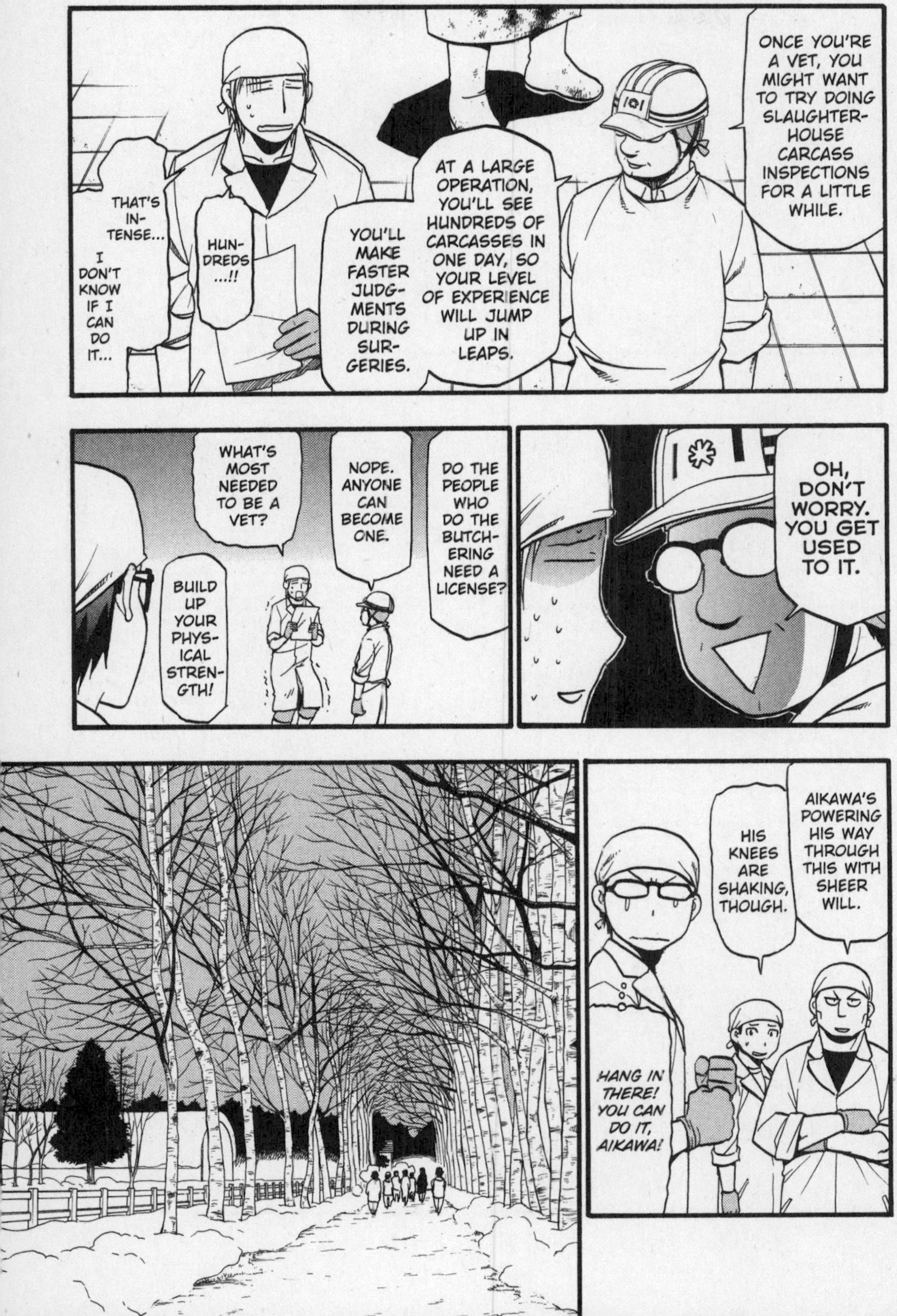
ONCE YOU'RE A VET, YOU MIGHT WANT TO TRY DOING SLAUGHTERHOUSE CARCASS INSPECTIONS FOR A LITTLE WHILE.
AT A LARGE OPERATION, YOU'LL SEE HUNDREDS OF CARCASSES IN ONE DAY, SO YOUR LEVEL OF EXPERIENCE WILL JUMP UP IN LEAPS.
YOU'LL MAKE FASTER JUDGMENTS DURING SURGERIES.
HUNDREDS ...!!
THAT'S INTENSE...
I DON'T KNOW IF I CAN DO IT...
OH, DON'T WORRY. YOU GET USED TO IT.
DO THE PEOPLE WHO DO THE BUTCHERING NEED A LICENSE?
NOPE. ANYONE CAN BECOME ONE.
WHAT'S MOST NEEDED TO BE A VET?
BUILD UP YOUR PHYSICAL STRENGTH!
AIKAWA'S POWERING HIS WAY THROUGH THIS WITH SHEER WILL.
HIS KNEES ARE SHAKING, THOUGH.
HANG IN THERE! YOU CAN DO IT, AIKAWA!

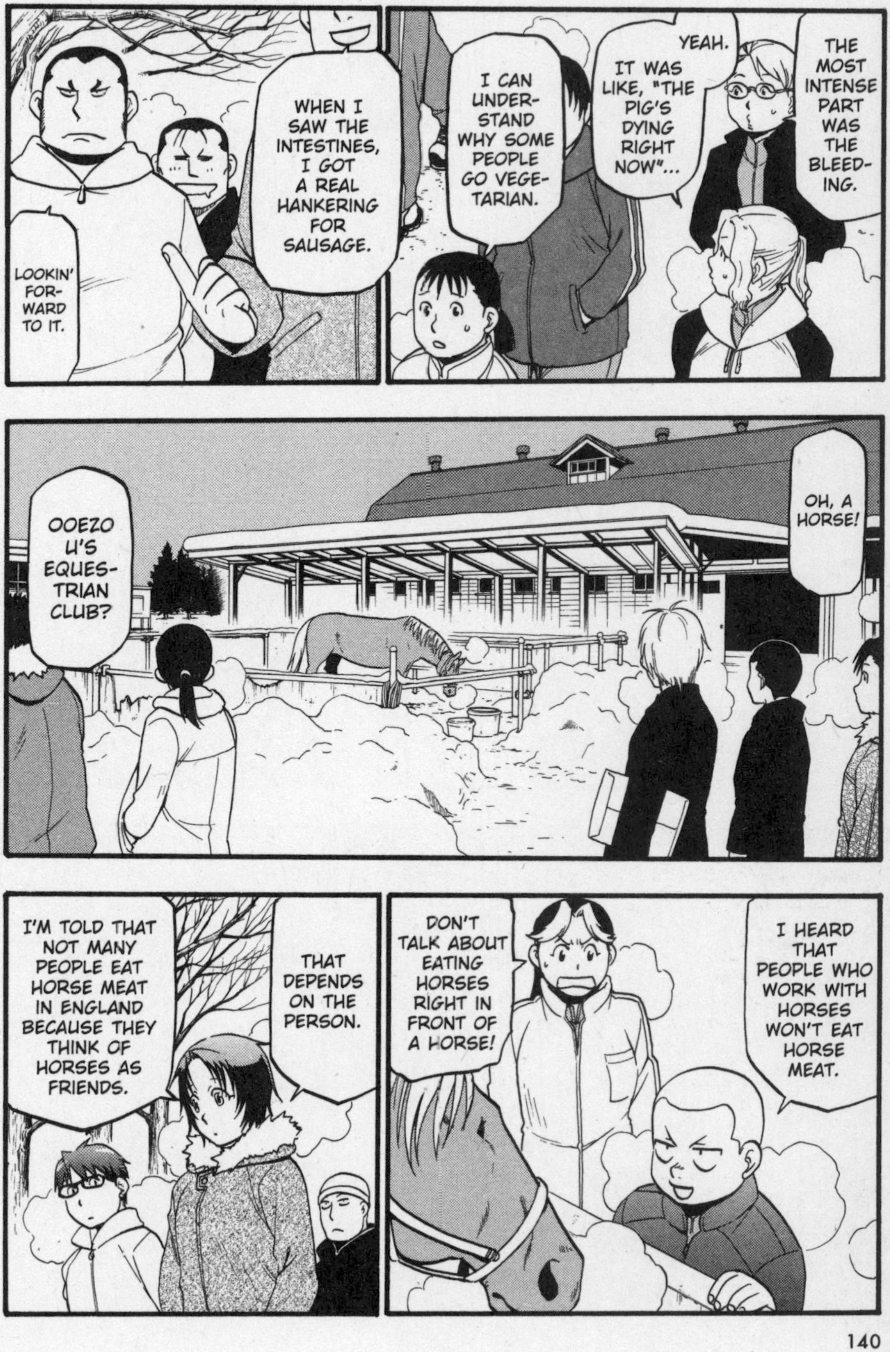
THE MOST INTENSE PART WAS THE BLEEDING.
YEAH.
IT WAS LIKE, "THE PIG'S DYING RIGHT NOW"...
I CAN UNDERSTAND WHY SOME PEOPLE GO VEGETARIAN.
WHEN I SAW THE INTESTINES, I GOT A REAL HANKERING FOR SAUSAGE.
LOOKIN' FORWARD TO IT.
OH, A HORSE!
OOEZO U'S EQUESTRIAN CLUB?
I HEARD THAT PEOPLE WHO WORK WITH HORSES WON'T EAT HORSE MEAT.
DON'T TALK ABOUT EATING HORSES RIGHT IN FRONT OF A HORSE!
THAT DEPENDS ON THE PERSON.
I'M TOLD THAT NOT MANY PEOPLE EAT HORSE MEAT IN ENGLAND BECAUSE THEY THINK OF HORSES AS FRIENDS.

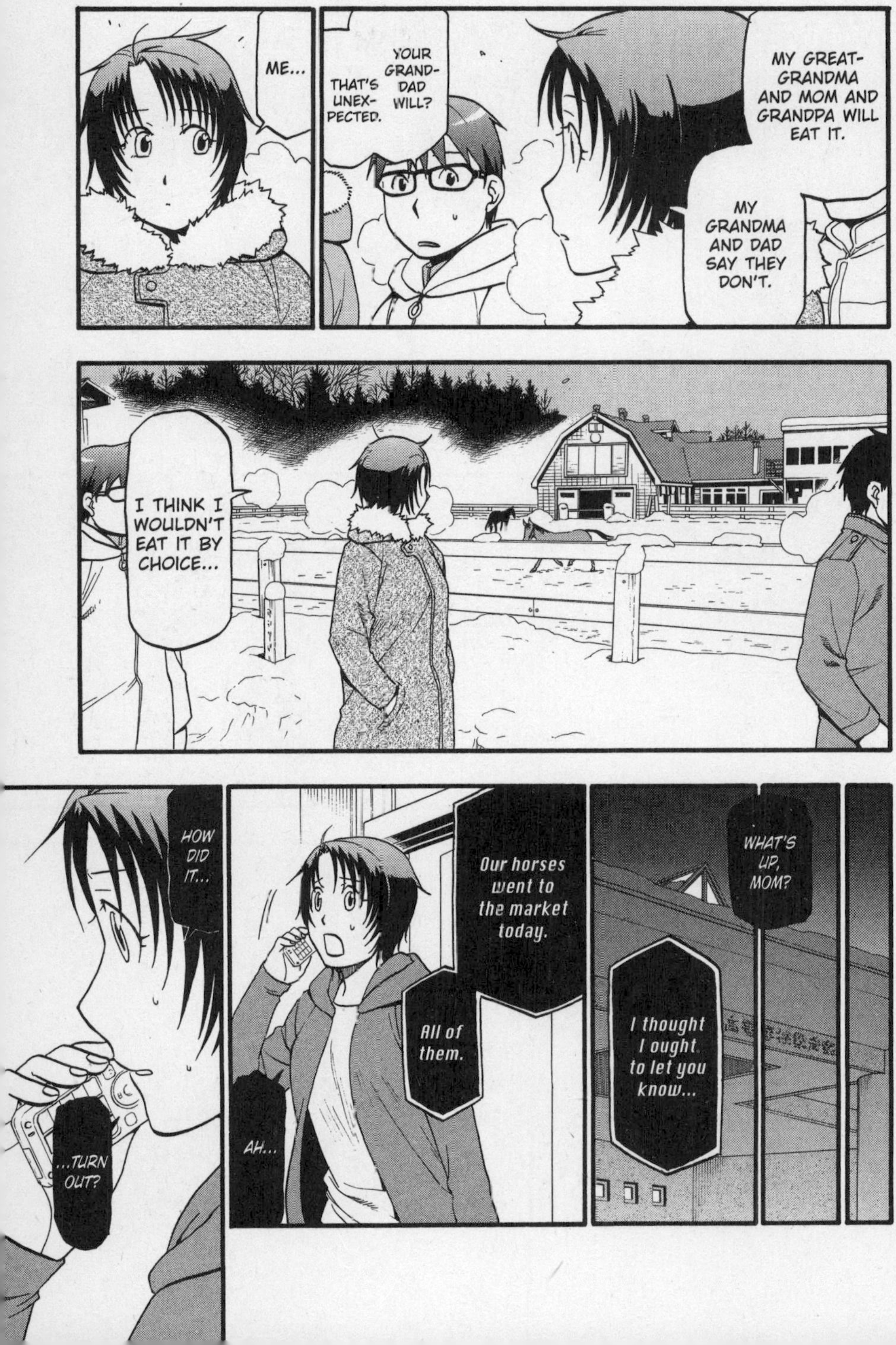
MY GREAT-GRANDMA AND MOM AND GRANDPA WILL EAT IT.
MY GRANDMA AND DAD SAY THEY DON'T.
YOUR GRAND-DAD WILL?
THAT'S UNEX-PECTED.
ME...
I THINK I WOULDN'T EAT IT BY CHOICE...
WHAT'S UP, MOM?
I thought I ought to let you know...
Our horses went to the market today.
All of them.
AH...
HOW DID IT...
...TURN OUT?

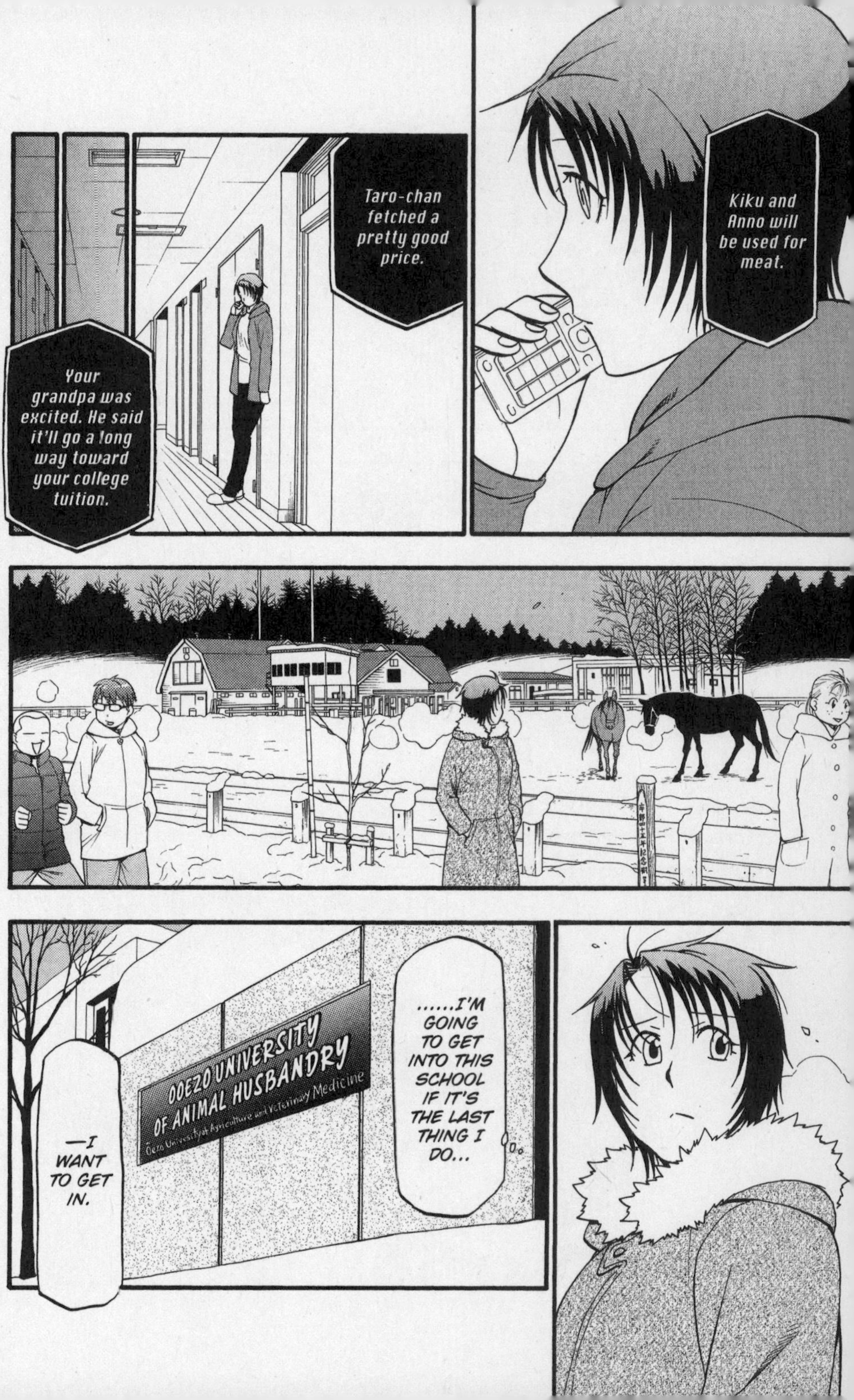
Kiku and Anno will be used for meat.
Taro-chan fetched a pretty good price.
Your grandpa was excited. He said it'll go a long way toward your college tuition.
......I'M GOING TO GET INTO THIS SCHOOL IF IT'S THE LAST THING I DO...
OOEZO UNIVERSITY OF ANIMAL HUSBANDRY
Ooezo University of Agriculture and Veterinary Medicine
—I WANT TO GET IN.

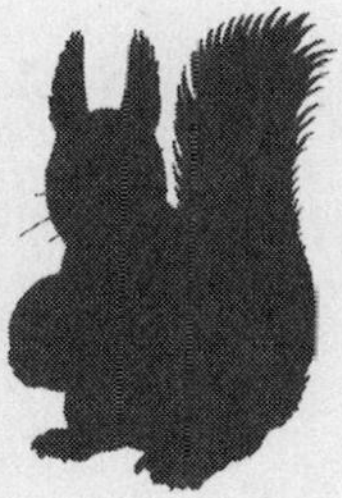

Silver Spoon

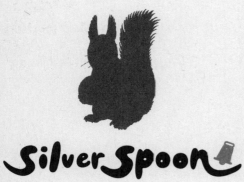

MISAKO HACHIKEN

HACHIKEN'S MOM
GOOD AT COOKING

Chapter 78:
Tale of Winter ⑮

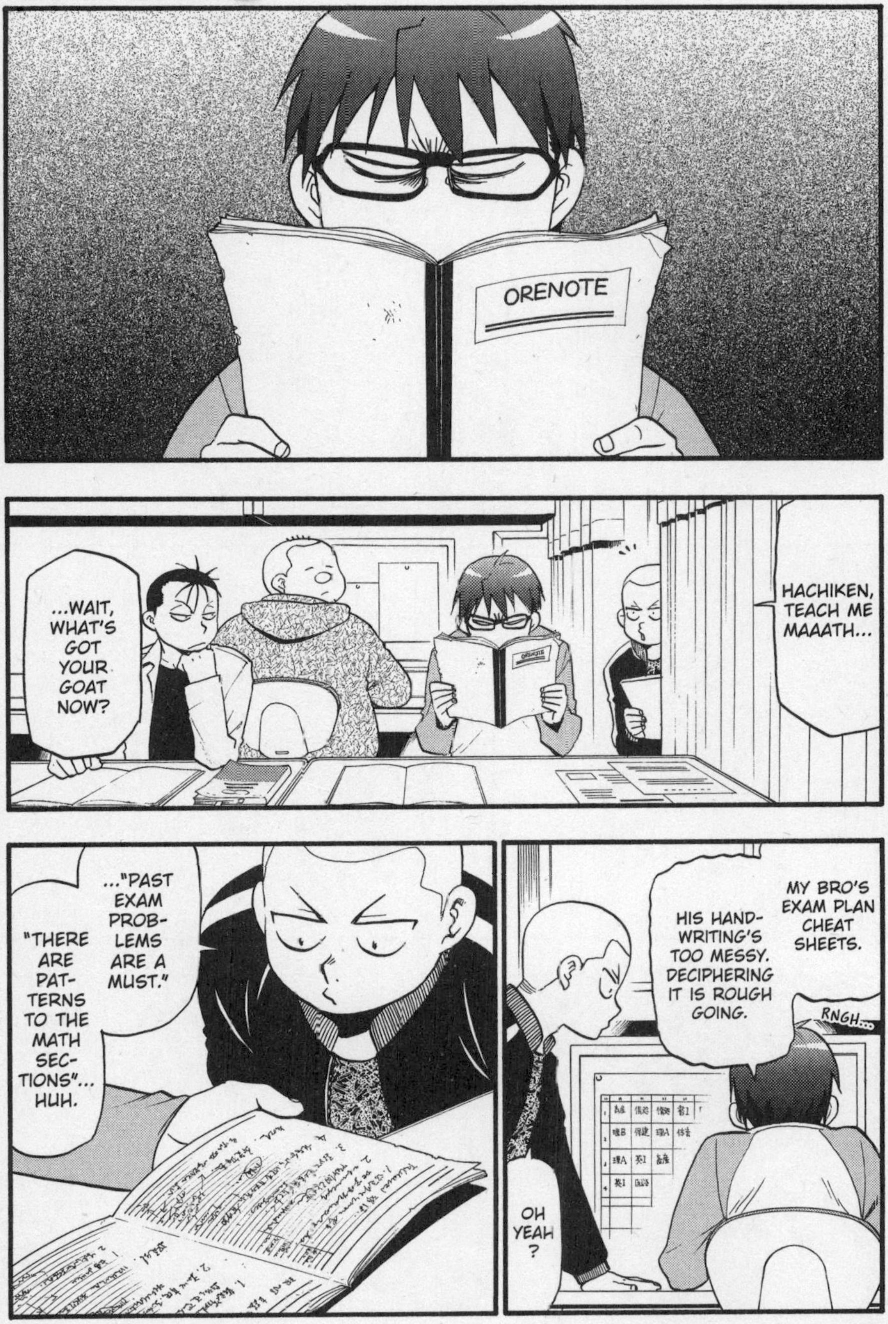
ORENOTE
HACHIKEN, TEACH ME MAAATH...
...WAIT, WHAT'S GOT YOUR GOAT NOW?
MY BRO'S EXAM PLAN CHEAT SHEETS.
HIS HAND-WRITING'S TOO MESSY. DECIPHERING IT IS ROUGH GOING.
RNGH...
OH YEAH?
..."PAST EXAM PROB-LEMS ARE A MUST."
"THERE ARE PAT-TERNS TO THE MATH SEC-TIONS"... HUH.

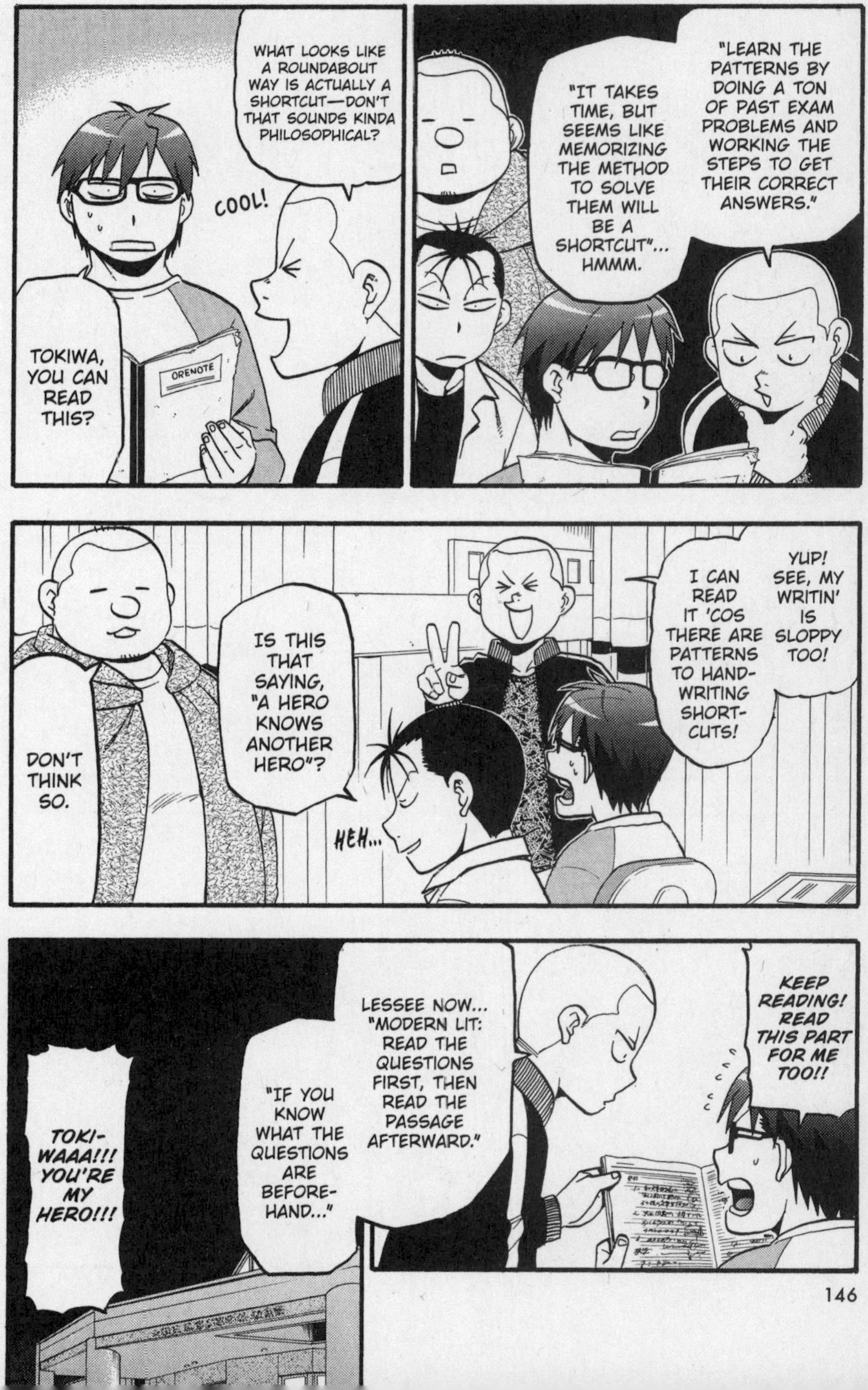
"LEARN THE PATTERNS BY DOING A TON OF PAST EXAM PROBLEMS AND WORKING THE STEPS TO GET THEIR CORRECT ANSWERS."
"IT TAKES TIME, BUT SEEMS LIKE MEMORIZING THE METHOD TO SOLVE THEM WILL BE A SHORTCUT"... HMMM.
WHAT LOOKS LIKE A ROUNDABOUT WAY IS ACTUALLY A SHORTCUT—DON'T THAT SOUNDS KINDA PHILOSOPHICAL?
COOL!
ORENOTE
TOKIWA, YOU CAN READ THIS?
YUP! SEE, MY WRITIN' IS SLOPPY TOO!
I CAN READ IT 'COS THERE ARE PATTERNS TO HAND-WRITING SHORT-CUTS!
IS THIS THAT SAYING, "A HERO KNOWS ANOTHER HERO"?
HEH...
DON'T THINK SO.
KEEP READING! READ THIS PART FOR ME TOO!!
LESSEE NOW... "MODERN LIT: READ THE QUESTIONS FIRST, THEN READ THE PASSAGE AFTERWARD."
"IF YOU KNOW WHAT THE QUESTIONS ARE BEFORE-HAND..."
TOKI-WAAA!!! YOU'RE MY HERO!!!

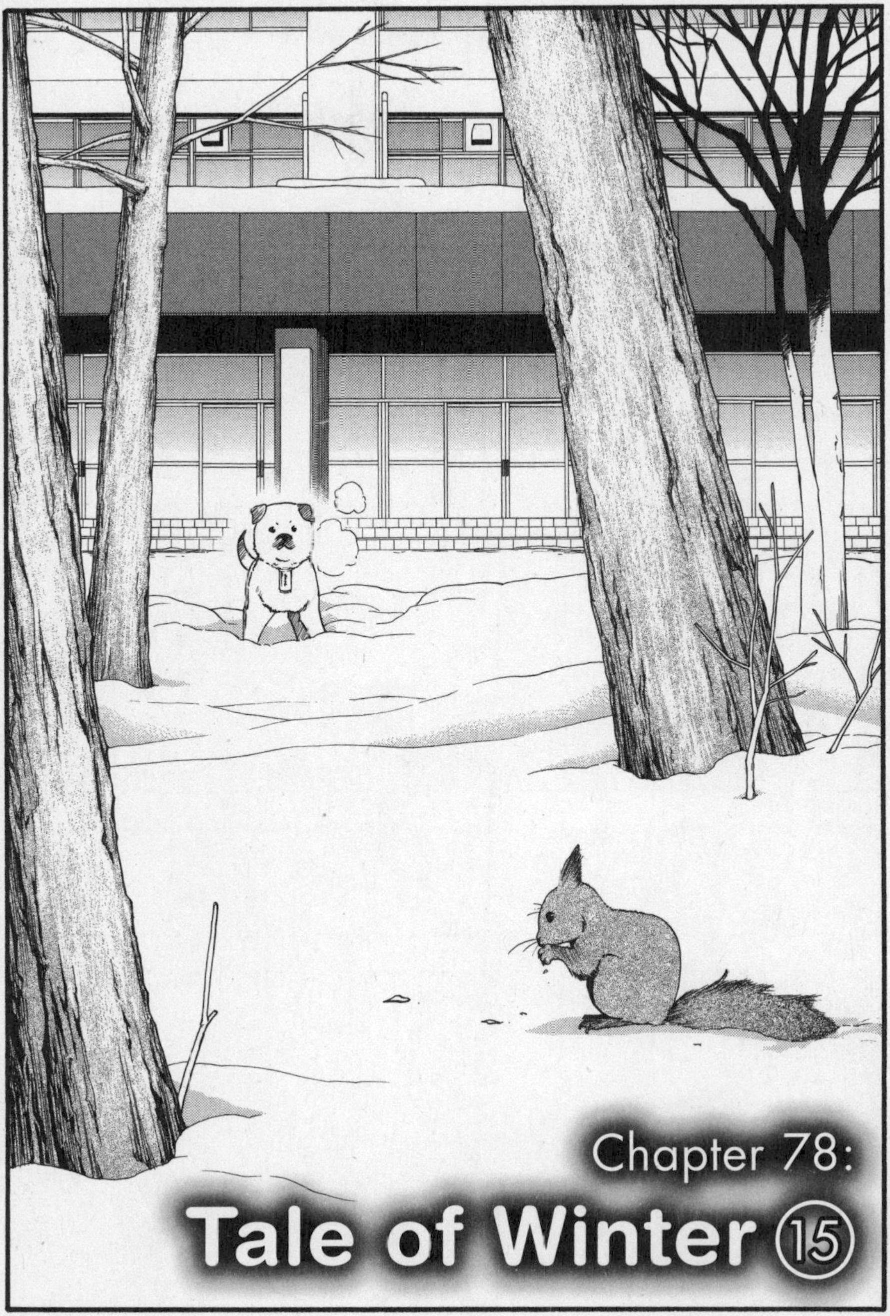
Chapter 78:
Tale of Winter ⑮

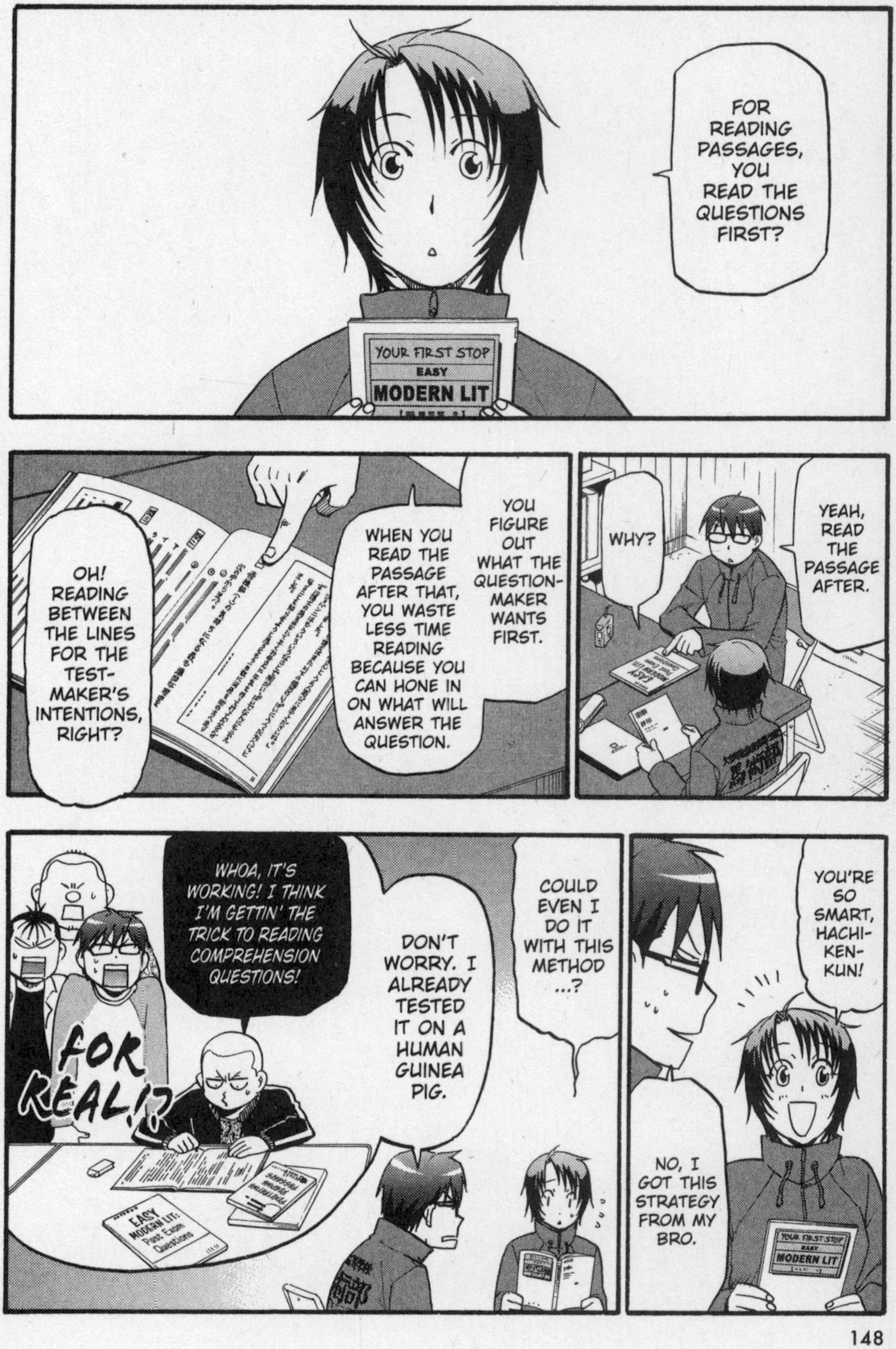
FOR READING PASSAGES, YOU READ THE QUESTIONS FIRST?
YOUR FIRST STOP
EASY
MODERN LIT
YEAH, READ THE PASSAGE AFTER.
WHY?
YOU FIGURE OUT WHAT THE QUESTION-MAKER WANTS FIRST.
WHEN YOU READ THE PASSAGE AFTER THAT, YOU WASTE LESS TIME READING BECAUSE YOU CAN HONE IN ON WHAT WILL ANSWER THE QUESTION.
OH! READING BETWEEN THE LINES FOR THE TEST-MAKER'S INTENTIONS, RIGHT?
YOU'RE SO SMART, HACHI-KEN-KUN!
NO, I GOT THIS STRATEGY FROM MY BRO.
YOUR FIRST STOP
EASY
MODERN LIT
COULD EVEN I DO IT WITH THIS METHOD ...?
DON'T WORRY. I ALREADY TESTED IT ON A HUMAN GUINEA PIG.
WHOA, IT'S WORKING! I THINK I'M GETTIN' THE TRICK TO READING COMPREHENSION QUESTIONS!
FOR REAL!?
EASY
MODERN LIT:
Past Exam
Questions

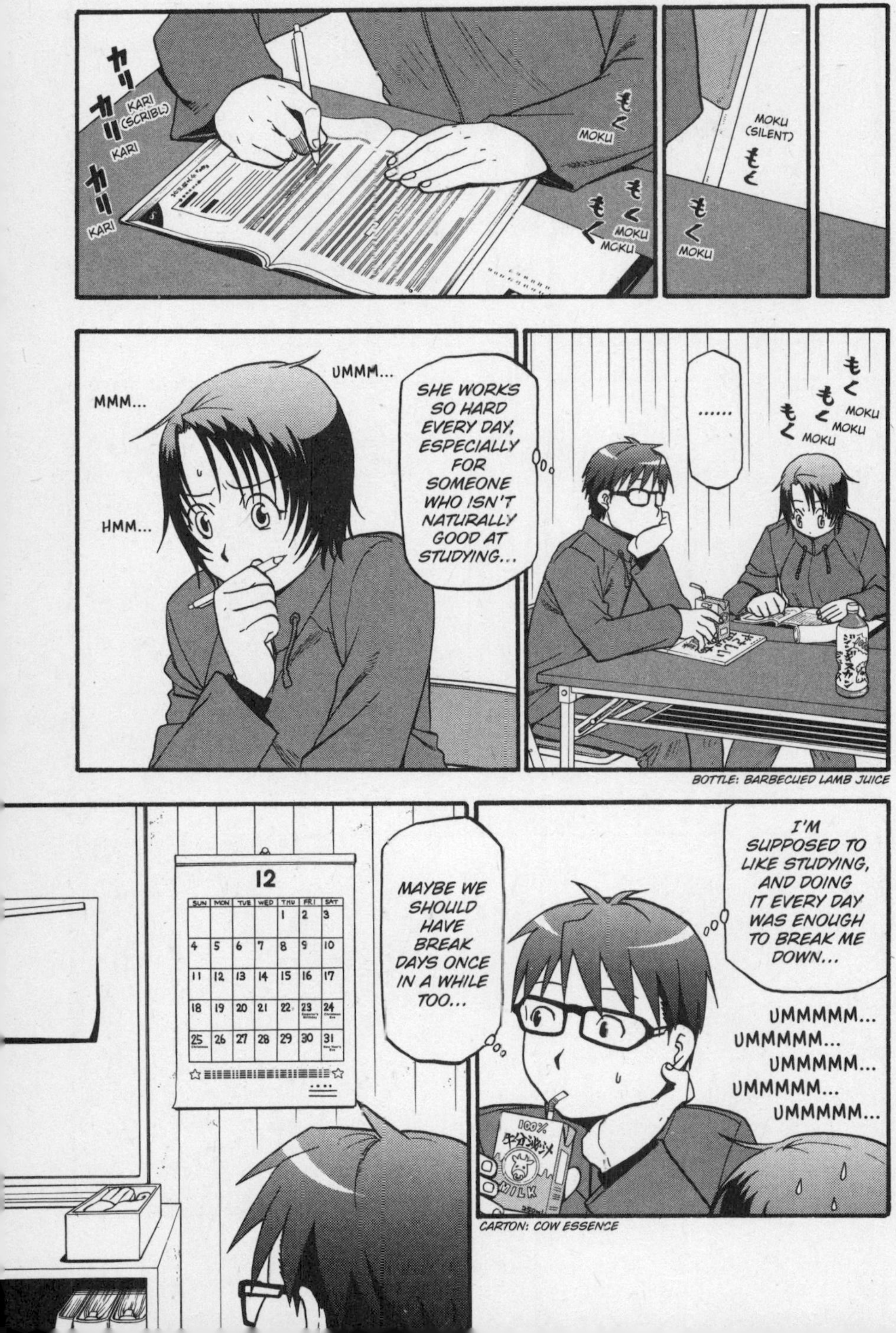
もく
MOKU (SILENT)
もく
MOKU
もく
MOKU
もく
MOKU
もく
MOKU
カリ
KARI (SCRIBL)
カリ
KARI
カリ
KARI
......
もく
MOKU
もく
MOKU
もく
MOKU
SHE WORKS SO HARD EVERY DAY, ESPECIALLY FOR SOMEONE WHO ISN'T NATURALLY GOOD AT STUDYING...
UMMM...
MMM...
HMM...
BOTTLE: BARBECUED LAMB JUICE
I'M SUPPOSED TO LIKE STUDYING, AND DOING IT EVERY DAY WAS ENOUGH TO BREAK ME DOWN...
UMMMMM...
UMMMMM...
UMMMMM...
UMMMMM...
UMMMMM...
100%
MILK
CARTON: COW ESSENCE
MAYBE WE SHOULD HAVE BREAK DAYS ONCE IN A WHILE TOO...
12
SUN MON TUE WED THU FRI SAT

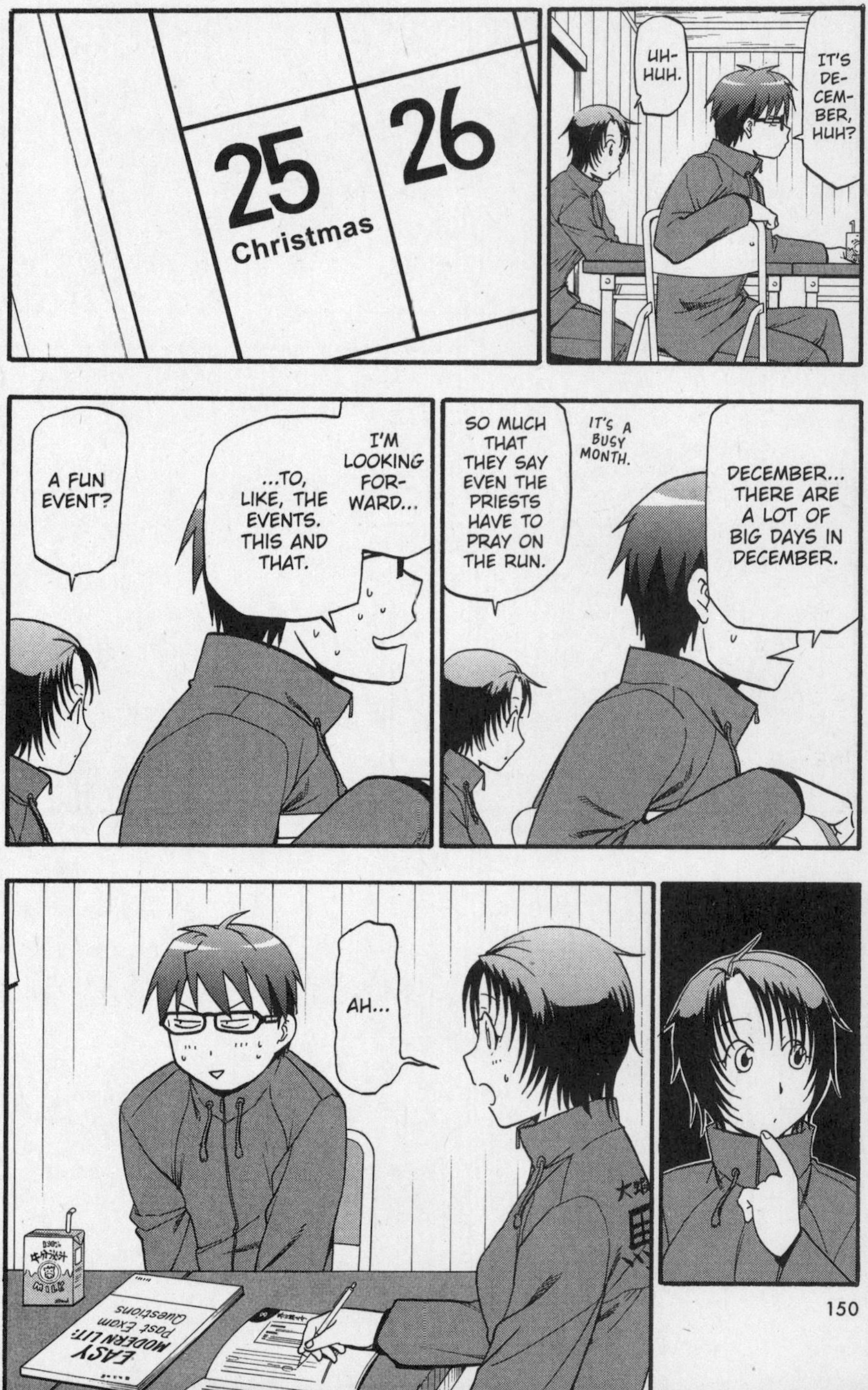
IT'S DE-CEM-BER, HUH?
UH-HUH.
25
Christmas
26
DECEMBER... THERE ARE A LOT OF BIG DAYS IN DECEMBER.
IT'S A BUSY MONTH.
SO MUCH THAT THEY SAY EVEN THE PRIESTS HAVE TO PRAY ON THE RUN.
I'M LOOKING FOR-WARD...
...TO, LIKE, THE EVENTS. THIS AND THAT.
A FUN EVENT?
AH...
EASY MODERN LIT: Past Exam Questions
MILK

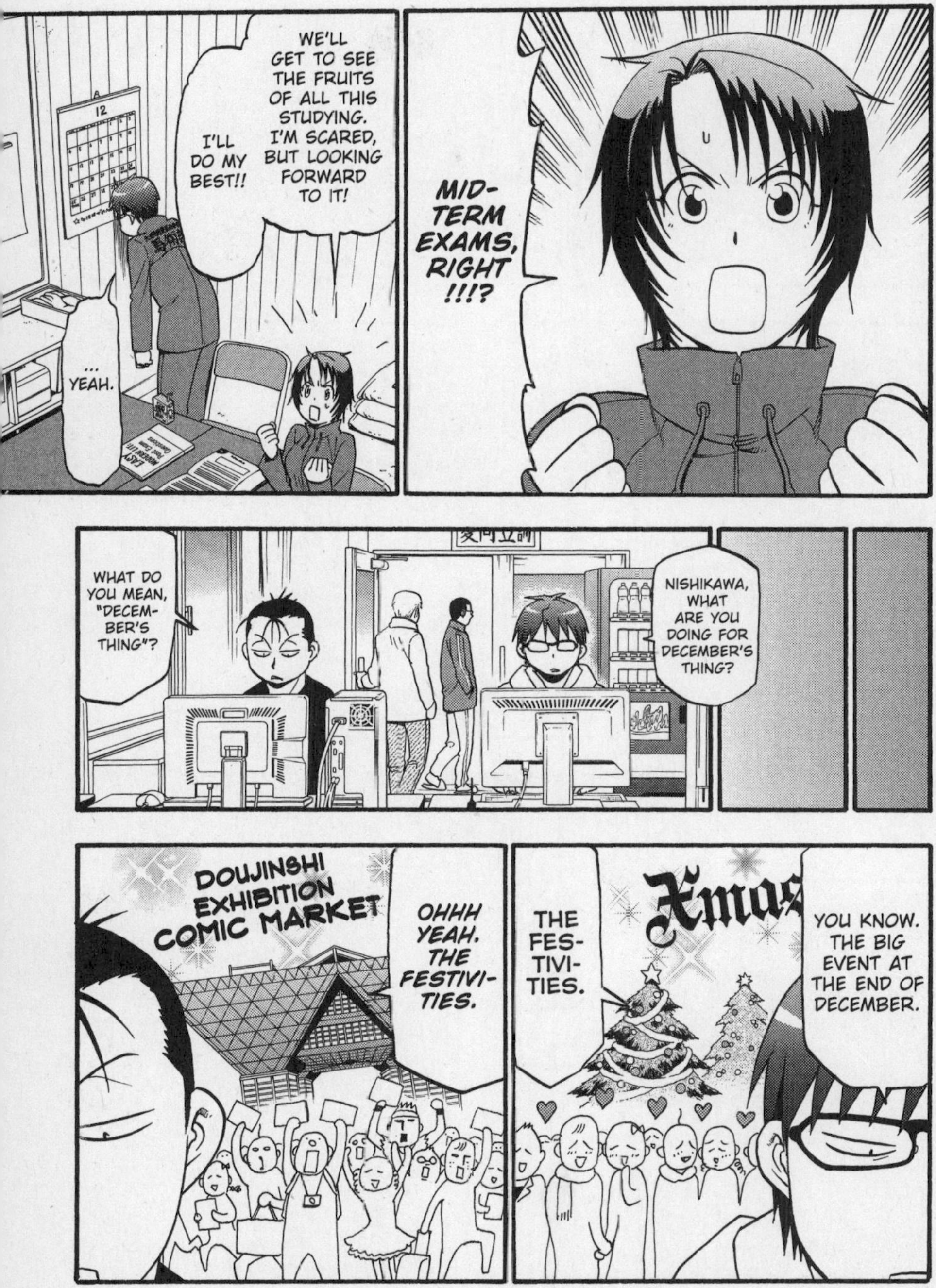
MID-TERM EXAMS, RIGHT!!!?
WE'LL GET TO SEE THE FRUITS OF ALL THIS STUDYING. I'M SCARED, BUT LOOKING FORWARD TO IT!
I'LL DO MY BEST!!
... YEAH.
NISHIKAWA, WHAT ARE YOU DOING FOR DECEMBER'S THING?
WHAT DO YOU MEAN, "DECEMBER'S THING"?
YOU KNOW. THE BIG EVENT AT THE END OF DECEMBER.
Xmas
THE FESTIVITIES.
OHHH YEAH. THE FESTIVITIES.
DOUJINSHI EXHIBITION COMIC MARKET

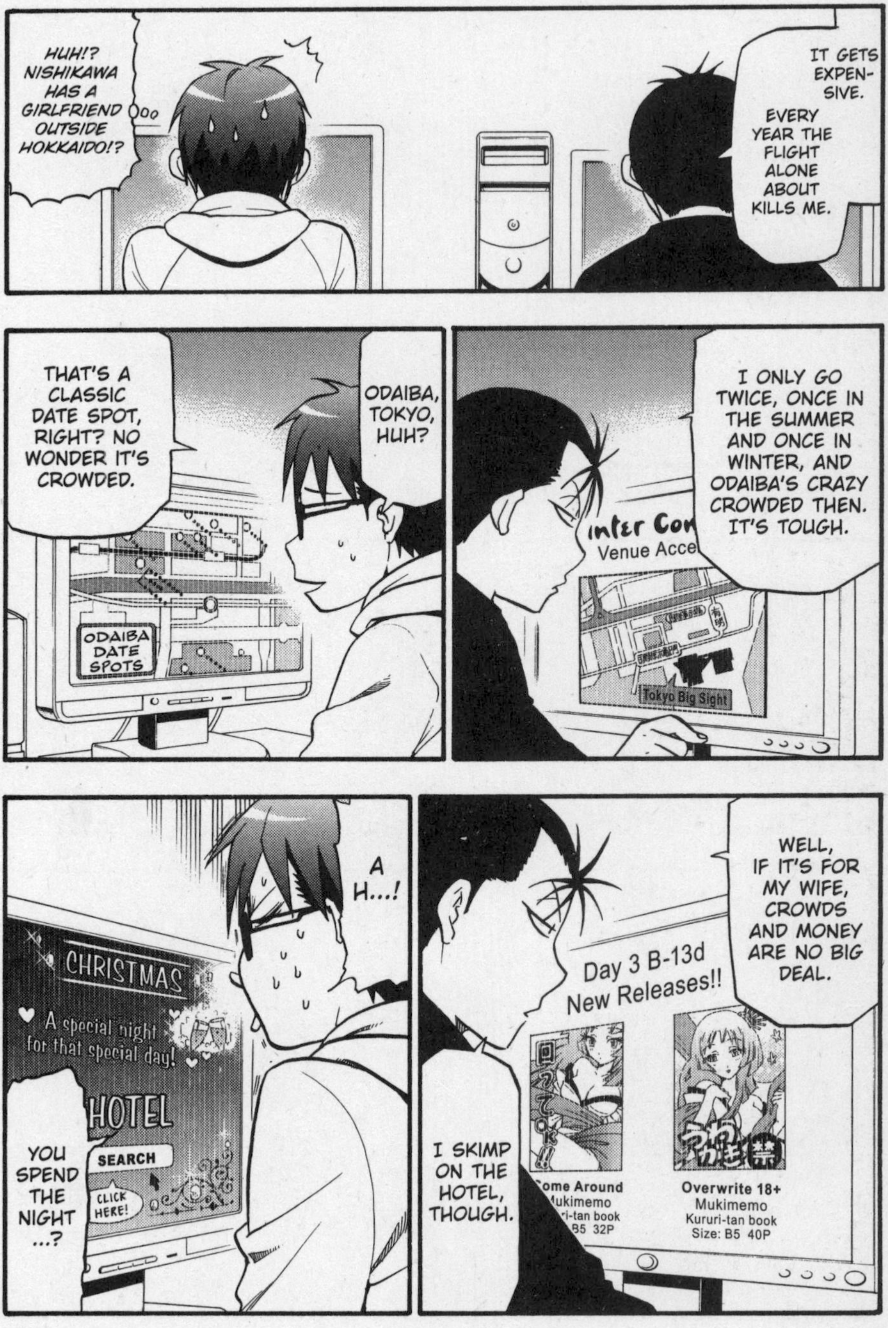
IT GETS EXPENSIVE.
EVERY YEAR THE FLIGHT ALONE ABOUT KILLS ME.
HUH!? NISHIKAWA HAS A GIRLFRIEND OUTSIDE HOKKAIDO!?
I ONLY GO TWICE, ONCE IN THE SUMMER AND ONCE IN WINTER, AND ODAIBA'S CRAZY CROWDED THEN. IT'S TOUGH.
Tokyo Big Sight
ODAIBA, TOKYO, HUH?
THAT'S A CLASSIC DATE SPOT, RIGHT? NO WONDER IT'S CROWDED.
ODAIBA DATE SPOTS
WELL, IF IT'S FOR MY WIFE, CROWDS AND MONEY ARE NO BIG DEAL.
Day 3 B-13d New Releases!!
Overwrite 18+
Mukimemo
Kururi-tan book
Size: B5 40P
I SKIMP ON THE HOTEL, THOUGH.
A H...!
CHRISTMAS
A special night for that special day!
HOTEL
SEARCH
CLICK HERE!
YOU SPEND THE NIGHT ...?

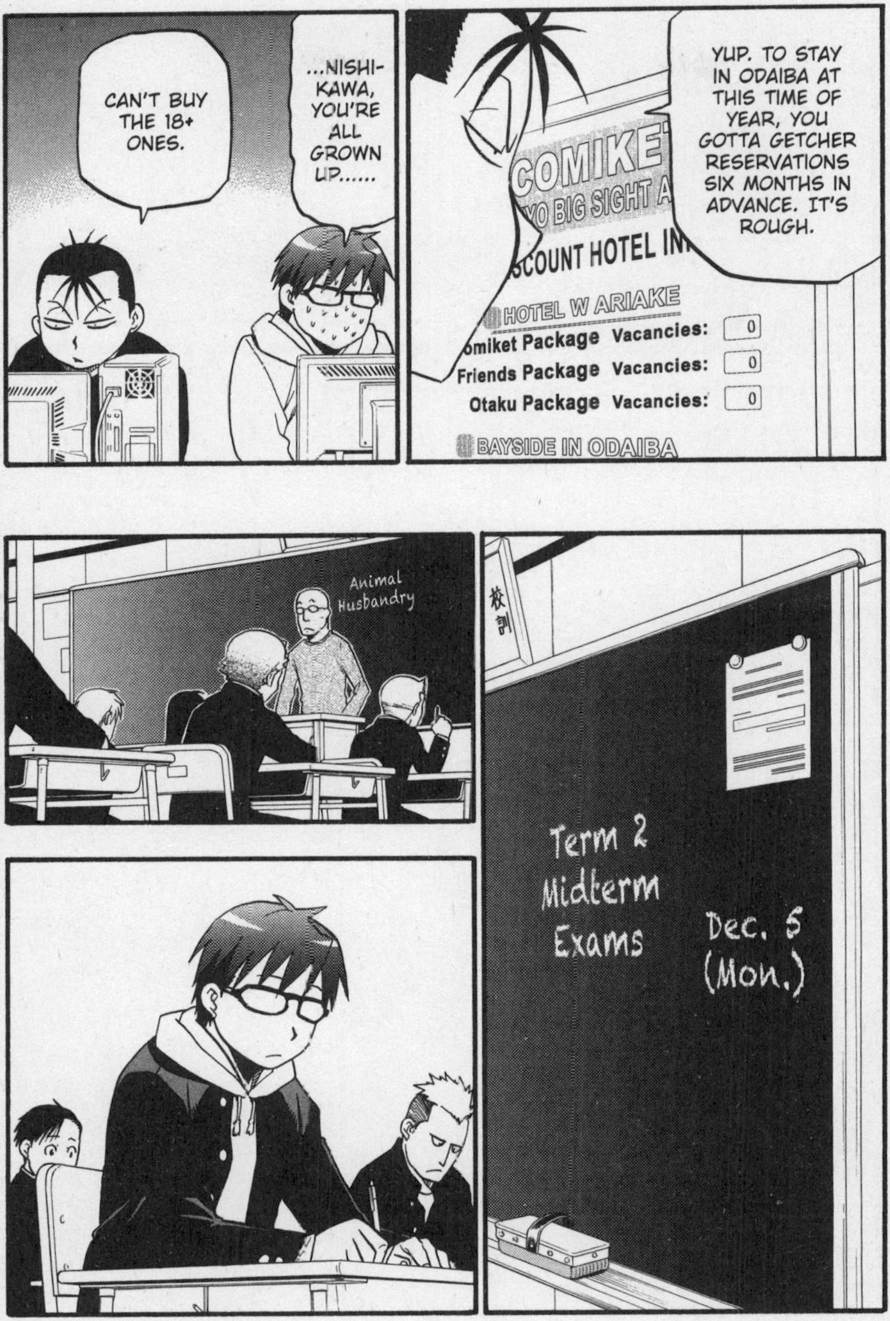
YUP. TO STAY IN ODAIBA AT THIS TIME OF YEAR, YOU GOTTA GETCHER RESERVATIONS SIX MONTHS IN ADVANCE. IT'S ROUGH.
COMIKET
YO BIG SIGHT A
SCOUNT HOTEL IN
HOTEL W ARIAKE
omiket Package Vacancies: 0
Friends Package Vacancies: 0
Otaku Package Vacancies: 0
BAYSIDE IN ODAIBA
...NISHI-KAWA, YOU'RE ALL GROWN UP......
CAN'T BUY THE 18+ ONES.
校訓
Term 2 Midterm Exams
Dec. 5 (Mon.)
Animal Husbandry

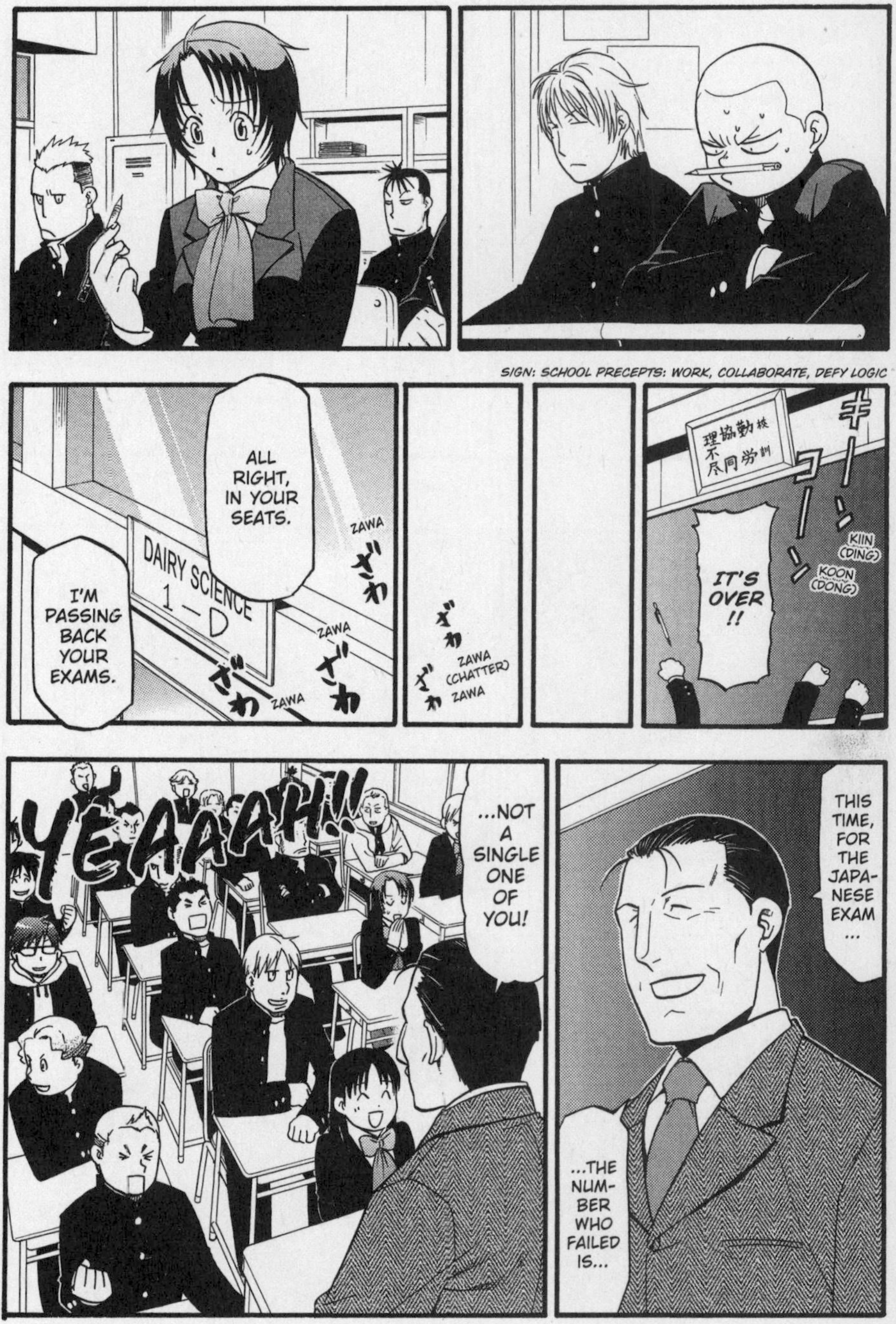
SIGN: SCHOOL PRECEPTS: WORK, COLLABORATE, DEFY LOGIC
KIIN (DING)
KOON (DONG)
IT'S OVER!!
ZAWA (CHATTER) ZAWA
ALL RIGHT, IN YOUR SEATS.
I'M PASSING BACK YOUR EXAMS.
ZAWA ZAWA ZAWA
DAIRY SCIENCE 1—D
THIS TIME, FOR THE JAPANESE EXAM...
...THE NUMBER WHO FAILED IS...
...NOT A SINGLE ONE OF YOU!
YEAAAH!!

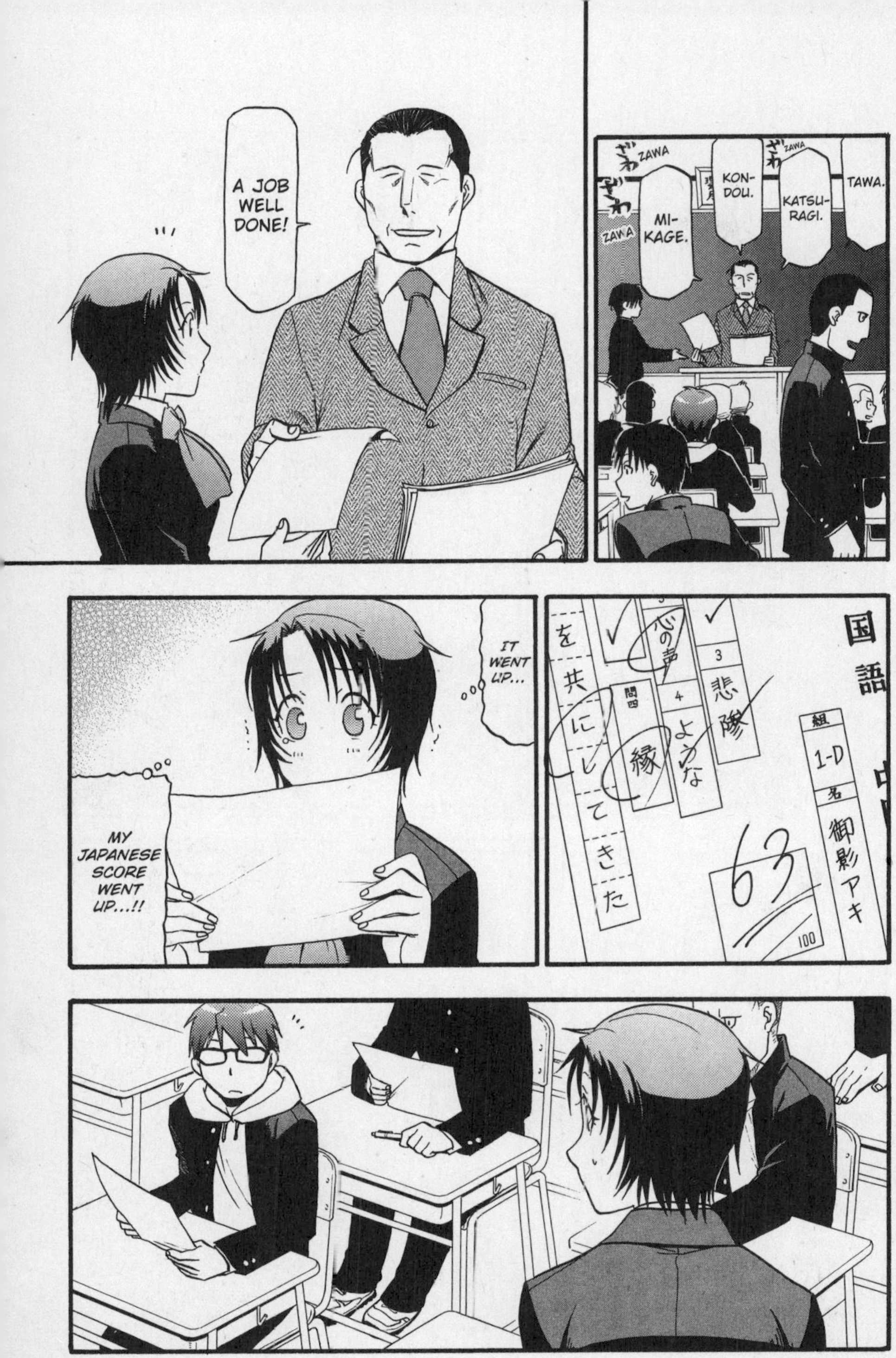
ZAWA
TAWA.
KATSU-RAGI.
ZAWA
KON-DOU.
MI-KAGE.
ZAWA
A JOB WELL DONE!
国語
組
1-D
名
御影アキ
63
100
IT WENT UP...
MY JAPANESE SCORE WENT UP...!!

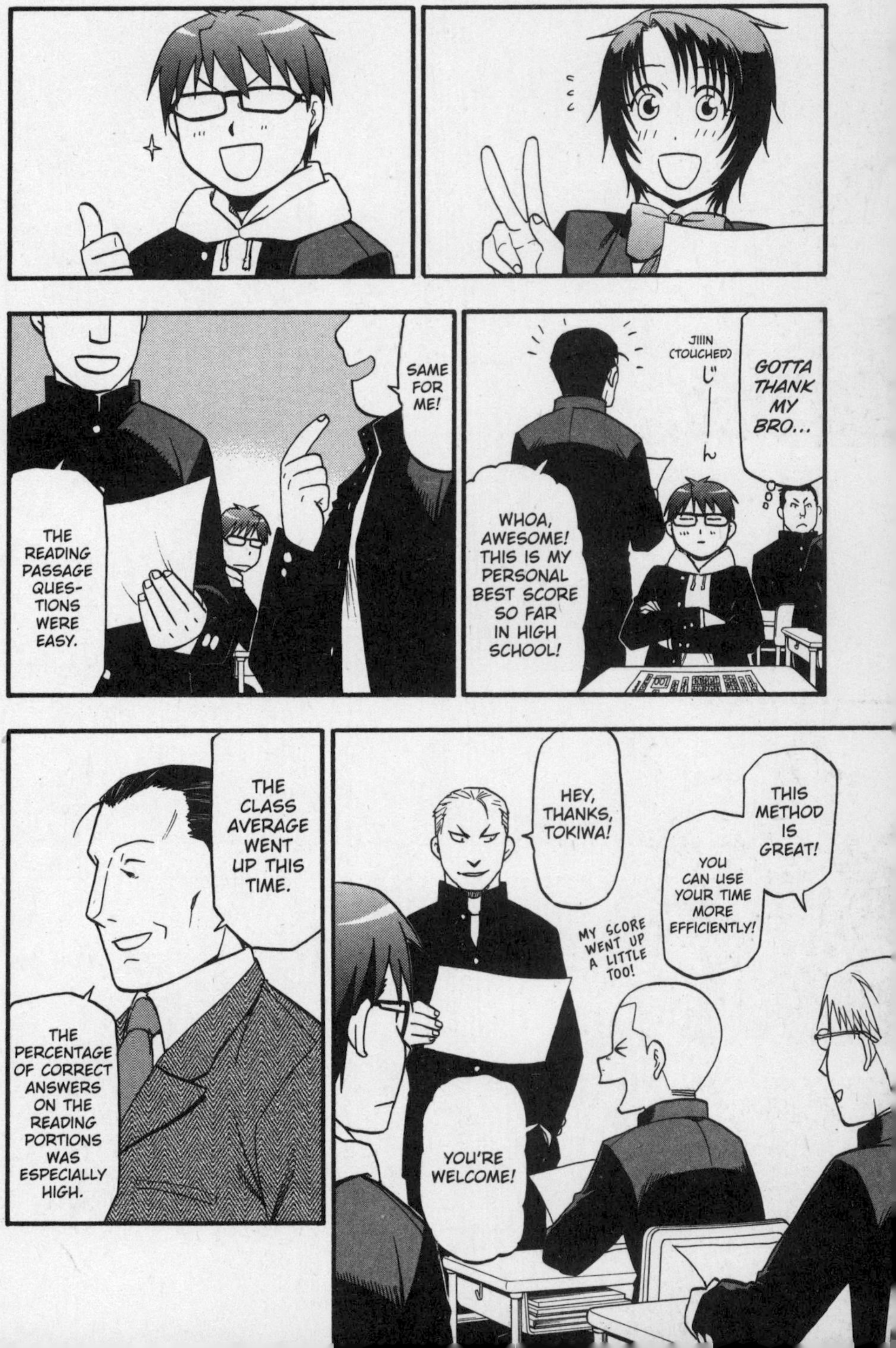
GOTTA THANK MY BRO...
JIIIN (TOUCHED) じーん
WHOA, AWESOME! THIS IS MY PERSONAL BEST SCORE SO FAR IN HIGH SCHOOL!
SAME FOR ME!
THE READING PASSAGE QUES-TIONS WERE EASY.
THIS METHOD IS GREAT!
HEY, THANKS, TOKIWA!
YOU CAN USE YOUR TIME MORE EFFICIENTLY!
MY SCORE WENT UP A LITTLE TOO!
YOU'RE WELCOME!
THE CLASS AVERAGE WENT UP THIS TIME.
THE PERCENTAGE OF CORRECT ANSWERS ON THE READING PORTIONS WAS ESPECIALLY HIGH.

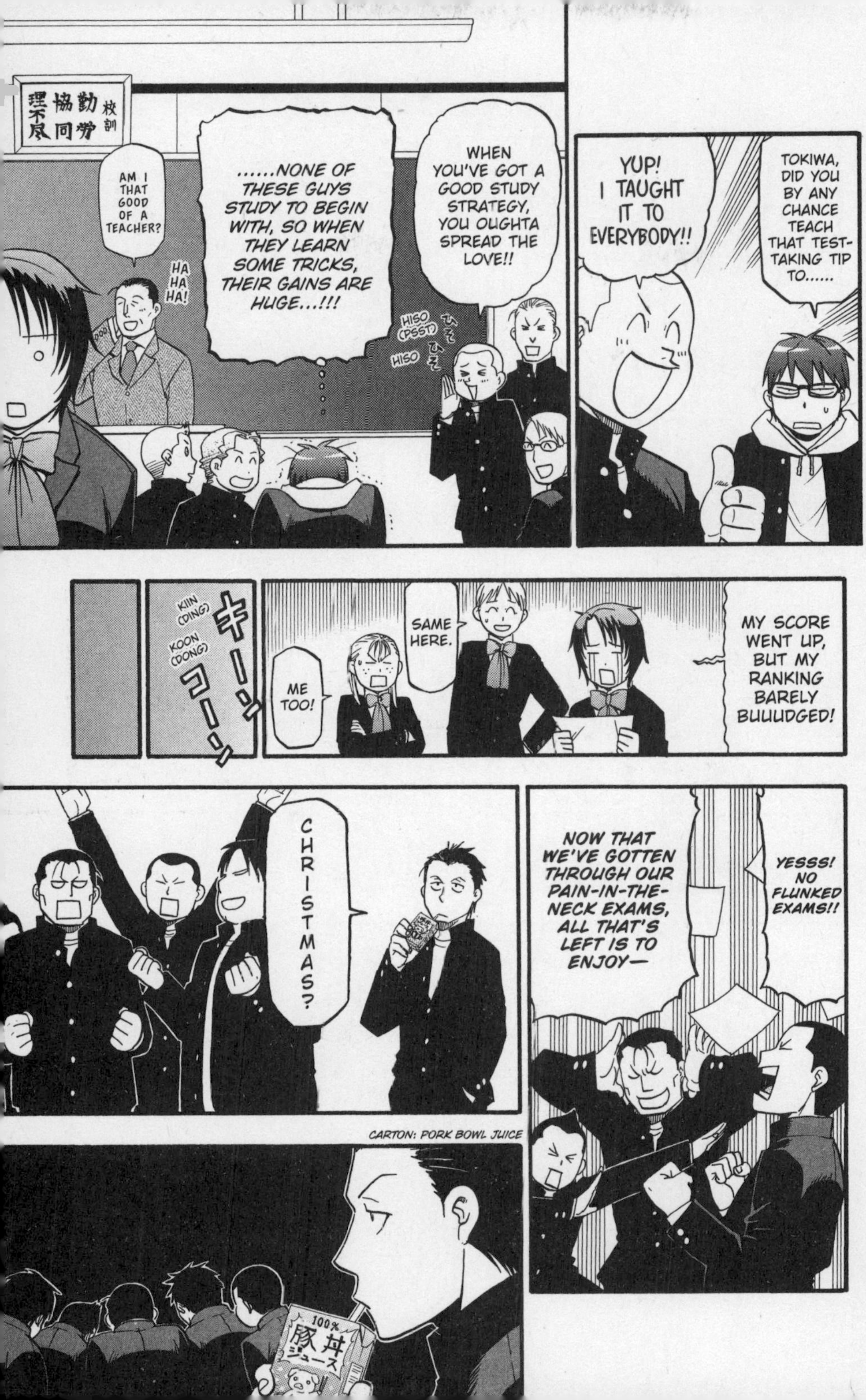
TOKIWA, DID YOU BY ANY CHANCE TEACH THAT TEST-TAKING TIP TO......
YUP! I TAUGHT IT TO EVERYBODY!!
WHEN YOU'VE GOT A GOOD STUDY STRATEGY, YOU OUGHTA SPREAD THE LOVE!!
HISO (PSSST) ひそ ひそ HISO
......NONE OF THESE GUYS STUDY TO BEGIN WITH, SO WHEN THEY LEARN SOME TRICKS, THEIR GAINS ARE HUGE...!!!
HA HA HA!
AM I THAT GOOD OF A TEACHER?
校訓 勤労 協同 理不尽
MY SCORE WENT UP, BUT MY RANKING BARELY BUUUDGED!
SAME HERE.
ME TOO!
KIN (DING) KOON (DONG) キーンコーン
YESSS! NO FLUNKED EXAMS!!
NOW THAT WE'VE GOTTEN THROUGH OUR PAIN-IN-THE-NECK EXAMS, ALL THAT'S LEFT IS TO ENJOY—
CHRISTMAS?
CARTON: PORK BOWL JUICE
100% 豚丼ジュース

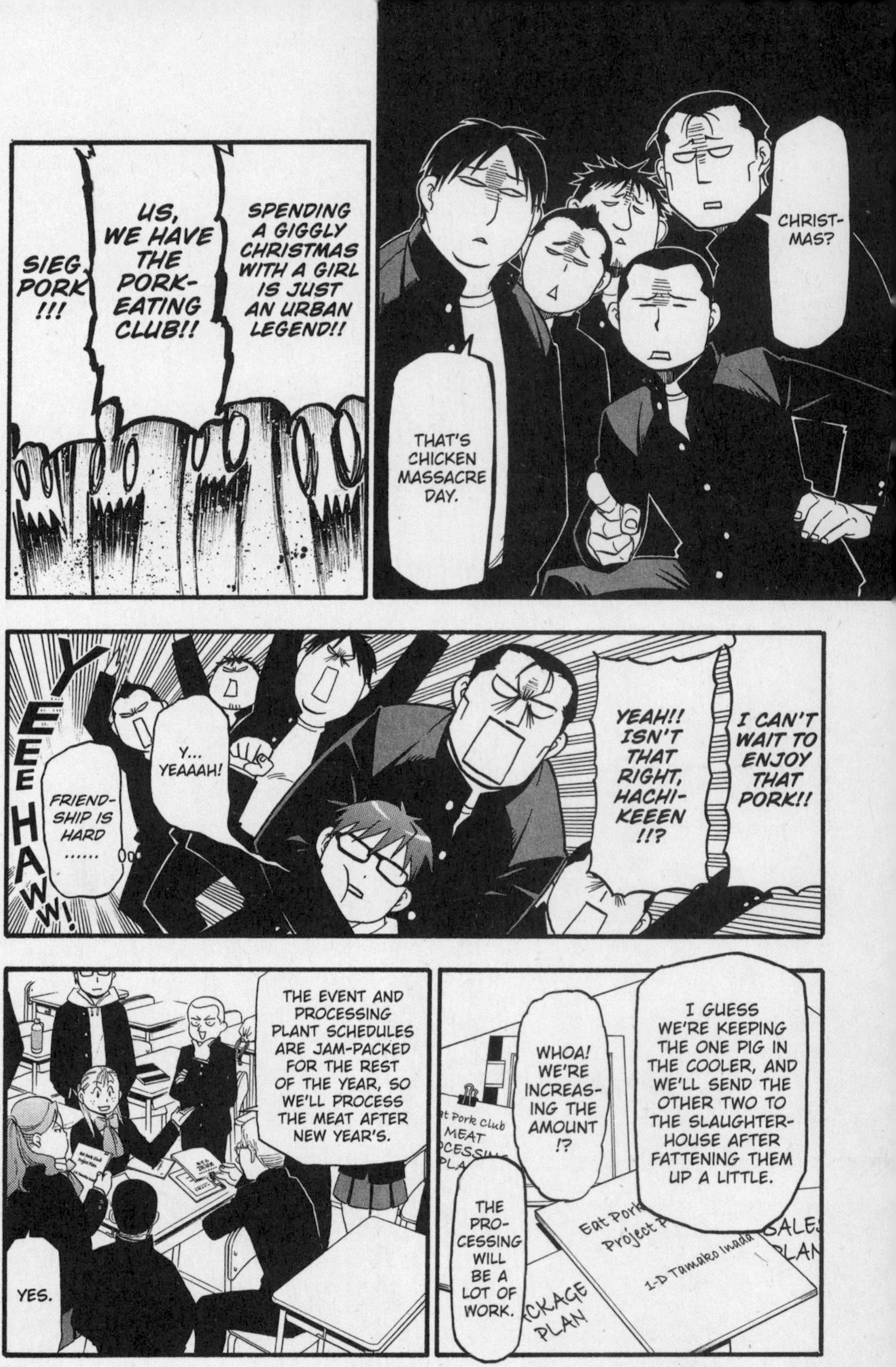
CHRIST-MAS?
THAT'S CHICKEN MASSACRE DAY.
SPENDING A GIGGLY CHRISTMAS WITH A GIRL IS JUST AN URBAN LEGEND!!
US, WE HAVE THE PORK-EATING CLUB!!
SIEG PORK!!!
I CAN'T WAIT TO ENJOY THAT PORK!!
YEAH!! ISN'T THAT RIGHT, HACHI-KEEEN!!?
Y... YEAAAH!
YEEEHAWW!
FRIEND-SHIP IS HARD ......
I GUESS WE'RE KEEPING THE ONE PIG IN THE COOLER, AND WE'LL SEND THE OTHER TWO TO THE SLAUGHTER-HOUSE AFTER FATTENING THEM UP A LITTLE.
WHOA! WE'RE INCREAS-ING THE AMOUNT !?
THE PRO-CESSING WILL BE A LOT OF WORK.
at Pork Club MEAT ROCESSING PLAN
Eat Pork Project P
SALES PLAN
1-D Tamako Inada
CKAGE PLAN
THE EVENT AND PROCESSING PLANT SCHEDULES ARE JAM-PACKED FOR THE REST OF THE YEAR, SO WE'LL PROCESS THE MEAT AFTER NEW YEAR'S.
YES.

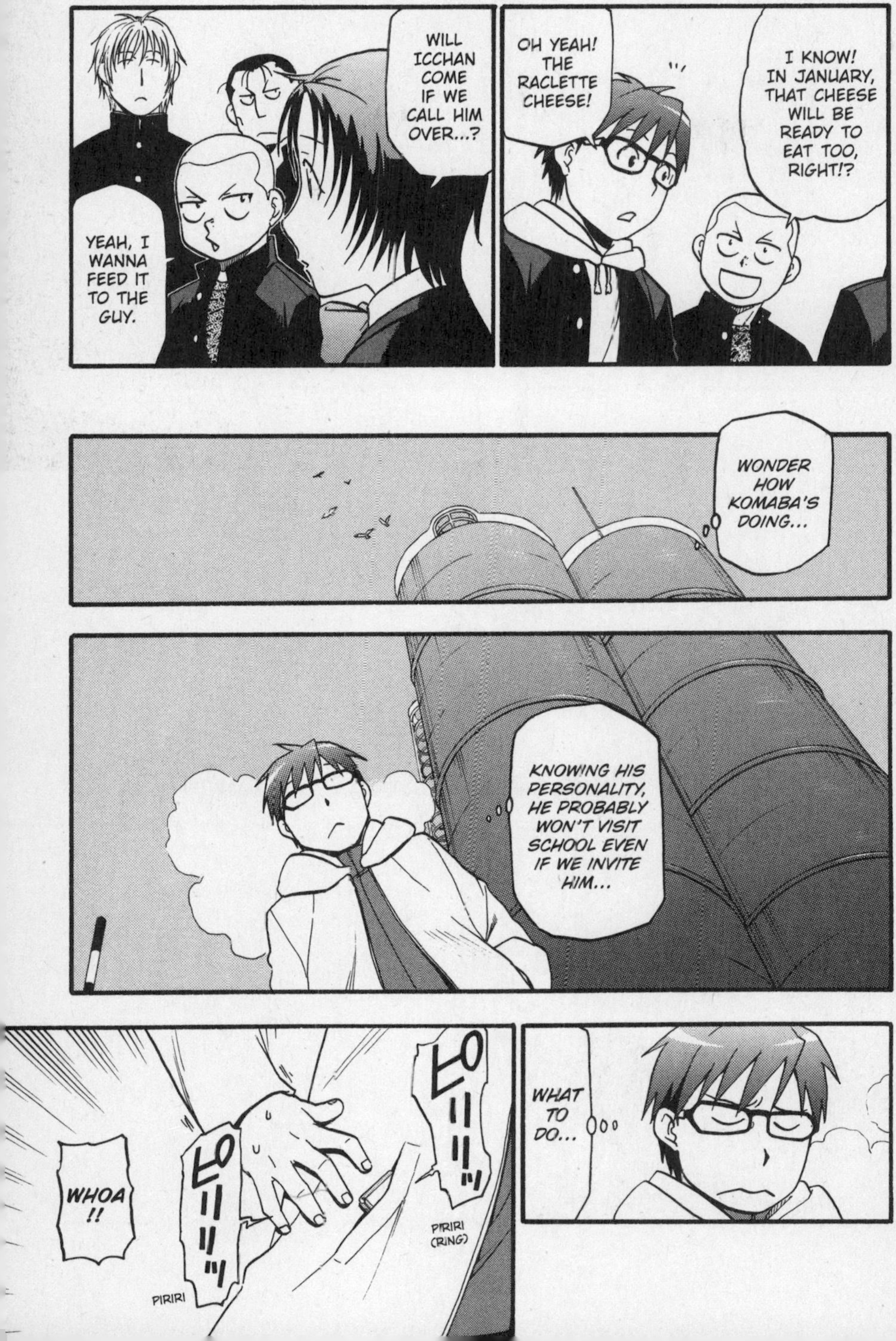
I KNOW! IN JANUARY, THAT CHEESE WILL BE READY TO EAT TOO, RIGHT!?
OH YEAH! THE RACLETTE CHEESE!
WILL ICCHAN COME IF WE CALL HIM OVER...?
YEAH, I WANNA FEED IT TO THE GUY.
WONDER HOW KOMABA'S DOING...
KNOWING HIS PERSONALITY, HE PROBABLY WON'T VISIT SCHOOL EVEN IF WE INVITE HIM...
WHAT TO DO...
PIRIRI (RING)
PIRIRI
WHOA!!

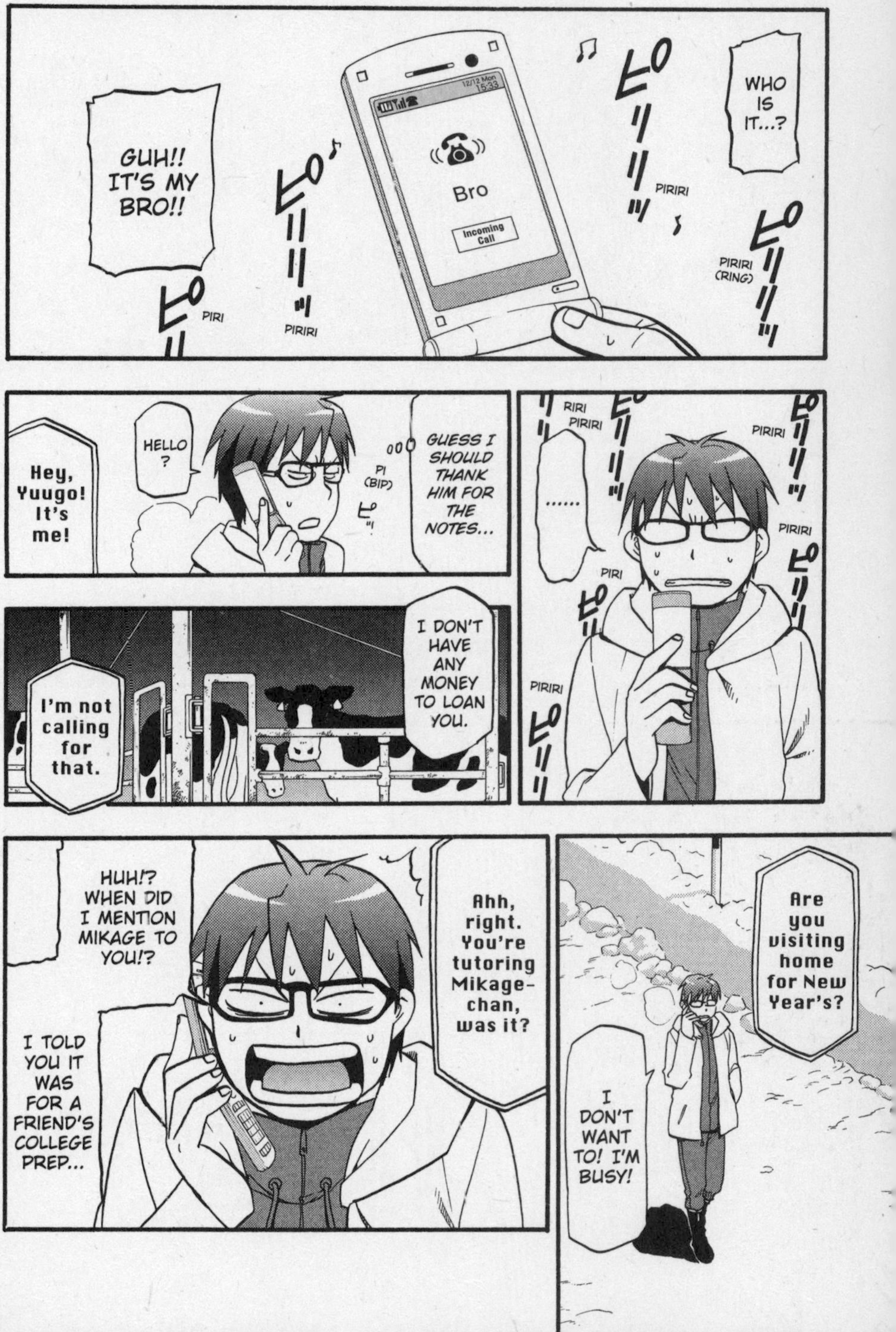
WHO IS IT...?
PIRIRI
PIRIRI (RING)
12/12 Mon 15:33
Bro
Incoming Call
PIRIRI
PIRI
GUH!! IT'S MY BRO!!
PIRIRI
PIRIRI
RIRI PIRIRI
PIRI
PIRIRI
......
GUESS I SHOULD THANK HIM FOR THE NOTES...
PI (BIP)
HELLO?
Hey, Yuugo! It's me!
I DON'T HAVE ANY MONEY TO LOAN YOU.
I'm not calling for that.
Are you visiting home for New Year's?
I DON'T WANT TO! I'M BUSY!
Ahh, right. You're tutoring Mikage-chan, was it?
HUH!? WHEN DID I MENTION MIKAGE TO YOU!?
I TOLD YOU IT WAS FOR A FRIEND'S COLLEGE PREP...

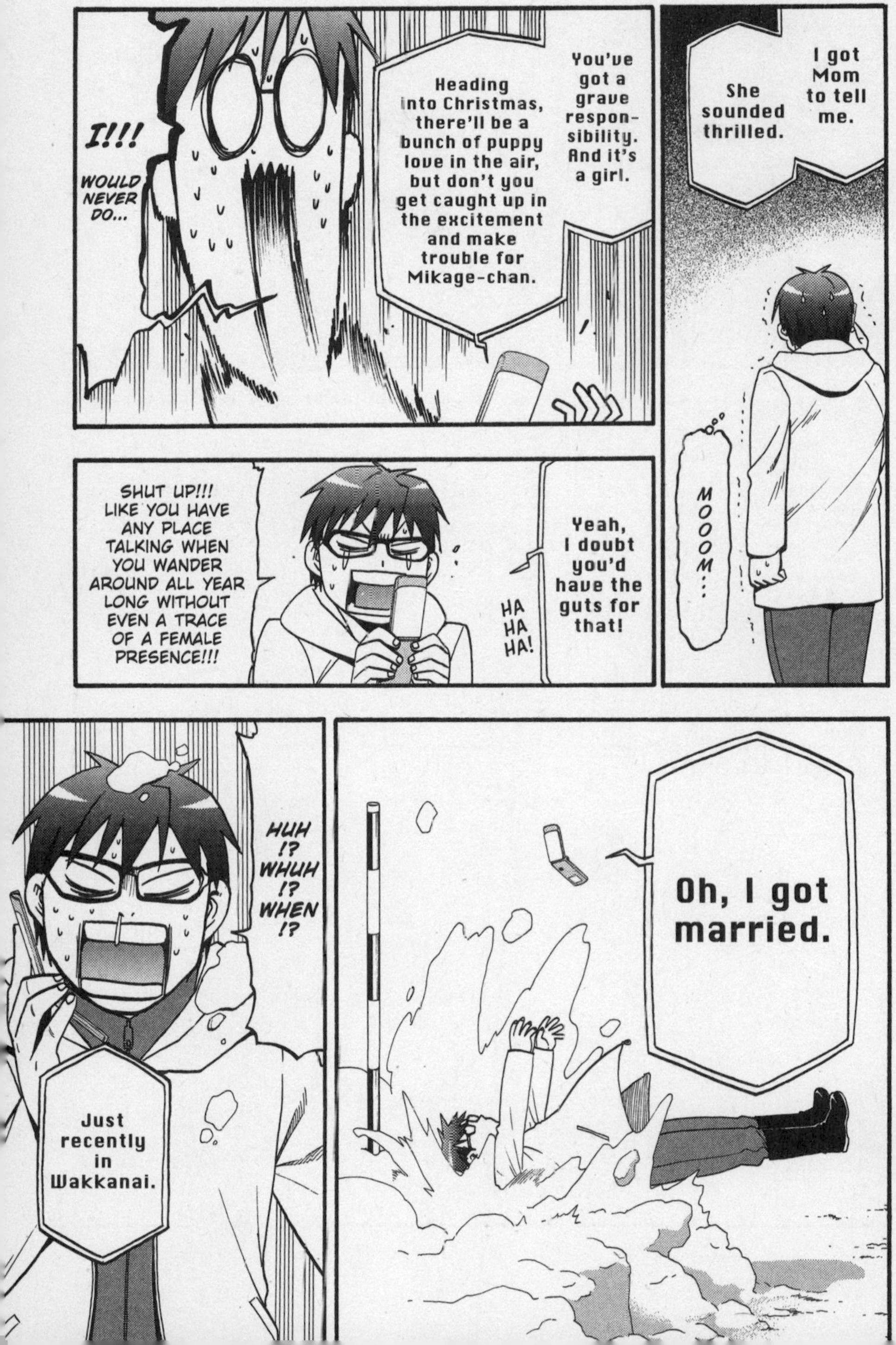
I got Mom to tell me.
She sounded thrilled.
MOOOM...
You've got a grave responsibility. And it's a girl.
Heading into Christmas, there'll be a bunch of puppy love in the air, but don't you get caught up in the excitement and make trouble for Mikage-chan.
I!!!
WOULD NEVER DO...
Yeah, I doubt you'd have the guts for that!
HA HA HA!
SHUT UP!!! LIKE YOU HAVE ANY PLACE TALKING WHEN YOU WANDER AROUND ALL YEAR LONG WITHOUT EVEN A TRACE OF A FEMALE PRESENCE!!!
Oh, I got married.
HUH!? WHUH!? WHEN!?
Just recently in Wakkanai.

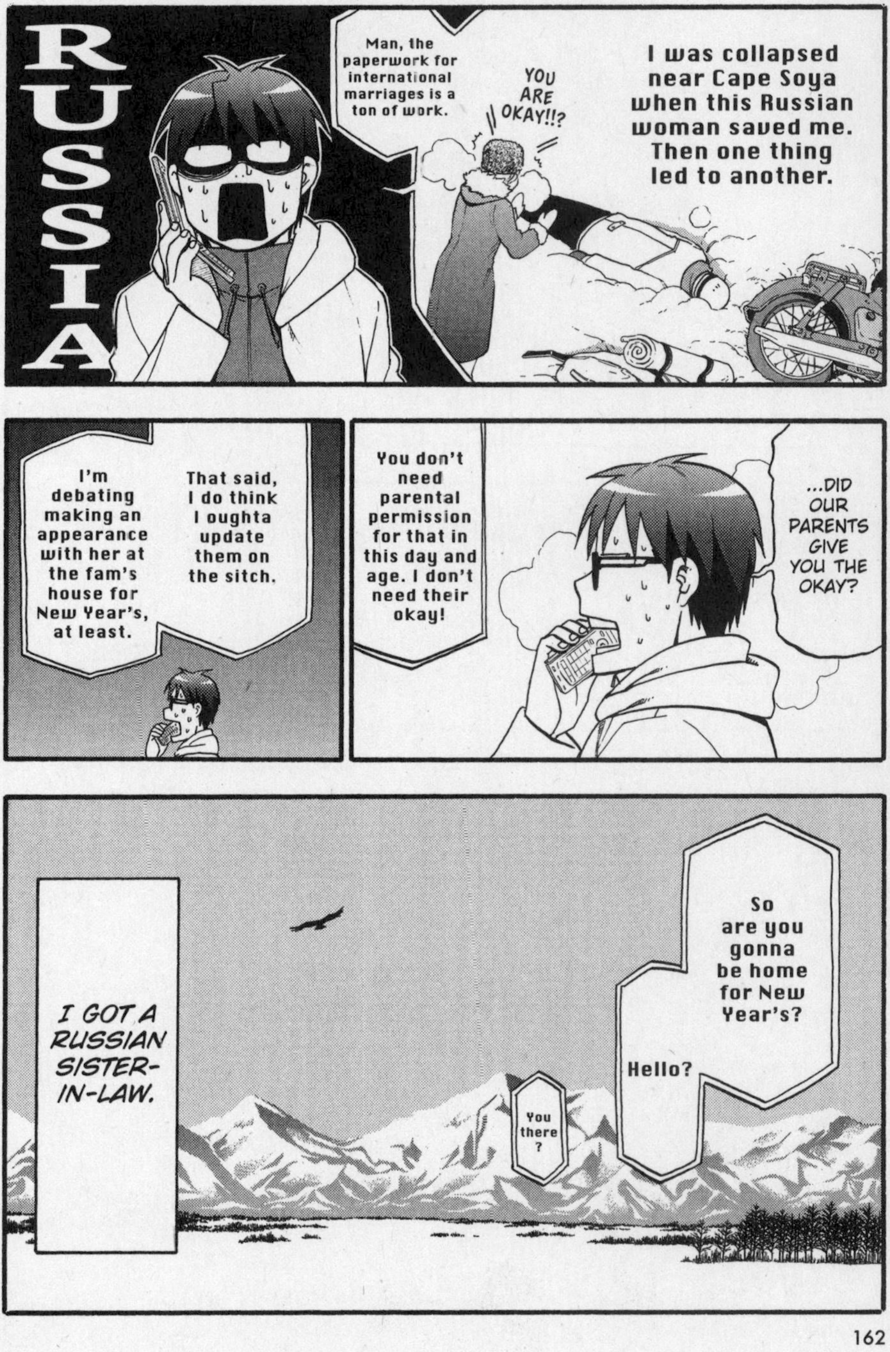
I was collapsed near Cape Soya when this Russian woman saved me. Then one thing led to another.
YOU ARE OKAY!!?
Man, the paperwork for international marriages is a ton of work.
RUSSIA
...DID OUR PARENTS GIVE YOU THE OKAY?
You don't need parental permission for that in this day and age. I don't need their okay!
That said, I do think I oughta update them on the sitch.
I'm debating making an appearance with her at the fam's house for New Year's, at least.
So are you gonna be home for New Year's?
Hello?
You there?
I GOT A RUSSIAN SISTER-IN-LAW.

Silver Spoon

DORM TEACHER
KOUJI HIRONO

LAZY

Chapter 79:
Tale of Winter ⑯

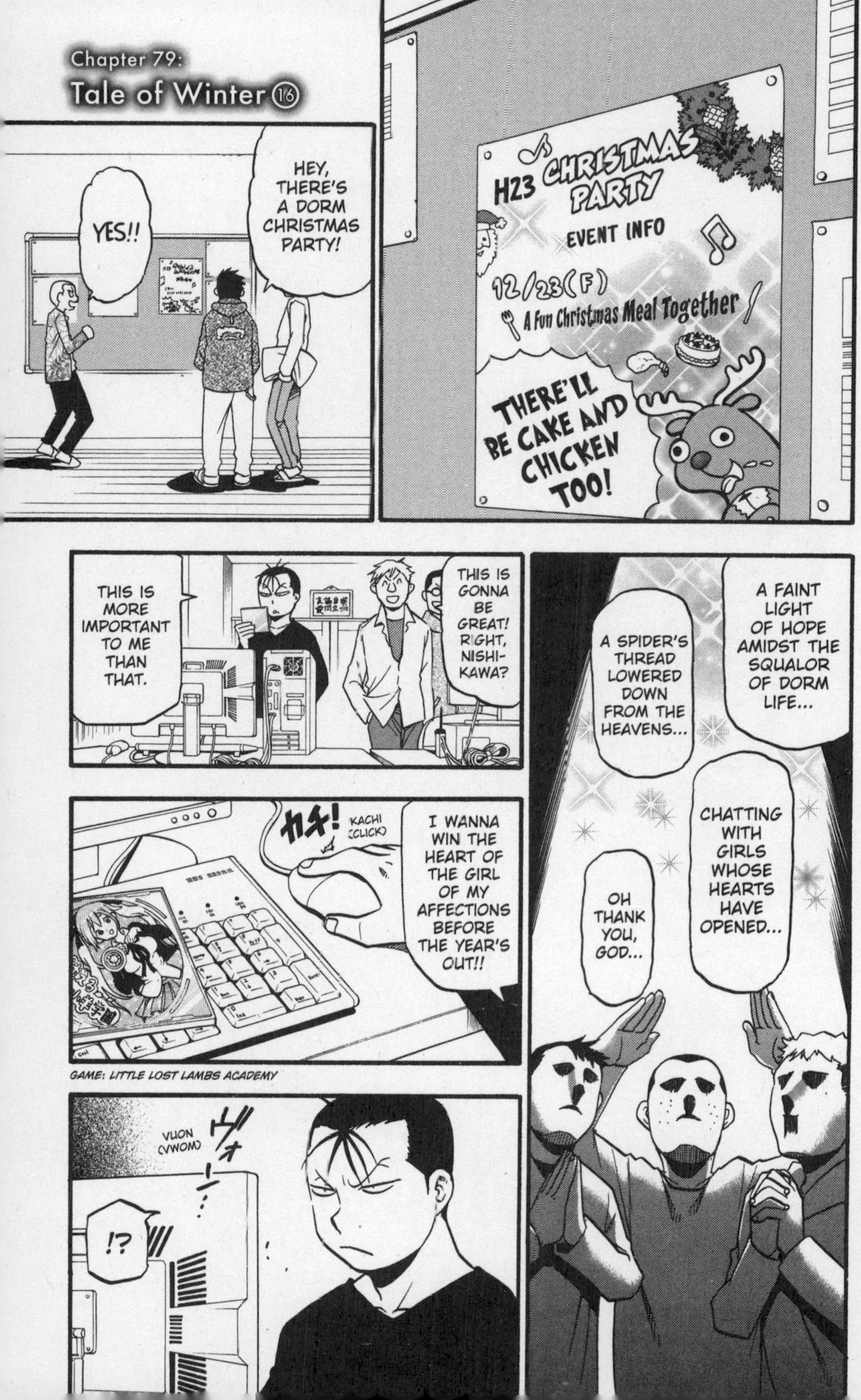

H23 CHRISTMAS PARTY
EVENT INFO
12/23 (F)
A Fun Christmas Meal Together
THERE'LL BE CAKE AND CHICKEN TOO!
HEY, THERE'S A DORM CHRISTMAS PARTY!
YES!!
A FAINT LIGHT OF HOPE AMIDST THE SQUALOR OF DORM LIFE...
A SPIDER'S THREAD LOWERED DOWN FROM THE HEAVENS...
CHATTING WITH GIRLS WHOSE HEARTS HAVE OPENED...
OH THANK YOU, GOD...
THIS IS GONNA BE GREAT! RIGHT, NISHIKAWA?
THIS IS MORE IMPORTANT TO ME THAN THAT.
I WANNA WIN THE HEART OF THE GIRL OF MY AFFECTIONS BEFORE THE YEAR'S OUT!!
カチ!
KACHI (CLICK)
GAME: LITTLE LOST LAMBS ACADEMY
ヴォー
VUON (VWOM)
!?

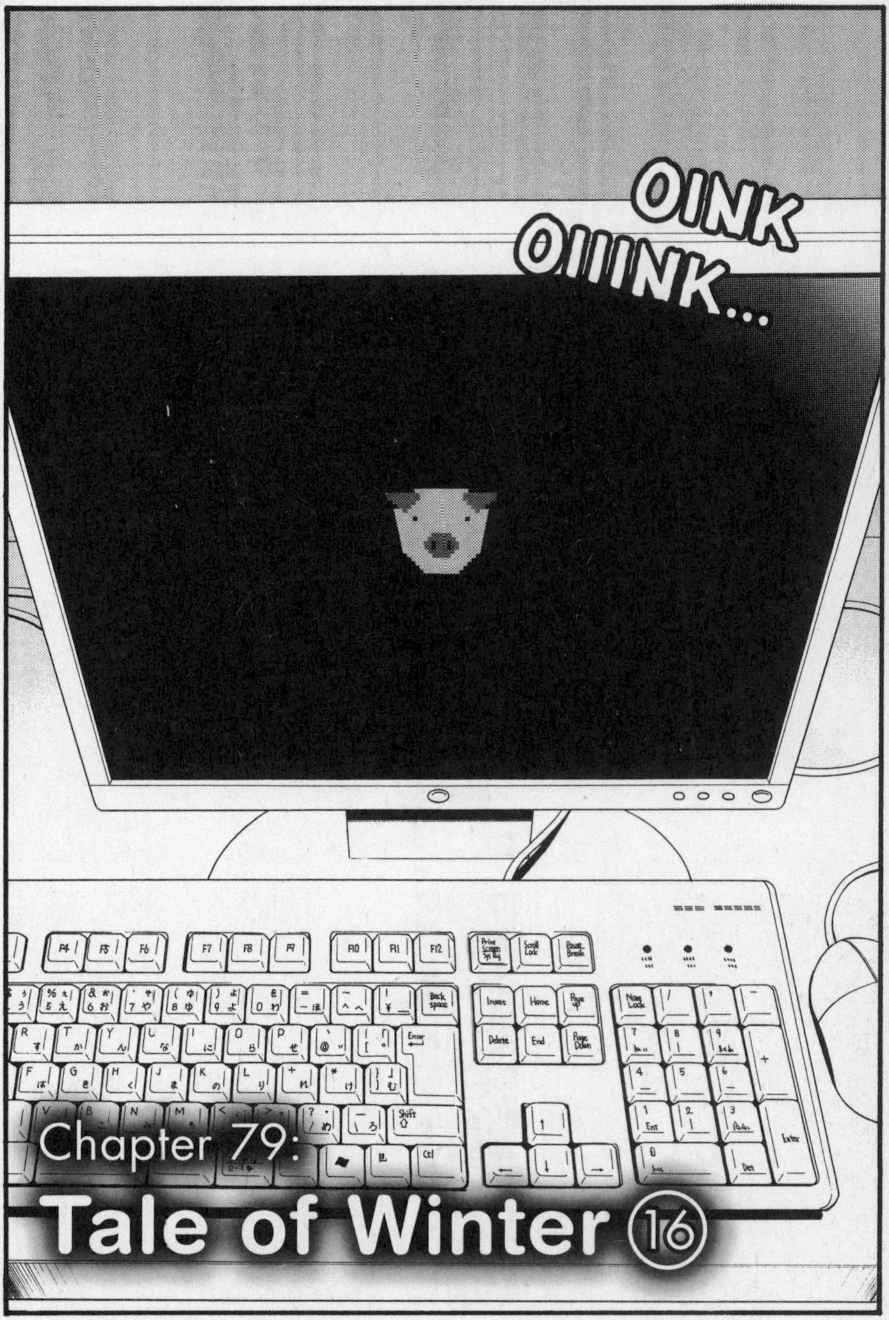
OINK
OIIINK...
Chapter 79:
Tale of Winter ⑯

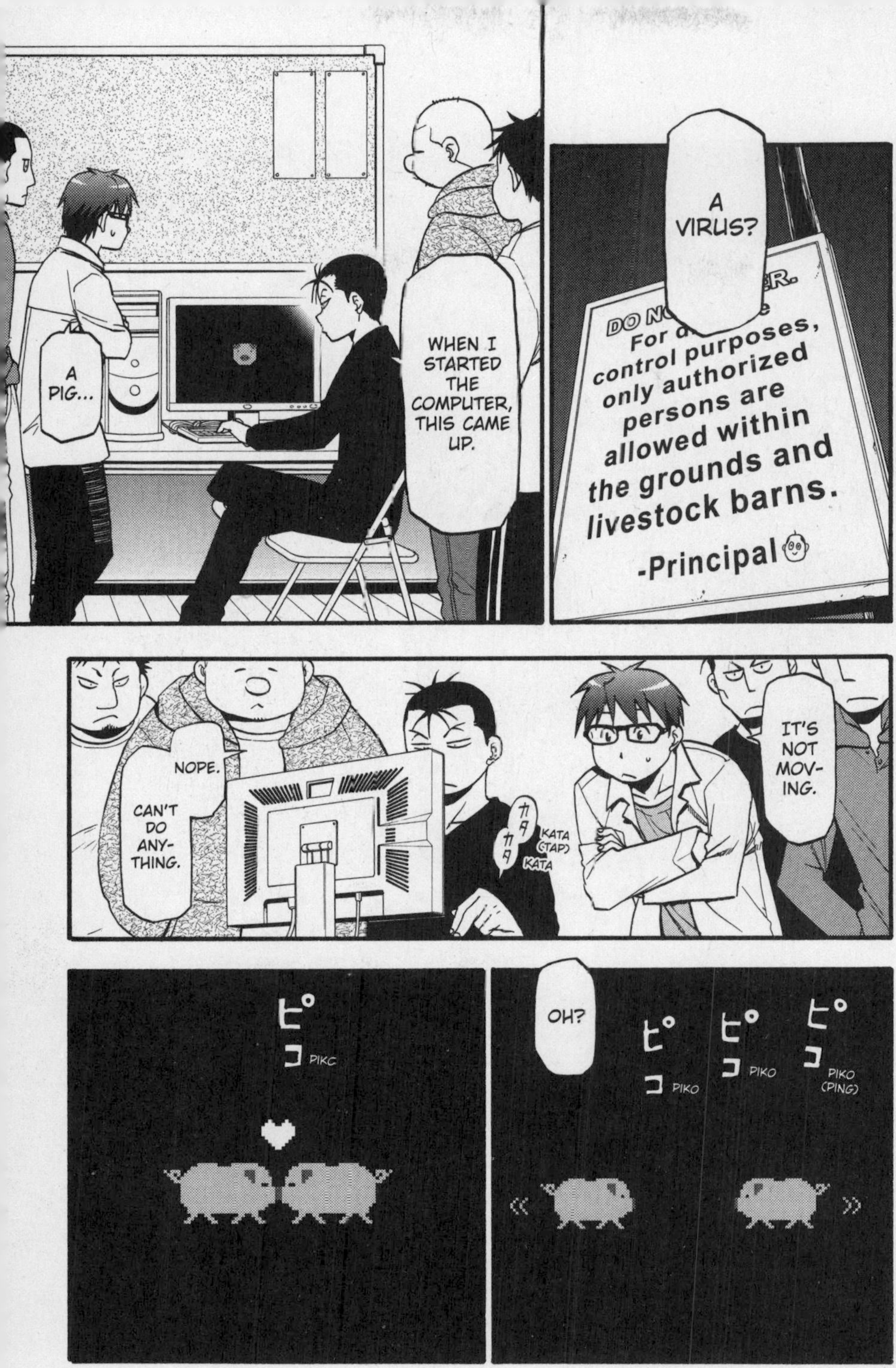
A VIRUS?
For
control purposes, only authorized persons are allowed within the grounds and livestock barns.
-Principal
WHEN I STARTED THE COMPUTER, THIS CAME UP.
A PIG...
IT'S NOT MOVING.
カタ カタ
KATA (TAP) KATA
NOPE.
CAN'T DO ANYTHING.
OH?
ピコ PIKO (PING)
ピコ PIKO
ピコ PIKO
ピコ PIKO

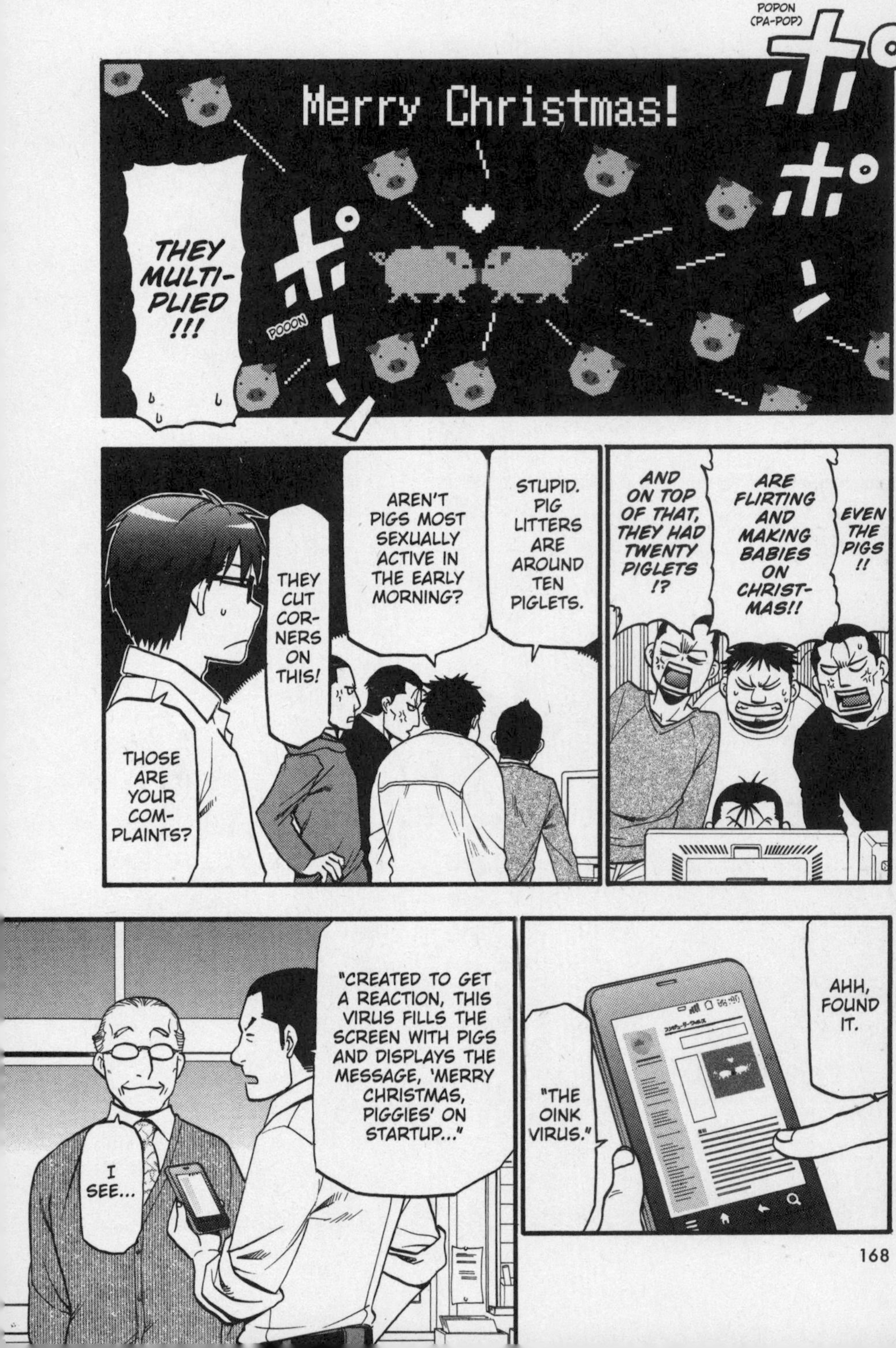
POPON (PA-POP)
Merry Christmas!
THEY MULTIPLIED!!!
POOON
EVEN THE PIGS!!
ARE FLIRTING AND MAKING BABIES ON CHRISTMAS!!
AND ON TOP OF THAT, THEY HAD TWENTY PIGLETS!?
STUPID. PIG LITTERS ARE AROUND TEN PIGLETS.
AREN'T PIGS MOST SEXUALLY ACTIVE IN THE EARLY MORNING?
THEY CUT CORNERS ON THIS!
THOSE ARE YOUR COMPLAINTS?
AHH, FOUND IT.
"THE OINK VIRUS."
"CREATED TO GET A REACTION, THIS VIRUS FILLS THE SCREEN WITH PIGS AND DISPLAYS THE MESSAGE, 'MERRY CHRISTMAS, PIGGIES' ON STARTUP..."
I SEE...

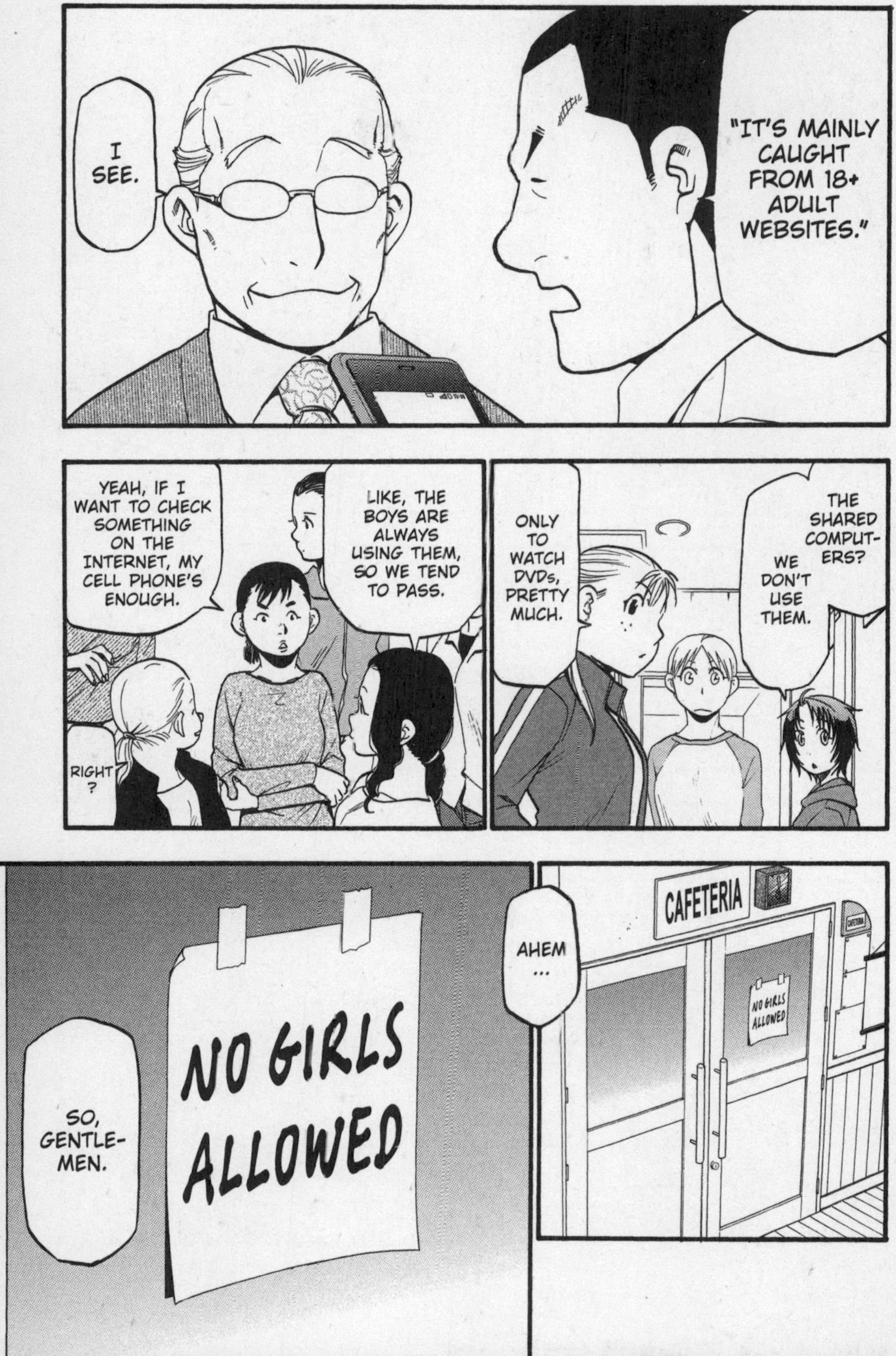
"IT'S MAINLY CAUGHT FROM 18+ ADULT WEBSITES."
I SEE.
THE SHARED COMPUTERS?
WE DON'T USE THEM.
ONLY TO WATCH DVDs, PRETTY MUCH.
LIKE, THE BOYS ARE ALWAYS USING THEM, SO WE TEND TO PASS.
YEAH, IF I WANT TO CHECK SOMETHING ON THE INTERNET, MY CELL PHONE'S ENOUGH.
RIGHT?
CAFETERIA
NO GIRLS ALLOWED
AHEM...
NO GIRLS ALLOWED
SO, GENTLEMEN.

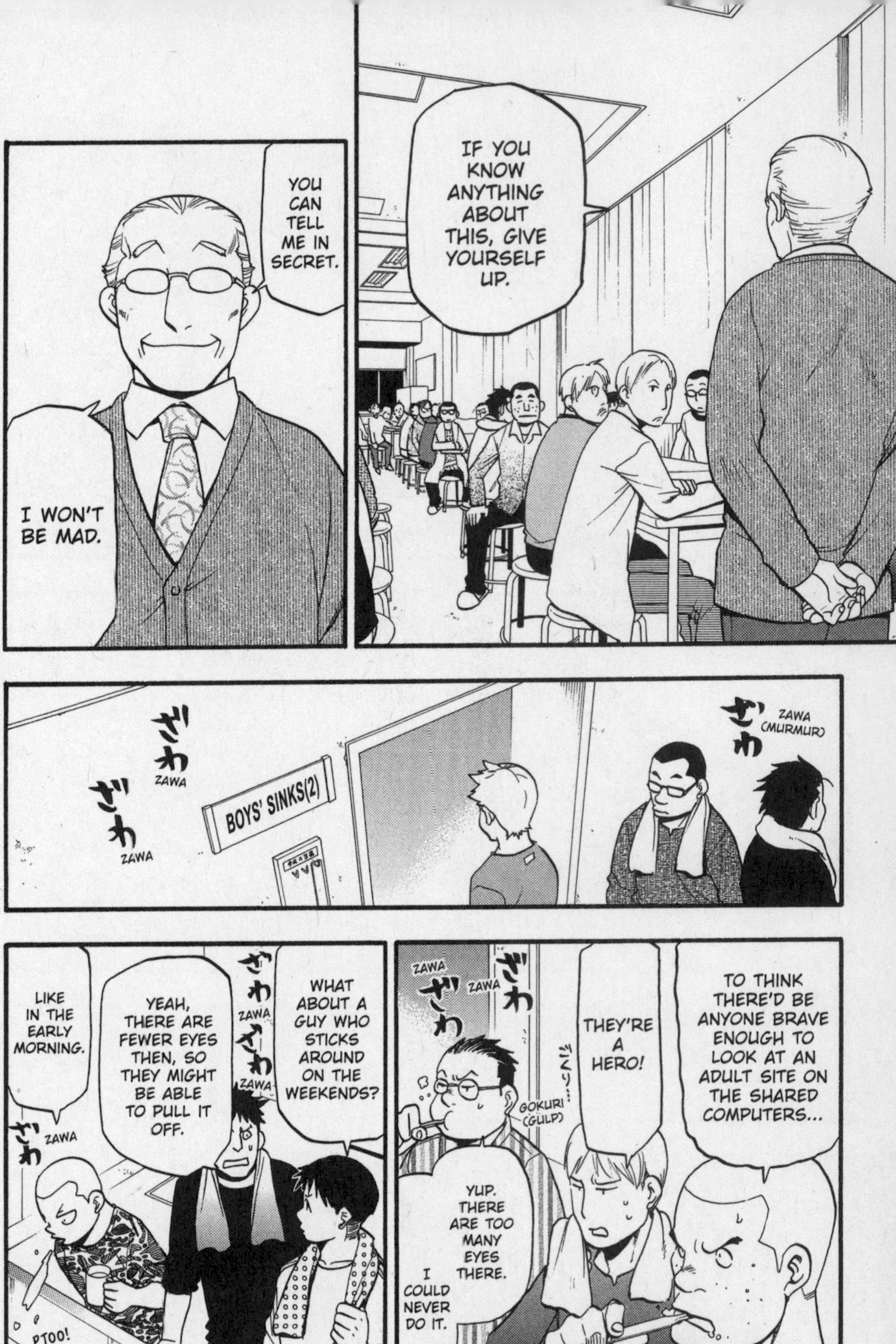

IF YOU KNOW ANYTHING ABOUT THIS, GIVE YOURSELF UP.
YOU CAN TELL ME IN SECRET.
I WON'T BE MAD.
ざわ ZAWA (MURMUR)
ざわ ZAWA
ざわ ZAWA
BOYS' SINKS(2)
TO THINK THERE'D BE ANYONE BRAVE ENOUGH TO LOOK AT AN ADULT SITE ON THE SHARED COMPUTERS...
ざわ ZAWA
ざわ ZAWA
THEY'RE A HERO!
GOKURI (GULP)
YUP. THERE ARE TOO MANY EYES THERE.
I COULD NEVER DO IT.
WHAT ABOUT A GUY WHO STICKS AROUND ON THE WEEKENDS?
ざわ ZAWA
ざわ ZAWA
YEAH, THERE ARE FEWER EYES THEN, SO THEY MIGHT BE ABLE TO PULL IT OFF.
LIKE IN THE EARLY MORNING.
ざわ ZAWA
PTOO!

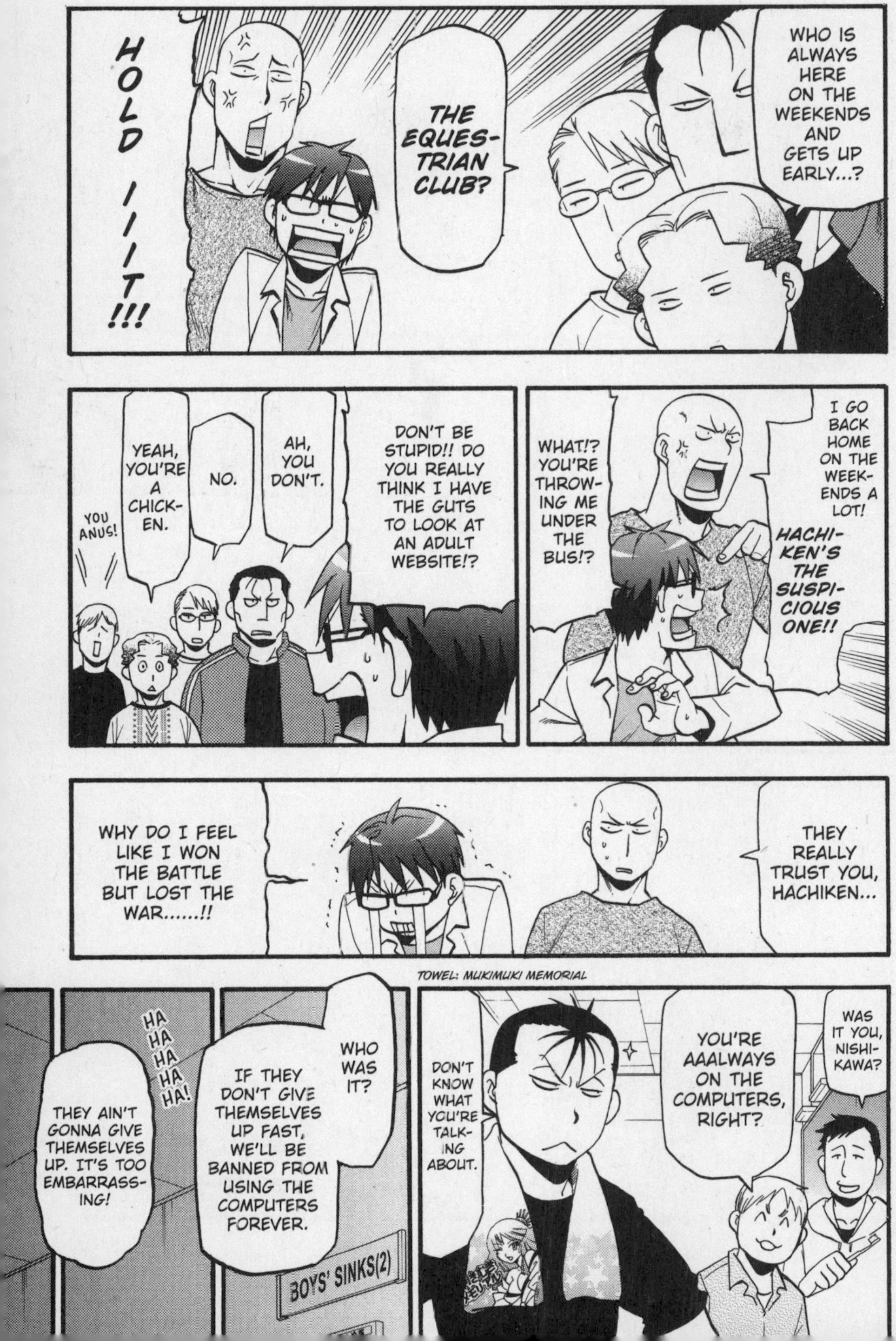
WHO IS ALWAYS HERE ON THE WEEKENDS AND GETS UP EARLY...?
THE EQUES-TRIAN CLUB?
HOLD IIIIT!!!
I GO BACK HOME ON THE WEEK-ENDS A LOT!
HACHI-KEN'S THE SUSPI-CIOUS ONE!!
WHAT!? YOU'RE THROW-ING ME UNDER THE BUS!?
DON'T BE STUPID!! DO YOU REALLY THINK I HAVE THE GUTS TO LOOK AT AN ADULT WEBSITE!?
AH, YOU DON'T.
NO.
YEAH, YOU'RE A CHICK-EN.
YOU ANUS!
THEY REALLY TRUST YOU, HACHIKEN...
WHY DO I FEEL LIKE I WON THE BATTLE BUT LOST THE WAR......!!
TOWEL: MUKIMUKI MEMORIAL
WAS IT YOU, NISHI-KAWA?
YOU'RE AAALWAYS ON THE COMPUTERS, RIGHT?
DON'T KNOW WHAT YOU'RE TALK-ING ABOUT.
WHO WAS IT?
IF THEY DON'T GIVE THEMSELVES UP FAST, WE'LL BE BANNED FROM USING THE COMPUTERS FOREVER.
HA HA HA HA HA!
THEY AIN'T GONNA GIVE THEMSELVES UP. IT'S TOO EMBARRASS-ING!
BOYS' SINKS(2)

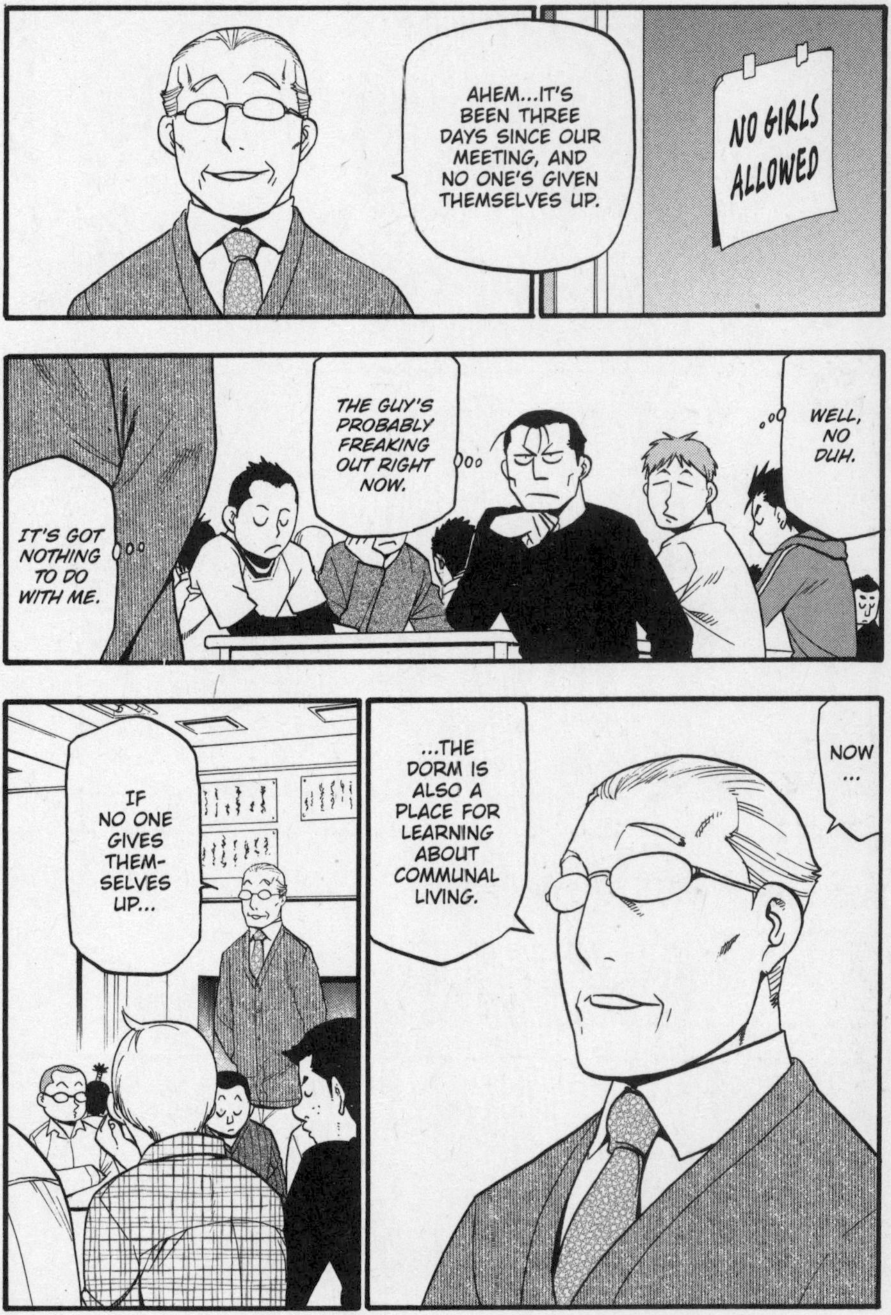
NO GIRLS ALLOWED
AHEM...IT'S BEEN THREE DAYS SINCE OUR MEETING, AND NO ONE'S GIVEN THEMSELVES UP.
WELL, NO DUH.
THE GUY'S PROBABLY FREAKING OUT RIGHT NOW.
IT'S GOT NOTHING TO DO WITH ME.
NOW...
...THE DORM IS ALSO A PLACE FOR LEARNING ABOUT COMMUNAL LIVING.
IF NO ONE GIVES THEM-SELVES UP...

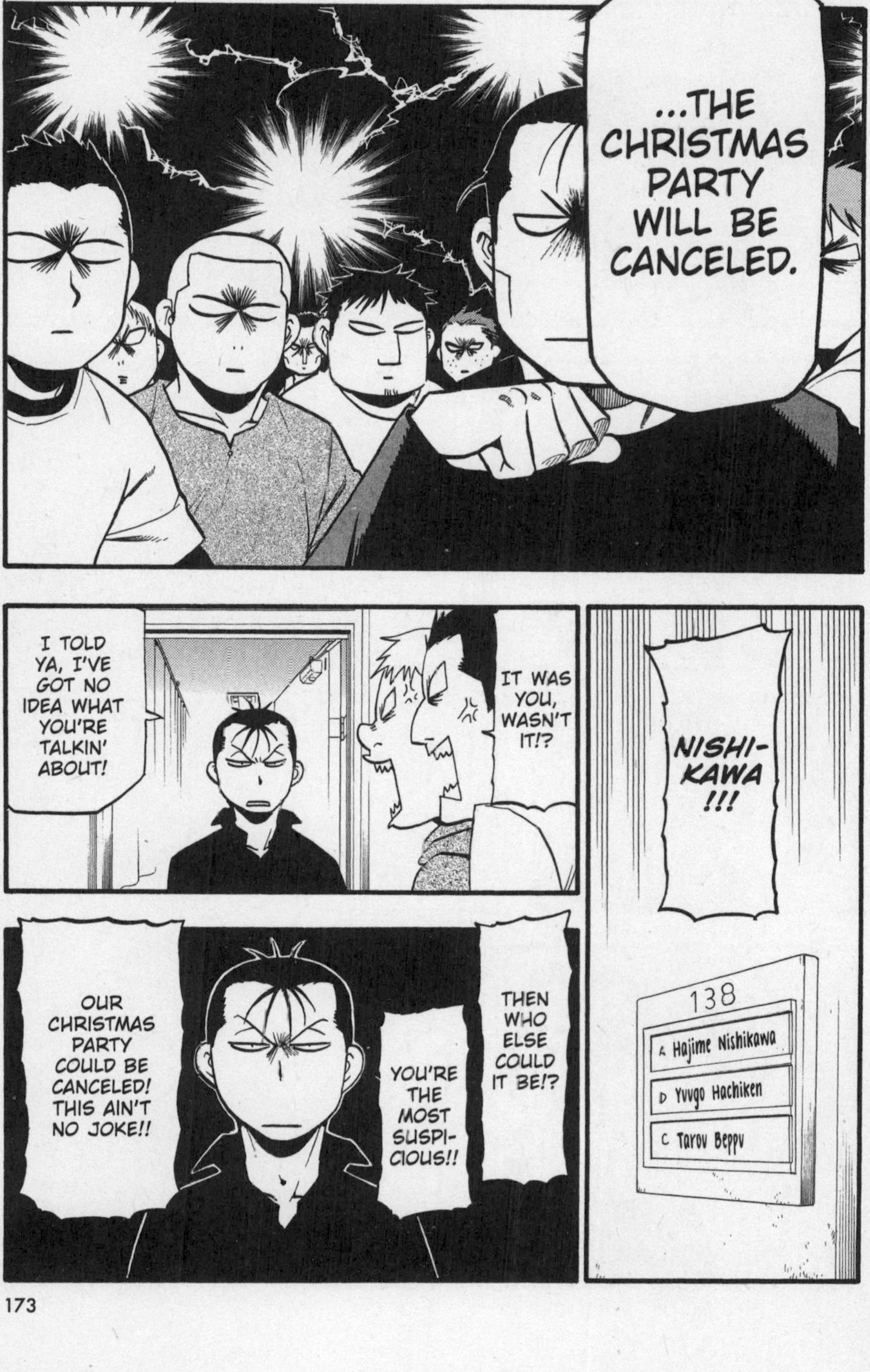
...THE CHRISTMAS PARTY WILL BE CANCELED.
NISHI-KAWA!!!
138
A Hajime Nishikawa
D Yuugo Hachiken
C Tarou Beppu
IT WAS YOU, WASN'T IT!?
I TOLD YA, I'VE GOT NO IDEA WHAT YOU'RE TALKIN' ABOUT!
THEN WHO ELSE COULD IT BE!?
YOU'RE THE MOST SUSPICIOUS!!
OUR CHRISTMAS PARTY COULD BE CANCELED! THIS AIN'T NO JOKE!!

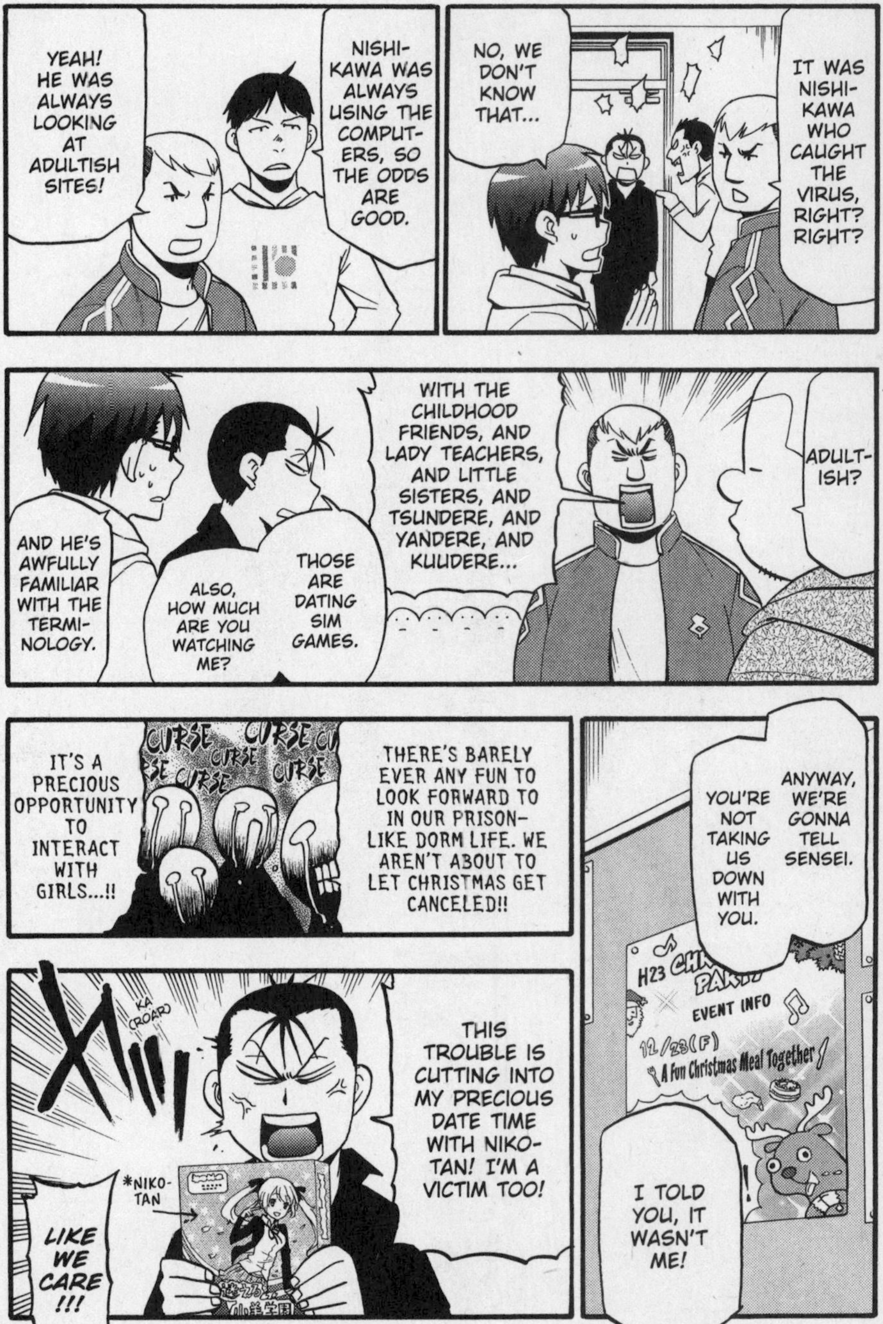
IT WAS NISHI-KAWA WHO CAUGHT THE VIRUS, RIGHT? RIGHT?
NO, WE DON'T KNOW THAT...
NISHI-KAWA WAS ALWAYS USING THE COMPUT-ERS, SO THE ODDS ARE GOOD.
YEAH! HE WAS ALWAYS LOOKING AT ADULTISH SITES!
ADULT-ISH?
WITH THE CHILDHOOD FRIENDS, AND LADY TEACHERS, AND LITTLE SISTERS, AND TSUNDERE, AND YANDERE, AND KUUDERE...
THOSE ARE DATING SIM GAMES.
ALSO, HOW MUCH ARE YOU WATCHING ME?
AND HE'S AWFULLY FAMILIAR WITH THE TERMI-NOLOGY.
ANYWAY, WE'RE GONNA TELL SENSEI.
YOU'RE NOT TAKING US DOWN WITH YOU.
EVENT INFO
12/23(F)
A Fun Christmas Meal Together
I TOLD YOU, IT WASN'T ME!
THERE'S BARELY EVER ANY FUN TO LOOK FORWARD TO IN OUR PRISON-LIKE DORM LIFE. WE AREN'T ABOUT TO LET CHRISTMAS GET CANCELED!!
CURSE CURSE CURSE CURSE CURSE CURSE
IT'S A PRECIOUS OPPORTUNITY TO INTERACT WITH GIRLS...!!
THIS TROUBLE IS CUTTING INTO MY PRECIOUS DATE TIME WITH NIKO-TAN! I'M A VICTIM TOO!
KA (ROAR)
*NIKO-TAN
LIKE WE CARE!!!

GAME: LITTLE LOST LAMBS ACADEMY

GAME: LIMITED FIRST EDITION

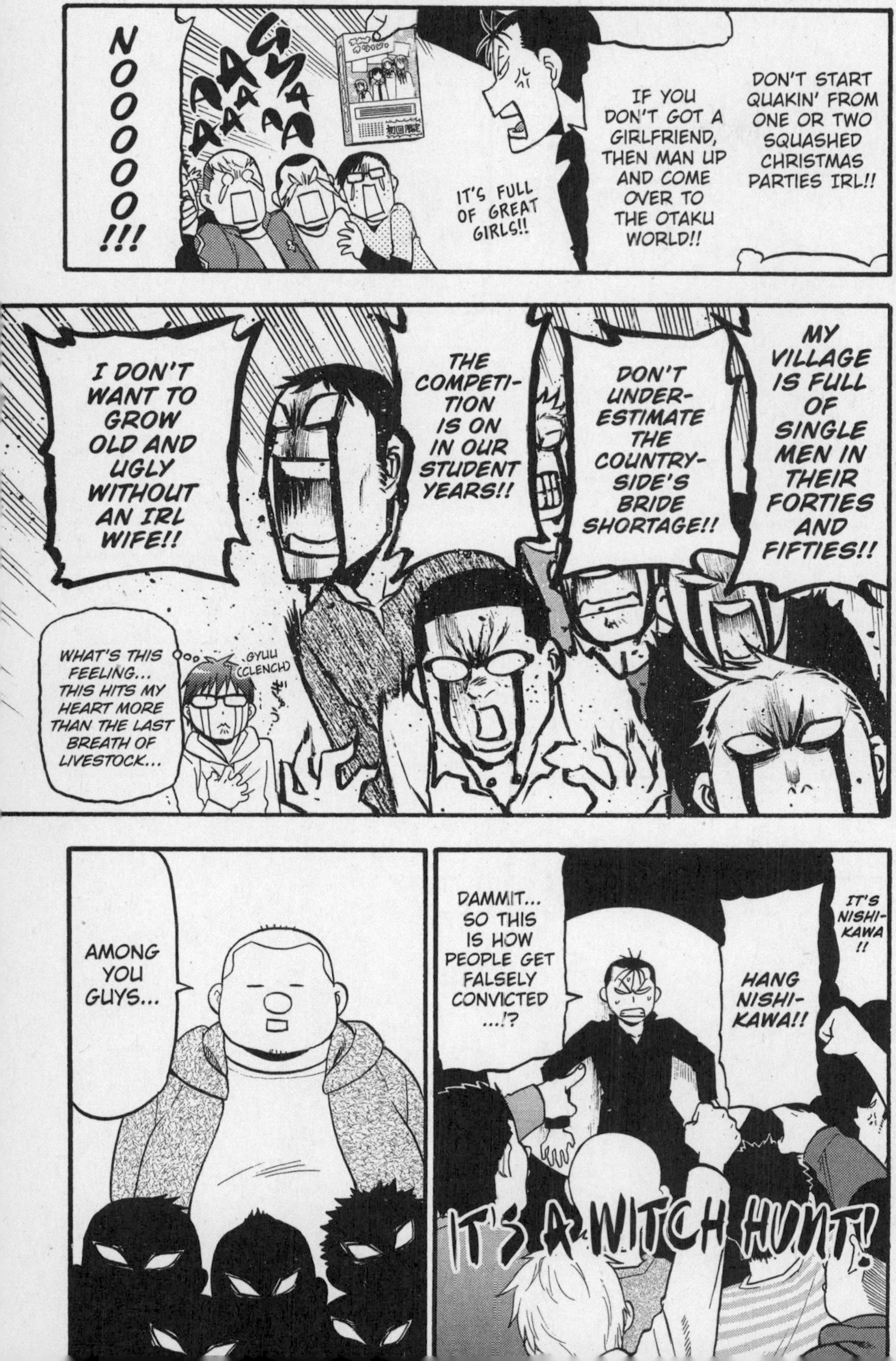
DON'T START QUAKIN' FROM ONE OR TWO SQUASHED CHRISTMAS PARTIES IRL!!
IF YOU DON'T GOT A GIRLFRIEND, THEN MAN UP AND COME OVER TO THE OTAKU WORLD!!
IT'S FULL OF GREAT GIRLS!!
NOOOOOOO!!!
MY VILLAGE IS FULL OF SINGLE MEN IN THEIR FORTIES AND FIFTIES!!
DON'T UNDER-ESTIMATE THE COUNTRY-SIDE'S BRIDE SHORTAGE!!
THE COMPETI-TION IS ON IN OUR STUDENT YEARS!!
I DON'T WANT TO GROW OLD AND UGLY WITHOUT AN IRL WIFE!!
GYUU (CLENCH)
WHAT'S THIS FEELING... THIS HITS MY HEART MORE THAN THE LAST BREATH OF LIVESTOCK...
IT'S NISHI-KAWA!!
HANG NISHI-KAWA!!
DAMMIT... SO THIS IS HOW PEOPLE GET FALSELY CONVICTED ...!?
IT'S A WITCH HUNT!
AMONG YOU GUYS...

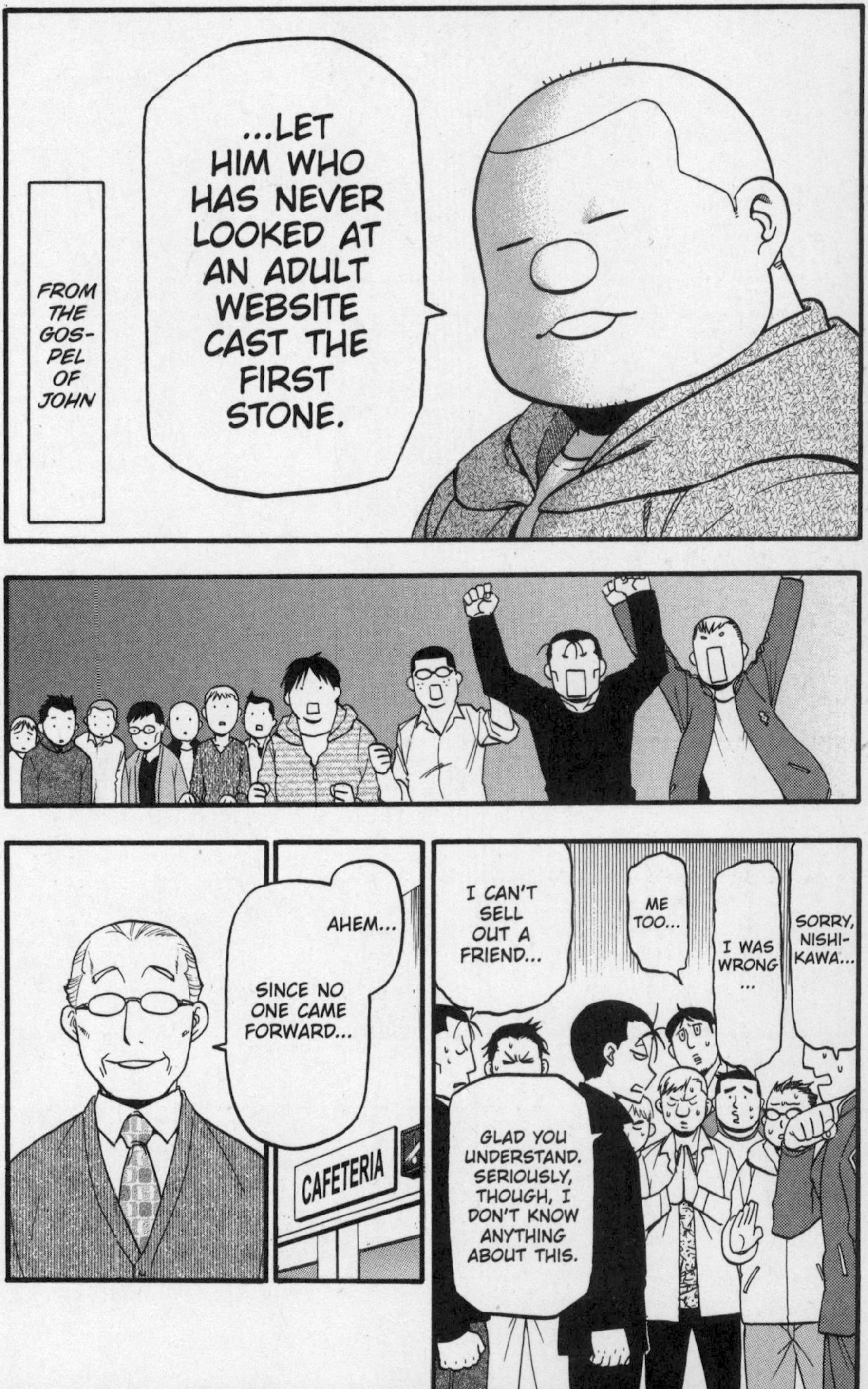
...LET HIM WHO HAS NEVER LOOKED AT AN ADULT WEBSITE CAST THE FIRST STONE.
FROM THE GOS-PEL OF JOHN
SORRY, NISHI-KAWA...
I WAS WRONG...
ME TOO...
I CAN'T SELL OUT A FRIEND...
GLAD YOU UNDERSTAND. SERIOUSLY, THOUGH, I DON'T KNOW ANYTHING ABOUT THIS.
AHEM...
SINCE NO ONE CAME FORWARD...
CAFETERIA

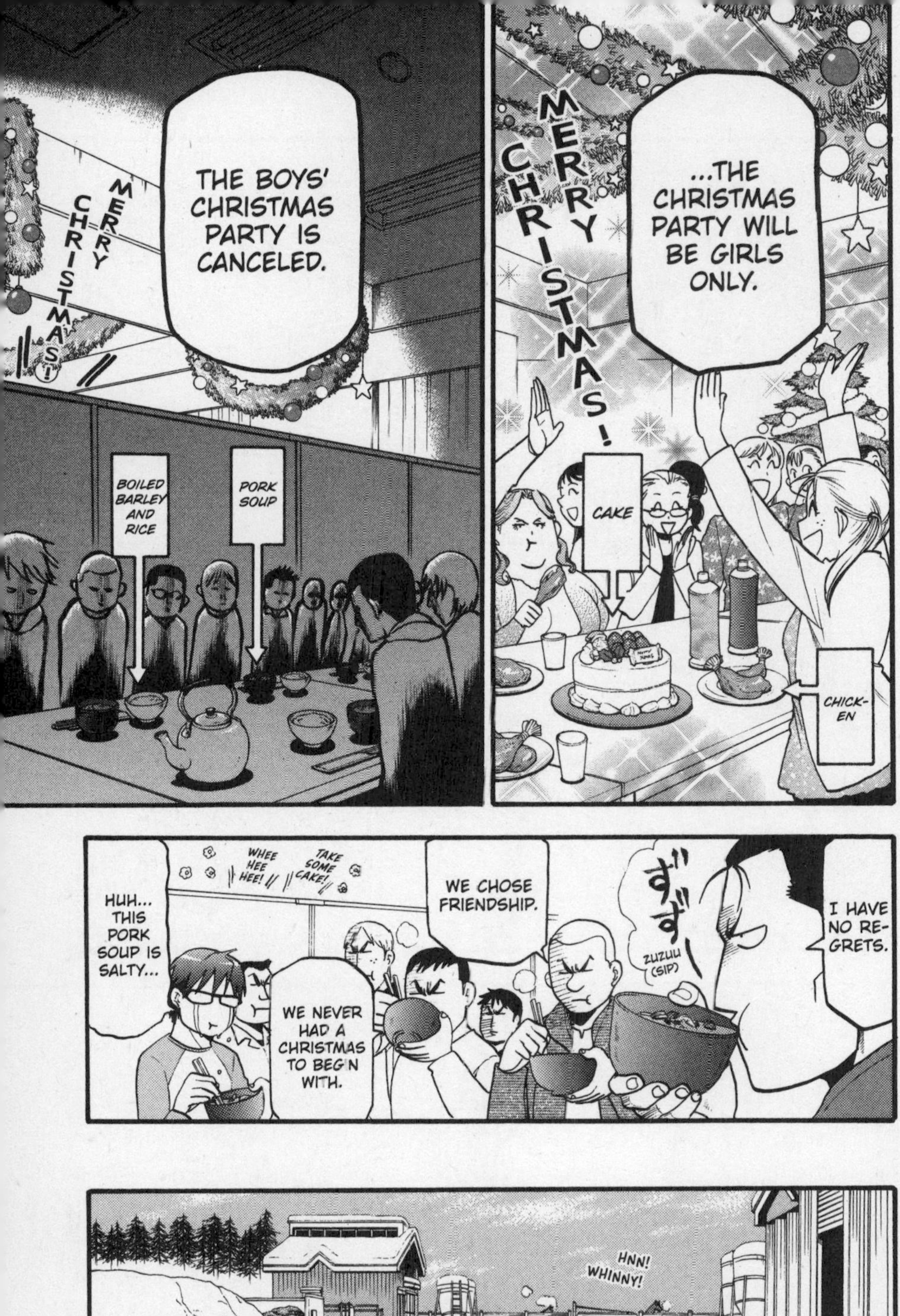

...THE CHRISTMAS PARTY WILL BE GIRLS ONLY.
MERRY CHRISTMAS!
CAKE
CHICK-EN
THE BOYS' CHRISTMAS PARTY IS CANCELED.
MERRY CHRISTMAS!
PORK SOUP
BOILED BARLEY AND RICE
I HAVE NO RE-GRETS.
ずず
ZUZUU (SIP)
WE CHOSE FRIENDSHIP.
TAKE SOME CAKE!
WHEE HEE HEE!
WE NEVER HAD A CHRISTMAS TO BEGIN WITH.
HUH... THIS PORK SOUP IS SALTY...
HNN! WHINNY!

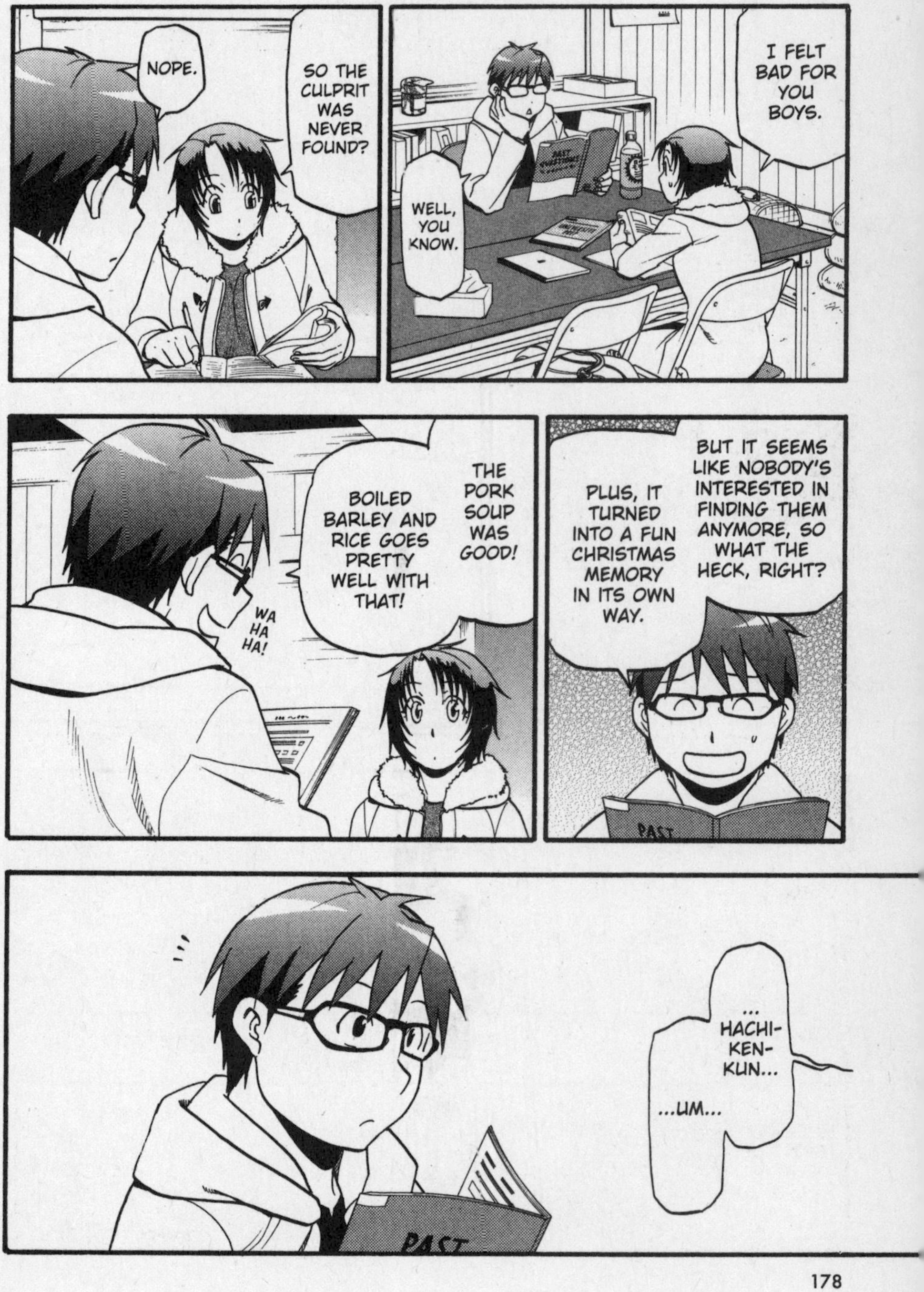
I FELT BAD FOR YOU BOYS.
WELL, YOU KNOW.
SO THE CULPRIT WAS NEVER FOUND?
NOPE.
BUT IT SEEMS LIKE NOBODY'S INTERESTED IN FINDING THEM ANYMORE, SO WHAT THE HECK, RIGHT?
PLUS, IT TURNED INTO A FUN CHRISTMAS MEMORY IN ITS OWN WAY.
PAST
THE PORK SOUP WAS GOOD!
BOILED BARLEY AND RICE GOES PRETTY WELL WITH THAT!
WA HA HA!
... HACHI-KEN-KUN...
...UM...
PAST

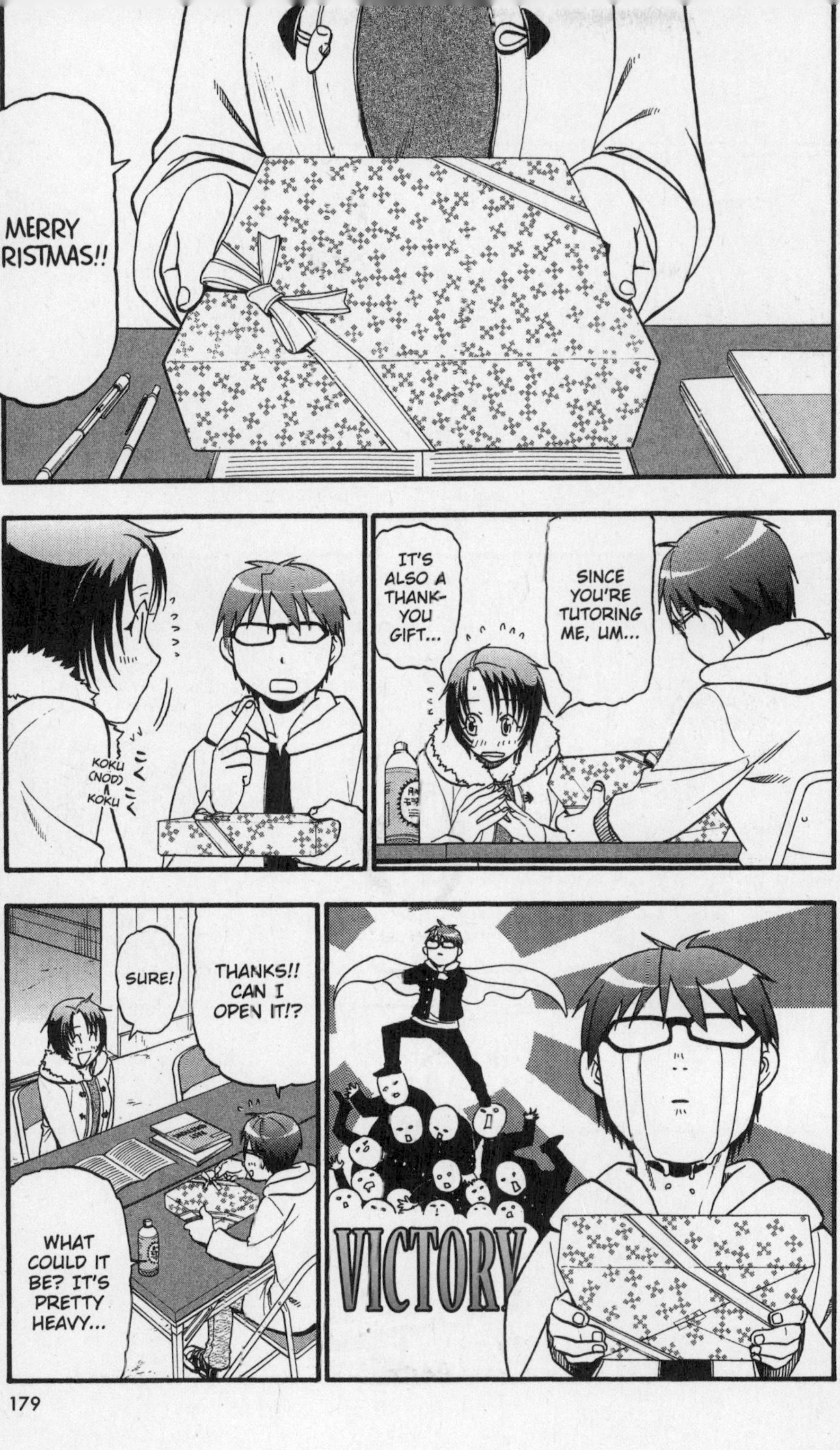
MERRY CHRISTMAS!!
SINCE YOU'RE TUTORING ME, UM...
IT'S ALSO A THANK-YOU GIFT...
KOKU (NOD) KOKU
VICTORY
THANKS!! CAN I OPEN IT!?
SURE!
WHAT COULD IT BE? IT'S PRETTY HEAVY...

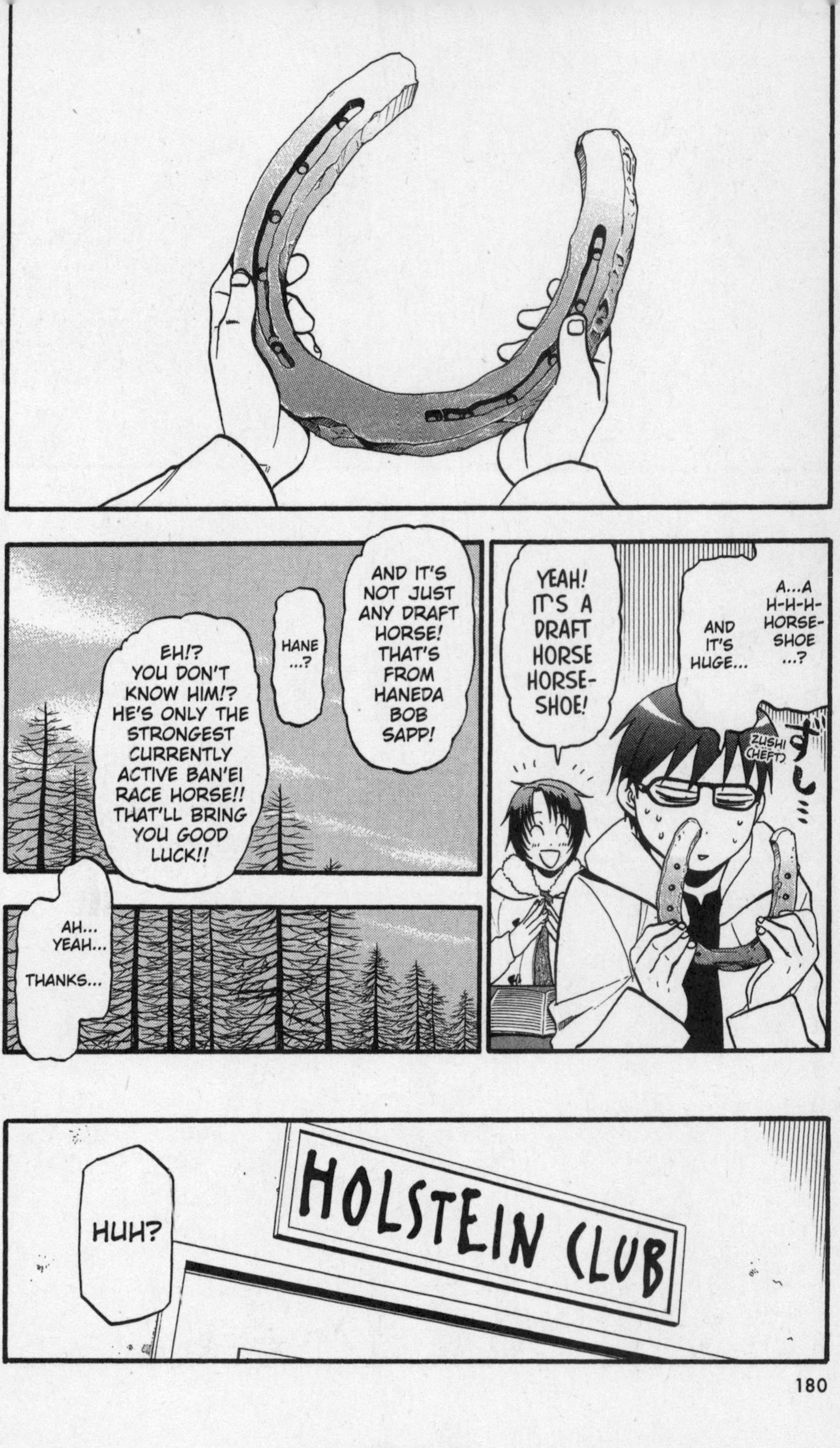
A...A H-H-H-HORSE-SHOE ...?
AND IT'S HUGE...
YEAH! IT'S A DRAFT HORSE HORSE-SHOE!
ZUSHI (HEFT)
AND IT'S NOT JUST ANY DRAFT HORSE! THAT'S FROM HANEDA BOB SAPP!
HANE ...?
EH!? YOU DON'T KNOW HIM!? HE'S ONLY THE STRONGEST CURRENTLY ACTIVE BAN'EI RACE HORSE!! THAT'LL BRING YOU GOOD LUCK!!
AH... YEAH...
THANKS...
HOLSTEIN CLUB
HUH?

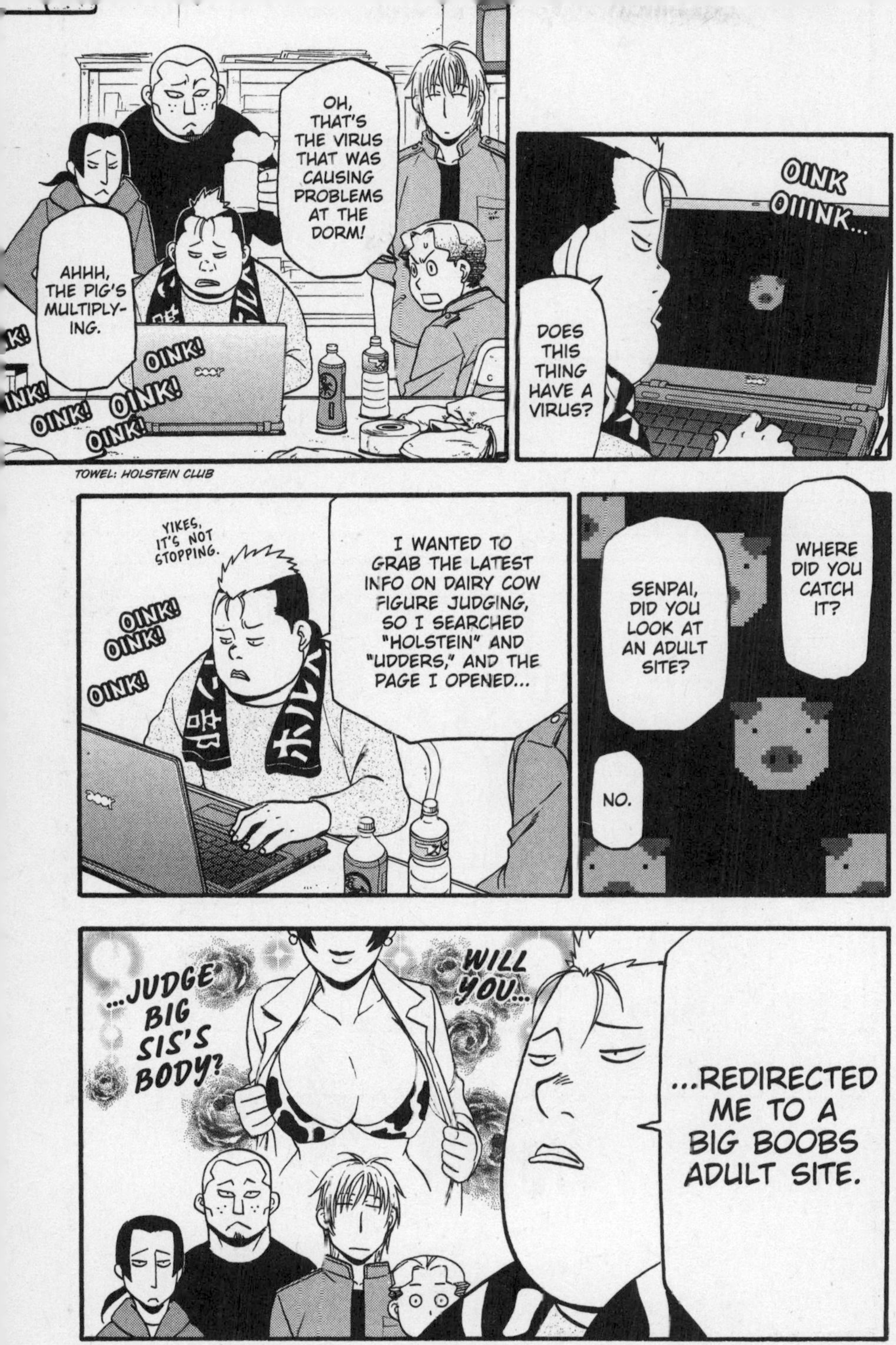
OINK OIIINK...
DOES THIS THING HAVE A VIRUS?
OH, THAT'S THE VIRUS THAT WAS CAUSING PROBLEMS AT THE DORM!
AHHH, THE PIG'S MULTIPLY-ING.
OINK!
OINK! OINK!
OINK!
WHERE DID YOU CATCH IT?
SENPAI, DID YOU LOOK AT AN ADULT SITE?
NO.
I WANTED TO GRAB THE LATEST INFO ON DAIRY COW FIGURE JUDGING, SO I SEARCHED "HOLSTEIN" AND "UDDERS," AND THE PAGE I OPENED...
YIKES, IT'S NOT STOPPING.
OINK! OINK!
OINK!
...REDIRECTED ME TO A BIG BOOBS ADULT SITE.
WILL YOU...
...JUDGE BIG SIS'S BODY?
TOWEL: HOLSTEIN CLUB

YUP.

....
AIKAWA...

YUP.

NOW THAT I THINK ABOUT IT, HAVEN'T WE SEARCHED "HOLSTEIN" AND "UDDERS" ON DORM COMPUTERS?

YUP.

AND IT REDIRECTED TO SOME WEIRD SITE?

MoOOooo!

...LET'S KEEP THIS TO OURSELVES.

YUP.

Silver Spoon **9** • END

Silver Spoon

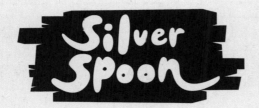

Chicken, Chicken, Chicken

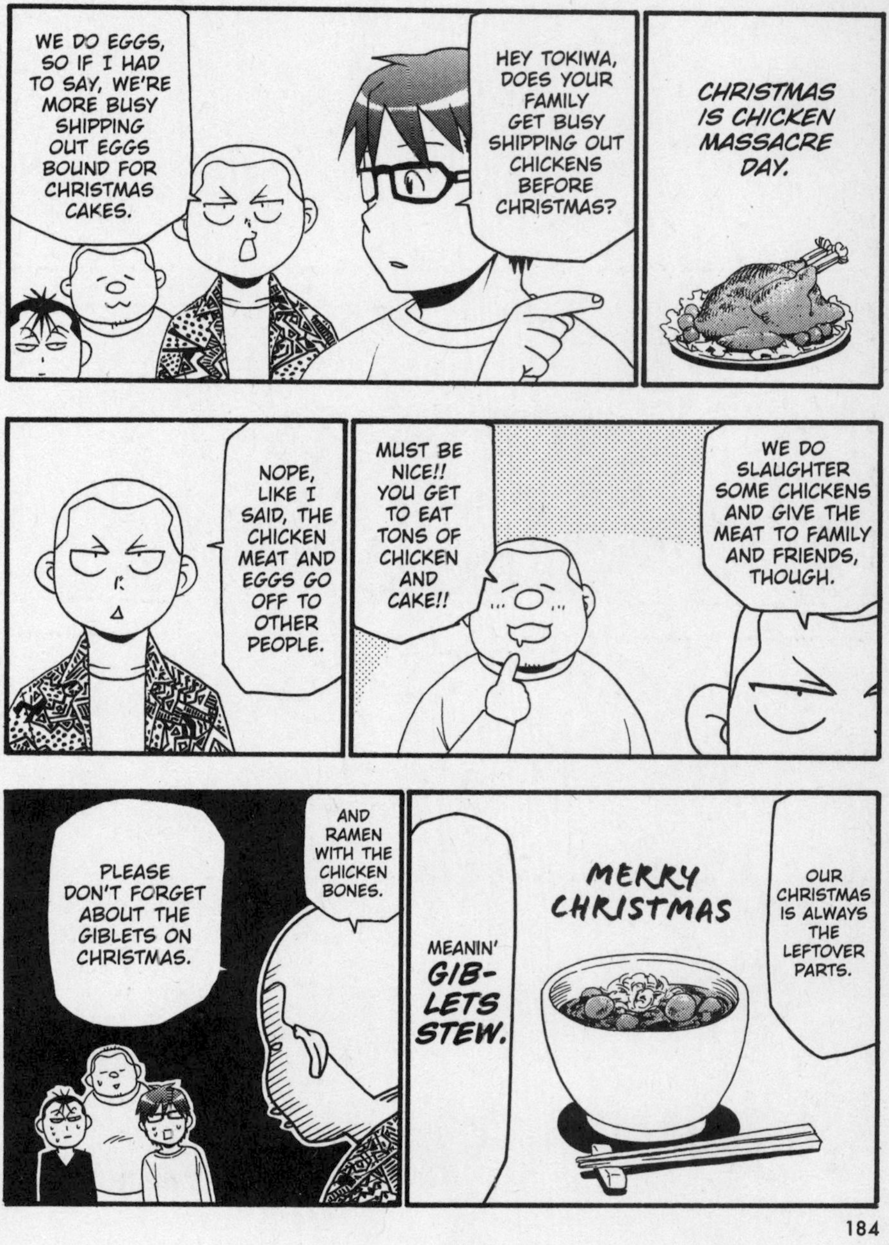
CHRISTMAS IS CHICKEN MASSACRE DAY.
HEY TOKIWA, DOES YOUR FAMILY GET BUSY SHIPPING OUT CHICKENS BEFORE CHRISTMAS?
WE DO EGGS, SO IF I HAD TO SAY, WE'RE MORE BUSY SHIPPING OUT EGGS BOUND FOR CHRISTMAS CAKES.
WE DO SLAUGHTER SOME CHICKENS AND GIVE THE MEAT TO FAMILY AND FRIENDS, THOUGH.
MUST BE NICE!! YOU GET TO EAT TONS OF CHICKEN AND CAKE!!
NOPE, LIKE I SAID, THE CHICKEN MEAT AND EGGS GO OFF TO OTHER PEOPLE.
OUR CHRISTMAS IS ALWAYS THE LEFTOVER PARTS.
MERRY CHRISTMAS
MEANIN' GIBLETS STEW.
AND RAMEN WITH THE CHICKEN BONES.
PLEASE DON'T FORGET ABOUT THE GIBLETS ON CHRISTMAS.

Cow Shed Diaries:
"That's the Hokkaido Trap!!" Tale

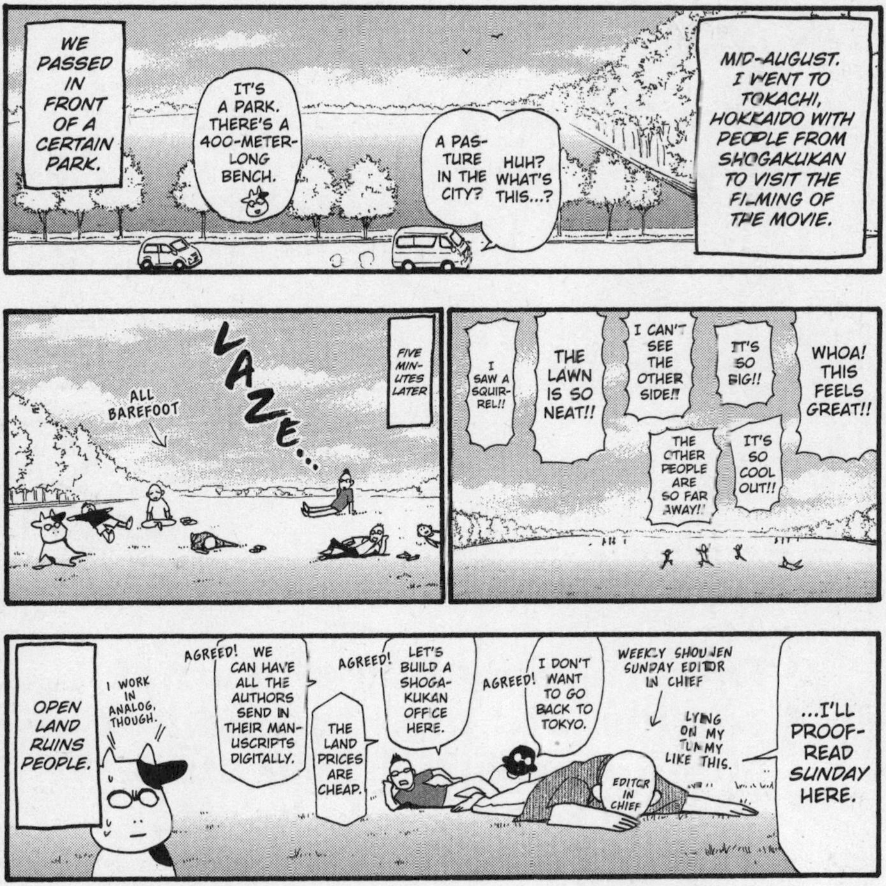
MID-AUGUST. I WENT TO TOKACHI, HOKKAIDO WITH PEOPLE FROM SHOGAKUKAN TO VISIT THE FILMING OF THE MOVIE.
HUH? WHAT'S THIS...?
A PASTURE IN THE CITY?
IT'S A PARK. THERE'S A 400-METER-LONG BENCH.
WE PASSED IN FRONT OF A CERTAIN PARK.
WHOA! THIS FEELS GREAT!!
IT'S SO BIG!!
IT'S SO COOL OUT!!
I CAN'T SEE THE OTHER SIDE!!
THE OTHER PEOPLE ARE SO FAR AWAY!!
THE LAWN IS SO NEAT!!
I SAW A SQUIRREL!!
FIVE MINUTES LATER
LAZE...
ALL BAREFOOT
...I'LL PROOFREAD SUNDAY HERE.
LYING ON MY TUMMY LIKE THIS.
WEEKLY SHOUNEN SUNDAY EDITOR IN CHIEF
EDITOR IN CHIEF
I DON'T WANT TO GO BACK TO TOKYO.
AGREED!
LET'S BUILD A SHOGAKUKAN OFFICE HERE.
AGREED!
THE LAND PRICES ARE CHEAP.
AGREED! WE CAN HAVE ALL THE AUTHORS SEND IN THEIR MANUSCRIPTS DIGITALLY.
I WORK IN ANALOG, THOUGH.
OPEN LAND RUINS PEOPLE.

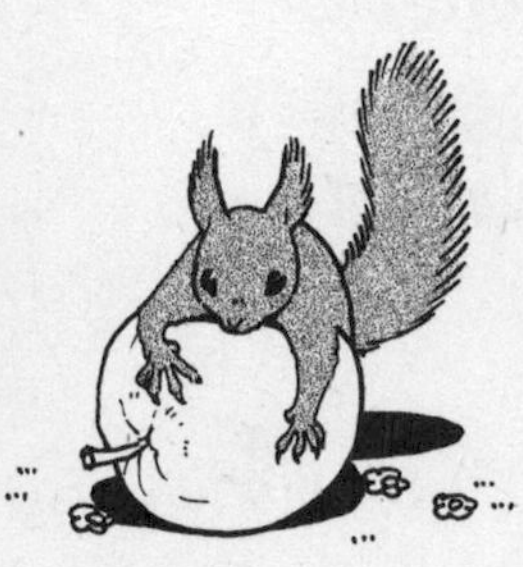

Silver Spoon 9!
In a flash, we're just before the double digits... Thank you so much for sticking with us.

あらかわひろむ
Hiromu Arakawa

~ Special Thanks ~
All of my assistants,
Everyone who helped with collecting material, interviews, and consulting,
My editor, Takashi Tsubouchi,

AND YOU!!

NEXT......

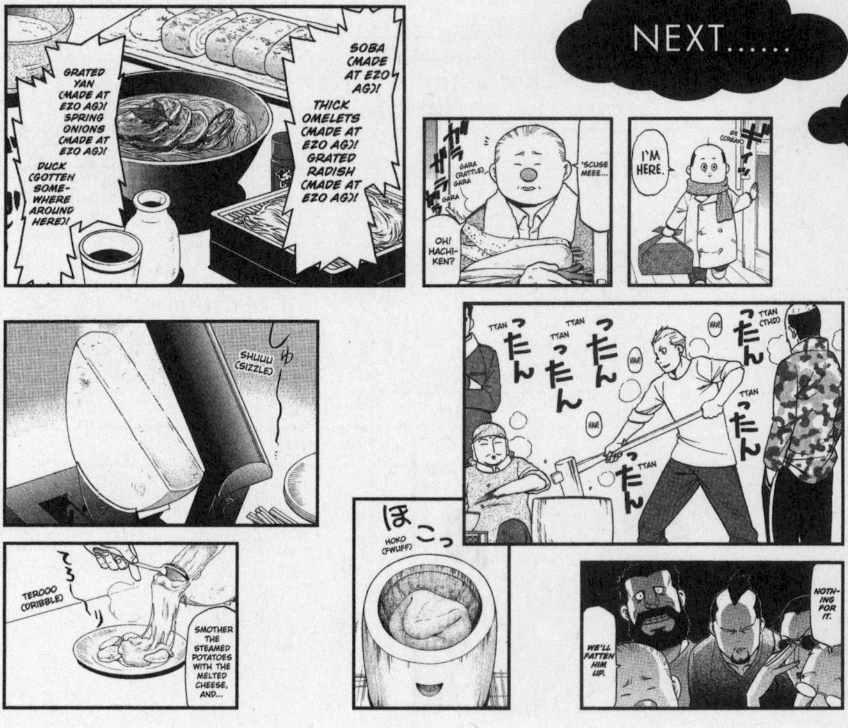
(CREAK)
I'M HERE.
GARA (RATTLE) GARA
GARA
'SCUSE MEEE...
OH! HACHI-KEN?
SOBA (MADE AT EZO AG)!
THICK OMELETS (MADE AT EZO AG)! GRATED RADISH (MADE AT EZO AG)!
GRATED YAM (MADE AT EZO AG)! SPRING ONIONS (MADE AT EZO AG)!
DUCK (GOTTEN SOME-WHERE AROUND HERE)!
TTAN (THD)
TTAN
TTAN
TTAN
TTAN
TTAN
SHUUU (SIZZLE)
NOTH-ING FOR IT.
WE'LL FATTEN HIM UP.
HOKO (PWUFF)
TEROOO (DRIBBLE)
SMOTHER THE STEAMED POTATOES WITH THE MELTED CHEESE, AND...

The students buy pigs...not live pigs, but pigs turned into meat. One boy's adventure moved everyone's hearts. After all, meat tastes better when you eat it together!! The bacon...the sausage...we made it with these hands.

YOU SHOULD DO BACON!
OOKAWA-SENPAI, WHICH ARE YOU DOING?
BACON!
OKAY, I'LL DO SAU-SAGE.
きゅっ
KYU (SQUEAK)
AND MIX!
WHOA...SO THE MEAT BLOCKS GIVE GROUND SAUSAGE ITS TEXTURE?
VUIIIIIII (VRRRR)
WHOA!
HANG THEM, AND AFTER WE DRY THEM A LITTLE ...
NYUIYUUU (STRETCH)
SINCE YOU CAN FINE-TUNE HOW MUCH COMES OUT WITH YOUR THIGH, YOU CAN USE BOTH HANDS.
Whoaaa! It's so looong!
YEAH.
LET'S FEED THOSE KIDS SOME-THING GOOD.

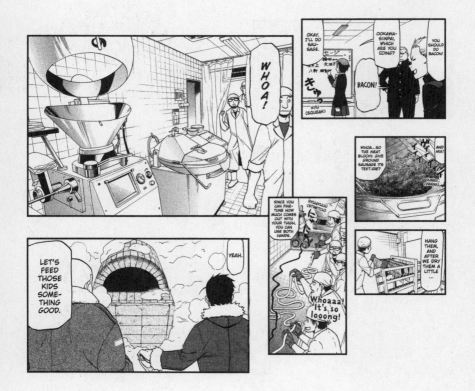

Now the Ezo Ag Carnival begins... Eat meat! Give the wine a pass and drink milk! Silver Spoon Volume 10 coming August 2019!

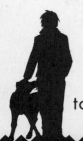

to be continued......

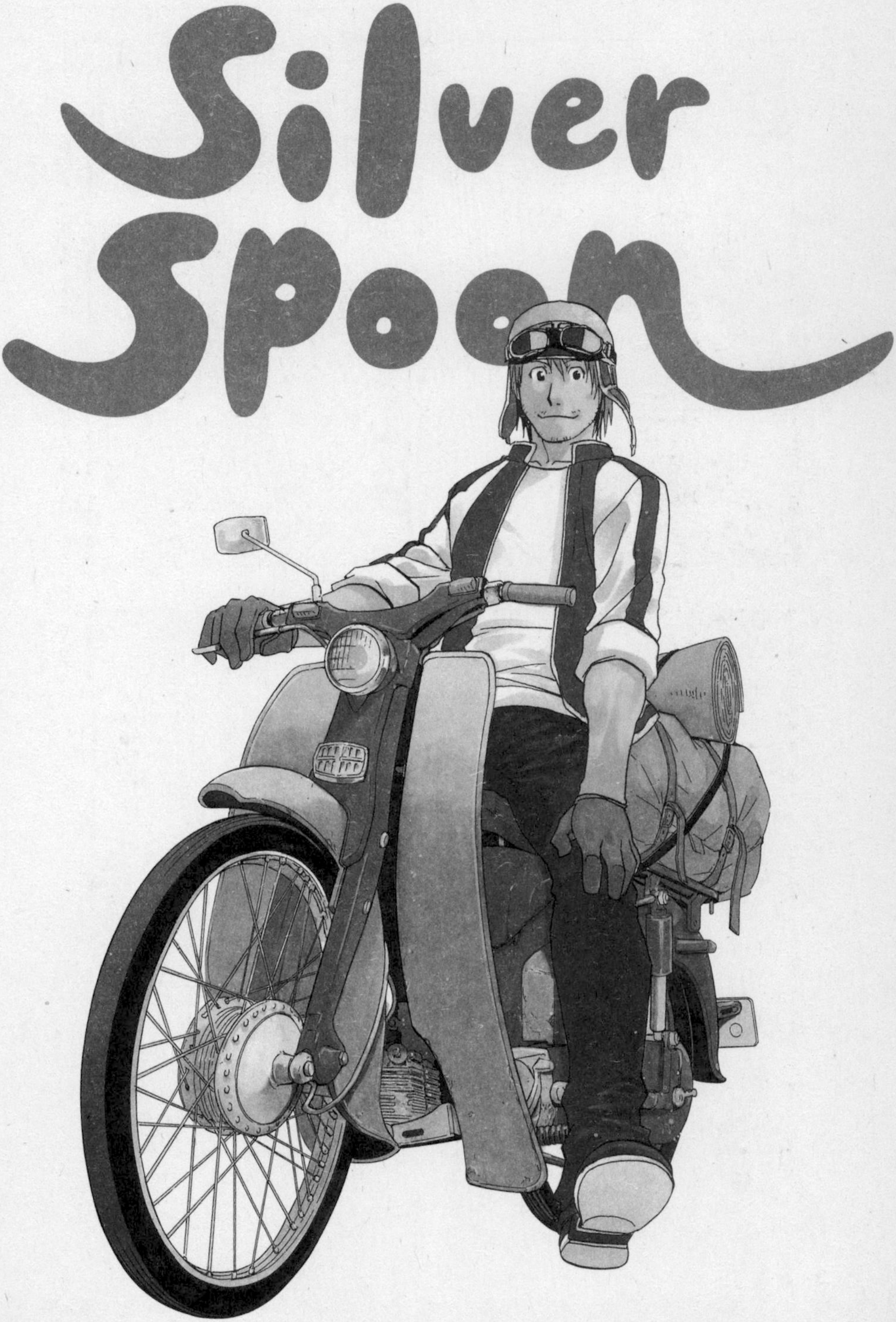
Silver
Spoon

Beware of Big Bro

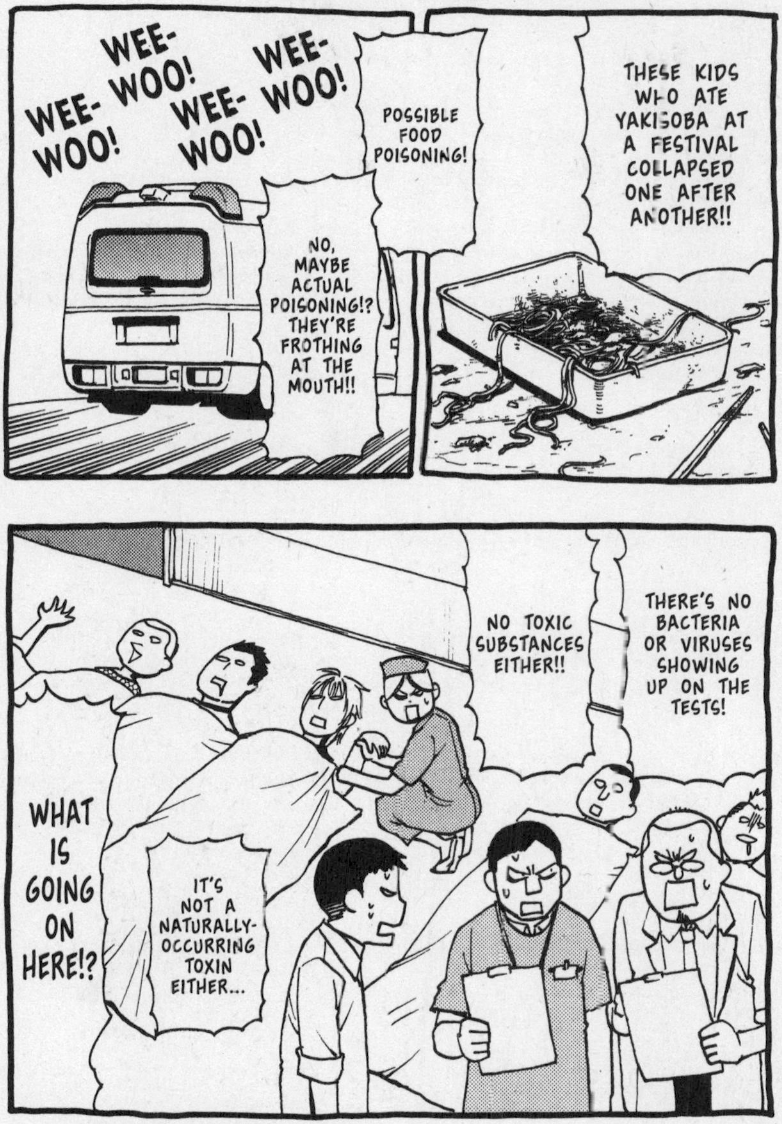
THESE KIDS WHO ATE YAKISOBA AT A FESTIVAL COLLAPSED ONE AFTER ANOTHER!!
POSSIBLE FOOD POISONING!
NO, MAYBE ACTUAL POISONING!? THEY'RE FROTHING AT THE MOUTH!!
WEE-WOO! WEE-WOO!
WEE-WOO! WEE-WOO!
THERE'S NO BACTERIA OR VIRUSES SHOWING UP ON THE TESTS!
NO TOXIC SUBSTANCES EITHER!!
IT'S NOT A NATURALLY-OCCURRING TOXIN EITHER...
WHAT IS GOING ON HERE!?

REALLY, WHAT'S GOING ON?

Translation Notes

Common Honorifics

no honorific: Indicates familiarity or closeness; if used without permission or reason, addressing someone in this manner would constitute an insult.

-san: The Japanese equivalent of Mr./Mrs./Miss. If a situation calls for politeness, this is the fail-safe honorific.

-sama: Conveys great respect; may also indicate the social status of the speaker is lower than that of the addressee.

-kun: Used most often when referring to boys, this honorific indicates affection or familiarity. Occasionally used by older men among their peers, but it may also be used by anyone referring to a person of lower standing.

-chan: An affectionate honorific indicating familiarity used mostly in reference to girls; also used in reference to cute persons or animals of either gender.

-sensei: A respectful term for teachers, artists, or high-level professionals.

-niisan, nii-san, aniki, etc.: A term of endearment meaning "big brother" that may be more widely used to address any young man who is like a brother, regardless of whether he is related or not.

-neesan, nee-san, aneki, etc.: The female counterpart of the above, nee-san means "big sister."

Currency Conversion

While conversion rates fluctuate, an easy estimate for Japanese Yen conversion is ¥100 to 1 USD.

Page 11
The kudan is a creature from Japanese folklore with the body of a bull and the head of a human that is said to predict misfortune.

Page 33
Natto is a traditional food made from fermented soy beans known for its powerful smell and strong flavor.

Page 150
The old Japanese name for December is "shiwasu," which is made up of the characters for "master/teacher" and "run." Some speculate the reason for this is because December is so busy that even priests must pray while running from one thing to another.

Page 151
Doujinshi are self-published works—sometimes fan work based around an existing property and sometimes original work. Though usually associated with self-published manga, doujinshi works include other forms of media too. Comic Market, or "Comiket" for short, is the biggest convention for doujinshi sales in Japan.

Page 152
Odaiba is an artificial island in the Tokyo Bay.

Serious fans will sometimes refer to their favorite anime/manga/etc. character as "my wife."

The suffix "-tan" is a cutesy form of "-chan" and is often used for a cute character's name.

Page 161
Wakkanai is the capital of the Soya subprefecture in Hokkaido. It's the northernmost city in Japan. Cape Soya is Japan's northernmost point.

Page 174

A *tsundere* is a character who acts proud and stuck-up on the outside, but is lovestruck on the inside.

A *yandere* is a character who is quite literally crazy about someone; they are often intensely jealous and may act out violently to "protect" their love.

A *kuudere* is a character who acts curt and uninterested around their love interest but is really lovestruck on the inside.

Page 185

Shogakukan is the Japanese publisher of *Silver Spoon,* and *Weekly Shounen Sunday* is the Shogakukan manga magazine in which *Silver Spoon* is serialized.

In Tokachi, Arakawa and the others visit Green Park, which is covered completely by lawns. Its 400-meter (1,312 feet) long bench once held the Guinness World Record for longest bench in the world.

Silver Spoon

Silver Spoon 9

HIROMU ARAKAWA

Translation: Amanda Haley **Lettering: Abigail Blackman**

GIN NO SAJI SILVER SPOON Vol. 9
by Hiromu ARAKAWA
© 2011 Hiromu ARAKAWA
All rights reserved.
Original Japanese edition published by SHOGAKUKAN.
English translation rights in the United States of America, Canada, the United Kingdom, Ireland, Australia and New Zealand arranged with SHOGAKUKAN
through Tuttle-Mori Agency, Inc.

English translation © 2019 by Yen Press, LLC

Yen Press
1290 Avenue of the Americas
New York, NY 10104

Visit us at yenpress.com
facebook.com/yenpress
twitter.com/yenpress
yenpress.tumblr.com
instagram.com/yenpress

First Yen Press Edition: June 2019

Yen Press is an imprint of Yen Press, LLC.
The Yen Press name and logo are trademarks of Yen Press, LLC.

The publisher is not responsible for websites (or their content) that are not owned by the publisher.

Library of Congress Control Number: 2017959207

ISBN: 978-1-9753-2764-4

10 9 8 7 6 5 4 3 2 1

WOR

Printed in the United States of America